I'M HERE TO ASK FOR YOUR VOTE

I'M HERE TO ASK FOR YOUR VOTE

HOW PRESIDENTIAL CAMPAIGN VISITS INFLUENCE VOTERS

CHRISTOPHER J. DEVINE

Columbia University Press
New York

Columbia University Press
Publishers Since 1893
New York   Chichester, West Sussex
cup.columbia.edu

Copyright © 2024 Columbia University Press
All rights reserved

Library of Congress Cataloging-in-Publication Data

Names: Devine, Christopher, 1984– author.
Title: I'm here to ask for your vote : how presidential campaign visits influence voters / Christopher J. Devine.
Description: New York : Columbia University Press, 2023. | Includes bibliographical references and index.
Identifiers: LCCN 2023020391 (print) | LCCN 2023020392 (ebook) | ISBN 9780231212342 (hardback) | ISBN 9780231212359 (trade paperback) | ISBN 9780231559331 (ebook)
Subjects: LCSH: Presidents—United States—Election—History—21st century. | Presidential candidates—United States—History—21st century. | Political campaigns—United States—History—21st century. | Campaign management—United States—History—21st century. | Voter turnout—United States. | Voting research—United States. | United States—Politics and government—2001–2009. | United States—Politics and government—2009–2017. | United States--Politics and government—2017–2021.
Classification: LCC JK528 .D483 2023 (print) | LCC JK528 (ebook) | DDC 324.7097309/05—dc23/eng/20230606
LC record available at https://lccn.loc.gov/2023020391
LC ebook record available at https://lccn.loc.gov/2023020392

Cover design: Julia Kushnirsky
Cover photo: Christopher J. Devine

FOR MY STUDENTS

CONTENTS

Acknowledgments ix

INTRODUCTION
1

1 A BRIEF HISTORY OF PRESIDENTIAL CAMPAIGN VISITS
16

2 WHEN AND WHY DO CAMPAIGN VISITS MATTER?
42

3 PRESIDENTIAL CAMPAIGN VISITS, BY THE NUMBERS
77

4 WHERE DO THE CANDIDATES GO—AND WHY?
119

5 WHAT DIFFERENCE DO CAMPAIGN VISITS MAKE?
160

CONCLUSION
209

Appendix A. Tables 223
Appendix B. Figures 251
Notes 259
Bibliography 297
Index 311

ACKNOWLEDGMENTS

About ten years ago, I was working with Kyle Kopko on a book about the vice-presidential home state advantage. To make the point that presidential campaigns *think* running mates can help win their home state (whatever the empirical reality may be), I wanted to show that in 2012 Republicans visited Wisconsin more often after Mitt Romney selected native son Paul Ryan as his running mate—and usually sent Ryan there, rather than Romney. In other words, I would use campaign visits as a window into campaign *strategy*.

Would the evidence bear out my expectations? (Yes, but that's not the point.) I remember the excitement—pure political science energy, here—of flipping open my computer to start collecting the data. Where to find it? I don't know. Surely, it's out there somewhere—probably on some academic's website. It'll be a big database with other elections, too—hey, why not test my hypothesis beyond 2012? I'll just run a quick Google search, start downloading the data, and find out soon enough.

But that didn't happen. I tried one search, then another. How could this be? The dataset that I assumed political scientists couldn't live without apparently didn't exist. Or at least not the one I imagined. I ended up building a workable dataset, for the time being, based on an online tracker from the *Washington Post*. But it wasn't detailed or accessible enough for my liking, and didn't even provide a definition—let alone a satisfactory one—of what made for a "campaign visit." Plus, it only pertained to 2012. Other online resources had similar limitations. At that point, I realized that if there was going to be a comprehensive database of presidential campaign visits, I might have to build it myself.

This book is the culmination of the work I started a decade ago. It introduces the Campaign Visits Database (CVD), which provides a detailed record of all presidential and vice-presidential campaign visits from 2008 to 2020 and is now available for download on my personal website (christopherjdevine.com/data). I use this dataset to present a comprehensive analysis of campaign visits over recent elections, focusing on their strategic objectives and effects on voting behavior. This research builds on a prior iteration of the CVD, which I have used in writing several journal articles and a book chapter on the 2016 presidential election.

In short, the book you hold in your hands has arrived here, safe and sound, after a long journey. But it has been a good one—and many good people have been a part of that journey. It is with joy and gratitude that I acknowledge their contributions here. But where to start?

With Trudy, of course. None of this would be possible without your patience and support. Much of that comes in the difficult times, when a chapter won't write—or when it will write, if only I could somehow find the time for it. Better yet are the good times—celebrating the much-anticipated completion of "my chapter" or an idea that has come to fruition. Sharing those moments with you makes them better. Thank you—for that and so much else.

Thanks, also, to my children—Hayes, Miles, Madison, and McKinley—who share in those moments, too, and inspire me to keep going. I love you all, and thank God for you.

At times, this book has felt like my other "baby." Giving it a good home, then, was extremely important to me. I am thrilled to publish it with Columbia University Press. My thanks go to everyone at CUP who has been a part of this process. In particular, I am grateful to Stephen Wesley for being a wonderful editor who, from the very start, got what I was trying to do with this book and shared my enthusiasm for it. For their assistance in the production and editing of this book, I am also grateful to Katherine Harper, Kathryn Jorge, Marisa Lastres, and Christian Winting.

Many excellent scholars also made invaluable contributions to this project. Andrew Reeves and Jay Wendland generously shared their encouragement and expertise on the study of campaign visits. Kyle Kopko, Carlos Algara, and Lee Hannah volunteered their time to help me solve seemingly intractable data problems. Kyle, as well as Aaron Weinschenk, also contributed to the development of this research as my coauthors on related projects. For valuable feedback at research conferences, I am grateful to Meena Bose, Daniel Ponder, Diane Heith, Seo-young Silvia Kim, Christopher Farris, and Ken Miller. Finally, I thank the three anonymous manuscript reviewers for providing exceptionally thorough and constructive feedback that went a long way toward preparing this book for publication.

This project probably would not have been possible without the support and guidance of my colleagues at the University of Dayton. Above all, I thank Grant Neeley, whose creativity and dedicated leadership as Political Science Department chair enabled me to complete this project right on time. Also, I thank Eileen Maloney, Nancy Martorano Miller, Autumn Lockwood Payton, Dan Birdsong, Heidi Gauder, Miranda Melone, and—in advance of all that will come in 2024—Meagan Pant and Shawn Robinson, for their important contributions to my work. Additionally, the University of Dayton's Research Council supported this project with a summer 2020 seed grant, for which I am grateful.

Finally, this book is dedicated to my students—those whom I have had the privilege to teach and learn from already, and those who are yet to come. You inspired this book; you inspire me often.

I'M HERE TO ASK FOR YOUR VOTE

INTRODUCTION

On May 7, 2020, Joe Biden—the Democratic Party's presumptive nominee for president of the United States—held his first general election campaign rally, in Tampa, Florida. Except that it didn't take place *in* Tampa. And was it really a *campaign rally*?

It had all the trappings of a typical rally, to be sure: state party leaders and elected officials were on hand to deliver remarks; a local high-school student led attendees in the Pledge of Allegiance; music blared from the DJ's speakers; and then came the moment they'd all been waiting for, when the candidate took the stage to address his jubilant supporters.

But Joe Biden wasn't standing in front of a cheering crowd. He wasn't in the same room as his supporters, let alone the same city. Nor were they gathered together in one room that night. Biden—like nearly everyone on this live stream—was at home, standing on a backyard patio in Wilmington, Delaware. When the big moment arrived, there was no raucous applause to cue his entrance—just an awkward silence, as Biden, sporting his signature aviator sunglasses, leaned against a trellis awaiting instructions. "Did they introduce me?" he said, finally, to someone offscreen. "Am I on?"[1]

Ten minutes later, Biden's speech—and, mercifully, this technological disaster of a "virtual rally"—was over.[2] Biden's image faded from the screen, to a musical outro (from Bruce Springsteen, of course), and within seconds, the live stream abruptly ended.

To anyone watching online who had experienced the excitement of an in-person rally, the contrast with this sterile, disembodied event must have been jarring. There was no ecstatic send-off for the candidate at the end. There were no applause lines, nor any audience interaction whatsoever—no feeding off of him, or him off of them. There were no rope lines, no handshakes, no selfies. Surely, no one would tell their friends or grandkids that they had *seen* Joe Biden that night, that he had come to *their* town, that *they* had witnessed history together. Indeed, it was anything but a social experience. There was no crowd—no collective voice or body in which to lose oneself to the intoxicating emotions of the moment, gathered physically in one space, joined with thousands of others, as one, in common cause. The attendees would not file out together to their cars or onto the surrounding streets, telling new friends it was nice to have met them and raising their voices in one last partisan chant. At the end, they just closed their computers or switched off their phones and returned to a more transparent state of pandemic-induced isolation.

What had just happened, exactly? According to the event's critics, of which there were many, the answer was not "a campaign rally."

"Biden's handlers approached the challenge of bringing a rally online too literally," wrote one of those critics, Andrew Ferguson, in *The Atlantic*. "They tried simply to list the elements of a typical rally and tick off the boxes—music, check; Pledge of Allegiance, check; candidate remarks, check . . .—and then throw them up in serial fashion." A campaign rally, Ferguson argued, is not merely the sum of its parts; whatever value it has—to mobilize supporters or persuade undecided voters, perhaps—comes from the uniquely galvanizing social experience that it provides. "Without applause, laughter, and the crush of swaying bodies, the conventions of a political rally come off as ludicrous."[3]

Why start a book on campaign visits here, with this utterly atypical illustration? It is not to take a cheap shot at the Biden campaign for its poor execution of an experimental online event. Clearly, holding virtual rather than in-person rallies was a matter of necessity, not choice: at that time, states generally prohibited large indoor gatherings and many Americans, including Biden, were under stay-at-home orders to limit the spread of COVID-19. Furthermore, as people the world over now know all too well, hosting or participating in an online event is logistically complicated and rarely, if ever, quite as good as "the real thing." Sure, this virtual rally was a bust. But how much better could Biden and his team have done at the time?

The purpose of this illustration, rather, is to introduce a popular narrative about Biden's presidential candidacy that speaks to the importance of in-person campaigning in modern elections: that Biden—at this early stage and even later, once he did start holding limited in-person events—was not *really* campaigning. Embedded in this critique (a go-to for Biden's Republican opponent, then-President Donald Trump, and his supporters, but also voiced by Democrats and some journalists) is the notion that a presidential candidate who does not conform to the traditional expectations of a campaign, defined in terms of the frequency and scale of his or her in-person appeals to voters, is not legitimately running for the presidency and therefore does not deserve to win it—or is "just asking to lose."

Much the same could be said about the familiar postmortem of Hillary Clinton's loss in the 2016 election: "She didn't even go to Wisconsin!" Of course, Clinton's failure to visit that state—a perennial battleground where every other presidential candidate has campaigned since 1972—did not cost her the presidency; to defeat Donald Trump in the Electoral College, she would have had to win there *and* in Michigan and Pennsylvania (both of which she visited, the latter quite frequently). But this fact did, and still does for many, serve as convenient shorthand for the broader argument that Clinton could have tried harder to win the election, and only has herself to blame for losing it.[4] The Wisconsin narrative's popularity also reveals a fundamental assumption about voting behavior that this book is designed to interrogate: that campaign visits *work*. In other words, so the argument goes, Clinton should have visited Wisconsin (and other states, such as Michigan, that she largely avoided) because by doing so, of course she would have won more votes, perhaps enough to take Wisconsin and even the presidency.

If Joe Biden had lost the 2020 presidential election, surely history (or at least the conventional wisdom) would have rendered a similar judgment: "What did Biden expect? He never even left his basement!" Of course, Biden did leave his basement during the campaign—quite often, in fact—although not at first. Much like the Clinton-didn't-go-to-Wisconsin line, however, this is not really a literal observation about the candidate's activity but shorthand for a more general attack on Biden's campaign strategy and his presidential legitimacy, built on similar empirical assumptions about the effects of campaign visits. While Biden held countless virtual and eventually many in-person events, still he did not campaign as aggressively in person as Americans have come to expect from a candidate seeking the highest office in the land—albeit due to personal and public safety concerns rather than a lack of ability or will. In that case, Ferguson's takeaway from the "virtual rally" in Tampa states the case more precisely: "The [COVID-19] crisis has forced [Biden] into being only a simulation of a presidential candidate."

"A SIMULATION OF A PRESIDENTIAL CANDIDATE"

It all began two months earlier, on March 10, when Joe Biden was scheduled to hold a campaign rally in Cleveland, Ohio, in a gymnasium jammed with supporters. Biden planned to celebrate his victories on that day in several key primary states, including neighboring Michigan, and ask Ohioans for their votes in the Democratic primary set to take place one week later. Six hours before the rally was to begin, however, Ohio Governor Mike DeWine called for the cancellation of all large indoor events in the state. Three Ohioans, each from the Cleveland area, had tested positive for COVID-19 the day before. Within two hours, Biden's campaign announced that it was canceling the Cleveland rally. Biden delivered his victory speech that night in Philadelphia, not far from his campaign headquarters, to a roomful of staffers.[5] Afterward, he returned to his home in Delaware. He would not appear in public again until late May, nor speak in public until June.

With hardly a choice in the matter, Biden became the first presidential candidate in one hundred years—since Warren Harding in 1920—to run a campaign out of his home. A poor internet connection ruined his first attempt to conduct a virtual town hall meeting from there, on March 13. Shortly afterward, campaign operatives set about converting the recreation room in his basement into a high-tech studio.[6] It was from here, in front of an elegant white bookcase and an American flag that had once flown atop the U.S. Capitol in honor of his deceased son, Beau, that Biden would speak to voters for the foreseeable future.

Biden did everything that a presidential candidate normally would do—but virtually, from his basement. That included hosting fund-raisers and town halls, conducting interviews with local and national media outlets, appearing on late-night talk shows, accepting endorsements from former presidential rivals, and, yes, eventually holding "rallies." In April, Biden even tried to simulate the most intimate moments of an in-person campaign event by speaking individually with six supporters on a "virtual rope line" for four minutes apiece.[7] In May, he and his wife, Dr. Jill Biden, embarked on "virtual travel days," hosting a flurry of online rallies and roundtable discussions targeting voters in a single battleground state.[8] Altogether, Biden's activities represented an impressive and innovative effort to re-create the essential elements of a modern presidential campaign within the strict confines of an online environment. But it was hardly a satisfactory substitute. Biden, indeed, seemed to be "only a simulation of a presidential candidate."

Donald Trump was stuck at home, too—but at the White House, where, as President of the United States in a time of grave national crisis, he commanded the public's attention on a regular basis. This was most evident when he emceed the daily COVID-19 news briefings, alongside top government officials and medical experts. Biden tried to counter Trump and keep himself in the public eye—for example, by holding his own "virtual news briefings" and launching a podcast—but, as a private citizen beaming in from his Delaware basement, he could hardly compete with the sitting president. This handicap became all the more apparent on May 5, when Trump—who had not left Washington, DC, for two months and desperately wanted to return to the campaign trail—visited a face mask manufacturing plant in the battleground state of Arizona, officially in his capacity as president. Soon he would make similar visits to Michigan and Pennsylvania. All the while, Trump proclaimed that the end of the pandemic was near.[9] How long would it take before he was again holding rock concert–style, in-person rallies?

It was at this time—after two months in lockdown, while struggling to get his message out to the public, his bully pulpit shrinking by the day—that a singular image of Biden's candidacy, capturing the anxiety of his supporters and the indignation of his opponents, crystallized, never to dissolve: *Joe Biden was hiding in his basement.* Trump himself would conjure up this image for the first time in a Fox News interview on May 8, just three days after his first trip outside Washington, DC, and one day after Biden's widely panned virtual rally.[10] By June, even after Biden began making in-person public appearances again, albeit on a limited basis, it had become Trump's favorite line of attack. For example, on June 11—the same day that Biden held an in-person roundtable discussion about the economy in Philadelphia—Trump tweeted: "Sleepy Joe Biden refuses to leave his basement 'sanctuary.'"[11] As this example shows, Trump used the "basement" narrative not as a literal observation about Biden's activities, but more as a vehicle for advancing related arguments against his opponent: namely, that Biden lacked the physical and mental capacity to serve as president and thus, if elected, could be easily manipulated by various left-wing goblins who would *really* be in charge of "his" administration. Trump's allies seized on this image, too, using it as the inspiration for myriad hashtags and nicknames, including #HidenBiden, "Joe Hiden," and "Punxsutawney Joe."[12] From June to August, Fox News aired more than three hundred references to Joe Biden hiding in his basement.[13] And in early August, the Trump campaign released an ad purporting to show Biden stuck at home, isolated and confused. "Deep in the heart of Delaware, Joe Biden sits in the heart of his basement," the narrator intoned. "Alone. Hiding. Diminished." With each word, a photoshopped image of Biden—mostly from pre-pandemic events, with people and objects removed and basement imagery swapped in—flashed across the screen, reinforcing the message.[14]

But it was not just Republicans who seized on the basement narrative. In May, many journalists invoked the same imagery to convey Democrats' concerns. On May 8, for example, a Reuters story reported: "As Trump Returns to the Road, Some Democrats Want to Bust Biden Out of His Basement."[15] Likewise, on May 13, the Associated Press announced: "Basement-Bound Biden Campaign Worries Democrats."[16] Even before Trump seized on the basement narrative, David Axelrod and David Plouffe, who had run Barack Obama's presidential campaigns in 2008 and 2012, published a *New York Times* op-ed calling for major changes to Biden's campaign strategy while referring to him as "the Man in the Basement."[17] Trump's press conferences, they argued, had made for "a striking contrast to the image of his solitary challenger, consigned to his basement." While Axelrod and Plouffe were not calling on Biden actually to leave his home and begin campaigning in person—instead, they argued, his campaign should find ways to reach voters more effectively through virtual platforms—the basement imagery served as a leitmotif for their strategic critique. At times, their belittlement of Biden was almost indistinguishable from that of Republicans: "Mr. Biden is mired in his basement, speaking to us remotely, like an astronaut beaming back to earth from the International Space Station."

By mid-2020, the image of Joe Biden hiding in his basement was baked in. It was not merely a partisan talking point, but a consensual narrative shared by political figures and media outlets from across the ideological spectrum. Moreover, because this narrative really was symbolic rather than literal (as indicated by the fact that Axelrod and Plouffe's intervention did not call on Biden to leave his basement, and that Trump's attacks did not abate once Biden did so), it could mean different things to different people and be used to make various strategic arguments for or against Biden's candidacy. It had become a rhetorical device, not a fact to be refuted or disproven. At that point, there was probably nothing Biden could do to shake this narrative or avoid having to defend himself against it. What could he say, really?

George Stephanopoulos of ABC News asked Biden in a May 12 interview: "When do you expect to get out on the campaign trail?" Biden answered defensively: "Well, we're on the campaign trail now. You know, everybody says, you know, 'Biden's hidin.'' Well, let me tell you something, we're doing very—very well . . . I reject the premise that somehow this is hurting me. There's no evidence of that. I'm following the rules. Following the rules. The President should follow the rules, instead of showing up at places without masks, and the whole—the whole thing."[18]

This response is telling in two respects. First, it underscores the Biden team's belief that his physical absence from the campaign trail—while motivated primarily by concerns about the candidate's health, and that of his staffers and supporters—served a strategic purpose. By complying with public health guidelines, including a stay-at-home order in place at that time in Delaware, Biden hoped to demonstrate that he was taking COVID-19 seriously and acting responsibly to combat its spread. From this, voters might make favorable inferences about how he would respond to this or other crises as president.[19] Also, by drawing a contrast to Trump's flouting of masking and distancing requirements, Biden hoped to signal to voters that he would handle the pandemic more effectively than the sitting president, for whom, according to polling then and throughout the campaign, this was a major electoral liability.[20]

Second, Biden refused to concede the point that, because he was not conducting *in-person* campaign activities at that time, he was "off" the campaign trail. Indeed, as described above, Biden was conducting the full range of presidential campaign activities—from rallies, town halls, roundtables, and fundraisers, to press conferences, media interviews, social media events, and rope lines—but doing so virtually, rather than in person. By maintaining that he *was* on the campaign trail, in essence Biden challenged the traditional (actually, modern) definition of "presidential campaigning."[21] Does it *have to* take place in person? Does it *have to* cross geographical boundaries? Why can't a campaign shorn of these two elements be legitimate and effective—under pandemic or, for that matter, any other conditions?

While Biden's comments here and at other points during the campaign[22] implicitly raised such questions, he probably did not intend to take the argument quite that far. As he clarified later in the interview: "I'm anxious to go out and campaign, George. I enjoy interfacing with people. I'm not trying to avoid it but I'm trying to set an example as to how we should proceed in terms of dealing with this health and economic crisis."[23] In other words, Biden indicated, this was not how he *wanted* to campaign for president. But it *was* a campaign, nonetheless.

"WHO LET ALL THESE PEOPLE INTO MY BASEMENT?"

As political pressure mounted and public health restrictions eased in the late spring of 2020, Joe Biden finally began making in-person public appearances: on Memorial Day, for a wreath-laying ceremony at a nearby veterans' memorial; on June 1, for a meeting with Black community leaders at an AME church in Wilmington, following George Floyd's murder; on June 2, for a speech on racial justice in Philadelphia. Biden would deliver three more speeches and hold three roundtable discussions in person that month—all within driving distance of his home in Delaware or just across the Pennsylvania border—and maintain a similar schedule in July.[24] At each event, Biden and his team tried to underscore their commitment to protecting public health, even while returning to "the campaign trail." For example, the campaign invited only twenty local community leaders and businesspeople to attend Biden's June 17 speech in Darby, Pennsylvania. Their chairs were spaced six feet apart and ringed by white tape to help enforce distancing requirements.[25] Trump, who would hold his first large indoor campaign rally three days later, gleefully retweeted a photo of the event. "Joe Biden's rally," he chuckled. "ZERO enthusiasm!"[26]

But small crowd sizes were a feature, not a bug, of the Biden campaign. In fact, the campaign regularly took dramatic steps to *avoid* drawing large crowds. On several occasions, it did not publicize an event or its location until just one day, or even hours, beforehand. Such was the case for Biden's first in-person campaign event after officially being nominated for president at the Democratic Party's virtual convention in mid-August. "Limited access to the event"—held at a converted steel mill in Pittsburgh on August 31—"was by design, [Biden's] campaign said, as a precaution in the coronavirus pandemic."[27] The campaign also capped attendance at its drive-in rallies at just fifty people in early September[28] and just under four hundred vehicles by October 30, as Election Day neared. Even at that late date—and for a drive-in rally, no less—the Biden campaign chose not to disclose the event's location to the general public in advance. It was, according to one report, "a formula designed to limit the number of people at the rally to ensure proper social distancing."[29]

The campaign also reduced risk by limiting how frequently Biden traveled. In September, for instance, he spent only one out of every three days physically on the campaign trail. Typically, when traveling, he would spend the day holding multiple events in one battleground state before flying home to Delaware at night.[30] On the other days, Biden—as well as his vice-presidential running mate, Kamala Harris, their spouses, and other surrogates—often targeted battleground states via virtual events and local media interviews.[31] Many times, though, the campaign called a "lid" by announcing to the press that their candidate would not be conducting any public events that day. Most notably, at the end of October, Biden devoted nearly an entire week to preparing for the second and final presidential debate, scheduling no other public events. Finally, he held two drive-in rallies in Pennsylvania that Saturday and then called another lid on Sunday.[32] (Over the next nine days, however, Biden would close the campaign by visiting seventeen cities in eight battleground states.)

Trump, by contrast, essentially conducted a traditional presidential campaign—holding large, in-person rallies nearly every day, often multiple per day, across every major battleground state (save for a ten-day stretch in early October when he contracted COVID-19 and required hospitalization). At those rallies, and in other public comments, Trump continued to disparage Biden for not leaving his basement—even though Biden frequently campaigned in person by this point. "While I travel the

Country, Joe sleeps in his basement," Trump tweeted on September 12. (One day earlier, Biden had appeared at 9/11 commemorations in New York City and Shanksville, Pennsylvania.) At a rally in Virginia on September 25, Trump scoffed: "I got a guy who stays in his damn basement all day long and I'm doing this." (Two days earlier, Biden had held multiple campaign events in North Carolina.) And at the first presidential debate, on September 29, Trump said about Americans' response to COVID-19: "We can't lock ourselves up in a basement like Joe does.... He has this thing about living in a basement."[33] (Trump, of course, was standing next to Joe Biden, on a stage in Cleveland, Ohio, when he said this. And, as campaign officials had announced that morning, Biden would visit seven cities in Ohio and Pennsylvania on the day after the debate.)

Trump's refusal to concede the basement narrative—indeed, his decision to double down on it—even after Biden began in-person campaigning further demonstrates that its utility was symbolic rather than literal in nature. *Sure, Biden's critics seemed to be saying, he finally left his basement and started to campaign in person. But that's not the point. His events are too small. And too quiet. And there aren't enough of them. This just doesn't feel like a presidential campaign. Is it a presidential campaign? How can anyone be elected president without even bothering to run for it?*[34]

The basement narrative, at bottom, is a contest over definitions: What is a campaign, really? Was Biden campaigning? If not, what would—or should—voters do about it? *Washington Post* reporter Josh Dawsey and his colleagues, in fact, raised this point in early September, when comparing the Trump versus Biden candidacies, respectively:

> [O]ne campaign [is] fueled by in-person events, raucous gatherings and defiant crowds flouting health rules; the other by quiet, small-bore events with everyone masked and spaced apart.
>
> These are more than just competing messages for a country riven by [the coronavirus] pandemic.... *The two sides don't even agree on what constitutes campaigning.*[35]

Biden also hinted at this debate in late October, when asked by a reporter to explain his "light" campaign schedule. "The reason it looks like we're not traveling," he said, is that "we're not putting on superspreaders." In other words, Biden argued, he *was* fully engaged in the campaign; indeed, he had said of his activity moments earlier, "There's not been a day that hasn't been a 12-hour day yet."[36] But many people perceived otherwise because he, in contrast to Trump, was not holding the jam-packed rallies that have come over time to define presidential campaigns. Once again, Biden was challenging that definition. Months earlier, he argued that a virtual presidential campaign was still a campaign. Now, aiming for the goalposts that his critics had moved downfield, he argued that a scaled-down presidential campaign—featuring fewer and smaller in-person events—was still a campaign. More than that, he suggested, it could work. And so it did: Biden defeated Trump in that year's presidential election.

By the end of the 2020 campaign, Joe Biden seemed to understand what all the talk about his hiding away in a basement was really about. A tweet of his from October 31 says it all. It shows Biden on the stage at a drive-in rally in Atlanta, held earlier that week.[37] He is smiling and pointing at a large crowd of supporters, as hundreds of cars fill the vast parking lot surrounding him.[38] Putting the lie to a narrative that defied refutation, Biden—virtually grinning—asks: "Who let all these people into my basement?"[39]

PLAN OF THE BOOK

As the preceding account of the 2020 election illustrates, candidate visits are central elements of modern presidential campaigns, which (it is widely assumed) significantly influence electoral outcomes. This book aims to provide a comprehensive analysis of when and why campaign visits matter, by explaining the historical development of in-person campaigning, the theoretical bases for campaign visit effects, the strategic implications of campaign visits in recent presidential elections, and their effects on presidential voting, measured at the aggregate and individual levels.

Such an analysis is unprecedented. Previous scholars have provided comprehensive analyses of only one such element—for example, the history of campaign visits[40]—or their effects in a different context, such as presidential primaries.[41] Only Daron R. Shaw has analyzed multiple elements (strategy and effects) and in more than one general election (2000 and 2004).[42] This book provides a rigorous analysis of presidential and vice-presidential campaign visits and their electoral effects over the four most recent (2008–2020) elections. In short, I try to explain why we should expect campaign visits to matter, with respect to presidential voting, and under what conditions they are effective.

First, in chapter 1, I describe the historical evolution of presidential campaign visits. Presidential candidates were not always expected to engage in in-person campaigning. In fact, for many years, doing so was widely considered to be inappropriate; candidates were supposed to merely "stand" for the presidency, not "run" for it. Only in the early 1900s did it become commonplace for presidential candidates—including incumbent presidents—to actively solicit votes, and in 1948 Harry Truman's "whistle-stop" tour showed, once and for all, that in-person campaigning could make the difference between winning and losing. After that point, it was expected that any candidate who really wanted to win the presidency—and therefore deserved it—would be as active as possible on the campaign trail. In other words, as Joe Biden's example in 2020 would show, in-person campaigning came to be seen as a prerequisite for presidential legitimacy.

In chapter 2, I discuss the theoretical bases for expecting campaign visits to influence presidential voting, and evidence of these effects in past scholarship. Specifically, I explain why visits might influence voting behavior due to local media coverage, campaign messaging, and mechanisms of mobilization versus persuasion—that is, stimulating turnout among latent supporters versus changing preferences among existing voters, respectively. Also, I consider how these effects might vary depending on the audience in question: for instance, among those who attend the event in person (direct audience) versus those who learn about it in a mediated fashion, such as through news coverage or word of mouth (indirect audience). Most previous studies found very limited evidence that campaign visits influence voting behavior and attributed those effects more often to mobilization than persuasion. I discuss those findings and the unique contributions that this study makes to the existing literature.

In chapter 3, I introduce an original dataset of presidential campaign visits in the 2008–2020 presidential elections: the Campaign Visits Database (CVD). Few previous studies have used consistent standards to evaluate campaign visits and their effects across multiple elections. Here, I provide a definition of campaign visits and explain my procedures for including and counting visits in the CVD. I also present descriptive statistics of campaign visits for recent presidential and vice-presidential candidates, in order to indicate their relative activity on the campaign trail and in what types of settings their visits took place. This analysis provides essential context for the discussions of campaign visit strategies and effects in the chapters that follow.

In chapter 4, I evaluate the strategies associated with presidential campaign visits. Specifically, I examine how two political institutions, the Electoral College and political parties, influence the allocation of campaign visits. First, I show that presidential candidates restrict their visits to a relatively small number of states that are most likely to provide a majority in the Electoral College, particularly those that are electorally competitive and have a greater number of electoral votes. Second, I try to discern the strategic objectives of each candidate based on the partisan inclinations of the geographic areas that they visited. Specifically, I evaluate whether the candidates tended to visit locales that, based on past voting behavior and demographic characteristics, can be described as part of the candidate's partisan constituency (thus indicating mobilization) or not (persuasion). I find that recent candidates have pursued strategies of mobilization and persuasion via campaign visits, but more often the former. By identifying an individual candidate's strategy, I can better evaluate the effectiveness of his or her campaign visits in the following chapter.

In chapter 5, I examine the effects of campaign visits in the 2008–2020 presidential elections. Specifically, I estimate the empirical relationship between presidential and vice-presidential campaign visits and presidential voting, at the aggregate (i.e., county) and individual (i.e., survey) levels. At both levels, I aim to determine not only *when*—that is, for which candidates—visits influence vote choice, but also *why* this occurs—that is, via persuasion versus mobilization. It is important to compare aggregate- versus individual-level estimates because, as I explain, both have methodological limitations, but can be used in a complementary fashion to derive greater confidence in core research findings. I also consider alternative data specifications with respect to variable measurement, units of analysis, and respondent samples. The empirical results are quite consistent. I find that campaign visits usually do not influence voting behavior, but, when they do so, it is more often by persuading rather than mobilizing voters. In some cases, these effects align with a candidate's overall strategy.

The conclusion discusses the significance of this research, particularly in terms of its practical relevance to campaign practitioners and scholars. To the former, I make three recommendations: don't stop campaigning; give persuasion a chance; and make the most of your vice-presidential candidate. To the latter, I recommend focusing on four areas of concern in future research on this topic: causal inference, dependent variables, qualitative research, and data collection. I conclude the book by arguing that in-person campaign visits are essential elements of American democracy, which—one should hope—will endure well into the future.

1

A BRIEF HISTORY OF PRESIDENTIAL CAMPAIGN VISITS

In June 1968, Richard Nixon's campaign manager (and future White House Chief of Staff) H. R. Haldeman delivered his boss a blunt message. "Times have changed," Haldeman declared, in a memo—"and ... the presentation of presidential candidates must change, too."[1]

His proposal? "Eliminat[e] ... all rallies, large public functions, press-the-flesh campaign techniques, plunging through the crowds, whistle-and-prop stops." Gone would be the days of presidential candidates "present[ing] themselves to large masses of people in person. They would, instead, utilize the mass communications media to carry their messages to the voters" via "direct speeches, telethons, televised press conferences, televised coffee hours with small groups of representative voters, televised interviews of all kinds, [and] documentary-type presentations." "In effect," Haldeman wrote, "the campaign would be conducted in individual living rooms instead of at public gatherings."[2] He was proposing no less than a revolution in presidential campaigning.

Haldeman's bold idea came in response to tragedy: just three days earlier, an assassin had shot and killed Robert F. Kennedy following a campaign rally to celebrate his victory in California's Democratic presidential primary. It was one in a series of political murders, beginning with President John F. Kennedy's five years earlier, that had traumatized the American public during the 1960s. Fearing even more bloodshed, Haldeman concluded that dramatic steps must be taken to protect present and future presidential candidates. Specifically, he proposed, Nixon should call upon President Lyndon Johnson to formally request that all presidential candidates, in the 1968 primary and general elections, agree to forego in-person campaigning.[3] This plan would help to ensure Nixon's safety without putting him at a competitive disadvantage should his opponents wish to remain on the campaign trail. It would be a unilateral disarmament.

Haldeman believed the American public would accept such a dramatic reimagining of the presidential campaign. In addition to protecting against security threats, he reasoned, this plan would help to improve political discourse by freeing presidential candidates from the physical burdens of campaigning so that they could concentrate more fully on the exchange of ideas.[4] Haldeman also questioned the utility of in-person campaigning; only a small proportion of the American public had direct contact with a presidential candidate, he noted, and most people who showed up to rallies had already decided how they would vote. Nor did Haldeman believe that campaign visits did much to help elect a candidate: "The reach of the individual campaigner doesn't add up to diddly-squat in votes," he said in 1960, while running Nixon's first presidential campaign.[5]

Alas, Haldeman's plan did not come to fruition in 1968. Nixon's opponents in that race, Democrat Hubert Humphrey and third-party candidate George Wallace, waged vigorous in-person campaigns. But Nixon—who campaigned tirelessly as a vice-presidential candidate in 1952 and 1956 and visited all fifty states as a presidential candidate in 1960—adopted elements of Haldeman's proposal anyway. He would continue to hold large rallies, but much less frequently than his opponents and mainly for the benefit of television audiences.[6] The Nixon campaign would be conducted primarily via television; indeed, it spent more money on TV than Humphrey's campaign spent altogether.[7] The centerpiece of Nixon's strategy was "Man in the Arena," a series of one-hour television programs in which the candidate—seated casually on stage, speaking in a conversational tone—answered questions from a carefully-selected audience of supporters who lived in the state or region where a given episode would air. This effort to reach voters in their "individual living rooms rather than at public gatherings" seemed to promise all the benefits of in-person campaigning—being seen among "the people," demonstrating popularity, attracting local news coverage, identifying with local concerns—but without taking on the associated risks of physical and mental exhaustion, gaffes, hostile audiences, and, yes, even assassination attempts.[8]

To Nixon and his advisers, this was not just a winning strategy for 1968; it represented a paradigm shift in the conduct of presidential campaigns. The conventional methods of in-person campaigning—of "rallies, large public functions, press-the-flesh campaign techniques, plunging through the crowds, whistle-and-prop stops"—would soon become things of the past, relics of a bygone era. In the words of Rogers Ailes, the television impresario who designed and executed much of Nixon's newfangled strategy: "[T]his is an electronic election. The first there's ever been. TV has the power now."[9]

What do Haldeman's memo and the 1968 Nixon campaign as a whole tell us about the history and contemporary significance of presidential campaign visits? Two things, I would argue. First, in-person campaigning is not inevitable. Second, while alternative methods have been tried, public expectations for in-person campaigning have proven resilient and defying them poses a considerable risk to a candidate's reputation.

To the first point, presidential candidates have not always campaigned aggressively and in person; in fact, it was considered inappropriate to do so throughout early American history. Only in the early to mid-twentieth century did it become acceptable and even expected for candidates in general, including incumbent presidents, to crisscross the country soliciting votes in person—so much so that what was, in reality, a profoundly *modern* method of presidential campaigning soon came to be regarded by the public as "traditional." Any subsequent deviation from this model would thus seem unduly "modern." As historian Gil Troy puts it: "[T]he stumping campaign became traditional and appropriate; the passive campaign, modern and illegitimate."[10]

Yet, this evolution in public expectations does not preclude trying something different—and some campaigns have done just that. Take Nixon's 1968 campaign, for example. Or his reelection campaign in 1972, when, according to journalist Theodore H. "Teddy" White, "It was easier to cover the President on campaign . . . by staying home and watching television with the rest of the people—[as] the President wanted it."[11] Or the "Rose Garden Strategy" adopted by incumbent president Gerald Ford in 1976, whereby (save for a two-week road trip to close the campaign) he communicated with voters via media coverage of daily White House events, including press conferences, bill signings, and other ceremonies.[12] Or the 2020 Joe Biden campaign, as detailed in this book's introduction.

The late establishment of a "tradition" of in-person campaigning, together with these deviant examples from subsequent elections, goes to show that there *are* different ways of conducting a presidential campaign, even today, that do not necessarily represent a fundamental break with the past. Moreover, it is hardly clear that alternative methods will prove ineffective or anathema to the American public: Nixon in 1968 and 1972, as well as Biden in 2020, were elected over opponents who ran more "traditional" presidential campaigns.

But, to the second point, despite such innovations, in-person campaigning remains the norm in American politics. Nixon's TV-centric run for president in 1968 did not, as some of his advisers suggested, spell the end of the "traditional" campaign. While television did become more central to mass communication strategies in subsequent elections, presidential candidates also continued to stump across the country, and in some cases, even more frequently than they did prior to 1968. By the late 1980s in-person campaigning persisted as a default strategy; as Troy describes it: "Even if candidates did not want to campaign, they often felt they had no choice."[13] In 2020, even as some Democratic strategists recast the limitations imposed by the coronavirus pandemic as an opportunity to "create a new paradigm for how presidential campaigns communicate" via digital media, and proclaimed "the death of the traditional campaign,"[14] Joe Biden consistently stated his preference to return to full-scale, in-person campaigning, if and when it became safe to do so, all the while presenting the alternative methods used by his campaign not as a rejection of traditional methods, but as a back-up plan forced upon him by the pandemic.

It is because of this consistent, long-term exposure to the traditional campaign model that Americans so clearly *expect* in-person visits and often draw negative inferences from their absence or infrequency.

Indeed, Troy writes that by the 1940s (surely as in the present day): "campaigning... was concerned not only with convincing Americans but with paying them respect. In this democratic era, the protocol of the stump illustrated the candidate's humility, his commitment to the democratic process, and his ties to the people. Rear-platform talks, handshaking, and speechmaking all served as symbolic exchanges, allowing the leader and the people to pay homage to each other."[15]

So engrained, so instinctive, did this expectation become that "Just as a politician worried that the people no longer appreciated him when his events were poorly attended, so did the people worry about being unappreciated if the politician refused to hold such events."[16]

Richard J. Ellis and Mark Dedrick offer perhaps the best description of what the American public expects from its presidential candidates: "We expect those who would be president to come to us, the people of the United States, and solicit our votes. We expect them to explain their positions on the issues, to mobilize the faithful, and to persuade the wavering. Every presidential candidate is expected to criss-cross this vast country in pursuit of votes. Would-be presidents do not stand for office, they run for it."[17]

No wonder Joe Biden's 2020 campaign, with its virtual rallies and scaled-down in-person events, seemed illegitimate to many people: the sorry effort of a candidate who wasn't trying very hard to earn their vote, and therefore may not deserve it. True, Biden was not just *standing* for the presidency, passively, as candidates once did. But he wasn't quite *running* for it, either. Biden seemed to be somewhere in between—as if he were merely jogging for the presidency.

STANDING FOR THE PRESIDENCY: EIGHTEENTH- AND NINETEENTH-CENTURY CAMPAIGNS

How times have changed.

In the late eighteenth century and for most of the nineteenth, the American public very much expected its presidential candidates *not* to campaign for office.[18] Adopting a precedent set by the nation's first president, George Washington—who was so intent on appearing to be "drawn reluctantly from private life by the irresistible summons of public service" that he refused even to privately discuss the possibility of being elected president—candidates took pains to convey that they were merely "standing" for the presidency, not "running" for it.[19] The presidency, as John Quincy Adams explained prior to his election in 1824, "is not in my opinion an office to be either solicited or declined"; rather, it must be "spontaneously bestowed" upon a man so disinterested in acquiring political power as to be worthy of the public's trust in exercising it.[20]

For decades to come, nearly all presidential candidates continued to present themselves to the public not as active promoters of their own cause, but as dutiful citizens merely submitting to calls from "friends" (i.e., political allies) to allow their names to be put forward for consideration by the voters. James Polk, for one, adopted Adams's formulation twenty years later, in 1844, when accepting the Democratic Party's nomination for president, by stating that "the office of President of the United States should neither be sought nor declined." Indeed, Polk assured the public, "I have never sought it, nor shall I feel at liberty to decline it, if conferred upon me by the voluntary suffrages of my fellow citizens."[21] Twenty years after that, in 1864, Democratic nominee George McClellan likewise wrote: "It is my firm conviction that no man should seek that high office, and that no true man should refuse it, if it is spontaneously conferred upon him."[22] Another twenty years later, in 1884, Democratic nominee Grover Cleveland wrote: "I have not a particle of ambition to be President of the United States. . . . If, however . . . I should be selected as the nominee, my sense of duty to the people and my party would dictate my submission to the will of the convention."[23]

"A SENSE OF DECORUM PREVAILS"

To maintain the fiction that presidential candidates at this time were merely "standing" for office, "A sense of decorum prevail[ed]," as John

Quincy Adams put it, enjoining interested parties "from active or even indirect canvassing of votes for himself."[24] Nonetheless, many presidential aspirants took an active role behind the scenes, even while publicly denying their ambitions. For example, in 1800, Thomas Jefferson—who had recently declared to a correspondent, "I protest before my God that I shall, from the bottom of my heart, rejoice at escaping" election to the presidency—privately orchestrated efforts to finance and distribute campaign literature on his behalf, meanwhile taking care to instruct his collaborator: "Do not let my name be connected with the business."[25] Likewise, Andrew Jackson—who boasted in an 1831 letter: "I meddle not with elections. I leave the people to make their own President"—published pseudonymous editorials promoting his candidacy.[26] Polk, his political protégé, pleaded with Jackson to resist taking an active role in the campaign, in hopes of convincing voters "that you live in retirement on your farm, calm and unmoved by the excitement around you, taking no part in the pending canvass for the Presidency, but committing yourself into the hands of your country."[27]

Jackson did, however, take a step toward campaigning publicly for the presidency in 1824, when he wrote a letter, intended for public consumption, explaining his policy views on the issue of tariffs. Careful to guard against accusations of wanton "electioneering," Jackson explained to his correspondent that because "[my] name has been brought before the nation for the first office in the gift of the people, it is incumbent on me, when asked, frankly to declare my opinion upon any political national question, pending before, and about which the country feels an interest."[28] With this reply, Jackson became "the first presidential candidate to acknowledge that the people had a right to question him on his views, in effect to concede that there could be a dialogue between the electors and the candidate."[29] This door, now cracked, would open more widely in subsequent campaigns. By the 1840s, presidential candidates, including incumbent presidents such as Martin Van Buren, frequently communicated their policy views to the public via letters to private correspondents that were, in fact, intended for publication. Also, by that time, it became customary for presidential candidates to accept their party's nomination by writing a public letter that, in many cases, also included comments on the party platform and other policy matters. "The letter of acceptance was one of the few exceptions to the unofficial 'no campaigning' rule for presidential candidate," presidential historian Benjamin Arrington explains, adding, "In a normal campaign, it was perhaps the only time a candidate could 'talk' directly to the electorate."[30]

It is no coincidence that presidential candidates' first tentative steps toward openly soliciting public support took place during the era of Jacksonian democracy, from the 1820s to the mid-1840s. Why? First, by that time it had become the norm for states to give voters, rather than legislators, the power to choose the presidential electors who would cast votes in the Electoral College. In 1789, only four states chose their electors by popular vote. By 1800, ten states (out of sixteen) did so, but by 1816 that was down to only nine (out of nineteen). By the time of Jackson's first election, in 1828, all but two states did so, and by 1836, all but one.[31] Thus, the strategic objective of presidential campaigns gradually changed from persuading small groups of political elites to persuading voters in their masses, through increasingly organized, public appeals. Indeed, the number of people casting presidential votes exploded in the early nineteenth century, from 67,000 in 1800 to more than 356,000 in 1824.[32] Also, technological advancements and internal improvements—particularly with respect to roads, canals, and eventually railroads—began easing travel and communication within and across states. Whereas once it had been logistically impractical for a presidential candidate to travel across states, speaking at various events before large crowds of voters, now it would be possible, perhaps even prescient, to imagine just such a campaign.

"FOR THE FIRST TIME IN THE HISTORY OF THIS COUNTRY"

In 1836, William Henry Harrison, a former general who had also served as a territorial governor and U.S. senator, became the first candidate to campaign for the presidency in person.[33] Harrison's campaign had multiple fronts. First, at home in North Bend, Ohio, he met "voters face to face ... throughout the campaign." Second, Harrison traveled west to Vincennes, Indiana, to speak at a public banquet.[34] Third, and most significantly, Harrison embarked on a tour of several Southern and Eastern states (specifically, Virginia, Maryland, Pennsylvania, New York, and New Jersey), where, on several occasions, he spoke to large gatherings of supporters—thirty thousand people, for example, near Independence Hall in Philadelphia.[35] While the candidate gamely protested that he was not "traveling for the purposes of Electioneering," few people were fooled.[36] As one opposition newspaper harrumphed: "For the first time in the history of this country, we find a candidate for the Presidency traversing the land as an openmouthed electioneer for that high and dignified station."[37] The historical significance of Harrison's 1836 campaign is undercut by the fact that he was but one of three regionally based Whig candidates running that year, and he did not win the presidency.

Four years later, as the Whig Party's official nominee for president, Harrison won. This time, too, he mounted the proverbial stump. At first, he stayed at home to receive visitors, while appointing a three-person committee to answer campaign correspondence on his behalf. But that changed when Harrison's Democratic opponents took to ridiculing him as "General Mum"—a man too feeble-minded to think or speak for himself—and "Old Granny"—one too old and frail to leave his home. Allegedly Harrison was "cut off from all intercourse with the people, refusing to answer their honest inquiries," while his "thinking committee," representing the Whig Party managers that—just you wait and see—would pull the strings in a Harrison administration, so feared what he might say or do that they "shut up the old gentleman in an iron cage."[38] One cannot help but note the historical parallel to Republican attacks on Joe Biden in the 2020 presidential campaign. Harrison was all but accused of hiding away in his basement! And just like Biden 180 years later, it was to counter these attacks that he hit the campaign trail.

Determined to prove his physical and mental fitness—at one point beseeching rallygoers: "You must have already perceived that I am *not* CAGED, and that I am *not* the old man on crutches . . . they accuse me of being"—in June Harrison began the first of several campaign tours across his home state of Ohio.[39] At the first event, ostensibly to commemorate the battle at Fort Meigs in the War of 1812, Harrison spoke for one hour to a crowd of thirty thousand people, including delegations from at least ten states.[40] While careful to stipulate that this was not a campaign speech—the "office of the President of the United States should not be sought after by any individual," of course—Harrison nonetheless discussed his support for expanded military pensions, his opposition to President Van Buren's subtreasury plan, and the Democratic Party's alleged abuses of executive power.[41] In subsequent speeches across Ohio—from Dayton to Columbus to Cleveland, and at numerous stops in between—Harrison discussed his views on topics including abolitionism, internal improvements, immigration, paper money, the spoils system, and the veto power.[42] By September, the candidate all but openly acknowledged that he was campaigning for office, while speaking ever more frequently and to even larger crowds, among them seventy-five thousand people in Dayton on September 10 and sixty thousand in Cincinnati on October 1.[43] All told, William Henry Harrison spent nearly fifty days on the campaign trail in 1840, delivering more than twenty speeches.[44]

"I AM NOT HERE TO ASK FOR YOUR VOTES"

Harrison told the audience at one campaign rally in 1840, regretfully: "I am not with you today, Fellow Citizens, in accordance with my own sense of propriety. . . . Indeed I sometimes fear that upon me will fall the responsibility of establishing a dangerous precedent to be followed in future [elections]."[45] As it turned out, his campaign would have no such legacy; aside from a few stray events, often with ambiguous political implications, subsequent candidates continued to "stand" for office rather than "run" for it. The first candidate after Harrison to depart from that tradition was Whig Party nominee Winfield Scott, in 1852. At that time, Scott also served as a commanding general in the U.S. Army. It was in this capacity that President Millard Fillmore, a fellow Whig, sent

Scott on a five-week trip to Kentucky, beginning in mid-September, ostensibly to select the site for a new army veterans' home. Scott's delegation took a circuitous route to its destination, just happening to hit a series of major population centers in battleground states—including New York City, Buffalo, Pittsburgh, Cleveland, Columbus, Cincinnati, and Louisville—along the way. Scott's speeches at each of these stops attracted extensive local and, thanks to the newly invented telegraph, national newspaper coverage.[46] But Scott publicly disclaimed any political motives. "Fellow citizens," he announced in Cleveland, "I am not on a political mission, but on business connected with my position."[47]

In 1860, Democrat Stephen Douglas—nominated for president by the Northern, unionist faction of his splintered party—campaigned for four months across more than twenty Northeastern, Midwestern, and Southern states. Like Scott and, at times, Harrison, Douglas was keen to portray his travels as anything but political in nature. A month-long tour of New England that summer, he insisted, was only to take care of family business: to attend his brother-in-law's graduation at Harvard, make a pilgrimage to his father's gravesite in Vermont, and visit his elderly mother in upstate New York. Douglas professed amazement when he was greeted by large crowds at railroad depots along the way and called upon to speak. Trumpeting his innocence, Douglas often concluded these remarks by noting apologetically that he had "been almost betrayed into making a political speech." Indeed, he told the citizens of Troy, New York, that "if I do not go home soon I shall get to making stump speeches before I know it."[48] Eventually, Douglas admitted to voters that he was, in fact, "tak[ing] the stump this year," but stipulated: "It is not personal ambition that has induced me" to do so. Rather, he claimed—somewhat plausibly, while touring Southern states after it became clear that he would lose the election—only to be campaigning for the preservation of the Union. Inverting what would become a standard line at future campaign rallies, he declared to an audience in St. Louis: "*I am not here to-night to ask for your votes for the presidency*. . . . I am here to make an appeal to you on behalf of the Union and the peace of the country."[49]

Only three more candidates would stump for the presidency before 1896. In 1868, Democratic nominee Horatio Seymour spent two weeks campaigning in New York, Pennsylvania, Ohio, Indiana, and Illinois.[50] In 1872, longtime newspaper editor Horace Greeley, nominated for president by the Democratic Party and a splinter faction of "Liberal Republicans," spent more than two months campaigning across nine states in the Northeast and Midwest. During that time, he delivered approximately two hundred speeches, averaging fifteen to twenty per day, typically from the rear platform of a train.[51] Finally, in 1884, Republican nominee James Blaine delivered approximately four hundred speeches, mostly in Ohio and New York, during the last six weeks of the campaign.[52]

Why did most presidential candidates in the late nineteenth century refuse to hit the campaign trail, even after Harrison and others had established a precedent for doing so? Simply put, it seemed to be a losing strategy.[53] Indeed, only Harrison in 1840 had campaigned for the presidency and won it. The risks of campaigning were obvious. First, it exposed the candidate to criticism—particularly from opposition newspapers, eager to style their partisanship as civic virtue—for breaking with tradition, and perhaps worse yet for insulting everyone's intelligence by pretending not to do so. In August 1860, for example, the *New York Times* accused Douglas of "Deplorably . . . degrad[ing]" the presidency by "soliciting his own elevation thereto . . . The Presidency is still a high office," the paper insisted, "too high to be reached by a mere stump-speaker, and too dignified to be canvassed for like a County Clerkship or a seat in Congress."[54] What's more, the *Charleston Courier* charged, Douglas had "not even the common honesty . . . to admit that he is on an electioneering tour for the presidency!"[55]

Campaigning also exposed the candidate to unpredictable and potentially embarrassing circumstances while in the public eye. One source of risk was the audience. At a campaign stop in Alabama, for instance, the crowd heckled Douglas and pelted him with eggs and tomatoes.[56] Fellow speakers at these events posed another risk. Blaine famously attended a campaign event in New York City in late October 1884 in which Presbyterian minister Samuel D. Burchard gave a speech branding Democrats as the party of "Rum, Romanism, and Rebellion"—that is, alcohol, Catholicism, and the Confederacy. Blaine—"appear[ing] exceedingly haggard" after forty days on the campaign trail—invited controversy, and the ire of Catholic voters, by failing to condemn the remarks at that time, and for three days afterward.[57] He lost the election one week later, by the narrowest of margins. Subsequent campaigns learned their lesson: keep the candidate at home or risk being "Burchardized."[58]

"A HAPPY MEDIUM"

Wary of the risks of campaigning and of failing to control campaign narratives, by the 1880s candidates had discovered a brilliant compromise: the front-porch campaign. It all started in July 1880, when small crowds of well-wishers gathered at James Garfield's 158-acre farm in Mentor, Ohio, to celebrate his unexpected nomination at the Republican Party's national convention. For decades, presidential nominees had welcomed small delegations to their home for private audiences. But the Garfields were not prepared to entertain guests that summer; the interior of their home was undergoing renovation, and the family had left its finest furniture and dishware at their residence in Washington, DC.[59] What could Garfield do? "I could not play dummy on my own doorstep," he explained, "when my yard was filled with voters from all parts of the country, hurling speeches at me on all subjects."[60] Garfield began addressing the crowds from his porch—as a formality, really, just to thank and welcome them. But soon it became a phenomenon. By mid-October, large delegations from Ohio and across the United States were arriving at Mentor's train depot and marching toward Garfield's home every day. Many delegations represented specific constituencies or social groups, including African Americans, German Americans, Civil War veterans, women, and businessmen. Journalists were on hand to record and report on each speech, in what became a symbiotic relationship: Garfield provided the newspapers with fresh copy; they provided Garfield with the opportunity to shape campaign coverage while his Democratic opponent, Winfield Scott Hancock, stayed at home, receiving visitors in private.

The front-porch campaign proved to be a winning formula, worthy of emulation. Indeed, eight years later, Benjamin Harrison, the Republican nominee for president and grandson of William Henry Harrison, campaigned from his front porch in Indianapolis, delivering ninety-four speeches to one hundred and ten delegations and at least three hundred thousand people.[61] Eight years later, in 1896, William McKinley—also a Midwestern Republican—elevated front-porch campaigning to an art form. McKinley welcomed seven hundred and fifty thousand people, from thirty states, to his home in Canton, Ohio, over five months' time, and delivered more than three hundred speeches.[62] On one day in late September, he spoke to twenty thousand people from thirty cities and six states.[63] Delegations of "ethnic societies, trade unions, women's clubs, business associations, veterans' and fraternal lodges, and religious denominations" arrived daily at Canton's train depot, where they were greeted by a brass band and paraded down Main Street to await their turn on McKinley's front porch.[64]

McKinley's campaign choreographed each visit to ensure message discipline and avoid embarrassments: the candidate met with delegation leaders weeks in advance of a proposed visit, requested submission of their written remarks seven to ten days beforehand, and returned each draft with edits. Yet on stage—on the porch, that is—everything looked natural, almost spontaneous. McKinley appeared "like a child looking at Santa Claus" as he listened serenely to each delegation leader's opening remarks.[65] When it was his turn to address the crowd, McKinley climbed onto a chair to announce his appreciation for the delegation's visit before pivoting to some favorite campaign themes. After concluding his remarks, he stepped down and invited each visitor onto his porch to share in a hearty handshake and a cold glass of lemonade. The McKinley campaign did all it could to maximize publicity for these events, printing the candidate's remarks and distributing them to journalists for publication in newspapers nationwide. It was, as historian Jeffrey Norman Bourdon aptly describes the front-porch campaign, "a happy medium between aggressively stumping for the presidency and doing nothing to seek it."[66]

"I MAKE NO APOLOGY FOR PRESENTING MYSELF"

McKinley's Democratic opponent in 1896, William Jennings Bryan, was not looking for a happy medium; he intended to campaign more aggressively than any prior presidential candidate, without apology or pretense. Bryan did just that—by his estimates, traveling 18,000 miles across nearly thirty states to deliver six hundred speeches to at least two to three million people. There were two simple reasons for Bryan's groundbreaking campaign. First, he was an extraordinary orator: if any candidate could win votes with his voice, it was Bryan. Second, McKinley had ten times as much money to spend on the campaign as he did.[67] In that case, Bryan's only hope of competing for the public's attention and getting his campaign message out to voters was to say something interesting as often as possible, in as many places as possible, to as many people as possible, so that newspapers simply had to print what he said every day—for free, no less. And so Bryan took to the campaign trail, boldly, proudly proclaiming, "I make no apology for presenting myself before those who are called upon to vote, because they have a right to know where I stand on public questions."[68]

From early August to Election Day, Bryan traveled the country by rail, speaking on every day but Sunday. He delivered most speeches from the train's rear platform, so great was the crush of onlookers seeking a handshake. Many had arrived hours or days in advance of his visit. Often, the candidate disembarked to speak at a large indoor venue as well. At one point, Bryan spoke to so many and such large audiences over three days in the area that one newspaper said he had put himself "practically in personal contact to the extent of sight and hearing of the entire population of Chicago."[69]

Bryan lost the election—quite handily, in fact—to a candidate who would not leave his front porch. Yet he was successful in demonstrating the potential for a new type of presidential campaign: one built on direct contact with "the people" via nonstop campaign events and free local, as well as national, media coverage of them. It was a glimpse into the future of presidential campaigning.

RUNNING FOR THE PRESIDENCY: TWENTIETH- AND TWENTY-FIRST-CENTURY CAMPAIGNS

Presidential campaigning underwent gradual, but marked, changes in the early twentieth century. In 1900, Bryan, again the Democratic Party nominee, nearly replicated his earlier feat, by traveling 16,000 miles and delivering six hundred speeches during the campaign. But this time he was outdone by the Republican vice-presidential nominee, Theodore Roosevelt, who traveled 21,000 miles and delivered 673 speeches.[70] In 1908, Republican William Howard Taft—a reluctant public speaker who had intended to conduct a front-porch campaign from his home in Cincinnati—became the first presidential candidate since William Henry Harrison in 1840 to stump for the presidency and win it. He traveled 18,000 miles across every region of the United States and delivered four hundred speeches.[71] In 1916, Woodrow Wilson became the first sitting president to stump for reelection, after initially planning to conduct a front-porch campaign from his summer home in New Jersey. But in October—with his Republican opponent, Charles Evans Hughes, on a 14,000-mile cross-country campaign tour—Wilson broke down and embarked on a series of campaign trips to Nebraska, Illinois, Indiana, Ohio, and New York.[72] Four years later, Republican Warren Harding undertook what would be the last front-porch campaign, from his home in Marion, Ohio. But he, too, gave in and launched a series of campaign trips that fall, under pressure from his Democratic opponents, presidential candidate James Cox and vice-presidential candidate Franklin Roosevelt, who, for their part, delivered four hundred and one thousand speeches, respectively.[73]

"RADIO HAS RENDERED THE CAMPAIGN OBSOLETE"

The introduction of radio in the 1920s would change everything—or so it seemed. Why, one had to wonder, would anyone bother campaigning from coast to coast, endlessly repeating the same speech but to different audiences, when soon it would be possible to speak to the entire nation, all at once? One expert, quoted in the *Literary Digest*, predicted the end of campaigning as Americans knew it: "Radio has rendered the 'front-porch' campaign and the 'swing around the circle' obsolete."[74] Indeed, the winning candidate in 1928, Republican Herbert Hoover, made only seven campaign speeches but reached a vast audience with them, via radio broadcasts. In 1932, while running for reelection, Hoover planned to do much the same; "except for a few major addresses expounding policies of the administration I will not take part in the forthcoming campaign," he announced that summer.[75] But Hoover ended up abandoning these plans and taking to the stump after all, delivering thirty speeches and "scores of talks" from the rear platform of his train in a coast-to-coast tour unlike any previously conducted by a sitting president.[76] Hoover's Democratic opponents in both races, Al Smith in 1928 and Franklin Roosevelt in 1932, also campaigned nationwide, by train. In 1936, as an incumbent president seeking reelection, Roosevelt spent sixty days on the campaign trail and delivered two hundred speeches.[77] Whatever the advantages of radio, it had not rendered in-person campaigning obsolete.

"A CHANCE TO SEE THEIR PRESIDENT FACE TO FACE"

In 1948, the in-person presidential campaign reached its zenith, with then-President Harry Truman's legendary "whistle-stop" tour of the United States. To that point, "whistle-stop" had been a derisive term—"railroad shorthand for a 'hick' town so trivial that it did not merit a regular stop, forcing conductors to toot their whistles in order to signal engineers when a stop *was* necessary."[78] It was in this context that Robert A. Taft, a leading Republican senator and the eldest son of William Howard Taft, fumed that Truman—on his first campaign tour, from Washington, DC, to California, that June—was "blackguarding [i.e., denigrating] Congress at whistle stops all over the country."[79] Truman shrewdly embraced the term as emblematic of his vision for the campaign: "I wanted the people in the out-of-the way places to have a chance to see their President face to face so that they could form their opinions of me and my program on the basis of firsthand acquaintance rather than on the basis of polls and propaganda."[80] Indeed, by meeting voters where they lived, no matter how small their hometown—by making plainly visible to the President of the United States those people and places that often seemed invisible to the powers that be—Truman had chosen "a method of campaigning that . . . fit with his message of sticking up for the little man against the special interests. His form followed function."[81]

To reinforce this message, Truman tried to make a personal connection with the people standing before him, to identify with them and with their community. At each stop, he wove local issues, as well as references to "local scenery, local history, local achievements and interests," into his campaign speech, drawing on briefings from his advisers delivered just prior to arrival.[82] Truman spoke without notes—"off the cuff," as he liked to say—and without pretense, signaling to voters that he was "one of us." As he told one audience, unapologetically: "I speak plainly sometimes. In fact, I speak bluntly sometimes. I am going to speak plainly and bluntly today."[83]

Truman's whistle-stop campaign was remarkably ambitious. "No President in history had ever gone so far in quest of support from the people. . . . Nor would any presidential candidate ever again attempt such a campaign by railroad."[84] In total, Truman traveled 31,700 miles, through every region of the country, delivering more than 350 speeches—sometimes as many as sixteen per day—to twelve to fifteen million people.[85] He drew massive crowds in major cities (one hundred thousand people attended a speech in Chicago and nearly one million lined the route from the train depot to his hotel in Los Angeles) and most of the local population in rural areas: for instance, Truman wrote, "They told me at a little town in Idaho at 5:15 a.m. the whole town was out. . . . At Pocatello, Id. at 7:15 there were 2000 people and at Ketchum . . . everybody in the county was there." Even "at remote [train] stations where no stops were scheduled people waited just to see the train go through."[86]

Truman was hardly the first president or presidential candidate to campaign aggressively and in person, or to draw enormous crowds while crisscrossing the country by train. It is not the method or even the scope of this tour that explains its profound and enduring significance, but rather the perception that *it worked*. Truman had gone into the 1948 campaign with relatively low approval ratings, and few people gave him any chance of defeating the Republican nominee, Thomas Dewey. Famously, leading pollsters were so sure of Truman's defeat that they stopped surveying the electorate in October. After Truman pulled off his shocking victory, politicians and journalists scrambled for an explanation. Naturally, most concluded that Truman's whistle-stop tour—an extraordinary, exhaustive effort, rapturously received by the public—was what made the difference. In time, historians and political scientists would reach the same conclusion.[87]

It was this combination of circumstances—a clear underdog who conducted an aggressive in-person campaign and won, apparently because of it—that finally put to rest lingering concerns about the propriety or wisdom of "stumping" for the presidency. With this precedent in place, how could any candidate afford *not* to campaign? To merely "stand" for office—to do anything but run, *sprint* for it—no longer signaled the dignity befitting a president, but rather a conspicuous lack of energy, commitment, and judgment marking that candidate as unworthy of the nation's highest office. This was the turning point, when the modern conception of presidential campaigning became dominant, so much so that later generations would innocently refer to it as "traditional." As Gil Troy summarizes: "Passivity was now considered more dangerous than campaigning; dignity could no longer keep the candidate from the people. The candidate's interactions with the millions he could reach really did matter, Americans decided."[88]

"THE EMPHASIS SHOULD BE ON TELEVISION"

At the same time, in the mid-twentieth century, technology was changing *how* presidential candidates reached the American public. First, in the 1950s, the growing popularity of television meant that presidential campaigns not only had to hold in-person events, but also, perhaps even more importantly, they had to make those events *look good* for the audience watching at home. Already, in 1952, Dwight Eisenhower's campaign made a practice of hiring "an advance man who visited each town on [the candidate's] route to insure [sic] newspaper, radio and TV coverage," followed by "a task force of crowd-builders ... to get up a telephone campaign, and recruit cheerleaders to throw confetti by the ton and give out campaign buttons and rally invitations."[89] In 1960, Richard Nixon—Eisenhower's vice president and that year's Republican presidential nominee—accosted campaign aides for putting "too much emphasis" on building crowds for his rallies, insisting, "The emphasis should be on the coverage for television rather than the live audience."[90] This became the new conventional wisdom in presidential campaigns. It would have profound effects on the strategy and content of future campaign visits.

With respect to strategy, campaigns began organizing their travel schedules around the goal of maximizing television news coverage, particularly at the local level. As journalist Teddy White observed in the early 1970s: "The traveling campaign is based on media markets—and the candidate's imperative is to expose himself to television networks for three shots every day, plus a few more exposures aimed at local or regional evening news shows at eleven o'clock."[91] This is still the case in the twenty-first century. As explained by Daron Shaw, a political scientist who also worked as a strategist on the 2000 and 2004 Bush/Cheney campaigns: "Most of the money in contemporary political campaigns ... is dedicated to television advertising, while most of the candidate's time is wrapped up in visiting cities and towns in an effort to win local media coverage. In planning both of these endeavors, the appropriate unit of analysis is the media market."[92]

This means that candidates do not spend much time on the ground, getting to know voters and the places where they live. Instead, they typically hold "one-off" events in a given media market, designed to reach local voters only indirectly, in most cases, via broadcast media. Additional visits within the same market are redundant. As one presidential campaign aide put it in 1972: "They're only going to show one event a day on TV in Los Angeles, so why should we do two?"[93]

With respect to content, television has encouraged campaigns to more tightly control the candidate's words, actions, and appearance at these events, in order to help ensure positive coverage by conveying attractive imagery to broadcast viewers and avoiding gaffes or controversies that might take over a news cycle. By and large, campaigns have been quite successful at doing so—but only by stripping these events of the spontaneity, authenticity, and personalization that made, for instance, Truman's whistle-stops so effective. By way of example, consider this description of George H. W. Bush's 1988 campaign: "His public appearances were choreographed. . . . His settings were chosen to flatter him on television, usually in sunshine, sometimes in shirtsleeves. His performances were stage-managed down to the last spontaneous gesture; an advance man down front would signal him when to flash a thumbs-up sign, when to fling his arms aloft and when to start speaking."[94]

Indeed, television has provided campaigns with powerful incentives to make their events as predictable as possible—particularly by avoiding those unscripted moments (e.g., a tough question from the audience or a revealing interpersonal exchange) that have the potential both to hurt a campaign by disrupting its message but also to educate voters about the candidate's policy views or character. In short, television has increased the reach of campaign visits while also making them less useful to the electorate.

"TO SWALLOW THE COUNTRY AT A GULP"

Since Truman's whistle-stop campaign, technology has also changed how candidates travel between events—specifically, by giving up trains for airplanes. This transition already was underway by 1948, when Truman's vice-presidential running mate, Alben Barkley, traveled 150,000 miles by air, in what has been called the first "prop-stop" campaign. Former vice president Henry Wallace, running as the Progressive Party's presidential nominee, also campaigned mostly by airplane that year.

Even Truman flew from Washington, DC, to a campaign event in Florida, and another in North Carolina.[95] Nor were these the first candidates to do so: Wendell Willkie traveled almost 9,000 miles by air—but nearly twice as far by rail—in 1940.[96] In 1952, Eisenhower tried to replicate Truman's success with a 21,000-mile cross-country whistle-stop tour. But he actually covered more ground (30,000 miles, to be exact) by plane.[97] His Democratic opponent, Adlai Stevenson, campaigned almost entirely by airplane.[98]

Nixon, who had traveled 46,000 miles by train while campaigning for the vice presidency in 1952, instead traveled mostly by airplane while seeking reelection in 1956.[99] In 1960, air travel made it possible for him to campaign for president in all fifty states. Nixon's Democratic opponent that year, John F. Kennedy, traveled "75,000 miles by jet, train, and motorcade," but "mainly by jet."[100] His opening days on the campaign trail would have been unimaginable to previous generations of candidates. In Teddy White's description, Kennedy took to the skies on September 2 "as if he meant to swallow the country at a gulp. Friday evening he campaigned in Maine; by Saturday noon he was campaigning in San Francisco; Saturday night he flew to Alaska and then, with only four hours' sleep, turned the big jet back to the continent and urged it on all day to Detroit."[101]

To this day, air travel fixes the pace and geographic scope of presidential campaigning. With private jets at the ready, candidates can visit any part of the country at any time they wish, and even cover large swathes of it in a single day. Strategy alone dictates where, when, and how often the candidate will campaign.[102] Of course, there are only so many hours in a day, and campaigning can take a tremendous physical and mental toll on the candidate. But the public expects presidential candidates to do what it takes to win—that is, if they really want to be president and if they're up to the job. And with the ability to travel anywhere, anytime, by air—well, the sky's the limit.

What does that mean, in practice? By way of example, consider John McCain—a seventy-two-year-old former prisoner of war and cancer survivor, no less—for whom the last three weeks of the 2008 presidential campaign "were a blur." As he later recalled:

We crisscrossed the country, stopping wherever we thought we were still competitive, staging several rallies a day, making my closing argument four, five, six times a day, which meant shouting myself hoarse, firing up supporters to fight for me. They were the most crowded days of the campaign, with the longest hours in the air and on the ground. It takes a special fortitude to get through it, and the ability to live completely in the moment, not thinking ahead to when it will be over.

McCain's efforts are all the more impressive because by that time he anticipated, correctly, that he would lose the election to Barack Obama. In one of the most telling statements about modern presidential campaigning, McCain explained why he persisted in such a grueling exercise despite its apparent futility: "[Y]ou can't phone in the end of the campaign. You have to appear to the world as if you can win and are fighting like hell to do it. . . . The country expects it."[103]

"AREAS NEVER VISITED IN MODERN PRESIDENTIAL CAMPAIGNS"

Flying from rally to rally has come to epitomize modern presidential campaigning, especially in the frenzied lead-up to Election Day. However, nearly every candidate finds other ways to reach voters in person, as well. Since the 1960s, for instance, numerous candidates have launched mini-whistle-stop tours, usually for only one day, in a single state (e.g., Gerald Ford in Illinois, 1976; Ronald Reagan in Ohio, 1984), or to attract media attention on their way to (Bill Clinton, 1996) or back from (George W. Bush and Dick Cheney, 2000) a national party convention.

In 1992, Bill Clinton and Al Gore—the Democratic presidential and vice-presidential nominees, respectively—updated the whistle-stop model by launching a post-convention *bus* tour across seven states. The initial tour was so successful at generating positive news coverage and public responses—particularly in those "small towns and rural areas never visited in modern presidential campaigns, which had become dominated by rallies in major media markets"—that Clinton and Gore embarked on six more bus tours that fall lasting one or two days each.[104] Bus tours would not replace air travel (Clinton spent the last twenty-nine hours of the 1992 campaign flying four thousand miles across eight states), but they did become part of the modern campaign repertoire.[105] Clinton and Gore—along with their spouses, Hillary Clinton and Tipper Gore—took another bus tour, but just once, in 1996. Bush and Cheney also did so, in 2000. Bringing it all full circle, in 2016, Hillary Clinton—now the Democratic Party's nominee for president, and Bill Clinton, the former president and aspiring First Gentleman—embarked on yet another bus tour, along with vice-presidential nominee Tim Kaine and his wife, Anne Holton.

Gore, for his part, also reimagined the whistle-stop campaign in 2000, by embarking on a four-day riverboat tour across four battleground states on the Mississippi River with running mate Joe Lieberman and their wives, Tipper Gore and Hadassah Lieberman. The trip was a great success, earning positive media coverage and, according to one scholarly analysis, improving Gore's standing in the polls in those states.[106] Yet the Gore campaign decided against scheduling another riverboat tour, and no other campaign has tried it since.

The final—or at least the most recent—adaptation of the whistle-stop campaign debuted in 2020, when Joe Biden and his wife, Dr. Jill Biden, visited seven cities in Ohio and Pennsylvania via Amtrak train. This was an innovative way to generate media attention as Biden returned home to Delaware from the first presidential debate in Cleveland, particularly given Biden's reputation as a loyal Amtrak passenger. Perhaps most importantly, in the spirit of the whistle-stop tour and its many derivatives, traveling by ground rather than air gave Biden the opportunity to visit remote areas in which voters rarely—if ever, these days—get to see a presidential candidate in person, or to know that the candidate sees them.

What is most remarkable about this catalog of recent campaign innovations is not how much has changed, but how much has stayed the same. For more than sixty years, presidential candidates have traveled primarily by airplane, from one major city (and media market) to another, a distant speck in the sky to most voters in between. In nearly every campaign, at least one candidate tries to revive the old tradition of touring small-town America, in the flesh. But that is the exception, not the rule; indeed, these visits often seem to be little more than stunts designed to win positive media coverage in the short term, rather than a new vision for campaigning among the people. Teddy White observed as much in the late 1960s, with words that still apply in the twenty-first century: "Whistle-stop campaigning in America has been obsolete since Harry Truman's campaign of 1948, but candidates still toss a salute to the past by a railway excursion now and then."[107] Much like the television productions that pass for campaign rallies these days, the point is to convey the candidate's presence among the people, rather than to actually *be present* with them for any sustained period of time.[108]

Notwithstanding such nostalgic head fakes, the basic contours of presidential campaigning—in-person events, designed to generate positive local news coverage, to which candidates travel by air—have remained constant throughout the late twentieth and early twenty-first centuries. A good indication of this comes from Dick Cheney, who saw little difference between the presidential campaign that he ran for Gerald Ford in 1976 and his own campaign for vice president in 2000. As he wrote in his memoirs, "The rallies, the speeches, the whistle-stop tour [in 2000] were the same kind of events we'd been doing in 1976."[109]

Candidate visits constitute one of the central features, if not the defining one, of today's presidential campaigns. Indeed, political scientists have described campaign visits, along with advertisements, as "the most obvious and visible manifestations of the campaign" and "the most obvious means by which candidates communicate with voters and articulate issues, themes, and agendas." Together, these activities "dominate our conception of presidential electioneering."[110] By themselves, campaign visits are reputed to be "[p]ossibly the most direct event for influencing voters," "one of the most important ways for candidates to shape public agendas and popular opinion," and "the most tangible evidence that a campaign is serious about winning voters in a specific locale."[111]

It is therefore all too easy to take campaign visits for granted, as if our inability to imagine a presidential election without an endless parade of candidate-centered, in-person events makes them automatic and necessary. The purpose of this chapter is to challenge such assumptions, by placing campaign visits in their proper historical context. This history demonstrates that the "traditional" model of campaigning for president exhaustively and in person—while clearly normative, in the present—is not inevitable, nor is it really traditional. In short, this is not the only way to conduct a presidential campaign. I point this out not in order to stake a claim as to whether visits are, in fact, necessary or effective features of modern presidential campaigns, but to emphasize that *we cannot take that for granted either*, simply because we expect the candidates to act accordingly and they so readily comply. The question that I introduce in the next chapter and develop throughout this book is: What difference does it make? Or, to be more precise: *when* and *why* do campaign visits matter?

2

WHEN AND WHY DO CAMPAIGN VISITS MATTER?

George W. Bush began nearly every presidential campaign speech with the same line: "I'm here to ask for your vote."[1] He said it while running for president in 2000, and while running for reelection in 2004. He said it to voters in Cuyahoga Falls, Ohio, and in Tampa, Florida, and in Alamogordo, New Mexico.[2] At a fall 2000 campaign stop in Springfield, Missouri, Bush prefaced this remark by smirking at the obvious: "I have a confession to make. I'm here to ask for your vote."[3] Apparently, he was feeling expansive. Deviating from the standard script, Bush paused to explain the significance of this line and, by implication, his presence in Springfield that day. After losing a congressional election in Texas in 1978—finishing "second in a two-person race," as he liked to say—Bush recalled that he was approached by a woman in his hometown who had disappointing news: she hadn't voted for him. Bush was taken aback. "Well, why not?" he demanded. She answered, simply: "Because you didn't bother to ask for my vote."

It's a good story. But is it true? By that, I don't mean: Did she really say this to George W. Bush? That, in itself, isn't important. I mean: Is this really *why* she didn't vote for George W. Bush? In other words, if Bush *had* come to ask for her vote in person—as he was doing in Springfield, Missouri, all these years later, lesson long since learned—*would that have made the difference*? More to the point, does it make a difference to voters, in general, whether a presidential candidate comes to ask for their vote in person—be it face-to-face or mediated by local news coverage and word of mouth? In short: Do campaign visits really work?

It may seem strange to ask such questions. After all, as noted in chapter 1, presidential candidates these days spend an extraordinary amount of time and effort—not to mention quite a bit of money—on campaign visits. Indeed, "the bulk of campaign dollars" are spent on visits and advertisements.[4] Why, with so much at stake, and the most capable political strategists on their payroll, would campaigns do this, if it wasn't a good investment of their precious resources? And why would voters, such as George W. Bush's candid neighbor, claim that campaign visits make a difference—perhaps *the* difference—for them, if that's not really the case? Why, for that matter, would so many people assume that Hillary Clinton lost Wisconsin in 2016, and in turn the election, because of all the campaign visits that she *didn't* make, or that Joe Biden might be forfeiting the 2020 election to Donald Trump by purportedly "hiding in his basement?"[5]

It is reasonable—in fact, necessary—to question the importance of campaign visits, because many of the things that we believe can and will (must!) determine the outcome of presidential elections actually don't matter much, if at all, or at least their effects may be greatly overstated. Take, for example, the vice-presidential pick, or the presidential debates, or presidential campaign advertisements.[6] While such effects can be difficult to measure, and may vary across campaigns, generally political scientists find that elections do not hinge on a series of strategic "game-changers" or other idiosyncratic events, as popular history and "horserace"-driven media coverage so often imply. Rather, election outcomes for the most part are shaped by a small set of basic contextual factors known as "fundamentals," including the strength of the national economy (e.g., GDP growth), the performance of the incumbent president (e.g., net approval ratings), and partisan considerations (e.g., how long the incumbent president and/or his or her party has held power).

Indeed, political scientists often "forecast" election outcomes quite accurately using fundamentals-based empirical models that do not account for—and, in many cases, collect data prior to—various campaign events that may seem decisive at the time or in retrospect.[7] Individual-level data also indicate that stability, rather than volatility, is generally the rule in presidential campaigns.[8] Most people, especially in recent years, seem to make up their minds about whether and for whom to vote well before these events take place, and even before the fall campaign begins, primarily based on partisan predispositions. For example, in 2016, most self-identified partisans and two-thirds of strong partisans reported deciding on a presidential candidate prior to the national conventions in July—this in a year when both parties nominated historically unpopular candidates following months-long, divisive primaries.[9] There must be little room, then, for events such as campaign visits to change voters' minds, let alone election outcomes.

Acknowledging the importance of electoral fundamentals, however, does not exclude the possibility of campaign effects or prove, in binary terms, that *campaigns don't matter*. Indeed, skeptical scholarship on this subject traditionally has been framed in terms of "minimal effects" rather than no effects at all.[10] In recent years, as Taofang Huang and Daron R. Shaw note, "a consensus has gradually been achieved that campaigns matter"[11]—or, as Henry E. Brady, Richard Johnston, and John Sides put it, "campaigns matter but in limited ways." Specifically, while fundamentals explain most of the statistical variation in presidential voting, campaign events (broadly construed) are responsible for about 1 to 5 percent of it.[12] As James Campbell explains, these effects "are neither large nor minimal in an absolute sense, but sometimes large enough to be politically important."[13] That is to say, campaign activities are quite unlikely to rescue a doomed candidate or topple an obvious favorite, but they may make the difference in a very close race.

To be sure, campaigns matter; but fundamentals matter a lot more. According to Thomas M. Holbrook's estimates, for example, national conditions had three times as much influence on presidential voting as campaign events in 1988 and 1992—and *fifty* times as much in 1984. He concludes: "The general level of support for candidates during a campaign season is primarily a function of national conditions. In other words, national conditions determine the context of a campaign, or what candidates have to work with."[14] Or, one might say, the electoral fundamentals establish an equilibrium of support for the major-party candidates heading into the fall campaign, from which subsequent events may cause (rather minor) deviations.[15]

In this context, as Brady and his colleagues note, whether presidential campaigns (or, by implication, specific activities such as campaign visits) *matter* isn't the right question. Rather, "a better question is this: When and how do campaigns matter?"[16] Or, as Gary Jacobson puts it: "where, when, for what, and for whom [do] they matter?"[17] Generally, scholars have concluded that campaigns are most effective at bolstering voters' preexisting electoral preferences or political dispositions. In some cases, these may be latent preferences that voters do not fully comprehend or have yet to connect to the choice between specific candidates and their policies. For example, a voter who is concerned about losing her job may not pause to articulate an assessment of the national economy and frame prospective judgments about the consequences of electing one candidate versus another as president, accordingly. Through a variety of activities, including speeches, debates, media interviews, advertisements, and, yes, candidate visits, campaigns may help to activate—that is to say, "enlighten" or make voters more fully aware of—such preferences and clarify their electoral implications.[18] By way of illustration, according to Richard Johnston, Michael G. Hagen, and Kathleen Hall Jamieson, Al Gore underperformed the fundamentals favoring his 2000 presidential campaign because, in the scramble to distance himself from Bill Clinton's personal scandals, Gore failed to activate, or "prime," voters' positive evaluations of the Clinton Administration's economic record.[19] He did not create these favorable economic conditions, but he did fail to capitalize on them. This is an instructive example as to when and why campaigns matter: by succeeding, or in Gore's case, failing to "produce congruence between fundamental political conditions and predispositions, on the one hand, and vote intention, on the other."[20]

It is also important to recognize that campaigns do not function in isolation; whether one campaign's activities are effective may depend on what its opponents are doing. Changing political attitudes and behaviors is difficult, but it is most likely to occur when people are exposed to a one-sided, or at least lopsided, flow of information.[21] Such imbalances often occur in races below the presidential level: for instance, congressional or state legislative elections in gerrymandered districts where the incumbent faces weak or even token opposition and enjoys tremendous advantages in terms of name recognition, fundraising, advertising, staffing, and media coverage. But that is not the case in presidential elections, where—because of the supreme importance of the office they seek—both candidates are virtually guaranteed to be well-funded, well-staffed, and extensively covered by national and local media.[22] As a result, presidential elections often look more like a "tug-of-war," in John Sides and Lynn Vavreck's description, with each campaign's activities more or less canceling out the effects of the other's.[23] This hardly proves that their activities do not matter; rather, as the two sides achieve relative parity, they help to maintain the fundamentals-based campaign equilibrium. In other words, while some campaign activities may be effective in and of themselves, if each side essentially counters the other (in roughly equal proportion, about as skillfully, and among the same or similar groups of voters), their net effects will be close to zero. Daron Shaw, however, warns against simply assuming that this will be the case in any given campaign. He states, "[A]lthough it is quite plausible that campaigns are equally competent in some aggregate sense, it is decidedly less plausible that they are equal in a given year. . . . Put another way, the volume of campaigning may be roughly equal . . . but the quality . . . may not be."[24]

Finally, to judge the effectiveness of a campaign in general (or a campaign visit in particular), one must understand its strategic objective. Of course, in presidential elections, the fundamental objective is to win by securing a majority in the Electoral College. But each campaign must devise a strategy for building that majority coalition, not just in terms of *where* to campaign but also *who* it is trying to reach. What is the target audience, so to speak? And what is the most effective way to try to win their votes? Political scientists and practitioners typically divide campaign strategies into two categories: persuasion versus mobilization. Persuasion strategies focus on changing people's minds, by getting undecided voters or those who support another candidate to support your candidate instead. But, as noted above, changing minds is difficult and most voters, particularly in recent years, make up their minds early in the campaign. That is why campaigns often prioritize mobilization over persuasion. Mobilization strategies focus on turnout—by getting people who are inclined to support your candidate, but who may sit out the election, to cast a ballot. In the simplest terms, persuasion is about influencing *who* a person votes for (vote choice), while mobilization is about influencing *whether* a person votes (turnout). It would be overstating the case to say that campaigns must choose between these strategies; in practice, campaigns can—and often do—pursue a mixture of both, particularly now that microtargeting makes it easier to personalize certain campaign appeals (e.g., online ads, fundraising emails, canvassing) based on a target's known political and demographic characteristics or consumer habits.[25] But broad public appeals, such as campaign visits, tend to force a choice between one strategy or the other, and since the early 2000s campaigns have become increasingly likely to pursue mobilization strategies.[26]

This chapter began with what might seem like a simple question: Do campaign visits work? The complexity of this question becomes apparent when put in its proper context. What do we learn? First, the opening question itself is problematic because—just like asking, "Do campaigns matter?"—it sets up a dichotomy that is not quite realistic or necessary. Campaigns, of which visits are an integral part, do not either determine election outcomes or have no effect at all; they matter, but their effects are limited and subject to constraints that may be outside of a candidate or campaign manager's immediate control. Indeed, campaigns do not take place in a vacuum; they operate within a context defined by electoral fundamentals that may favor or disfavor a given candidate, and in which their activities may be countered by an opponent. In that case, we should not expect to find that campaign visits simply work or do not work—that they decide election outcomes or else add up to a big waste of time. Rather, we must ask: under what conditions, and by what mechanisms, do they influence voting behavior? In other words, *when* and *why* do campaign visits matter?

Second, consider that campaign visits do not always serve the same strategic purpose for the same target audience. Rather, campaigns may vary in terms of what they want to accomplish and who they want to reach with these visits. We ought to judge their successes or failures accordingly. That is to say, we can measure visits' effectiveness in relation to campaign strategy, specifically in terms of whether (mobilization) and how (persuasion) people vote. In practical terms, this means that empirical assessments of campaign visit effects may use as their dependent variable voter turnout and/or vote choice at the aggregate or individual level. Effects may vary across candidates, depending on the strategic choices they make about where and how to campaign.

This book presents an original analysis of campaign visit effects in the 2008–2020 presidential elections, designed to clarify when and why visits matter, particularly in relation to strategies of persuasion versus mobilization. But this is hardly the first study of campaign visits, and it cannot be taken for granted that—simply because they are part of the campaign—visits should be expected to influence voting behavior, and specifically to persuade or mobilize the electorate. In that case, we cannot proceed to the empirical analysis that follows in subsequent chapters without first gaining a proper understanding of its theoretical underpinnings, the existing body of scientific knowledge that precedes it, and the unique scholarly contributions yet to be made.

The rest of this chapter is designed to achieve those objectives. It is organized around three questions, corresponding to theory, literature review, and gaps in the literature: first, why should we expect presidential campaign visits to influence voting behavior?; second, what do we already know about their effects?; third, what do we have left to learn?

WHY SHOULD WE EXPECT CAMPAIGN VISIT EFFECTS?

"The logic underlying the impact of direct campaigning is straightforward," Thomas Holbrook explains:

> Campaign appearances provide candidates with an opportunity to deliver their messages in a setting that may or may not generate national

media coverage but is almost guaranteed to generate extended local and state coverage. The local and state coverage of campaign activities translates into more localized exposure to the campaign rhetoric and, hence, greater opportunities for persuasion and mobilization at the state and local level. Also, since the candidates' stump speeches and other local activities are delivered in a relatively uncontested format, direct campaigning provides a great opportunity for candidates to convey their messages without interference from the other side.[27]

Three mechanisms for campaign visit effects are at work here: (local) media coverage; campaign messaging; persuasion and mobilization. Let's consider each one, in turn.

MEDIA COVERAGE

According to Daron Shaw and James Gimpel, "the underlying point of [campaign] appearances it to drive local [news] coverage."[28] This is a matter of consensus among scholars studying campaign visits. Why do campaigns focus on *local* media coverage? Why not try to reach as many voters as possible, via national media coverage?

First, consider the institutional context in which presidential campaigns take place. The objective is to win a majority in the Electoral College, not to win the national popular vote. In other words, presidential candidates must focus their efforts on winning over state electorates—enough to cobble together a total of 270 electoral votes—rather than the US electorate as a whole. The point is not to reach everyone, equally, but to reach people *in the right places*. Plenty of people, of course, live in "safe" states that (based on past voting behavior, as well as recent political, economic, and social dynamics) can be expected to vote for one party's presidential nominee, almost no matter what. It makes sense, then, for campaigns to target their resources (e.g., visits) and try to attract media attention primarily in those "swing" or "battleground" states that seem open to voting for either party's nominee. Attracting national media coverage, which reaches voters in safe and swing states alike, is all well and good, but quite beside the point.[29]

Second, campaign visits are much more likely to attract news coverage at the local rather than the national level. Frankly, most campaign visits are not that newsworthy to Americans as a whole. How many times, and in how many different ways, can national media outlets report on the same basic stump speech? And why should people care about an event happening in another part of the country if it doesn't yield any real *news* or directly affect their community? A local campaign visit is different. For voters, the fact that a candidate is coming to *their* city or part of the state is newsworthy in and of itself. Many people take it as a sign of respect, even an honor. As Shaw and Gimpel explain: "[C]ampaigns believe that in-person appearances send a signal to voters that the candidate cares about a particular set of local interests or concerns"—and, by extension, about *them*. Furthermore, local voters may conclude that the candidate, if elected, "is more likely to deliver individual or group benefits" that will directly affect their lives.[30]

Local media outlets help voters to make these connections in a way that national outlets cannot be expected to do, by highlighting the candidate's positions on issues of local importance, as articulated at an event or in response to questions posed during one-on-one interviews and press conferences. It is all the more likely that viewers will internalize the candidate's message when it is communicated in this context, because they tend to be more trusting of and attentive to local, versus national, news coverage.[31] As David C. King and David Morehouse put it: "a candidate's interview with a trusted local columnist or news anchor is often more compelling than an Associated Press interview by a remote reporter in Texas or Tennessee."[32] It is also the case that campaign visits often draw *sustained* coverage in local media outlets—not just on the day of an event, but before and after it takes place. For example, President Bill Clinton's visit to Chillicothe, Ohio, while running for reelection in 1996, was, according to one local newspaper editor, "lead story material for nine days." This included interviews, ticket information, and the solicitation of readers' questions for the candidate.[33]

Finally, presidential campaigns probably expect "softer" (that is, less critical or challenging) coverage from local, versus national, media outlets. Thomas Wood is a political scientist who worked on Mitt Romney's

2012 presidential campaign. As he explains: "a presidential campaign will often regard a political correspondent at a local TV affiliate as a 'soft touch' whose reluctance to grill a national political figure promises a receptive media setting for the campaign."[34] At times, candidates may be led astray by this expectation and expose themselves to embarrassment.[35] But in general, it is true that local media provide more positive campaign coverage.[36] Why is this the case? According to Shaw and Gimpel, "[C]ampaigns believe that local news media are so grateful when candidates pay a visit to their city that they eschew the hardball coverage that so often accompanies political reportage. Instead, reports are more positive, with relatively little cynicism in the description of the event itself and fewer quotes from the other side."[37] That is to say, local journalists may be so flattered by the candidate's attention to their local area, or by the rare opportunity to interview a national political figure, as to avoid exchanges that might ruin the moment—in contrast to, say, an interview with a CNN or *New York Times* reporter who regularly travels with the campaign.

In short, campaign visits give candidates the opportunity to earn extensive, largely positive—not to mention free—media coverage directly targeted at the voters who most urgently need to hear their message.

CAMPAIGN MESSAGING

Campaign visits might help to attract local voters' attention, but that in itself is not enough. Candidates must also have something worthwhile to *say*—something that will motivate voters to respond in ways that align with the campaign's strategic objectives, such as persuading those who are undecided or mobilizing latent supporters. In other words, candidates must communicate a campaign *message*. As Jeffrey M. Jones describes it, "[C]andidates use campaign visits to inform, to exhort, and to influence."[38] Campaign visits are ideal for this purpose because, as Holbrook indicates in the passage quoted above, at these events candidates speak directly to voters—without their message being diluted by interlocutors in an attempt to summarize or interpret. Candidates may also be able to speak directly to those who do not attend in person, because local broadcast media often air these events live or stream them on their websites. Finally, as noted above, candidates might have the opportunity to address voters in their own words through the local media interviews that typically accompany campaign visits.

Candidates communicate a message to voters not only by what they say at campaign events, but also by where they choose to hold these events. Which state or part of a state the candidate visits can send a message to voters. Take John McCain, for example, in 2008. After becoming the Republican Party's presumptive nominee that spring, McCain's campaign scheduled a two-part national tour designed to educate voters about who he was and what he stood for. First was a "biography tour"—in the candidate's words, to "reintroduce myself to voters" by giving mostly biographical speeches "in locations that had been important in my life," such as the U.S. Naval Academy and near the naval base in Pensacola, Florida, where he had trained as a pilot years earlier. Second was an "economic tour" of "places that hadn't shared in the prosperity of the previous quarter-century," including the site of a closed steel mill in Ohio, a coal mining region in Eastern Kentucky, and New Orleans' Ninth Ward. Both tours were designed to convey core elements of McCain's campaign message, the first "emphasizing my service to the nation" and the second "show[ing] I cared about every American community."[39]

Furthermore, the venue—that is, the actual facility or outdoor setting—chosen for a campaign event may help communicate a message to voters. Take a campaign memo sent by adviser Ted Van Dyk in August 1972, arguing that the campaign message or "principal theme . . . that George McGovern and the Democratic Party"—then struggling in a doomed effort to defeat President Richard Nixon's bid for reelection—must adopt is that they "deeply care about the well-being of decent hardworking people." To convey this message, he recommended that McGovern schedule, without any geographic specificity, "visits to assembly lines, bowling alleys, supermarket checkout counters, blue-collar shopping centers, [and] plant cafeterias."[40] Likewise, in 1980, nearly all of President Jimmy Carter's campaign advisers recommended that, in order to more effectively communicate to voters his first-term accomplishments and second-term objectives, he reinforce the substance of his speeches by delivering them at venues such as "an automobile plant with new American cars; a steel plant that was being modernized; [and by] . . . the signing of bills like mental health in a major mental hospital."[41]

Campaign visits present extraordinary opportunities for candidates to reach the voters they need to reach, in their own words. Sometimes it isn't even what they say, but where they go that gets a message across to voters.

PERSUASION AND MOBILIZATION

Campaign visits, and the messages they communicate, cannot be expected to have uniform effects across target populations. First, some people—particularly those with higher levels of education and political interest—are more likely than others to receive these messages by attending the actual event or by learning about it through local media coverage or interpersonal networks. Second, those people who do receive the campaign's message may vary in terms of their electoral dispositions: some are already planning to vote but are undecided or favor another candidate; others prefer the visiting candidate but have not yet decided to cast a vote. In that case, campaign visits may be effective at influencing one group of people while failing to influence another—for example, by persuading undecided voters to support the candidate while failing to mobilize turnout among marginal supporters, or vice versa. It seems unlikely that a campaign visit, or the message advanced by it, could achieve significant persuasion *and* mobilization effects all at once: the former requires empathy for those who do not already agree with the candidate, and often some indication of compromise or moderation, while the latter requires affirming not only existing points of agreement but also the candidate's commitment to governing accordingly and, in many cases, the dangers posed by electing someone with different views. In the simplest terms, persuasion usually requires appealing to the political center, while mobilization usually requires appealing to one's partisan base. In that case, campaign visits must either persuade *or* mobilize voters—right?

To be sure, previous studies of presidential campaign visits have tended to emphasize their mobilizing effects. Often, this approach is justified in terms of the expectations of campaign strategists and political experts. For example, J. Paul Herr explains: "Most political observers hold that campaign appearances succeed by increasing the turnout of supporters and less by changing preferences."[42] Thomas Holbrook and Scott McClurg, however, justify their expectations in theoretical terms. "Campaign activity increases participation," including voter turnout, they argue, primarily "by reducing information costs and creating interest in the campaign"—for instance, by educating voters about the candidates (e.g., their policy positions, professional qualifications, and personal qualities) and/or the election itself (e.g., registration deadlines or the election date). But not everyone pays attention to the campaign, and those who do are more likely to be politically interested enough already to favor one party or the other. Thus, "core party voters are more likely to receive and respond to campaign information," which, in effect, mobilizes partisans by "translat[ing] their natural predispositions into actual votes." Furthermore, campaign visits should be particularly effective at mobilizing partisan supporters—even more so than advertisements—"because they are targeted more directly at partisans and include more explicitly partisan cues."[43]

But this is not to say that campaign visits *only* have mobilizing effects. In fact, many studies explicitly allow for both possibilities. For example, Herr states that "one of the most important objectives of appearances . . . by a presidential candidate [is to] increase the turnout of supporters at the polls. . . . [Another] effect of appearances . . . is that they sway undecided voters toward the visiting candidate."[44] Holbrook and McClurg criticize Herr and other scholars—as well as some of Holbrook's earlier work—for "generally . . . not distinguish[ing] between the *persuasive* and *mobilizing effects* of campaigns in their analysis." It is important to do so, they argue, in order to identify the causal mechanism linking campaign activities to voting behavior: "Understanding which type of effect exists is central to our substantive understanding of the electoral process."⁴⁵ Holbrook and McClurg are right to call for greater clarity when analyzing the causal mechanisms undergirding campaign effects. However, much like the question of whether campaigns matter, it may not be entirely constructive or accurate to frame the debate in dichotomous terms—in this case, by seeking to identify "which type of effect exists." Indeed, while I share their expectation that campaign visits are most likely to have mobilizing effects, and for the same reasons, nonetheless I would argue that both effects are likely to "exist" for campaign visits in general, and even in a single instance. How can that be?

First, candidates may vary in terms of their ability to persuade or mobilize voters via campaign visits. Indeed, campaigns differ with respect to their relative emphasis on achieving such effects. Some campaigns strategies, in general, emphasize persuasion more than others, for instance.⁴⁶ The same is true when it comes to the geographic distribution of presidential campaign visits, with some candidates mostly visiting electorally competitive counties and others partisan base counties— thus indicating a strategic focus on persuasion versus mobilization, respectively.⁴⁷ For that matter, campaigns may shift their emphasis on persuasion versus mobilization as the campaign progresses, in response to electoral (e.g., polling, current events) or internal campaign dynamics (e.g., personnel changes, power struggles).⁴⁸ Even if it is the case (as Holbrook and McClurg argue, and I would also expect) that campaign visits in general are more effective at mobilizing than persuading voters, we should expect some persuasion effects, particularly from those candidates who organize their activities around this strategic goal. After all, a campaign may choose to focus on persuasion because this plays to the candidate's natural strengths.⁴⁹ Also, a campaign may design its events— for example, in terms of geographic location and venue, speech content, and the nature of the candidate's interaction with voters and local media—in such a way as to maximize the potential for achieving persuasion effects. Even if campaign visits in general mobilize more than persuade, these effects are not mutually exclusive and they are unlikely to be uniform across candidates.

Second, campaign visits have multiple audiences, and there is good reason to suspect that their effects will vary across audiences. Teddy

White, for example, references this dynamic in *The Making of the President 1960*, when he distinguishes between "personal" versus "strategically calculated" audiences for campaign events.[50] The former describes the relatively small group of people attending a given event in person, the latter the much larger group of people who learn about the event through newspaper, television, and other, mostly local media coverage. Shaw and Gimpel refer to this as "direct exposure" versus "indirect exposure" to campaign information.[51] King and Morehouse explicitly link this distinction to differential campaign effects: "Candidate visits have direct and indirect effects on voters. Some are personally persuaded by a candidate (the direct effect). Many more voters in an area that has been recently . . . visited by a candidate, however, are moved by the local media coverage [the indirect effect]."[52]

How, exactly, should these audiences and effects differ?

The "personal"—or as I will call it, "in-person"—audience is essential, even definitional, according to most Americans' conception of legitimate presidential campaigning.[53] It is a civic ideal that many people at these events will be undecided voters who attend in hopes of making up their virtuous, open minds. This may have been more common in the days of the whistle-stop tour, when anyone could crowd around the candidate's train to hear him speak—and many did so, out of curiosity more than anything else. But in recent years, candidates typically have held their events in closed indoor or outdoor spaces, where attendees are screened in advance (for instance, when requesting tickets), and troublemakers may be ejected from the premises. Moreover, the campaigns must reserve venues, and thus plan their events, well in advance. The upshot is that, because they often require attendees to engage in partisan networking and/or advanced planning, these events are not really designed to attract the less partisan and less politically engaged persuadable voter. Rather, in-person audiences tend to be made up of committed partisans who already plan to vote, and to vote for the visiting candidate. In other words, the potential for mobilization, let alone persuasion, effects among this audience would seem to be quite limited. In that case, what's the point?

One function of the in-person audience is to make the candidate look good for the "strategically calculated"—or, as I will call it, "target"—audience. As Holbrook and McClurg explain, campaign visits "place the candidate in front of sympathetic, partisan audiences," which "produce[s] the kind of good visuals campaign professionals strive for."[54] This is the more numerous, and thus more consequential, audience for campaign events. Among other things, a supportive in-person audience—who greet the candidate like a rock star, cheer when they are supposed to cheer, and boo when they are supposed to boo—give the target audience, who are following the event live or watching clips broadcast later, and perhaps even the journalists covering the event, the impression of fervent popular support for the visiting candidate. Also, it has become common in recent years for event organizers to carefully select and arrange attendees for placement behind the candidate, in the camera's view, in such a way as to help convey a favorable campaign message—for instance, that its supporters are diverse in terms of gender, age, and/or race and ethnicity.

In these respects, campaign events are typically not designed to influence the in-person audience so much as the in-person audience is designed to influence the target audience. This is part of the campaign's broader objective to exert indirect effects via media coverage and word of mouth. King and Morehouse explain: "Campaign visits can have very large multiplier effects through local outlets. Television, especially, reaches voters, but the free local media generated by candidate visits are especially valuable."[55] Here is where persuasion effects are most likely to occur, among people who do not attend an event but hear positive accounts of it, second-hand. Mobilization effects may be indirect, as well—for instance, if a candidate uses the event to convey a partisan message. But mobilization effects are more likely than persuasion effects to occur among other audiences.

Indeed, another function of the in-person audience is to engage in behavior outside of the event itself that may change how *other people* vote. This is a distinct form of mobilization, expanding the term as I described it previously to include "encourag[ing] people to participate by voting *or* joining the local campaign effort."⁵⁶ Campaigns are well aware of the potential for such mobilization effects via campaign visits, and they try hard to encourage it. Wood affirms, "It is campaign lore to expect a spike at a field office after a candidate visit is announced. Similarly, following a successful visit, campaigns attempt to capture the available information from those who have attended a rally, for example, so that they may be cajoled into providing volunteer labor, giving financial support, or just receiving a reminder to vote."⁵⁷

Jay Wendland's description of this mobilization effect, in the context of presidential primary campaigns, may be the most perceptive:

> Campaign visits are likely going to appeal to party activists—or at least those that are already paying attention to the campaign. Nonetheless, this is where we may see visits have a *two-step effect*, in that these activists will likely speak with neighbors, friends, family, and coworkers about the candidate they support. *By energizing activists through a visit, candidates are also hoping to gain grass roots volunteers to help inspire further support and more volunteers.*⁵⁸

Is this a direct or indirect effect of campaign visits? Here, I prefer to define "effects" in terms of concrete electoral outcomes: whether and for whom a person votes. A direct effect, in this context, would describe making one or both of those decisions as a result of experiencing the event itself, first-hand. An indirect effect would describe making one or both of those decisions as a result of experiencing the event in a mediated, or secondhand, fashion, by hearing someone else's account of it (e.g., media report, conversation with a friend or coworker). Volunteering for a campaign, or donating money to it, does not add a vote to the candidate's total by itself. But clearly it has the potential to cause such outcomes—for example, by inspiring attendees to distribute campaign literature or make phone calls to potential supporters, or funding television advertisements, which might persuade undecided voters and/or mobilize partisan sympathizers to vote. If and when such activities add a vote to the candidate's tally, it is not as a consequence of the event itself but rather the changes in behavior that the event brought about among attendees (with firsthand, or direct, exposure) or those who learned about it from someone else (with secondhand, or indirect, exposure). At such a distant remove from the original source, I would call this a "downstream effect" of campaign visits.

DISCUSSION

To summarize: campaign visits may have persuasive as well as mobilizing effects, although, based on Holbrook and McClurg's reasoning and the strategic tendencies of recent campaigns, I suspect that the latter is more common.[59] These effects are also likely to vary depending on the audience in question. For the in-person audience, I argue, campaign visits are unlikely to cause changes in vote choice (i.e., persuasion effects); more likely to cause changes in voter turnout (i.e., mobilization effects); and especially likely to cause increased activism among already committed voters that may influence other people's voting behavior. For the much larger and more heterogeneous target audience, campaign visits are likely to cause each of these effects. But, to the extent that persuasion effects occur, they are most likely among members of this audience.

At least, that is how campaign visits *might* work—in theory. But what does the evidence show?

WHAT DO WE ALREADY KNOW?

Do we know whether campaign visits matter—or, more precisely, when and how they influence presidential voting? There is no simple answer to this question. An accurate but admittedly unsatisfying assessment of the academic literature would be: it depends (on research design). Do we analyze campaign visits across multiple elections, or in just one? For presidential candidates only, or their vice-presidential running mates, too? Do we measure these effects at the aggregate level (i.e., voters within a particular state, county, or media market), or at the individual level (i.e., survey respondents)? Across every state, or only in electoral battlegrounds? Do we estimate these effects based on how people actually voted (i.e., aggregate election returns or, more problematically, self-reported vote choice and turnout) or how their preferences changed during the campaign (i.e., state polling averages or self-reported vote intentions)? What research methods should we use to estimate the effects of campaign visits, and what other factors must we statistically control for in our models?

There are good reasons to answer these questions differently based on, for instance, one's theory of campaign visit effects or the data available to study them in a given election or set of elections. Indeed, political scientists and other scholars often do just that. As a result, sometimes they reach different conclusions.

In this section, I provide an overview of scholarly research on the electoral effects of presidential campaign visits—first, in terms of vote choice; second, turnout; third, other relevant outcomes.[60] At this point, I do not present detailed discussions of research methodology or any original evidence; that is for later chapters, after introducing my dataset and providing a descriptive analysis of campaign visits in recent elections. Before doing so, it is essential to review the existing body of knowledge on this subject, in order to appreciate others' contributions and to identify opportunities for further contributions.

VOTE CHOICE

Boris Heersink and Brenton D. Peterson aptly summarize: "The existing political science literature on campaign visit effects has found mixed results . . . To the extent that there is any consensus within the literature, it appears that campaign visits—at best—have short term effects, but are unlikely to have major effects on the outcome of elections."[61] In terms of "mixed results," it is true that few studies find evidence that presidential campaign visits in a given election or set of elections exclusively influence or do not influence vote choice.[62] Most studies find that campaign visits influence presidential vote choice in some elections but not others, or for one candidate in a given election but not another. This is true for studies of the presidential election(s) of 1948, 1980–1988, 1996, 2000, 2000–2004, 2000–2008, 2012, and 2008–2016.[63] For example, in their analyses of the 1948 election, both Holbrook and Heersink and Peterson find that Harry Truman gained votes via campaign visits, while his Republican challenger, Thomas Dewey, did not. Holbrook estimates that Truman's visits added 0.25 percent to his state vote share, on average. Heersink and Peterson estimate that they added 3.0 percent to his county vote share, on average.[64]

Why might some candidates win votes via campaign visits, but not others? It is possible, for one thing, that some candidates are just more effective campaigners. Heersink and Peterson suggest this is why Truman's, but not Dewey's, visits made a difference; both outcomes align with the candidates' reputations on the stump.[65] Much the same could be said for Bill Clinton and Bob Dole in 1996: the former, like Truman, had the reputation of being an excellent campaigner and the latter, like Dewey, anything but. Sure enough, Herr estimates that Clinton's visits gained him votes, while Dole's did not.[66] Similarly, James M. Snyder and Hasin Yousaf find that in 2016, Donald Trump's visits increased support for his candidacy, but Hillary Clinton's had no such effect.[67] However, they also estimate that Barack Obama—like Trump, a prolific campaigner who drew enormous crowds of passionate supporters to his rallies—generally did not gain support via campaign visits in 2008 or 2012. Other factors may explain differential visit effects. For example, previous studies have examined the role of electoral fundamentals, favoring the incumbent (party) in good times and the challenger in bad times; partisan asymmetries, favoring Democrats, whose coalitional dynamics offer greater opportunities for mobilization; and campaign visit imbalances, favoring the more active candidate.[68]

In terms of literature review, to the extent that campaign visits influence candidate preferences, the effects seem to be short-lived. This suggests that visits may not cause changes in actual vote choice unless they occur close to Election Day, or just before voters cast early or absentee ballots. It is important to note that campaign effects, in general, tend to fade fairly quickly, as yesterday's news competes with today's greedy news cycle.⁶⁹ Direct evidence of this, with respect to campaign visits, is limited because tracking dynamic effects requires especially complex, costly, and thus less common data-collection efforts (e.g., panel studies, daily tracking polls) and methods of analysis (e.g., vector autoregression). However, two sophisticated analyses of visit effects in recent elections demonstrate the point. Snyder and Yousaf find strong evidence—based on survey data from the Cooperative Congressional Election Study—that, in 2016, Trump's campaign visits increased his support among respondents by about five percentage points in swing states, for two days afterward. But then these effects disappeared. The authors conclude: "Trump['s] rallies had a short-lived effect on the intention to vote for Trump that dies out at most three days after the rally."⁷⁰ Wood finds minimal evidence of visit effects in the 2012 election, mostly among independents and only for a day or two afterward. "These effects are not only small," he explains, "they are also ephemeral."⁷¹

Even if the effects of a campaign visit are fleeting, we cannot say they are irrelevant; it may just be a matter of timing. This seems to be the case in other studies that use state vote share as their dependent variable. Herr finds that only Bill Clinton's visits in the last month of the 1996 campaign had a statistically significant effect on vote choice; his earlier visits had no discernible effect.⁷² Jones finds that Democrats' campaign visits in the 1980–1988 elections generally had a significant effect on vote choice, while Republicans' visits did not. However, both parties' visits had stronger effects closer to Election Day.⁷³ Snyder and Yousaf also find evidence of temporal variation: Trump's rallies during the last week of the 2016 campaign significantly increased his vote share in visited media markets, while earlier rallies did not. They find a similar effect for Obama in 2008, but not in 2012 or for McCain in 2008, Romney in 2012, or Hillary Clinton in 2016.⁷⁴ Heersink and Peterson also do not find that Truman or Dewey's campaign visits were more effective later in the 1948 campaign.⁷⁵

We must recognize, then, that campaign visits have the potential to decide presidential elections, but usually they don't. This is because, as detailed above, most candidates' visits do not have discernible effects on vote choice, and those that do seem to be only, or perhaps most, effective toward the end of the campaign. When visit effects do occur, they tend to be small in magnitude—probably too small to make the difference in a given state, let alone the election as a whole. For example, the average effect of campaign visits on state vote share or intended vote choice, when this occurs, is usually around 0.5 percentage points or lower, but sometimes closer to one or even three percentage points.[76] When focusing on narrower geographic units, such as counties, in at least some states visits have been found to increase a candidate's support by around one percentage point or as many as three.[77]

If campaign visits are to decide an election, one or more exceptional factors must be in place. First, one candidate may gain votes via campaign visits while the opposing candidate does not, or does so but to a much lesser extent, giving the former an exclusive or exaggerated electoral advantage. Second, one candidate may campaign much harder than the opposing candidate, at least in a given geographical area, effectively winning the "tug-of-war" that Sides and Vavreck credit with maintaining electoral equilibria.[78] Third, electoral conditions must be competitive enough that even fairly small campaign effects could make the difference between one candidate's winning or losing. As previously noted, political scientists generally agree that electoral fundamentals establish a competitive equilibrium from which campaign effects may cause relatively minor deviations. To the extent that this is true, only in a naturally competitive environment will campaign visits be able to make the electoral difference.[79] Wood provides a fitting synthesis: "On balance . . . campaign events are found to have only a modest effect on voter behavior, such that only in the most marginal elections would the pattern of campaign visits prove decisive."[80]

VOTER TURNOUT

Fewer studies analyze the effects of presidential campaign visits on voter turnout, in comparison to vote choice. Those that do also tend toward mixed results. For example, Jones finds that, in the 1980–1992 elections, Democratic candidates' visits generally increased turnout (by

1.20 percentage points, on average, per media market) while Republican candidates' visits did not.[81] Likewise, Snyder and Yousaf find that, in 2016, Trump's visits increased intended voter turnout among survey respondents by 5.1 percentage points, while Hillary Clinton's visits—as well as those of Obama in 2008 and 2012, McCain in 2008, and Romney in 2012—had no effect.[82] However, in both cases, the timing of these visits mattered. In 1980–1992, visits by Democratic *and* Republican candidates had a greater effect on turnout later in the campaign. And in 2016, Trump's visits only influenced expected turnout for about two days. As is the case with vote choice, visits by Trump in 2016 and Obama in 2008 had a statistically significant effect on intended turnout in the last week of the campaign, but not beforehand, while Obama in 2012—like McCain in 2008, Romney in 2012, and Clinton in 2016—had no such effect at either point in the campaign. Other studies find only that campaign visits do or do not increase voter turnout.[83]

INDIRECT EFFECTS

Campaign visits may also have effects that indirectly influence vote choice and voter turnout—for example, via media coverage and campaign contributions. In terms of the former, Wood finds that visits had a "very modest" effect on local television and newspaper news coverage in 2012, resulting in three extra reports, on average.[84] Snyder and Yousaf's analysis of the 2016 election indicates that Trump and Clinton caused a significant increase in their local television and newspaper coverage on the day of a campaign visit and the following day, but not afterward.[85]

As for campaign donations, Snyder and Yousaf also find that Trump's visits caused a spike—of about 41 percent in swing states—for two days afterward, but then went away. Clinton in 2016, and both presidential candidates in 2008 and 2012, experienced no gains in campaign donations following their visits.[86] Boris Heersink, Brenton Peterson, and Jordan Carr Peterson, however, find that visits by Trump and Clinton—as well as Democratic vice-presidential candidate Tim Kaine—inspired an increase in campaign donations, in terms of the number of contributors and the total amount donated. At the same time, candidate visits sometimes inspired reactions from their opponents: Trump's visits caused an increase in donations to Clinton, in terms of the total amount and number of contributors, as did Clinton's visits for Trump.[87]

MOBILIZATION AND PERSUASION

It would appear from previous studies that campaign visits usually do not move votes. But when they do so, we must ask: *why*? Do they persuade undecided voters, mobilize partisan sympathizers, or both? First, let's ask: *how would we know the difference?* Previously, I framed persuasion effects primarily in terms of vote choice and mobilization effects primarily in terms of turnout. In that case, one might think that studies linking campaign visits to changes in a particular candidate's vote totals or polling numbers within a state, county, or media market provide clear evidence of persuasion effects and changes in overall vote totals or intended turnout, clear evidence of mobilization effects. But, as a matter of what social scientists call "ecological inference," one must be cautious when drawing conclusions about individual-level behaviors, such as vote choice and turnout, based on geographical or other *aggregations* of those behaviors (e.g., state election returns or polling averages). In short, that's because states, media markets, and counties don't vote: people do.

Consider, for example, Holbrook's estimate that Harry Truman's 1948 campaign visits increased his vote total within a given state by 0.25 percentage points, on average.[88] It is *not* safe to assume, as one might be tempted to do, that Truman's gains therefore came from winning over 0.25 percent of people in that state who had already planned to vote but for a different candidate, or had not chosen one until Truman's train rolled into town (i.e., persuasion). Another possibility, in the simplest theoretical terms, is that Truman's visits instead inspired enough people who favored him but had not planned to vote to cast a ballot, so that their addition to the otherwise existing electorate, by itself, increased his overall vote share by 0.25 percentage points (i.e., mobilization). For that matter, Truman's visits—based on what he said, how local media covered it, or other factors—at the same time might have alienated portions of the electorate, persuading previously favorable or undecided voters to choose a different candidate or mobilizing latent Republicans to cast a vote. Or, finally, his visits might have galvanized local Republican officials and activists to increase their persuasion and mobilization efforts.

In reality, campaign visits probably have all of these effects, to some degree.[89] To the extent that one type of effect (e.g., persuading undecided voters) overwhelms another (e.g., the other party mobilizing latent supporters in response), we should find evidence of an overall campaign visit effect (e.g., a 0.25 percentage-point increase in Truman's vote share). And, to the extent that one type of effect (e.g., persuading undecided voters) is canceled out by another (e.g., alienating other undecided voters), we should find no overall visit effect (e.g., Dewey in 1948).[90] In each case, we may credibly estimate the overall effects of campaign visits. However, disentangling the underlying causes of those effects and estimating their relative weight is difficult and, in some cases, practically impossible, especially when working with aggregate-level data. Often, studies of campaign visits do not even try to do so.[91]

Some studies of campaign visits have tried to identify persuasion and mobilization effects. One way of doing so has been to compare their effects in geographic areas that differ in terms of aggregate partisanship—essentially, in safe versus swing states or counties. For example, Heersink and Peterson find that Truman's visits gained him votes in safe Republican and swing counties, but most of all in safe Democratic counties (in each case, defined by their partisan vote share in the previous election).[92] This suggests that Truman persuaded but even more so mobilized voters via campaign visits. Jeffrey S. Hill, Elaine Rodriguez, and Amanda E. Wooden compare visit effects in battleground versus safe states, again suggesting the possibilities of persuasion versus mobilization, respectively.[93] Their evidence is quite mixed: in most cases, visits had no apparent effect on voters' preferences, but when they did, the results were about equally likely to suggest persuasion versus mobilization. For example, in 2008, Hill and his colleagues find that Obama's visits increased his support in battleground states, indicating persuasion, *and* in safe Democratic states, indicating mobilization, while having no effect in safe Republican states. However, visits by Bush in 2000 and Cheney in 2004 appear to have mobilized voters in safe Republican states while failing to persuade voters in battleground and safe Democratic states. Finally, with respect to turnout, Damon Cann and Jeffrey Bryan Cole find that the indirect effects of campaign visits are much greater in battleground states, which would seem to indicate persuasion.[94]

Shaw provides a more direct test of persuasion versus mobilization effects in the 1988–1996 presidential elections, by regressing the Republican candidate's state vote share on a variable interacting the net difference in candidate visits to that state with the percentage of undecided (persuasion) *or* partisan (mobilization) voters in its electorate. In most cases, he finds evidence of persuasion and mobilization effects, but a bit more of the latter.[95] However, his analysis of the 2000–2004 elections does not yield comparable results. Here, he finds "little evidence for the sorts of interactive effects—mobilization and persuasion—that I found for 1988 through 1996."[96] Holbrook and McClurg use the partisan composition of the electorate as their dependent variable. They do not find that campaign visits cause a surge in independent voters (persuasion) or in net partisanship among voters (mobilization).[97]

The best way to isolate persuasion and mobilization effects is to use individual-level data, whereby scholars may directly examine how exposure to campaign visits combines with partisan predispositions to affect voting behavior. To date, only one study has done so. Snyder and Yousaf separately regress vote choice and turnout in the 2016 presidential election on the interaction of party identification—separated into five dichotomous variables, indicating strong partisanship, weak partisanship, or independence—and exposure to a Trump campaign rally—also a dichotomous variable, indicating whether Trump had or had not visited the survey respondent's media market in the ten days prior to an interview. This innovative analysis provides evidence of mobilization effects; Trump's rallies are associated with increased support among strong and weak Republicans and increased turnout among strong

Republicans—as well as strong Democrats! By contrast, we see no evidence of persuasion effects: Trump's rallies did not increase support for his candidacy or turnout among independents or weak Democrats.[98]

DISCUSSION

What do we know about the effects of presidential campaign visits? Quite a bit, but not nearly enough. Indeed, there have been many studies of their effects on vote choice, voter turnout, and other electorally relevant outcomes, some of which try to distinguish between persuasion versus mobilization effects. In every respect, these results are not consistent enough to deliver an authoritative yes-or-no answer as to whether campaign visits matter, let alone when or why. Rather, the results are best described as "mixed"—not just across but even within studies, owing to a range of factors including differences in research methodologies, units of analysis, election years, and candidates. A concise and comprehensive synthesis of the literature is not possible. But a reasonable attempt might go like this: campaign visits can win votes and get people to the polls, but usually they don't; and if effective, it is probably because they mobilized partisans rather than persuading undecided voters.

WHAT IS LEFT TO LEARN?

Given the central role that campaign visits play in contemporary presidential elections, it is vitally important that we understand their effects on voting behavior. Previous studies yield important insights into these effects. But there is still much to learn. This book is designed to address some of the limitations of the existing literature, and to provide a more comprehensive analysis of the electoral significance of presidential campaign visits. Specifically, it improves upon previous analyses of visit effects by analyzing multiple elections, using the same data sources and research methods, to enhance generalizability; focusing on more recent elections that capture campaigns' shift toward mobilization over persuasion strategies; including the 2020 election, in which the candidates' disparate approaches to campaign visits provide a unique opportunity to observe visit effects; using individual-level data to estimate persuasion and mobilization effects across multiple candidacies, and compare estimated effects to those based on aggregate-level data; and directly linking campaign strategies to campaign visit effects.

GENERALIZABILITY

The fundamental goal of this book is to understand the electoral significance of presidential campaign visits *in general*, not just within one particular election. That requires examining multiple elections—in this case, the four most recent ones, from 2008 to 2020. The existing literature on campaign visit effects includes several studies that encompass multiple—from as few as two to as many as five—elections.[99] More often, studies of this topic focus on a single election.[100] This makes it difficult to draw more general conclusions about visit effects, especially because many of these studies use different criteria or time frames for identifying campaign visits, as well as different units of analysis, dependent variables, control variables, and research methodologies. Greater consistency on these points should make it more practical to compare effects across elections and reach more broadly applicable conclusions.

However, one should not expect campaign visits to have the same effects in each election, for each candidate, and across each state. As the preceding literature review indicates, these effects may vary depending on such factors as the candidate's campaigning abilities or the context of a given election. Indeed, Shaw cautions against making direct comparisons across election years. He notes that

> one could analyze and compare several campaigns, with an eye toward developing a broader conceptualization of presidential electioneering.... However, it is not clear that comparing multiple cases is a wise strategy. For starters, the technical innovations occurring

between 1988 and 2004—the internet, e-mail, cell phones, and the like—are staggering. Campaigning simply looks different today than it did as recently as a decade ago.[101]

I agree that it is unrealistic to strive for a comprehensive, overall judgment about the effectiveness of campaign visits: that they win votes or do not, increase turnout or do not. But the alternative, of judging each election in isolation from another, without drawing any broader conclusions, is even less appealing. In this book, I make comparisons across elections, in hopes of identifying general patterns of visit effects, but with the caveat that each election—whether because of fundamentals, technological developments, or other idiosyncrasies—differs in fundamental ways from another. In other words, I attempt to strike a balance between drawing general conclusions about campaign visit effects and recognizing the unique electoral context in which those visits occur.

TWENTY-FIRST-CENTURY CAMPAIGNING

Another important goal for this book is to provide the most updated and relevant possible analysis of campaign visit effects. Of course, one could make such an argument at any time. But it is particularly compelling in the present context. Specifically, I say this because twenty-first-century campaigning has taken a noticeable (and much commented-upon) turn toward mobilization. Costas Panagopoulos documents this trend, particularly in terms of grassroots campaigning, and traces its origins to the 2000 and 2004 presidential elections.[102] Shaw, who worked for the Bush campaigns in both elections, observes that "most scholars would now agree that campaigns are more about mobilization than they are about persuasion."[103] In that case, it is reasonable to suggest that the effectiveness of campaign visits, or at least the mechanism whereby these effects occur, might have changed in the time since many of the studies discussed in the preceding literature review were conducted.

In the same book, Shaw makes an interesting observation regarding the relationship between campaign financing and campaign effects. At the time, he noted, "federal law imposes spending limits on the candidates' campaigns in exchange for public funding." As a result, "This public funding supposedly puts the major party candidates on roughly equal footing—certainly in the aggregate—and makes it difficult to achieve an advantage in terms of campaign volume in a given state or locale. Sometimes this equality is 'rougher' than not . . . but it holds as a general condition."[104]

Since that time, the campaign financing landscape has changed considerably. In 2008, Barack Obama became the first presidential candidate to forgo federal funding and the attendant campaign spending limits, a precedent that each subsequent major-party candidate has followed. Also, U.S. Supreme Court rulings since 2010 have opened the door for individuals and corporations to make unlimited campaign contributions in support of a political figure or cause, albeit not directly to an individual campaign committee. In that case, if Shaw's earlier analysis was correct, one might suspect that these changes have given presidential candidates greater opportunities to establish financial advantages over their opponents, and thus to achieve greater campaign effects (via visits, among other things) than in past elections. Again, this makes it all the more important, and not just in a generic sense, to provide an updated analysis of the role that campaign visits play in U.S. presidential elections.

THE 2020 PRESIDENTIAL ELECTION

At the time of this writing, no other study has analyzed the effects of campaign visits in the 2020 presidential election. In that sense alone, this book makes an important contribution. But again, this is not just a generic contribution—as in, "the more up-to-date, the better." Rather, the 2020 election provides an extraordinary opportunity to analyze the effects of presidential campaign visits. In short, this is because, as detailed in this book's introduction, the candidates' approaches to in-person campaigning differed more in 2020 than in any other recent election. Specifically, Donald Trump campaigned that fall as any candidate normally would—by holding large in-person rallies, almost nonstop—while Joe Biden held less-frequent, often small-scale and sometimes strictly virtual events, in response to the COVID-19 pandemic. In that sense, the 2020 election comes closer than any other recent precedent to approximating a "natural experiment" that might help answer a persistent but, to this point, mostly fanciful question in the campaign visits literature: *what if the presidential candidates just stayed home?*

Indeed, some scholars—unimpressed by the demonstrable effects of campaign visits, or lack thereof—have raised such provocative questions. Wood, for example, imagined this "thought experiment: if visits have only a moderate impact on voters but consume vast amounts of the candidates' and their staff's time, attention, and resources, why not neglect visits and instead redouble candidates' attention to fundraising?"[105] To be clear, Wood's question is not rhetorical; he goes on to weigh the pros and cons of adopting such a risky strategy. But it is a compelling hypothetical, with clear implications for the 2020 campaign; after all, while Joe Biden largely stayed at home in Delaware that spring and summer, he raised an enormous amount of money, not only overcoming Trump's initial financial advantage but far surpassing him by the fall. Other scholars had speculated about the advantages of virtual campaigning years earlier. Specifically, Scott L. Althaus, Peter F. Nardulli, and Daron R. Shaw wrote at the dawn of the twenty-first century: "The potential for candidates to personally connect with millions of voters via the Internet could significantly change the nature and scope of candidate travel and profoundly affect the future conduct of presidential elections. 'Virtual' town halls might serve as a focal point of the campaign and dramatically reduce 'in the flesh' appearances."[106]

Of course, this would not be the case unless campaigns perceived an advantage in moving toward virtual campaigning—assuming either that doing so would not diminish the effectiveness of their campaign "visits," or that the difference would be so minimal that other advantages gained, in terms of travel costs and the candidate's well-being, would overwhelm it.

Other scholars, while not going so far as to actually call for an end to in-person campaigning, have raised the point even more bluntly. Shaw and Gimpel, for example, offer this assessment of the previous literature on campaign visits: "Put succinctly, little hard evidence exists that would dissuade a skeptic from asking whether a candidate's time and energy might be better spent at home rather than on the road."[107] Also, reflecting on their research showing that Trump's campaign visits did nothing to help Republican candidates during the 2018 midterm elections, Alan I. Abramowitz and Costas Panagopoulos state: "Our findings suggest that whether or not presidential candidates are able to conduct traditional campaign events may have little impact on the behavior of the electorate."[108]

The COVID-19 pandemic so altered the 2020 presidential campaign—at least for Democrats—that it in some ways it represents a unique opportunity to estimate what happens when one side in the quadrennial "tug-of-war" lets go of the rope. For instance, Joshua Darr observes that the Biden campaign's decision not to open any in-person field offices, in stark contrast to his opponent, presents researchers with a natural experiment for studying their electoral significance. He explains: "Political scientists are trained to look for campaign effects in situations with unequal effort by campaigns: for example, if one candidate is airing way more ads or receiving outsized media attention."[109] Or, for that matter, if one—and only one—candidate dramatically scales back the size and scope of his campaign visits, as Biden did in 2020. If any election could show that in-person campaigning is a waste of time—or well worth it—this is the one.

INDIVIDUAL- VERSUS AGGREGATE-LEVEL DATA

As discussed in the previous section, it is most appropriate to use individual-level data (e.g., survey responses) when evaluating the causes of individual-level behaviors such as whether and for whom to vote. However, only a few studies use individual-level data to evaluate campaign visits effects; the rest use aggregate-level data, such as state election returns or polling averages.[110] Furthermore, only Snyder and Yousaf use individual-level data to identify the persuasive versus mobilizing effects of campaign visits.[111] Theirs is a critical contribution to the relevant literature, and not just for this reason. But it is also limited in several respects, each of which I address in this book.

First, Snyder and Yousaf analyze persuasion and mobilization effects for only one candidate (Trump) and in one election year (2016); I analyze these effects for four candidates (the major party presidential and vice-presidential candidates) in each of the 2008–2020 elections. Second, they measure exposure to campaign visits dichotomously (i.e., whether or not Trump visited a respondent's media market within the previous ten days), and do not account for the potentially countervailing effects of an opponent's visit(s) to the same area. I measure campaign visits cumulatively, and statistically control for the opposing presidential and vice-presidential, as well as the copartisan vice-presidential candidates' visits. Third, they restrict the respondent sample only to those with a stated preference for one of the two major-party candidates prior to the election, thereby excluding undecided voters and minor party supporters who might be swayed by campaign visits, particularly in a tumultuous election year such as 2016. I use actual, rather than intended, vote choice and voter turnout as my dependent variables, thereby including many previously undecided voters who ended up choosing a major-party candidate. Finally, to better understand the inferential implications of using aggregate- versus individual-level data, I use both approaches to analyze visit effects for each candidate in each election, and then compare substantive conclusions accordingly.

Most election surveys include too few respondents by state, let alone county or media market, to permit robust analyses of geographically targeted activities such as candidate visits. Recognizing that in most cases it is therefore more practical for researchers to use aggregate-level data, my analysis may be useful to future researchers as they weigh the costs and benefits of using one type of data source versus the other for this purpose.

CAMPAIGN STRATEGY AND CAMPAIGN EFFECTS

This book is unusual—with Shaw's *The Race to 270* being one kindred spirit—in that it pairs detailed analysis of the strategy of presidential campaign visits with detailed analysis of their effects. Specifically, in chapter 4, I use data on presidential campaign visits in the 2008–2020 elections, as well as county-level demographic and political characteristics, to identify whether a given campaign prioritized persuasion over mobilization, or vice versa. Indeed, previous studies indicate that presidential campaigns, even in the same election year, often pursue different strategies, as judged by visit patterns.[112] To the extent that some campaigns are more effective at achieving persuasion versus mobilization effects, this may not be random; rather, it may reflect the strategic intentions of a given campaign and the way that it conducts visits (e.g., geographic location, venue, speech content, crowd and media interaction, follow-up contact with attendees). This is an important step toward understanding the effectiveness of campaign visits, because it answers an essential question: effective at doing what, exactly?

Presidential campaigns influence voting behavior, and thus election outcomes, on the margins, competing to achieve favorable deviations from an equilibrium established by electoral fundamentals such as economic conditions and presidential incumbency. As is the case with campaigns in general, the question is not whether campaign visits matter, but when and why they matter. To the extent that visits influence vote choice and voter turnout, as well as other behaviors with downstream effects on the same, this is likely to come from persuading undecided voters and/or mobilizing latent partisans via local media coverage, interpersonal networks, and grassroots activism, all of which amplify the campaign's message.

Based on the existing literature, it seems that campaign visits more often than not fail to influence voting behavior—or, at best, have countervailing effects (e.g., persuasion *and* alienation; mobilization of supporters *and* opponents) that essentially cancel each other out. But in some cases, their effects are consequential, perhaps even decisive, and apparently caused by persuasion or, more often, mobilization. However, the literature has significant limitations, which this book seeks to address. Specifically, I provide a comprehensive account of campaign visit effects, by analyzing the four most recent presidential elections, including the anomalous 2020 Trump–Biden campaign, using uniform methods of analysis, as well as individual- and aggregate-level data. Furthermore, I evaluate the effectiveness of these visits in relation to each campaign's strategic emphasis on persuasion versus mobilization, as indicated by its visit allocation patterns.

The rest of this book is designed to achieve the objectives just stated. In chapter 3, I introduce an original dataset of presidential campaign visits in the 2008–2020 elections and present a descriptive analysis of those visits. In chapter 4, I analyze the geographic distribution of campaign visits, particularly with respect to local political and demographic characteristics, for the purpose of identifying persuasion versus mobilization strategies. In chapter 5, I analyze campaign visit effects—specifically, in terms of vote choice and voter turnout, while empirically distinguishing between the causal mechanisms of persuasion versus mobilization—in the 2008–2020 presidential elections. Finally, in the concluding chapter, I discuss the implications of this research for the future conduct and study of presidential campaigning.

3

PRESIDENTIAL CAMPAIGN VISITS, BY THE NUMBERS

The principal objective of this book is to evaluate the strategy and effectiveness of presidential campaign visits. The next two chapters present empirical evidence toward that end. But first, it is essential to describe the data upon which those analyses are based. This chapter introduces the Campaign Visits Database (CVD)—an original dataset including 1,440 campaign visits from the 2008–2020 presidential elections.[1] After explaining the criteria used to identify and count campaign visits, I present a descriptive analysis of the data. Specifically, I describe *how many* campaign visits take place in a typical election year, as well as *when* and—in terms of host venues—*where* they take place. This overview provides necessary context for the more complex empirical analyses presented in subsequent chapters.

WHAT *IS* A CAMPAIGN VISIT?

I define campaign visits as *any public, in-person appearance apparently organized or initiated by the candidates or their campaign, for the purpose of appealing to a localized concentration of voters.* This definition excludes nationally oriented events (e.g., national party conventions, national conferences, presidential debates, and historical commemorations), as well as events in which the public and/or the press are prohibited from participating (e.g., private fundraisers, closed press conferences).

To understand how I put this definition into practice—and, for that matter, why defining campaign visits is a more complex task than one might think—consider one eventful week from Donald Trump's 2020 campaign.

DONALD TRUMP, 2020

On Friday, October 2, 2020, President Donald Trump announced via Twitter that he had tested positive for COVID-19. White House physician Sean Conley reported that Trump and his wife, Melania, who also contracted the virus, were "both well at this time, and they plan to remain at home within the White House during their convalescence."[2] But, with Trump's symptoms worsening, that evening he was hospitalized at the Walter Reed National Military Medical Center, in Bethesda, Maryland. He would recover, following significant health scares and aggressive medical treatments, and return to the White House three days later.

Trump campaign manager Bill Stepien issued a press release that Friday, stating: "All previously announced campaign events involving the President's participation are in the process of being moved to virtual events or are being temporarily postponed."[3] These included two events scheduled for that day: a roundtable discussion with supporters in Washington, DC, and an airport rally in Sanford, Florida. Trump would not return to the campaign trail until October 12. By all accounts, he was desperate to do so. As *Politico*'s Nancy Cook put it later that month: "Trump views rallies in battleground states as the linchpin of his closing argument, a means to excite his supporters and ensure they vote on Nov. 3."[4] For their part, "[Trump's] advisers were hoping to close the gap [on Democratic frontrunner Joe Biden] in upcoming weeks with an aggressive travel schedule."[5]

Indeed, Trump had been quite active over the previous week. On Saturday, September 26, the President hosted 150 guests in the White House's Rose Garden for a ceremony followed by an indoor reception to announce his nomination of Judge Amy Coney Barrett to the U.S. Supreme Court. That evening, he held a rally at the Harrisburg International Airport in Middletown, Pennsylvania. It was attended by "perhaps a few thousand" supporters, many of whom had watched the announcement ceremony while waiting outside, for hours, in the rain. In an eighty-minute speech, Trump touted Barrett's credentials while also addressing several major campaign themes and predicting victory in Pennsylvania—by "a lot more" than in 2016. "The only way they [Democrats] can win Pennsylvania is to cheat on the ballots," Trump claimed. Nonetheless, he pleaded with supporters to get to the polls. "All I am asking is people to go out to vote, go out to vote."[6]

Trump returned to Washington, DC, that night. On Sunday, after playing a round of golf at one of his courses in northern Virginia, he held two events at the White House: a press conference and an East Room reception for Gold Star military families. On Monday, he held a press conference in the Rose Garden to introduce his administration's new COVID testing strategy, following an event on the White House's South Lawn to promote Lordstown Motors' new electric pickup truck. This event was clearly intended to appeal to voters in northeastern Ohio, where Trump had promised to bring back jobs at a recently closed General Motors assembly plant—the very plant that Lordstown Motors was using to manufacture its new pickup (albeit with many fewer workers).[7]

On Tuesday, Trump was at Case Western Reserve University in Cleveland for the first presidential debate. It was an ugly affair from the start, with Trump interrupting his opponent so often that Biden finally blurted out: "Will you shut up, man? This is so unpresidential." One subject of debate—or argument, really—was Trump's campaign rallies. When pressed on the lack of masking and social distancing at these events, Trump insisted: "We've had no negative effect, and we've had thirty-five to forty thousand people at some of these rallies." Biden insisted that it was "totally irresponsible" to hold such events, to which Trump responded: "If you could get the crowds, you would have done the same thing. But you can't."⁸

On Wednesday, Trump held two events in Minnesota. First, he attended a fundraiser at the lakeside home of Cambria Countertops CEO and supporter Marty Davis, in the Minneapolis suburb of Shorewood. Trump was expected to raise $7 million at the event, which was closed to the media and the public.⁹ Second, that evening, he held a rally about 150 miles to the northeast, at the Duluth International Airport. At least one thousand supporters braved the wind and rain to hear Trump speak. He touched on several major campaign themes, including the Barrett nomination and policing, but also emphasized local issues. Speaking from a stage flanked by tractor trailers bearing signs that read "Make Logging Great Again," Trump boasted of his support for mining and oil pipeline projects in Minnesota, while blaming Biden for mine closures that took place while he was vice president. Appealing to local pride, Trump said that Minnesota had "the greatest iron ore anywhere in the world" and took credit for reviving the industry: "After I put tariffs on foreign steel, the iron range came roaring back." He also criticized refugee resettlements in the state, and the Somali-American congresswoman from Minneapolis, Ilhan Omar. Summing up his appeal to voters, Trump said: "[Y]ou have a president who is standing up for America and standing up for the great people of Minnesota. . . . So get your friends, get your family, get your neighbors and get your workers and get out and vote. We've got to win."¹⁰

Trump's speech in Duluth lasted only forty-six minutes, which was rather brief by his standards. He seemed tired and his voice was raspy. For a busy candidate, this was hardly unusual. But there was reason to be concerned: Hope Hicks—one of Trump's closest advisers, who had spent much of the past week traveling and meeting with him, usually indoors and without a mask—developed COVID-like symptoms that evening and had to isolate herself from others on the flight from Minnesota to Washington, DC. The next morning, on Thursday, Hicks tested positive for the virus. Trump was informed of this, but, in violation of Centers for Disease Control guidelines requiring self-isolation following close contact, he left shortly thereafter to attend a fundraiser at the

Trump National Golf Club in Bedminster, New Jersey.[11] After speaking to about three hundred donors at an outdoor reception, Trump met indoors—unmasked, albeit socially distanced—with about forty donors of $50,000 or more at a VIP reception, and eighteen donors of $250,000 or more for a roundtable discussion. Trump raised approximately $5 million at the fundraiser, which attracted donors from across the United States.[12]

That evening, Trump—as well as Biden—appeared via video recording at the Al Smith Memorial Foundation dinner, an annual New York City charity event held virtually in 2020 due to the pandemic. Following unofficial reports of Hicks' diagnosis, at 9:30 p.m., Trump called in to Fox News' *Hannity* show to say that he was awaiting the results of a COVID-19 test. A few hours later, at 12:54 a.m. on Friday, Trump announced that he and Melania had tested positive for the virus.[13]

It was a dramatic conclusion to a busy week, in which Trump made a dozen public appearances in Washington, DC, and across the United States. For our purposes, the question is: how many *campaign visits* did he make?

DEFINING CAMPAIGN VISITS

Answer: It depends on how you define campaign visits. But, by my count, it would be two.

Again, I define campaign visits as *any public, in-person appearance apparently organized or initiated by the candidates or their campaign, for the purpose of appealing to a localized concentration of voters.* This definition distinguishes "campaign visits" from the broader concept of "campaign events"—which Daron R. Shaw, for example, defines as "an occurrence that conveys distinct political information about the presidential candidates to the electorate," such as a campaign speech, debate, party convention, or gaffe.[14] Many of these events are national in scope and take place at sites not directly chosen by an individual candidate or campaign. Therefore, they are not conducive to making geographically oriented inferences about campaign strategy or comparing effects across "treated" versus "untreated" audiences. In other words, including such events in my data would not align well with the principal objectives of this book: to evaluate the strategy and effectiveness of presidential campaign visits.[15]

This definition also requires that the apparent purpose of an event be to win votes in the locale that the candidate has chosen to visit—whether directly, by interacting with voters, or indirectly, by attracting local media coverage. This is why I do not treat fundraisers as campaign visits: the apparent purpose of such events is to raise money, not win votes; whatever indirect effects those funds have on voters is not likely to be locally concentrated, since they go into the campaign's general treasury and can be spent anywhere; and there is little chance of influencing local voters because most fundraisers are private events closed to the news media and anyone but the candidate's financially committed supporters.[16] Also, while some fundraisers take place in swing states, many take place in safe states and particularly in areas where wealthy donors are concentrated (e.g., New York City, Hollywood). Clearly, the purpose of such travel is to rake in money, not to add votes in places where the race is effectively over already. Treating these events as "campaign visits," therefore, would distort my analysis of campaign strategy in chapter 4. Similarly, I would not treat White House events hosted by the incumbent president—or, for example, analogous events held by an incumbent governor in the state's capital—as campaign visits, unless there was clear evidence that the event was campaign-oriented and targeted toward local voters.

Finally, my definition of campaign visits encompasses events that are "apparently organized *or* initiated by the candidates *or* their campaign" (emphasis added). Essentially, this allows me to include unannounced stops, such as surprise visits to a restaurant, another local business, or a school. For example, on October 27, 2016, Democratic presidential candidate Hillary Clinton followed up a speech at Wake Forest University in Winston-Salem, North Carolina, by making surprise visits to two nearby universities. First, at the University of North Carolina-Greensboro, she greeted students at an early voting site. Then, at North Carolina A&T State University, she appeared on stage as the guest speaker at a homecoming rally.[17] Clearly, these visits were calculated to increase voter turnout among favorable constituencies—specifically, college students and (in the case of North Carolina A&T) Black students, in particular. There is no question that these should qualify as "campaign visits." But they would not be included if I required that visits be announced in advance, as some studies at least seem to do—"A campaign event is an appearance . . . at a publicly announced event"—or if I relied on official campaign itineraries or some popular online resources to identify visits.[18] Conversely, I do not include visits that were scheduled but did not take place.

Thus, by my definition, Donald Trump made only two "campaign visits" between September 26 and October 2, 2020, those being the airport rallies in Pennsylvania and Minnesota. Both events clearly fit the specified criteria. They were: 1) public, in-person appearances; 2) organized by the Trump campaign; and 3) apparently held for the purpose of appealing to a localized concentration of voters. In Minnesota, particularly, Trump and his campaign tailored their message to emphasize local issues and identity.

Each of the other events from that week fail to qualify for at least one reason. Trump's White House events (the Barrett announcement, the Gold Star families reception, and the two press conferences) were clearly not designed to appeal to a localized concentration of voters. The other White House event promoting the Lordstown Motors pickup truck on the South Lawn was, in fact, designed to appeal to voters in northeastern Ohio. Had Trump appeared in person in Ohio and held the same event, this would have qualified as a campaign visit. By my criteria, however, he could not "visit" Ohio from Washington, DC. Likewise, his virtual appearance at the Al Smith dinner does not count as a campaign visit to New York City. Nor do the two fundraisers he attended, or the two cancelled appearances on October 2. Trump's golf outing in Virginia on September 27 might qualify if there were evidence that he used the opportunity to engage with voters and attract local media attention. But I know of no such evidence. It seems that Trump simply wanted to play golf, and chose this course because it was the closest one that he owned.

DISCUSSION

Political scientists do not agree on a common definition of "campaign visits," nor is there an official, centralized resource from which to draw data for an analysis such as this. As Jay Wendland aptly states: "Visits data is harder to collect because candidates do not have to report their visits schedules to a central organization like they do campaign spending."[19] Even with reliable information on candidates' overall activities, analyzing campaign visits can be an uncertain exercise because "It is difficult to pin down the variable of interest, both practically and conceptually."[20]

To reach well-founded conclusions about the strategy and effectiveness of campaign visits, scholars must begin by providing and faithfully applying an appropriate conceptual definition. Some studies of campaign visits provide no definition at all.[21] Others provide only a cursory definition: for example, Eric M. Appleman, creator of the popular online resource Democracy in Action—from which several prominent studies obtain their data—states simply: "A visit is fairly straightforward. If a candidate enters a state, does an event or events and then leaves the state, that is a visit."[22] Other studies define campaign visits only by listing which types of events are included ("visits include campaign rallies, town hall meetings, stump speeches, and stopping by a local restaurant or pub to talk with voters") or excluded (visits are "public, nonfundraising, campaign stops") from their data.[23] A few studies provide clearer and more comprehensive definitions: for example, "Campaign appearances are defined to be events at which a candidate either makes some public address to an audience (whether the address takes the form of a major speech or brief remarks, but excluding news conferences) or participates in some public activity like a parade, motorcade, or fair."[24]

I have provided my own definition of campaign visits, and explained its central features.[25] Furthermore, I have demonstrated how this definition can be applied to a diverse range of candidate activities, using one week from Donald Trump's 2020 reelection campaign as a point of reference. This information is essential to understanding the Campaign Visits Database. In short, it explains why certain events are included in the dataset as "campaign visits" while others are not. But that is only one part of the data-collection process.

WHOSE VISITS COUNT—AND *HOW OFTEN*?

To illustrate what, according to my definition, constitutes a "campaign visit," in the previous section I described a week in the life of then-president and presidential candidate Donald Trump. But what if the candidate in question were not running for *president*? And what if he or she made multiple stops in the same state, even the same city, on a single day? How many "campaign visits" would that candidate have made? Let's try another example.

JOE BIDEN, 2012

At 4:00 p.m. on October 23, 2012, Vice President Joe Biden bounded onto the stage at Triangle Park in Dayton, Ohio. Sporting his trademark aviator sunglasses and a dress shirt with rolled-up sleeves, Biden appeared (as his boss liked to say) fired up, ready to go. "*Hello, Ohio!*" he called out—a rock star's words, in a politician's voice. The vice president beamed as he admired the sea of cheering supporters before him—9,500 in total. "Hello, everybody in the county over there!" he exclaimed. "What a great crowd." But Biden knew they weren't there to see him; he was the warm-up act. It was the day after the final presidential debate, and Biden's job, as always, was to assist the President of the United States. After talking up his boss for several minutes—praising him for the debate and everything from foreign to economic policy—Biden finally said the words that everyone listening to him had been waiting for: "So, ladies and gentlemen, join me in welcoming my friend, our president, Barack Obama!"

Obama emerged, to rousing applause. But he did not *take* the stage; he shared it with Joe Biden. After greeting his vice president with something enthusiastically in between a high five and a handshake, then adding a slap on the shoulder for good measure, Obama offered Biden a seat on a nearby stool—just a foot or so away, right in the thick of things—for the rest of the event. It was clear from the start that this was *their* campaign rally. Indeed, after the obligatory, "*Hello, Ohio!*" Obama directed everyone's attention to the man sitting beside him. "I want everyone to understand this," he said. "I could not ask for a better partner than my vice president, Joe Biden. There's nobody who knows more about foreign policy than my vice president. There's nobody who gives better advice than my vice president . . . I could not do what I do without him having my back every single day." The crowd responded with chants of: "Joe! Joe! Joe!" Obama joined in, too.[26]

Biden had Obama's back that day, indeed. While the president was holding a rally in Florida, near the site of the previous night's debate, the vice president was courting voters throughout western Ohio on behalf of the Democratic ticket. Biden's long day on the campaign trail began at 11:00 a.m. with a rally at the University of Toledo. Appearing before 1,500 students, faculty, staff, and community members at the Student Union Auditorium, Biden made the case for Obama and against his Republican opponent, Mitt Romney. Biden tailored his message to the audience, focusing on issues of importance to Ohioans—such as the auto industry and job growth in the state—and college students in particular—such as expanding access to student loans, reducing tuition growth, promoting job training at community colleges, and recruiting new math and science teachers ("hopefully some of you from this great university"). The crowd responded enthusiastically, giving every indication that it regarded a visit from the Vice President of the United States as a major event. Indeed, junior Guyton Matthews, who introduced Biden, said later: "I think it was super important that he was here. . . . It just showed how much our vote matters, and how much our vote counts." Another student, Christopher Morrow, agreed: "I think it's a good thing he's coming to UT because it shows us, as college students, that, like, they care to hear what we have to say."[27]

After the rally, Biden directed his driver to pull over just four miles down the road, at Schmucker's Restaurant. "I hear they've got great coconut custard pie," he explained. Of course, Biden was hungry for votes, too—and at just before 1:00 p.m., with lunch hour winding down, he had come at the right time: "The diner was packed." Owner Doug Schmucker greeted Biden at the door, eager to show him around. They started at the lunch counter. "What pie do you like best?" Biden asked Doug Roloff, a local AT&T repairman sitting nearby, who described himself agreeably as "an Obama person." Before Roloff could answer, the server arrived with Biden's custard pie. Undeterred, Biden asked the same question of two other customers, Ernest and Linda Vasquez—who, also happily for him, described themselves as Democrats. Biden's luck ran out when he reached the next customer, who snapped: "Just because you're a good guy doesn't mean you're a good vice president," before adding that he should "enjoy his last couple of months" in office. Biden picked up his pie and moved along to a nearby table. There, he met Ed Nazar, a businessperson who planned to vote for Romney, and his wife, Ann Monaghan Nazar, an undecided voter who, following their brief conversation, judged the vice president to be "a pretty straight up guy." They parted with a promising high five. Finally, Biden met Dawn Metzger, a social worker from Toledo, and her parents. When Metzger mentioned that her children attended Catholic schools, Biden—sensing a connection—shared that he had, too, many years ago. But it wasn't enough; afterward, Metzger "said she's undecided and Mr. Biden's visit didn't sway her."[28]

Following the afternoon rally in Dayton, Biden made two "surprise" stops just to the northeast, in Springfield, Ohio, first picking up pizza at a family restaurant and then delivering it to campaign volunteers at a nearby Democratic field office. Biden was greeted warmly by the Catanzaro family when he arrived at their restaurant, and snapped photos with some of the employees. When one of them thanked him for coming, Biden shot back: "Are you kidding me? I'm a pizza guy!" Not long afterward, Biden arrived at the campaign office, where eighty volunteers were busily making phone calls. He talked with the volunteers and posed for photos before finally calling it a day.[29]

To recap: Biden engaged with Ohio voters on five different occasions that day—twice in Toledo, once in Dayton, and twice in Springfield.

Again, my question is: how many *campaign visits* did he make?

COUNTING CAMPAIGN VISITS

Answer: It depends on whose visits count, and how many times per day. But I say five.

First, consider that Joe Biden was a *vice*-presidential candidate in 2012. Should his visits count at all, then? No, according to many previous studies of campaign visits that include data on presidential candidates only.[30] Many other studies of campaign visits, however, include data on presidential *and* vice-presidential candidates—in some cases, combining their visits, by party, and in others analyzing them separately, by candidate.[31] Some studies also include data on visits by the candidates' spouses alone, or in addition to the presidential and vice-presidential candidates.[32]

I count vice-presidential candidates' visits, for two reasons. First, presidential and vice-presidential candidates run together, as a presidential *ticket*; formally speaking, one's election is inseparable from that of the other. Of course, presidential candidates are the focal point of campaigns and have much more influence on the election's outcome than their running mate. With respect to campaign visits, frankly, they should draw a bigger crowd. But vice-presidential candidates also influence voters, albeit in nuanced ways.[33] Moreover, as the preceding account shows, they are quite capable of drawing large crowds and local media coverage and, by their very presence, making voters feel important and visible to the campaign. In some cases, the vice-presidential candidate might actually be more popular than the presidential candidate, at least among certain audiences (e.g., Sarah Palin, 2008; Kamala Harris, 2020). Categorically excluding vice-presidential candidates, therefore, might result in a limited or inaccurate assessment of the strategy and effectiveness of campaign visits. If vice-presidential candidates are to be excluded from the data, this decision should at least be justified by clear evidence—rather than mere assumptions—that their visits are inconsequential.

Second, on that point, previous studies indicate that presidential and vice-presidential candidates' campaign visits *are* distinguishable in important ways. For example, both Daron R. Shaw and the team of Jeffrey S. Hill, Elaine Rodriguez, and Amanda E. Wooden find that campaign visits by George W. Bush and Dick Cheney in 2000—the Republican Party's respective presidential and vice-presidential nominees—had different effects on state polling averages, with Bush's visits often proving inconsequential and Cheney's actually hurting the ticket.[34] Boris Heersink, Brenton D. Peterson, and Jordan Carr Peterson find that, in 2016, Trump's visits increased donations to his campaign, while visits by his running mate, Mike Pence, had no effect.[35] In terms of vote choice, my own 2018 study finds that Trump's visits did not gain Republicans votes in battleground states, but Pence's visits to Ohio did.[36] On the Democratic side, presidential candidate Hillary Clinton's visits to Pennsylvania gained votes there, whereas visits by her running mate, Tim Kaine, had no effect. Finally, in terms of campaign strategy, Kyle C. Kopko and I find several significant differences between the counties visited by presidential versus vice-presidential candidates in 2016. For example, on the Republican side, Trump visited less-educated and more conservative counties than Pence, while Clinton visited faster-growing and more liberal counties than Kaine.[37]

Including vice-presidential candidates' visits in my dataset raises other questions. First, should presidential and vice-presidential candidate visits count equally? I say yes. While the former typically attract greater attention from voters and the news media, that is not always the case. For example, in 2008, the vice-presidential debate between Biden and Palin (clearly, because of the latter) drew more viewers than any *presidential* debate since 1992, including the first one between John McCain and Barack Obama one week earlier.[38] And, as I show later in this chapter, McCain apparently tried to capitalize on Palin's stardom by making joint appearances with her on numerous occasions. Perhaps most important, there is no clear answer as to how presidential versus vice-presidential campaign visits should be differentially weighted, particularly when collecting data on both parties' tickets across several elections. As a rule, is 2:1 the right ratio? 1.5:1? The fact is, any standard other than treating these visits as numerically equivalent would be arbitrary.

Speaking of joint appearances, how should those visits be counted? Take Obama and Biden's joint appearance in Dayton, described above. Should that count as one visit or two for the Democratic ticket? I say two (i.e., one visit each). Admittedly, this is counterintuitive: how could one event count as two visits to the same place? Fair enough. But what is the alternative? If this only counts as one campaign visit, which candidate gets the credit? Obama, surely. But by erasing Biden's visit from the dataset, we will underestimate his contributions to the campaign. For a running mate such as Palin, who made many joint appearances, that would result in a significant distortion of her activities and influence. Furthermore, *is* the appearance of both candidates at the same event equivalent to just one of them showing up? I think not. To the extent that voters see a candidate's visit to their hometown as a sign of respect and a signal of importance—which clearly is the case—they should regard it as that much more significant when *both* candidates converge on their community together, knowing full well that they could be maximizing their presence elsewhere by being in two places at once. For that matter, voters probably recognize that it is not typical for the candidates to campaign jointly. The fact that both are appearing *here*, at the same time, suggests that these voters are *especially* important. Does that amount to double the normal campaign visit, when only one candidate shows up? Maybe not. But I'm confident that the two circumstances are not equivalent. And, again, any other numerical formula would be arbitrary.

If vice-presidential candidates' visits count, why not visits by the candidates' spouses and other surrogates? Indeed, they typically play an active role in presidential campaigns. In 2020, for instance, Joe Biden's wife, Jill Biden, and Kamala Harris's husband, Doug Emhoff, made numerous campaign visits, as did Donald Trump's son, Don Jr., and daughter-in-law, Lara Trump. Obama, the former president under whom Biden served as vice president, also made several visits on behalf of the Democratic ticket. There is good reason to believe that these visits, at least in some cases, are consequential, given the time and money invested in them. However, because the individuals in question are typically less well-known than the presidential and vice-presidential candidates, they are likely to attract much smaller crowds and much less media attention. For practical reasons that will become evident in the next section, this would also make it harder for me to reliably document their visits. Also, while some spouses seem to enjoy being on the campaign trail and regularly hold their own events, others (e.g., Melania Trump, Janna Ryan) rarely, if ever, make campaign visits—as I have defined them—and still others (e.g., Todd Palin, Karen Pence) almost always appear jointly with their candidate-spouse. In that case, very often it would be difficult, if not impractical, to precisely estimate the strategy or effectiveness of these visits. Also, whereas each candidate may have one spouse whose credentials as such are objectively, legally defined, there can be any number of campaign surrogates and it may not be obvious exactly who should or should not qualify for that category when collecting data on a particular campaign. If there is any hard-and-fast rule to apply here, it is one that I reference above: the presidential and vice-presidential candidates run as a ticket, and they are elected to office together. This is not true of anyone else. That is why both of their visits—and only their visits—belong in the data.

Another conceptual issue applies to presidential and vice-presidential campaign visits alike: how many times can a candidate "visit" the same geographic area (e.g., state, county, or city) in one day? In other words, if a candidate participates in two or more events in the same locale on the same day, is that one "visit" or more? Take Joe Biden, for example. He made *five stops* in *three cities* across *one state* on October 23, 2012. So did he make five visits that day? Or three? Or one? Some studies count visits in terms of the number of *days* spent in whichever geographic area serves as the unit of analysis.[39] As Jeffrey M. Jones explains: "For the purposes of this study, any public appearance(s) by a presidential candidate in a particular media market per calendar day is considered a visit."[40] Jones, therefore, would credit Biden with two campaign visits: one to the Toledo media market and one to the Dayton media market (encompassing Dayton and Springfield). More restrictive is Appleman, at Democracy in Action, who would credit Biden with just one visit that day, even if he had briefly left Ohio and returned; "In this study, if a candidate does an event or events in a state, drives over the border and goes out of the state for a nearby event or events, and then comes back in state the same day such a trip is considered as one visit."[41]

I follow most other studies by crediting the candidate with one campaign visit per qualifying event in which he or she participates, even if it takes place within the same geographic area as other such events on the same day.[42] That is to say, I would credit Biden with five visits: two in Toledo, one in Dayton, and two in Springfield. As Shaw explains: "The logic here is that one wants to measure the 'earned' (or 'free') news media coverage an appearance generates, thus additional events on a given day warrant additional weight."[43]

Of course, there is good reason to question this approach. Do two stops in one city really mean double the local media coverage and public awareness—or triple or quadruple, in some rare cases? Perhaps not. But the alternative creates a false equivalency that, in my opinion, is less defensible. As Darrell M. West puts it, counting visits per day rather than per campaign stop "is misleading . . . because it equates half-hour visits with day-long appearances."[44] For example, on October 11, 2008, presidential candidate Barack Obama held *four* large outdoor rallies in Philadelphia—each attracting up to fifteen thousand people, in what one report described as a "campaign blitz."[45] To treat this as one campaign visit would dismiss each rally after the first one as irrelevant, and put all of the day's events on par with any other campaign stop in the city, no matter how minor or brief.

There is no perfect solution here. But, given the range of choices, I think it is most reasonable to count each time that a candidate visits a distinct location and interacts with a distinct group of voters, even if they happen to live within the same city or state that plays host on the same day.

DISCUSSION

Having defined "campaign visits," it might seem that counting them would be a simple matter. But, as this section makes clear, it isn't. First, one must decide *whose* campaign visits count—those of the presidential candidate only, or the presidential *and* vice-presidential candidates. I count both, as do most previous analyses of campaign visits. Second, when a candidate participates in multiple events in the same geographical area on the same day, one must decide whether to count visits by the day or by each distinguishable event. Again, I follow most previous studies in opting for the latter. Therefore, when counting campaign visits in Ohio for October 23, 2012, not only do I credit Barack Obama with one visit (in Dayton), but also his vice-presidential candidate, Joe Biden, with five visits (two in Toledo, one in Dayton, and two in Springfield). And so on, for all other entries in the Campaign Visits Database.

CAMPAIGN VISITS DATABASE

The Campaign Visits Database (CVD) includes 1,440 presidential and vice-presidential campaign visits from the 2008–2020 elections. Specifically, this database reports the following details about each campaign visit: timing (year, date); participants (name, party, presidential or vice-presidential candidate, solo or joint visit); location (state, city, county, address); host site (venue name, venue type); and links to two documentary sources.

Campaign visits are defined and counted in accordance with the criteria described in the preceding sections of this chapter. The CVD includes only those visits that took place between September 1 and Election Day of a given election year. Most studies of campaign visits use September 1 or a date shortly thereafter, usually corresponding to Labor Day, as a starting point for analysis.[46] As Shaw notes, September 1 "serves as both a legal and historical starting point for the fall campaign."[47] Other studies focused on a single election year have used the announcement of the vice-presidential candidates as a starting point for data collection.[48] However, the dates for this announcement varied widely across the 2008–2020 elections—from as early as July 16 (Mike Pence, 2016) to as late as August 29 (Sarah Palin, 2008). Using September 1 as a starting point at least ensures that all eligible (i.e., presidential and vice-presidential) candidates are available to make campaign visits during this period, and maximizes comparability across election years given that the final date for inclusion, Election Day, varies by only a few days (from as early as November 3, in 2020, to as late as November 8, in 2016).

To identify potential campaign visits, I began by searching campaign websites and other reliable online sources announcing upcoming or past events in which the presidential and/or vice-presidential candidate was scheduled to participate. Then I identified at least two reputable sources—typically national or local media reports, but in some cases videos or social media posts from journalists or the candidates themselves—to confirm not only whether, but (based on one source, at least) *where* the event took place. This strategy, of starting with advance announcements and then cross-checking via subsequent media coverage, is common within the campaign visits literature. For instance, Scott L. Althaus and his colleagues explain: "We compiled appearance data . . . by first recording the dates and locations of every major-party candidate speech for our time period . . . [and] then verified that speeches were actually made by confirming the dates and locations of stops made by both campaigns."[49] In some cases, this process reveals that a scheduled event did not take place, or that it was moved to a different location. For example, on October 27, 2008, a Sarah Palin rally in Salem, Virginia, was moved from the Salem Civic Center to Salem High School's football stadium when the event's organizers realized that attendees would be double the former venue's seating capacity.[50] In many other cases, this process reveals that a candidate made one or more unannounced stops, such as Joe Biden's in Springfield, Ohio, on October 23, 2012 as described above.

It is important to identify exactly where—in terms of the host site, not just the city or state—each campaign visit took place. I say this for two reasons, in particular. First, toward the end of this chapter, I describe how often campaign visits take place at various types of venues (e.g., universities, airports), and how these patterns vary across parties and candidates. Second, when empirically evaluating the strategy (chapter 4) and effectiveness (chapter 5) of campaign visits, I use counties as the geographical unit of analysis. In most cases, cities and towns are contained entirely within one county. But in plenty of other cases, municipalities are split across two or more counties. For example, in 2012, Republican vice-presidential candidate Paul Ryan made a campaign visit to Young's Jersey Dairy, a working dairy farm in Yellow Springs, Ohio. While most of Yellow Springs is within Greene County, this particular location is *just* over the county line, in Clark County. Here and in several other cases, it is only by identifying the *exact* location of a campaign visit, including its address, that I am able to determine the county in which a visit took place.

Identifying the correct address is usually straightforward. In some cases, it is specified in one or more of my documentary sources. In most other cases, I was able to find an address simply by Googling the name of the host site (e.g., "Young's Jersey Dairy").[51] But sometimes I had to get creative. Occasionally my documentary sources did not provide an address or an identifiable location, and so I had to rely on public announcements posted prior to the event by local media sources or campaign affiliates. There were other cases in which the site of a visit was identifiable but not associated with a permanent address (e.g., a temporary campaign office or street festival). If a permanent address was not available, I had to find another document or webpage—perhaps for a different campaign-related event—in which it was listed. For example, John McCain visited what newspaper accounts described as his "New Mexico Campaign Headquarters" in Albuquerque on Election Day, 2008. Because campaign offices often close down after Election Day, I could not simply look up a building by this name. Instead, I found a newspaper announcement from earlier in the 2008 campaign specifying locations where Republicans could pick up tickets for a different campaign event, one of which was listed as "NM Victory Main/McCain HQ" and accompanied by an address.[52]

In a few particularly difficult cases, I had to play detective. For example, in 2020, Joe Biden visited a Cook Out ice cream shop in Durham, North Carolina. The problem is, there are several Cook Outs in Durham, and none of the documentary sources provided an exact location. To determine where Biden's visit took place, then, I had to compare photos and videos of Biden's visit with Google Street View images of Durham's various Cook Out establishments. Based on the surrounding buildings (including a Subway restaurant, visible in a window reflection in a C-SPAN video), I was able to determine exactly where Biden visited.

Also in 2020, Biden held an event in a parking lot near of one of his campaign offices in Fort Lauderdale, Florida. One source specified the street where this office was located, but not its street *number*. By examining video footage of the event from C-SPAN, I saw that Biden was standing near the back door of a local business, which had written on it the business's name and street number. I confirmed via Google Street View that this was, in fact, the correct location.

Finally, my favorite example: Sarah Palin and her husband, Todd, took their young daughter, Piper, trick-or-treating on Halloween 2008—not at home, in Alaska, but among swing state voters in Dauphin, Pennsylvania. Media coverage of this "visit" (a borderline case, but acceptable within the parameters of my definition) was substantial, but provided little in the way of geographic details. However, one account, from the *York Daily Record*, quoted the resident of a house that the Palins had visited that night on what type of candy she had given Piper. Public records data indicate that a woman by the same name recently lived at 503 High Street in Dauphin, which matched the number visible in a *New York Times* photo of the Palins trick-or-treating and talking with residents. Google Street View confirmed that the house on that street matched the one from the photo, down to the sticker on the mailbox reading "503."

A DESCRIPTIVE ANALYSIS OF CAMPAIGN VISITS

The CVD makes it possible to answer several fundamental questions about campaign visits—not just for one specific candidate or party ticket, but more generally, across candidates and election years. *How many* campaign visits do candidates make? *When* do they make these visits? And *where*, in terms of host sites, do they choose to visit?

This analysis is particularly important because, as noted in chapter 2, most studies of campaign visits focus on just one election; thus, whatever descriptive statistics they provide—on the number of visits made by each candidate, for instance—cannot be generalized beyond that election year. Nor can we simply compare such data across studies of different elections, because there are sure to be differences in how one study versus another defines or counts visits, or the time frame used for analysis, and so forth. While several studies analyze campaign visits across multiple election years, few provide much in the way of descriptive statistics, and usually no more than the total number of visits made by the candidates or party tickets overall, and perhaps by state or media market. No previous study describes—as I do, here—exactly when (i.e., visits per calendar date) and where (i.e., host venues) campaign visits took place, across multiple elections. What follows, then, is a unique empirical overview of modern presidential campaign visits.

FREQUENCY

Figure 3.1 presents the total number of campaign visits, by candidate, in the 2008–2020 presidential elections. On average, I find that candidates make ninety campaign visits per general election period (defined, for the purposes of this analysis, as September 1 through Election Day). Curiously, campaign visits have decreased steadily over time—from an average of 110.8 (total of 443) in 2008, to 95.0 (380) in 2012, to 90.3 (361) in 2016, to 64.0 (256) in 2020. Different election dates do not explain the discrepancy; starting on September 1, the candidates had sixty-five days to campaign in 2008, sixty-seven in 2012, sixty-eight in 2016, and sixty-four in 2020. Clearly, there were fewer visits in 2020 due to the COVID-19 pandemic. But it is not immediately clear why visits began declining prior to that election, or what this might portend for future elections.

Barack Obama, in 2008, made the most campaign visits of any candidate in the dataset (115), followed closely, in the same year, by Sarah Palin (114) and John McCain (113). Donald Trump, in 2016, made the most visits in any subsequent election (113).[53] Kamala Harris (57) and Mike Pence (58) made the fewest visits of any candidates in the dataset—in fact, well behind their respective 2020 running mates, Joe Biden (66) and Donald Trump (75). These numbers are notable for two reasons. First, as described in this book's introduction, Biden—and Harris, once she joined the Democratic ticket in August—intentionally limited the number and scope of their campaign events due to concerns about COVID-19. Biden, in particular, was ridiculed—most of all, by

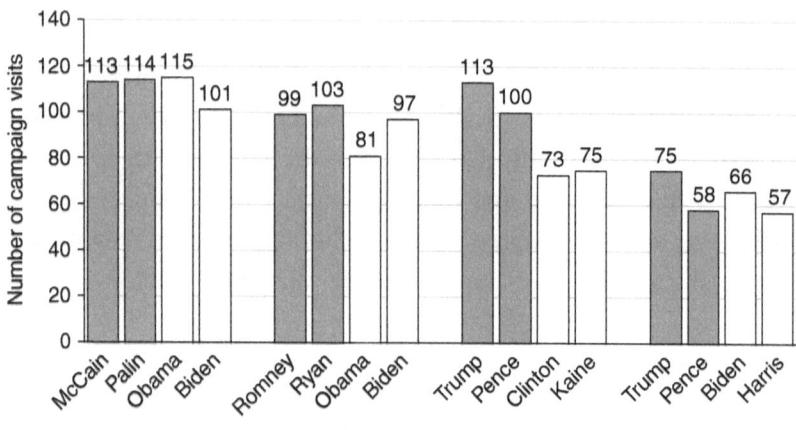

FIGURE 3.1 Presidential campaign visits by candidate, 2008–2020

Source: Campaign Visits Database, available for download at christopherjdevine.com/data.html

Trump—for purportedly "hiding in his basement." Yet Biden outpaced his much younger running mate, Harris, on the campaign trail, and made only nine fewer visits than Trump.[54] Of course, as described earlier in this chapter, Trump lost ten precious days on the campaign trail due to COVID-19. Excluding those days, he averaged 1.4 visits per day throughout the rest of the campaign. This suggests that Trump, had he not been infected, would have made fourteen more visits (10 × 1.4), for a total of eighty-nine. That is much higher than any other candidate in 2020, but well behind his own pace in 2016. It is, however, on par with the prior incumbent president to run for reelection, Barack Obama in 2012 (81).

Second, it is notable that Pence made so few campaign visits in 2020—nearly tying Harris for last place and trailing eight visits behind Biden! For Biden and Harris, it is no mystery why their totals fall well short of candidates in other election years; again, their scheduling made explicit concessions to COVID-19. But the Trump campaign did not advocate or enact any such policy, and Trump spent much of the fall eagerly contrasting his frenetic pace with that of "Sleepy Joe Biden." To the extent that Trump ever slowed down, it was only because he contracted COVID. Pence did not; in fact, there was no period in which he left the campaign trail, even when Trump was hospitalized. All of this is to say: what was Pence's excuse? For all the talk about Biden and Harris not campaigning hard enough, his numbers were as bad or worse.

Now, let's move beyond individuals to compare different *groups* of candidates. Figure 3.2 presents the average number of visits made by the Democratic versus Republican presidential or vice-presidential candidates in the 2008–2020 elections. This evidence indicates that Republicans made more visits (97.4) than did Democrats (82.6) during these recent campaigns, on average. According to a t-test (a test of probability when a variable is unknown), this difference is statistically significant ($p = 0.002$). It is not obvious why there would be a systematic difference between the parties, in terms of campaign visits. For that matter, Obama made the most visits in 2008 and, overall, the Democratic

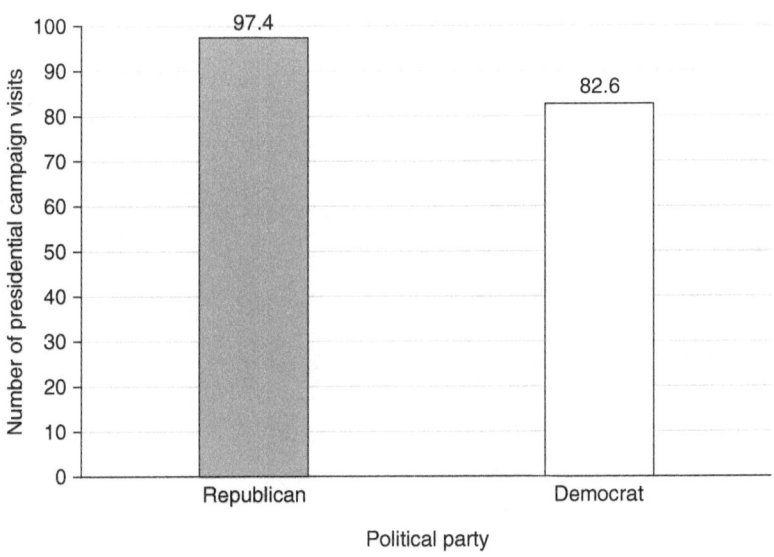

FIGURE 3.2 Presidential campaign visits by party (average), 2008–2020

Source: Campaign Visits Database

candidates' visits were about on par with Republicans' in 2008 and 2020. Democrats' overall deficit seems to be mostly attributable to the elections in 2012—when Obama and Biden, running as incumbents, surely had less time to campaign—and 2016—when Hillary Clinton and Tim Kaine campaigned quite a bit less than Trump and Pence.

Next, are presidential candidates more active on the campaign trail than their vice-presidential running mates? It would be reasonable to expect this, given that the presidential candidate is the focal point of the campaign, running for the most powerful office. If campaigns therefore view the head of the ticket as a more effective salesperson—that is, someone who can attract the biggest crowds and the most media attention—perhaps they deploy him or her (much) more often on the campaign trail. Figure 3.3 suggests this is the case. It shows that, on average, presidential candidates made slightly more campaign visits (91.9) than did vice-presidential candidates (88.1) from 2008 to 2020. This difference, however, is not statistically significant, according to t-testing (p = 0.399). Figure 3.1 reinforces that there is no clear pattern in the data. While in some cases

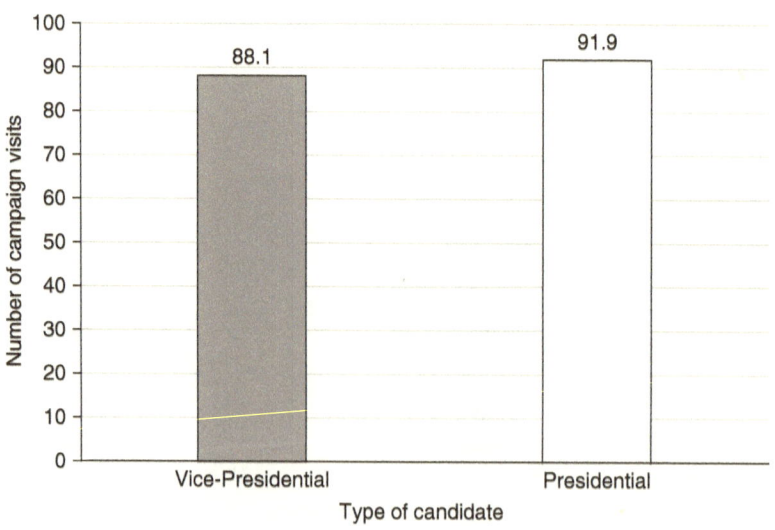

FIGURE 3.3 Presidential campaign visits by candidate (average), 2008–2020

Source: Campaign Visits Database

the presidential candidate makes many more visits than the vice-presidential candidate (Obama–Biden 2008; Trump–Pence 2016 and 2020), we also see the inverse (Obama–Biden 2012). And in other cases, the running mates are about equally active (McCain–Palin 2008; Romney–Ryan 2012; Clinton–Kaine 2016).

Finally, how common is it for presidential and vice-presidential candidates to make joint campaign visits, such as the Obama–Biden rally in Dayton described earlier in this chapter? As figure 3.4 shows, Obama and Biden rarely appeared together on the campaign trail—just four times in 2008 and three times in 2012. The same was true for the two subsequent Democratic tickets, Clinton–Kaine in 2016 and Biden–Harris in 2020. Joint visits are much more common among Republicans. Most notably, in 2008, McCain and Palin made nearly one-quarter of their campaign visits together (23.8 percent, or twenty-seven visits each). Clearly, the campaign believed that Palin's popularity, especially early

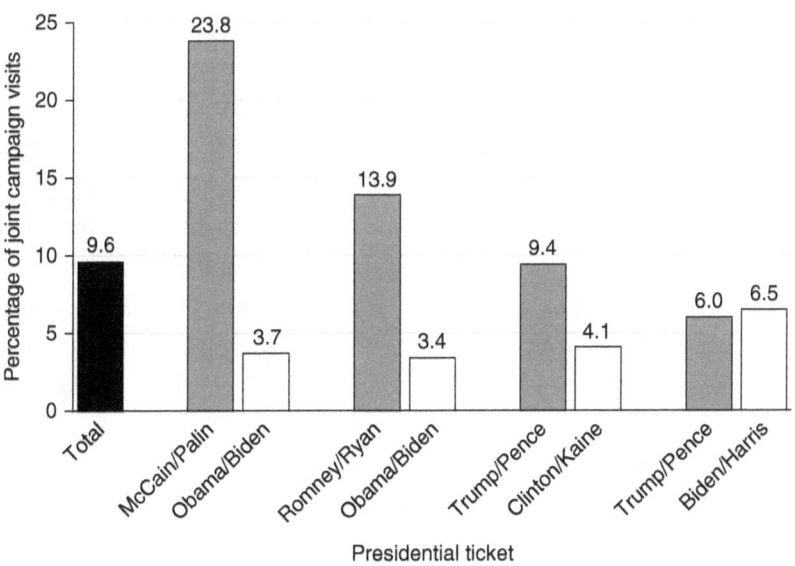

FIGURE 3.4 Joint campaign visits by presidential ticket, 2008–2020 (percentage of total visits)

Source: Campaign Visits Database

in the general election campaign and among the party's base, might help to excite voters and the (local) news media about McCain's rallies and resuscitate his campaign. While the McCain–Palin ticket is an outlier in figure 3.4, Mitt Romney and Paul Ryan also made many of their visits together: 13.9 percent of them, to be exact, or fourteen apiece. Trump and Pence made ten joint visits in 2016 (9.4 percent), but only four in 2020 (6.0 percent). In total, about one in ten campaign visits (9.6 percent) are made jointly by the presidential and vice-presidential candidates.

TIMING

The conventional wisdom holds that presidential candidates initiate their general election activities around Labor Day—"the kickoff of the fall campaign"—and then, after several weeks of steady travel, media appearances, and debates, in mid- to late-October start sprinting toward the finish line, scheduling as many rallies in as many different places as possible, right up to the very end. But is this accurate? Even if it was at one time, what about more recently, as the expansion of early voting, absentee voting, and vote-by-mail laws have disrupted the traditional campaign timeline, so that in some states large percentages or even the majority of voters already have cast their ballots well before Election Day?

Figure 3.5 presents the average number of campaign visits made by the presidential and vice-presidential candidates, combined, for each day of the 2008–2020 campaigns. In other words, it shows the *total* number of campaign visits typically made by the candidates—all four of them, together—on any given day, from September 1 to Election Day. Take September 1, for example. I sum the total number of visits made by all four candidates on September 1, 2008; September 1, 2012; September 1, 2016; *and* September 1, 2020. This gives me the total number of visits made on September 1, across all four elections. Next, I divide that total by four to derive the *average* number of visits made on September 1 in the 2008–2020 election cycles. I do this for each date until Election Day. Because election dates vary across years, averages from November 4 to November 8 exclude any candidate for whom Election Day had already passed.

For example, in 2020, Election Day was November 3. So, when calculating the average for November 4, I total only the campaign visits from 2008, 2012, and 2016, then divide by three.

The evidence from figure 3.5 is more or less in line with traditional understandings of the pace of a presidential campaign. Recognizing that Labor Day falls on a different date each year—but always on the first Monday in September—there does seem to be an initial spike in campaign visits at that time, totaling four to six (i.e., at least one visit per candidate, on average) at several points during the first week of September. It is not until mid-October that the candidates typically make a total of six visits again. For all of that time in between, the candidates combine for only two to four campaign visits (i.e., one or fewer per candidate) on most days. But then they suddenly come to life, with the total number of visits increasing to nearly eight just a couple of days later, on October 21, then nine on October 23 and 24 and eleven on October 27, albeit in fits and starts. As the calendar turns to November, we see a spike in activity, to a total of twelve visits on October 31, or three per candidate, on average; fourteen on November 2, and—with the caveat that

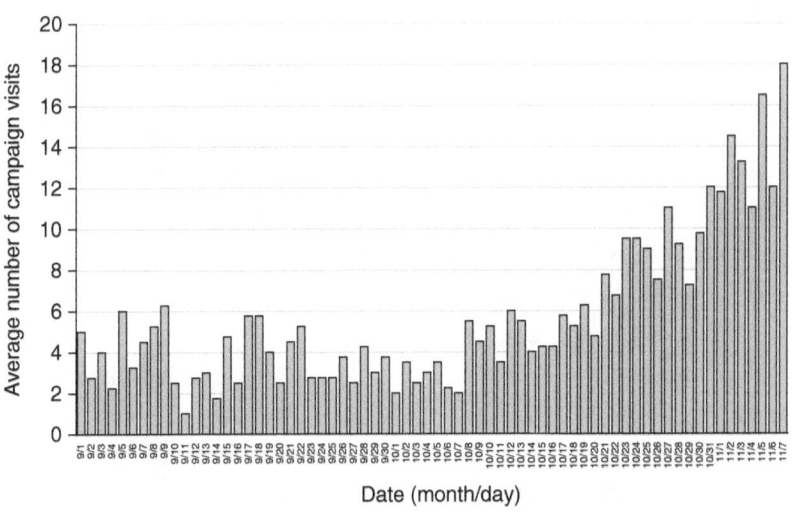

FIGURE 3.5 Presidential campaign visits by date (average), 2008–2020

Source: Campaign Visits Database

only some elections are included at this point—sixteen on November 5 (for 2012 and 2016) and eighteen on November 7 (2016). Indeed, the candidates make a mad dash to the finish line.

But each campaign is different. And each candidate works at his or her own pace. Some spend nearly every day on the campaign trail, while others are on and off. Some pace themselves evenly throughout the campaign, making a visit or two per day and a bit more at the end, while others pack their schedules while on the road with numerous visits. The totals from figure 3.1 cannot differentiate between such approaches; indeed, two candidates may appear just as active based on total visits, when in fact they campaign in radically different ways. The only way to tell the difference is to look at how individual candidates' visits were distributed throughout the campaign. I do this for each of the presidential candidates in figures 3.6–3.13.[55]

Several interesting patterns emerge from these data. First, candidates vary widely in terms of the number of days on which they make campaign visits. Only two candidates, Barack Obama in 2008 (86.2 percent) and Donald Trump in 2016 (77.9 percent) logged visits on at least three-quarters of the days between September 1 and Election Day. John McCain and Mitt Romney were just behind that pace, each at 73.1 percent. Obama spent many fewer days on the campaign trail (53.7 percent) when running for reelection in 2012, but again this is probably because he was also serving as president at that time—which, for example, kept him off the campaign trail while responding to Hurricane Sandy in late October. Likewise, in 2020, Trump's activity dropped considerably (60.9 percent). However, remember that he was unable to campaign for ten days while battling COVID-19; excluding those days brings Trump more in line with his 2016 pace (72.2 percent).

Joe Biden, in 2020, spent the fewest days of any candidate on the campaign trail—only twenty-nine out of sixty-four (45.3 percent). Three times that fall, he had stretches of five or six days without a single campaign visit. While Biden clearly was not holed up in his basement throughout the campaign, as some people imagined it, there is something to the criticism that he too frequently called a "lid" on events for a given day. But, given that Biden had nearly as many total visits as Trump, and more than Pence or Harris, the flip side is that he usually packed his days on the campaign trail with multiple events—including seven on his day-long Amtrak tour while returning home from the first debate in Cleveland (see Introduction).

Then there's the curious case of Hillary Clinton. In 2016, Clinton spent only half of her days on the campaign trail (thirty-four of sixty-eight, exactly). This is higher than Biden, of course, but the cases are not comparable because he intentionally scaled back campaigning due to COVID-19. Clinton had no apparent reason to campaign so lightly. What is most striking about her schedule is that over the first fifty days of the campaign, from September 1 to October 20, she spent *only sixteen days* making campaign visits (32.0 percent). On most of those days, she logged only one visit. With a total of only twenty-four visits over the first fifty days of the campaign, she averaged only 0.48 per day. Suddenly, on October 21, after *eight consecutive days* without a campaign visit, Clinton flipped the switch. On each of the remaining eighteen days, she logged at least one visit, usually multiple, and in several cases four or five per day. After moving at a leisurely pace for most of the campaign, finally she sprinted to the finish line—only to lose. One can't help but think of the tortoise and the hare.

The second interesting pattern to observe from figures 3.6–3.13 is that each presidential candidate except for Donald Trump in 2020 (1.9) averaged at least two visits per day on those days that he or she made a campaign visit.[56] Of course, this includes the two candidates who made visits on the fewest days, Clinton (2.1) and Biden (2.3)—suggesting that they at least tried to make up for time spent off the campaign trail by keeping a busy schedule while on it. Of all the candidates, John McCain (who, at seventy-two years of age in 2008, many people considered too old to be president) packed in the most visits per day (2.4), while also spending three-quarters of that fall on the campaign trail. No wonder, as quoted in chapter 1, McCain described the end of the campaign as "a blur"—recalling, we can now say accurately, that the campaign "stag[ed] several rallies a day, making my closing argument four, five, six times a

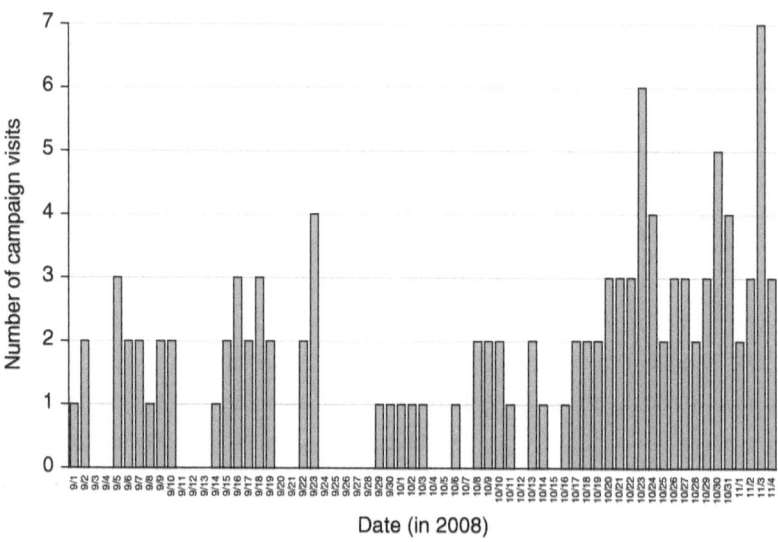

FIGURE 3.6 John McCain's campaign visits by date, 2008

Source: Campaign Visits Database

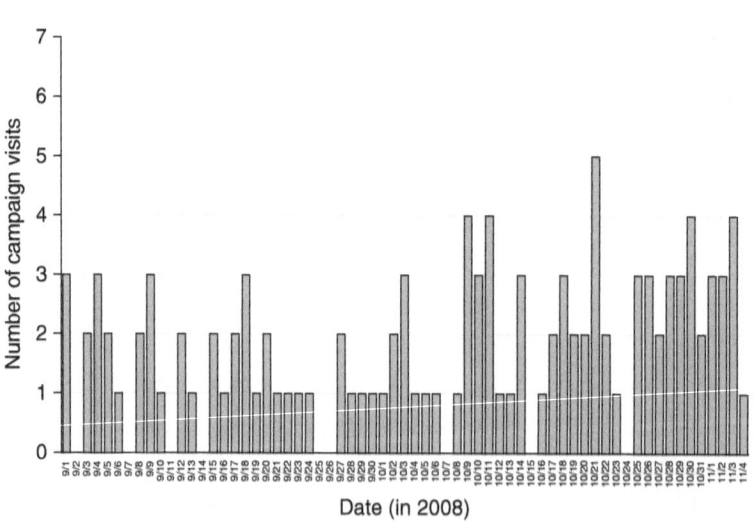

FIGURE 3.7 Barack Obama's campaign visits by date, 2008

Source: Campaign Visits Database

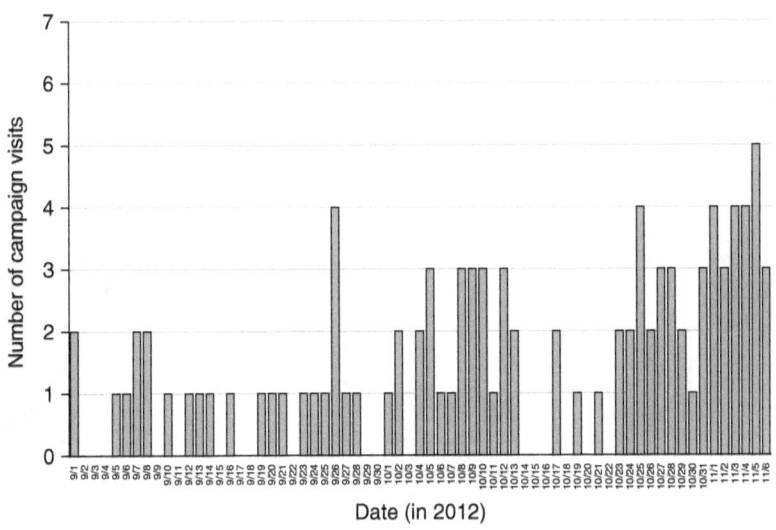

FIGURE 3.8 Mitt Romney's campaign visits by date, 2012

Source: Campaign Visits Database

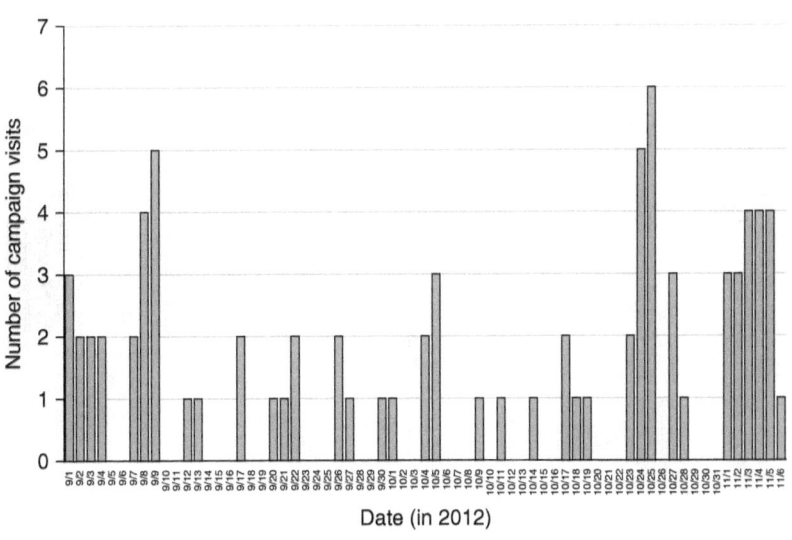

FIGURE 3.9 Barack Obama's campaign visits by date, 2012

Source: Campaign Visits Database

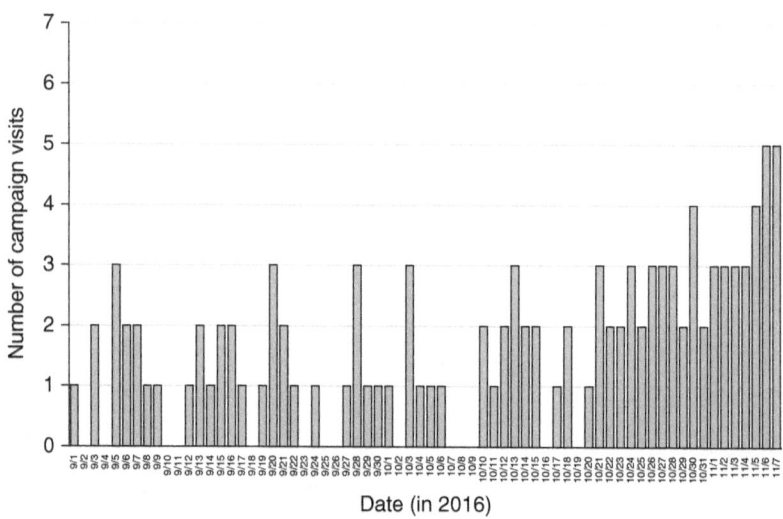

FIGURE 3.10 Donald Trump's campaign visits by date, 2016

Source: Campaign Visits Database

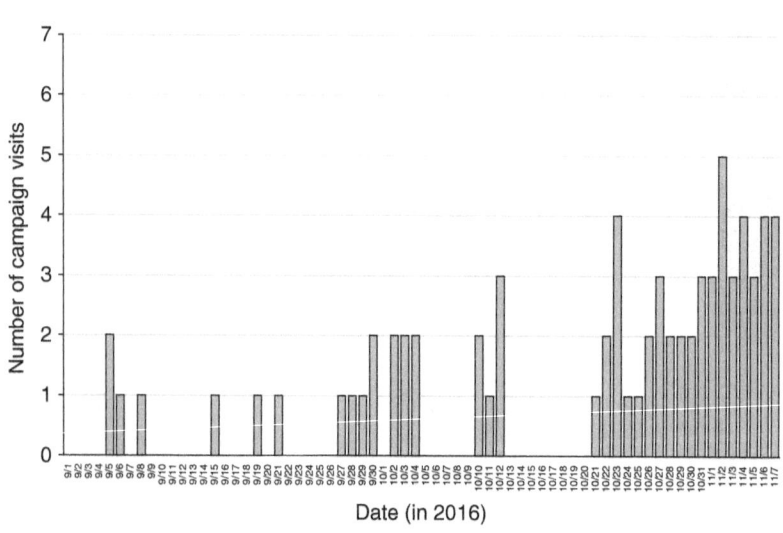

FIGURE 3.11 Hillary Clinton's campaign visits by date, 2016

Source: Campaign Visits Database

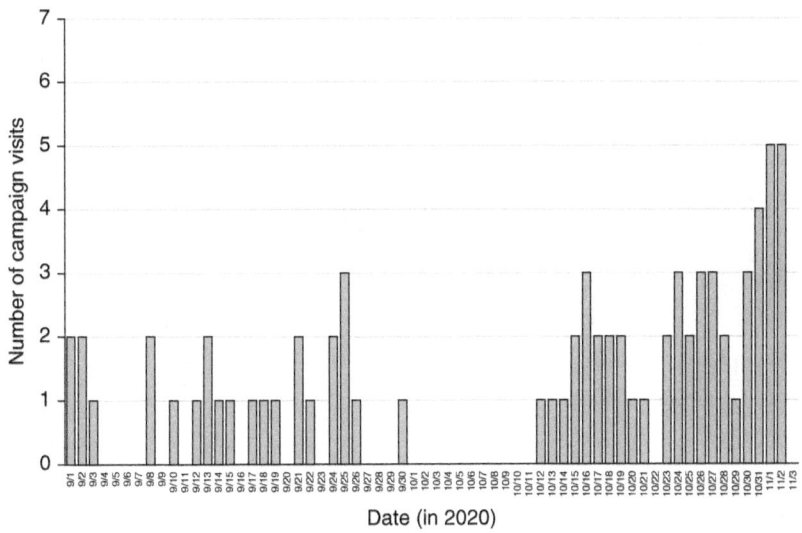

FIGURE 3.12 Donald Trump's campaign visits by date, 2020

Source: Campaign Visits Database

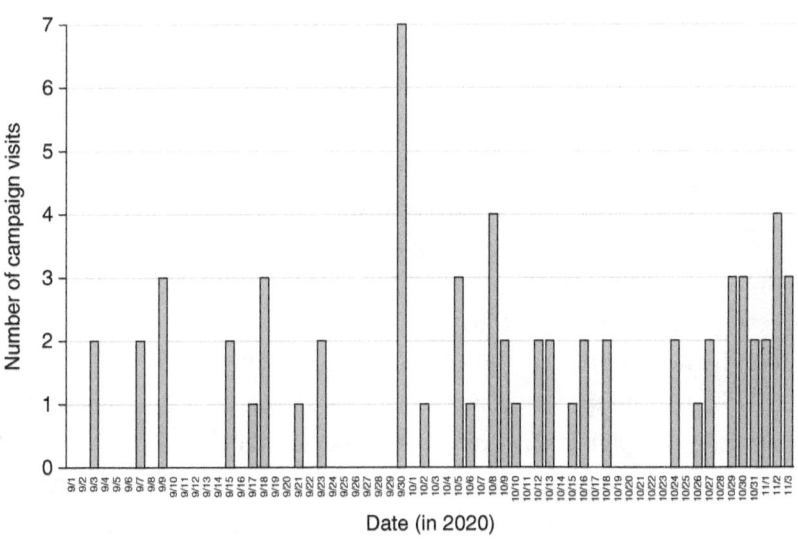

FIGURE 3.13 Joe Biden's campaign visits by date, 2020

Source: Campaign Visits Database

day."⁵⁷ That is probably how most people picture the campaign; as McCain said, "The country expects it." However, as this evidence shows, not everyone follows the same schedule.

VENUES

Picture a "campaign visit." What do you see?

Chances are, you envision a candidate onstage, surrounded by cheering supporters. But what about the details? Is this event being held outside, perhaps in a park or on the town square? Or is it inside, in a large sports arena or convention center? What about the crowd of people in attendance? Is this a representative cross-section of the local population, or at least those who would attend a rally for the candidate you've imagined? Or is this a more specific audience—for instance, full of union workers or college students?

While each of us has some sense of what campaign visits look like, the reality is that they happen in many different places, before different types of audiences. For that matter, campaign visits—by my definition, or any other plausible one—are not always large rallies. Of course, many of them are just that: for example, Donald Trump's rallies at the Pennsylvania and Minnesota airports or Obama and Biden's at the park in Dayton, referenced earlier. But other visits are more targeted and intimate: for example, Joe Biden's stops at the Toledo diner and the Springfield campaign office. When trying to gain an overview of campaign visits, then, it is important to ask: what *is* the typical setting for these events? And, to the extent that we can generalize across elections, how do individual candidates deviate from the norm?

Also, describing the specific sites for campaign visits creates a bridge to the next chapter, where I use the CVD to evaluate campaign strategy. Consider that even when the candidates or their campaigns want to hold a certain type of event—say, the traditional mass rally—in a particular city or town, they must decide precisely *where* it will take place. Sometimes, depending on the available facilities and the anticipated crowd size, they may have only one good option. But typically campaigns do have choices, and those choices may provide important indications of strategy. Take Biden's previously mentioned speech at the University of Toledo (UT). A mid-sized city such as Toledo, Ohio, has any number of venues that would accommodate a crowd of 1,500 people. Is it a coincidence that the Obama–Biden campaign chose to hold this rally at a university? Probably not, given the Democratic Party's advantage among younger voters and the many explicit appeals to college students made by Biden and others at this event. Of course, it is possible that the campaign chose UT for other reasons: perhaps because its location was convenient, it had better security and amenities than alternative sites, and so forth. With a sample size of one, we can only guess as to the real cause. But if we aggregate across campaign visits and compare across parties, we can make reasonable inferences about the strategic elements of site selections such as this one.

My analysis in this section builds on the only previous study to categorize presidential and vice-presidential candidates' campaign visits in terms of the host venue.[58] In that study, I found that campaign visits in 2016 most often took place at universities (16.9 percent), arenas or convention centers (16.7 percent), and places of business (12.6 percent). Also, I provided strong evidence that some of these choices were strategically motivated: Democrats visited universities (29.5 percent) far more often than did Republicans (8.2 percent), and were significantly more likely to do so as registration and voting deadlines neared. In other words, the Democratic candidates apparently targeted universities in order to mobilize a friendly constituency of voters.

I followed the methodology from my previous work, as well as that of Darrell West, by using an inductive approach to categorize host venues.[59] That is to say, I began by separating venues into more obviously distinct categories (e.g., arenas versus airports versus churches). Along the way, as new examples pressed on the boundaries of my current scheme, I divided some categories into two and merged others. For example, initially I grouped together all general-purpose spaces where large public events typically take place, such as sports arenas or stadiums, convention centers, and banquet and events centers. But it soon became apparent that these spaces were not quite alike, particularly in terms of size and configuration: the first two are typically designed to hold several thousand people, often in stadium seating, in stark contrast to the latter. To treat these spaces as more or less interchangeable did not seem appropriate, so I separated them.

Conversely, I was tempted to separate restaurants (think of Joe Biden visiting the folks at Schmucker's) from commercial manufacturing sites (think of a candidate touring an auto assembly plant). However, I found that some of the former were not just meet-and-greets; in many cases, the candidates used these events to demonstrate their support for small businesses and their owners or employees, which to me seemed conceptually indistinguishable from the objectives of visiting a manufacturing site. Therefore, I combined these visits into one category, highlighting attention to commerce and industry.

Finally, in many cases, I had to distinguish venues based on the overall environment in which they were embedded. Take universities, for example. When visiting campuses, candidates often speak in large arenas that, from the internal environment, are essentially indistinguishable from other large arenas where, say, the local professional sports team might play. But on other occasions, candidates speak in large outdoor spaces, such as The Ohio State University's iconic Oval. If Joe Biden, for example, speaks at UT's Savage Arena (capacity: ten thousand), I have to ask: what is the most important commonality here—that this arena hosts sporting events and holds thousands of people, like Toledo's local Glass City Center (formerly the SeaGate Convention Center), where several other candidates in the dataset held events, or that it is located on the UT campus, in a space familiar and accessible to university students who are thus more likely to attend events there? To put it another way, what would be most distinguishable from this event: if Biden spoke at the local convention center, or if he spoke outside somewhere at UT, say on a lawn space? Which of these is most unlike the other? I think it's clear that the convention center would be a greater departure. I would treat this as a university visit.

I identified sixteen distinct categories of host venues, most conforming to those from my previous study, but diverging in some areas where the inclusion of new events from other election years necessitated modifications. Below, I list each of these categories and the subset of venues that they comprise.

- **Airports**—including hangars and tarmacs
- **Arenas/Convention Centers**—including arenas, stadiums, convention centers, conference centers, exposition centers, sports complexes, and sports training centers
- **Banquet and Events Centers**
- **Campaign Offices**
- **Churches**
- **Fairgrounds**—including county or state fairgrounds and their arenas or pavilions, and street fairs or festivals
- **Government Facilities**—including community centers, recreation centers, fire stations, military facilities, town halls, train stations, and publicly owned museums
- **Hotels/Resorts/Clubs**—including hotels, resorts, casinos, privately owned country clubs, social clubs, and community clubhouses
- **Nonprofit Facilities**—including nonprofit museums, markets, medical centers, family service centers, arts education centers, retirement communities, Boys and Girls Clubs, and Fraternal Order of Police, American Legion, and Chamber of Commerce buildings
- **Places of Business**—including restaurants, cafés, bars, commercial farms, privately owned markets, retail stores, service centers, manufacturing sites, corporate offices, and for-profit museums
- **Private Residences**—including private homes and estates
- **Public Spaces**—including public streets, parks, markets, and town squares[60]
- **Schools**—including public, private, and charter schools (pre-K or K–12)
- **Theaters**—including performing arts centers, studios, pavilions, and amphitheaters
- **Union Offices**—including union halls, training centers, and education centers
- **Universities**—including public or private four-year colleges and universities, community colleges, and higher-education centers

Figure 3.14 presents the percentages of presidential campaign visits by venue across the 2008–2020 elections. It is clear from this evidence that there is no "typical" venue for a campaign visit; indeed, not even one-sixth of visits take place at any one type of venue. Moreover, the two most common sites for presidential campaign visits—places of business (16.3 percent) and universities (15.4 percent)—are not generic spots for communities to gather, but ones that specifically implicate a certain type of voter or issue. While I suspect that most people, when asked to picture a typical campaign visit, see the candidate at an arena (11.6 percent), airport (11.1 percent), or public space such as a park or town square (9.9 percent), more often they are somewhere else.

Of course, we should not expect that each candidate will conform to the same patterns evident in figure 3.14. For example, as noted above, my previous study found that, in 2016, Democratic candidates were much more likely than Republican candidates to visit colleges and universities. But is that typical? And do certain candidates diverge from these general trends? To find out, in table 3.1, I present a breakdown of the

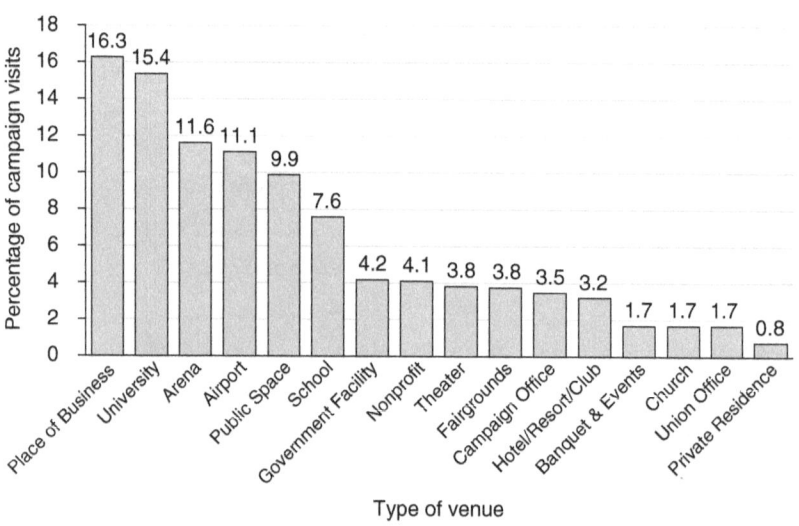

FIGURE 3.14 Percentage of presidential campaign visits by venue (average), 2008–2020

Source: Campaign Visits Database

TABLE 3.1 Percentages of Presidential Campaign Visits by Venue, 2008–2020

	2008		2012		2016		2020	
Venue	GOP	Dem	GOP	Dem	GOP	Dem	GOP	Dem
Airport	10.1	0.0	14.9	1.1	8.9	0.7	62.4	1.6
Arena/Convention Center	21.2	12.0	7.9	6.2	22.5	3.4	4.5	5.7
Banquet & Events Center	0.0	0.5	1.5	1.7	6.1	2.0	0.8	0.0
Campaign Office	0.4	3.2	5.5	9.6	1.9	5.4	0.8	0.8
Church	0.0	0.5	0.0	0.0	2.8	6.1	2.3	4.1
Fairgrounds	2.6	3.2	5.0	1.7	8.5	0.7	3.0	4.1
Government Facility	2.2	3.2	2.5	5.1	4.2	7.4	0.0	11.4
Hotel/Resort/Club	2.2	0.9	1.0	1.1	10.3	2.7	4.5	2.4
Nonprofit Facility	3.5	4.2	4.0	5.1	3.8	2.7	3.8	6.5
Place of Business	19.8	12.0	23.3	21.9	10.8	8.8	12.8	19.5
Private Residence	0.4	1.4	0.5	0.0	0.0	0.0	1.5	3.3
Public Space	10.1	21.3	9.9	10.1	1.9	10.8	1.5	10.6
School	9.3	13.0	7.4	14.6	3.8	4.1	0.8	3.3
Theater	4.4	1.9	4.0	3.4	7.5	6.1	0.0	1.6
Union Office	0.0	1.9	0.0	1.1	0.0	2.7	0.0	11.4
University	13.7	20.8	12.9	17.4	7.0	36.5	1.5	13.8

Note: Campaign visits are those made by the presidential or vice-presidential candidate on a given party ticket, between September 1 and Election Day in a given election year. Entries are in percentages, calculated as the ticket's total visits held at a particular type of venue, divided by its total number of visits.

venues data by presidential ticket. I do not pool the data by party, across all four elections, in large part because of the effects of the COVID-19 pandemic in 2020. Notably, the data show that Donald Trump and Mike Pence—most of whose visits took place at (usually indoor) arenas and convention centers in 2016—held the majority of their events (62.4 percent) at airports in 2020. There is no mystery as to why they did so; many (swing) states prohibited or significantly restricted large indoor gatherings, thus forcing some events outdoors. Airports provided a relatively accessible location where large crowds could gather outside, while giving campaign staff the ability to control entrances and providing access to hangars or other overhead coverings if weather conditions required them.

What general conclusions can we draw from table 3.1? First, the Republican ticket's preference for airports in 2020 is exceptional; no other presidential ticket hosted even 40 percent of its visits at any one type of venue, let alone airports specifically. Even Trump and Pence, in 2016, held only 8.9 percent of their visits at airports—fewer than their Republican predecessors, Mitt Romney and Paul Ryan in 2012 (14.9 percent) or John McCain and Sarah Palin in 2008 (10.1 percent). If there is any point of comparison, it is the Democratic ticket in 2016, which held 36.5 percent of its campaign visits at colleges and universities, versus only 7.0 percent for the Republican ticket.[61] We see a similar pattern in 2020, with Democrats holding 13.8 percent of their visits at colleges and universities, versus only 7.0 percent for Republicans. Despite popular conceptions of college students as Democratic partisans, this phenomenon was not evident before Trump's candidacies; in previous elections, Republicans visited college campuses far more often than Trump and Pence did (13.7 percent in 2008, 12.9 percent in 2012), although not as often as Obama and Biden did (20.8 percent in 2008, 17.4 percent in 2012). Republican candidates, for their part, were much more likely than Democrats to visit places of business in 2008, and slightly more likely to do so in 2012 and 2016, but not in 2020. The only other instance in which we see clear partisan differences is in terms of visiting union offices; no Republican candidate visited a union office during the 2008–2020 campaigns, while Democrats visited them a few times from 2008–2016 and much more often (11.4 percent) in 2020. This is no surprise, given that unions tend to support Democratic candidates. But, together with the evidence on university visits, it does suggest that the candidates were more focused on mobilizing allies than persuading skeptics.

DISCUSSION

What do we learn from this descriptive analysis of presidential campaign visits? First, in terms of frequency, the total number of visits has declined steadily over recent elections—and not just because of the COVID-19 pandemic in 2020—but with quite a bit of variation across candidates. One noteworthy finding on this point is that Joe Biden was not, in fact, "hiding in his basement" in 2020, but actually made more campaign visits that year than Kamala Harris or Mike Pence and only nine fewer than Donald Trump.

Second, in terms of timing, the conventional wisdom regarding the pace of presidential campaigning is about right: candidates hit the campaign trail hard around Labor Day but slow down over the next month or so before sprinting toward the finish line in the closing weeks. However, there is quite a bit of variation across candidates, with some spending nearly every day on the campaign trail (e.g., Obama and McCain in 2008) and others no more than half (e.g., Clinton in 2016, Biden in 2020). Clinton, in particular, deviated from the expected pace of a presidential campaign, making visits on only one-third of the first fifty days of the campaign before ramping up her activities toward the end.

Third, there is no "typical" venue for a presidential campaign visit. In fact, the most common settings for these visits—places of business and universities—are often selected for the purpose of mobilizing a specific group of supporters rather than appealing to voters in general. The large rallies that most people associate with presidential campaigning, perhaps held indoors at sports arenas or outdoors at airports, are not so typical, after all. Many or most events that could be reasonably defined as campaign visits take place in more modest settings, often with more targeted audiences in mind.

This chapter introduces an original database of presidential campaign visits, the CVD, and explains the criteria for including and counting visits therein. Based on these data, I provide a unique descriptive analysis of campaign visits in the 2008–2020 presidential elections. This analysis yields several important conclusions about the frequency, timing, and host sites for presidential campaign visits, in general as well as across parties and specific candidacies. In short, I find some general patterns regarding, for example, the pace of campaigning and the diversity of host sites, with some indication of choosing venues that are conducive to partisan mobilization, but also significant variation across election years and individual candidates. In some cases, these findings diverge from common understandings of when, where, and how often campaign visits take place.

This chapter provides essential context for the two that follow it, wherein I present more complex empirical analyses of the strategy (chapter 4) and effectiveness (chapter 5) of presidential campaign visits. In the next chapter, I provide a descriptive analysis of the geographical settings for these visits, focusing on the frequency with which candidates travel to different states and drawing connections to the incentive structure created by the Electoral College. Then I use the county-level demographic and political factors associated with each candidate's campaign visits to assess whether they pursued a strategy more indicative of the intent to persuade versus mobilize voters. This allows me to evaluate, in chapter 5, whether the campaigns were effective at reaching their strategic goals via campaign visits.

4

WHERE DO THE CANDIDATES GO—AND WHY?

This chapter analyzes the geographic distribution of presidential campaign visits in the 2008–2020 elections, using data from the Campaign Visits Database (CVD) introduced in chapter 3. My objective is to discern the strategic purpose of campaign visits, generally speaking and for individual campaigns.

This chapter is divided into two parts. First, I examine how political institutions—particularly, the Electoral College, in combination with a "winner-take-all" electoral system, and political parties—shape strategic decisions about where candidates, in general (that is, regardless of party or election year), make campaign visits. Specifically, I describe which states hosted visits (and the most of them) in recent elections, to what extent both parties visited the same battleground states, and how institutional factors such as electoral votes and competitiveness influenced candidate travel.

Second, I characterize individual campaign strategies (in terms of mobilization versus persuasion) based on the political and demographic characteristics of visited counties. Specifically, I describe whether the presidential and vice-presidential candidates tended to visit counties that favored (mobilization) or did not favor (persuasion) their political party, independent of other political or demographic factors. This analysis provides essential context for chapter 5, in which I evaluate the effectiveness of campaign visits. It is only by determining what a candidate was trying to achieve strategically via campaign visits that we can judge whether those visits were effective.

POLITICAL INSTITUTIONS, ELECTORAL STRATEGY, AND CAMPAIGN VISITS

How do we know which electoral strategy guided a campaign? Most studies, including this one, are not conducted by direct campaign participants such as candidates and advisers, with authoritative, inside knowledge of the motives behind strategic decisions.[1] Therefore, we can only make informed judgments—or, in social science terms, causal inferences—about strategy based on the allocation of campaign resources.[2] Such resources may include candidate visits, advertising expenditures, paid staff, online and social media communications, field offices, and polling.

Scholars and practitioners alike typically identify visits and advertisements as the two most important of these resources—indeed, the campaign equivalents of "time" and "money"—with particular emphasis on the former.[3] As Taofang Huang and Daron R. Shaw put it: "Campaign experts agree that the candidate's time is the most valuable campaign resource."[4] Candidates and campaign strategists, such as Dick Cheney (who ran Gerald Ford's re-election campaign in 1976 before successfully running for vice president in 2000 and 2004) and Tad Devine, (who ran John Kerry's 2004 presidential campaign) have confirmed this in their own words, respectively identifying the candidate's time, in reference to campaign visits, as "our most precious commodity" and "our most precious resource."[5]

Why are visits—"the principle means by which campaigns commodify the candidate's time"—particularly useful when trying to discern strategy?[6] As Steven J. Brams and Morton D. Davis explain, time is "the one resource which imposes the same implacable restraints on the campaign behavior of all candidates."[7] That is to say, there are only so many hours in a day (twenty-four, to be exact) and so many days in a general election campaign (approximately from Labor Day to Election Day). Time, in this sense, is an egalitarian resource; each candidate has the same amount of time to make campaign visits or engage in other campaign activities as does his or her opponent.

Campaign visits are also a centralized resource. The candidates' ability to spend time with voters, and to decide when, where, and how often they do so, generally does not depend on external actors. True, campaign visits cost money—for transportation, venues, vendors, staff, and so forth. But they are so cost-efficient in comparison to ads and other campaign activities that travel decisions are unlikely to hinge on the state of a campaign's finances (see chapter 2). Indeed, Darrell M. West makes the distinction that "unlike financial resources, which depend on willing contributors, time is contributed by candidates and therefore controlled by them."[8] In comparison to other resources, therefore, it is particularly reasonable to make inferences about the inner workings of a campaign (i.e., its strategy) based on visit allocation patterns.

Because time is a finite resource, however, campaigns must make discrete choices about when, where, and how often visits take place. Not only are they limited in terms of how many to schedule in a given day or week, but also the candidate can physically inhabit only one space at a time. In that sense, visits differ from advertisements, which can air simultaneously in multiple media markets within or across states. When scheduling visits, campaigns must prioritize certain states and locales, in essence asking: "What is the *most important* place for our candidate to be today?"[9] How a campaign answers that question should tell us a great deal about its strategic goals.

Before making such inferences, however, we must consider the strategic context in which decisions about allocating campaign resources are embedded. That is to say, what are the rules of the game that the candidates are trying to win? And what are the resulting incentives that shape campaign strategy, in general, and decisions about candidate travel, in particular? Specifically, we must consider the influence of two institutions: the Electoral College and political parties.

THE ELECTORAL COLLEGE

On July 28, 1960, the Republican Party nominated Vice President Richard Nixon for the U.S. presidency. In his acceptance speech that night at the Chicago convention, Nixon did something unusual: he discussed where he'd be making campaign visits. The press, Nixon claimed, had been clamoring to know: "Mr. Vice President, where are you going to concentrate? What states are you going to visit?" He proclaimed, "This is my answer. In this campaign we are going to take no states for granted, and we aren't going to concede any states to the opposition. I announce to you tonight, and I pledge to you, that I, personally, will carry this campaign into every one of the fifty states of this Nation between now and [Election Day]."[10]

Nixon wasn't lying (this time); he made it to all fifty states. But keeping such an ambitious pledge would prove difficult. For instance, it required a long detour to Alaska on the final weekend of the campaign. With that, Nixon became the first presidential candidate to visit every state in the Union. No candidate has done it since then, nor is one likely to do so again. There's a good reason for that. It's called the Electoral College.

How the Electoral College Works

Article II, Section 1 of the U.S. Constitution—modified by the Twelfth Amendment in 1804—established the Electoral College. Whereas nearly every other election in the United States is won by the candidate for whom most voters cast their ballot (i.e., by popular vote), the Electoral College awards the presidency and vice presidency to whichever candidates secure the majority of votes cast by presidential electors chosen solely for this occasion by each state, in proportion to its number of votes in the U.S. House and Senate.[11] In that case, the goal for presidential candidates is not to win the national popular vote, but to win at least 270 electoral votes (out of 538) in the Electoral College.

The Constitution does not specify how states must allocate their electoral votes; as a matter of federalism, those decisions are left to them.

But today, with just two exceptions, states award all of their electoral votes to whichever candidate wins the plurality—i.e., the most, even if less than 50 percent—of popular votes cast in that state. This is called a "winner-take-all" electoral system, or sometimes the "unit rule." Only Nebraska and Maine use a different system, whereby two electoral votes are awarded to the plurality winner in that state, equaling its number of U.S. senators, and each remaining vote is awarded to the plurality winner within individual U.S. House districts. With the unit rule prevailing in most states, however, presidential candidates generally do not need to win over a majority of voters in order to gain a state's electoral votes; they just need to get more votes than any other candidate.

How the Electoral College Shapes Campaign Strategy

These institutions—the Electoral College, established by the U.S. Constitution, and the winner-take-all system, established by law in most states—function together to create the incentive structure that guides campaign strategy among presidential candidates, in general. Specifically, it dictates that campaigns concentrate their resources, including visits, primarily or exclusively in "battleground" states, where it is uncertain which candidate will win the plurality of popular votes and thus (except in Maine and Nebraska) all of the electoral votes.

That is why Nixon's pledge to visit all fifty states in 1960 was so foolish, no matter the public relations boost it might have given him at the time. In many states, he was so far ahead or behind that spending time there wouldn't make any material difference. In Alaska, it is possible that Nixon's last-minute visit was decisive; he won the Frontier State by just 1.9 percentage points. But Alaska had only three electoral votes that year, and Nixon lost the Electoral College by a much wider margin, 303–219. In other words, winning Alaska was not going to win him the presidency. Where *should* Nixon have spent his time, if he wanted to affect the election's outcome? In competitive states with many more electoral votes, such as New York (forty-five), Illinois (twenty-seven), and New Jersey (sixteen). That's where Kennedy campaigned on the final weekend, while Nixon flew to Alaska.

Typically, both parties seem to agree on which states are battlegrounds, and they allocate campaign visits accordingly. This is evident in Daron Shaw's research, much of which draws upon his experience working within Republican presidential campaigns. Generally speaking, Shaw finds that, across the 1988–2008 elections, both campaigns classified the same states as battlegrounds, versus safe for or leaning toward one party.[12] For example, in 2000 the Al Gore and George W. Bush campaigns identified the same states as "Base Republican" or "Base Democratic," and in only two cases disagreed on which states were "Battlegrounds" (with the Gore campaign classifying two Bush battlegrounds as "Lean Democratic"). In 2004, the campaigns differed more, but not in any fundamental sense; it was never the case that one campaign classified a state as a battleground and the other as safely Democratic or Republican.

The vast majority of campaign visits take place in battleground states. In 2008, for instance, Huang and Shaw find that the Republican presidential candidate, John McCain, averaged 14.1 visits to states that his campaign designated as battlegrounds, versus about three visits to Democratic- or Republican-leaning states and about two to safe states. The Democratic candidate, Barack Obama, averaged about ten visits to states classified by his campaign as battlegrounds, and about eight visits to Democratic-leaning states, but virtually no visits to safely Republican states and only 3.6 to safely Democratic states.[13] Visits by both parties to competitive states or other geographic areas also tend to be highly correlated. For example, Brams and Davis find that the number of visits per state made by the Democratic versus Republican candidates were highly correlated in 1960 (0.92), 1964 (0.83), 1968 (0.90), and 1972 (0.74).[14] Likewise, in their analysis of the 1972–2000 elections, Scott L. Althaus, Peter F. Nardulli, and Daron R. Shaw find that "the two major-party presidential candidates in each election have been going to the same places fairly consistently since at least 1972, with the exception of state-level visits in 1996."[15]

This, critics of the Electoral College say, is exactly the problem: candidates know which states matter and which ones don't, and they have no incentive to spend precious campaign resources, including their time, on the latter. Indeed, reform advocates seeking to abolish the Electoral College and replace it with a national popular vote system often cite the skewed distribution of campaign visits to help make their case. One such organization, FairVote, regularly tracks campaign visits for this very purpose. One analysis posted to FairVote's website, which showed that three-quarters of visits during the early stages of the 2020 campaign took place in just six states, concludes:

> This inequity in attention between "safe" and "battleground" states is a consequence of America's winner-take-all system . . . [which makes] it fruitless to campaign in any state that leans too much to either party. . . . The ultimate effect of this system is that, election after election, the attention of America's presidential candidates is not on all voters but rather exclusively on voters in battleground states that can swing the Electoral College in their favor.[16]

In other words, the electoral system makes it rational for candidates to ignore voters in safe states—which, by the way, have represented a majority of the American electorate in recent years.

The Electoral College also incentivizes allocating campaign resources to battleground states with a greater number of electoral votes. As George C. Edwards III explains: "Candidates are not fools. They go where the electoral college makes them go, and it makes them go to competitive states, *especially large competitive states*. They ignore most small states; in fact, they ignore most of the country."[17] Indeed, campaigns are likely to weigh electoral votes *and* competitiveness when allocating resources such as campaign visits, but give greater weight to the former (because winning one large state can deliver as many or more votes than winning multiple small states).[18] We should therefore expect an interactive effect, whereby candidates are most likely to visit very competitive states with many electoral votes, while also, but less often, visiting more populous states that are only somewhat competitive and less populous states that are highly competitive.[19]

POLITICAL PARTIES

Political parties—which Marty Cohen, David Karol, Hans Noel, and John Zaller define as "coalition[s] of interest groups, social group leaders, activists, and other 'policy demanders' working to gain control of government on behalf of their own goals"—constitute one of the central institutions in American politics.[20] One of their most important functions is to nominate candidates for the presidency and other offices, who appear with their party's label on general election ballots. That label means something: it is a *brand* label that gives voters a high degree of confidence, if not absolute certainty, about what a candidate stands for, and with whom (e.g., which social groups) he or she stands. For example, it is well known that ideological liberals, African Americans, Latinos, women, Jews, poorer people, and urban residents, among other groups, tend to favor the Democratic Party. Likewise, ideological conservatives, white evangelical Christians, wealthier people, and rural residents tend to favor the Republican Party.[21] Americans have become increasingly likely to draw connections between their party identification and various social identities, which in turn influences their political opinions and voting behavior.[22] Indeed, party identification is the strongest predictor of vote choice in presidential and other elections.

What does this have to do with the allocation of campaign resources, particularly candidate visits? Simply put, partisanship in past elections provides a baseline for expectations about the current election, even when an incumbent president is not running for reelection. In 2016, for example, Hillary Clinton's campaign was reticent to treat Wisconsin, Michigan, and Minnesota as battleground states. Donald Trump's campaign was bold to do so—not because these states had voted for *Clinton* in the past (she had never appeared on their general election ballot), but because for decades they had voted for other presidential candidates from *her party*.[23]

It might be difficult to imagine this, but if parties were not so central to our politics—or, theoretically, if parties did not exist—campaigns (as well as the rest of us) would have to assess a candidate's chances in a particular state based on individual factors, such as how well his or her policy views aligned with voters there and the relative presence of social groups that, for policy or other reasons, were inclined to support his or her candidacy. Past elections, with different candidates, would essentially be irrelevant; the question would be: how well do *these* candidates appeal to the state electorate? For instance, Trump's populist appeal to white working-class, non-college-educated, and rural voters, together with their significant share of the state population, should have suggested that he had a real shot at winning Rust Belt states such as Wisconsin, Michigan, and Minnesota—that is, if he were being judged as an individual candidate, based on present conditions alone.

What made it improbable that Trump would win these states—and what made his visits there seem almost ridiculous to many observers at that time—was the fact that he was a *Republican*, and in recent history these states simply would not vote for Republican presidential candidates. Nor had the types of voters that would make the difference in those states favored Republicans in past elections. Trump's hope seemed to be that he could win by mobilizing voters who were favorable to the Republican Party, or at least his version of it. As MSNBC analyst Steve Kornacki explained:

> [T]he Trump campaign [has] been seeing . . . unusual strength in rural areas, unusual strength with sort of white non-college voters. So they look at Minnesota. They look at the iron range in Minnesota. They look at the Upper Peninsula in Michigan . . . They look at the rural parts of Pennsylvania . . . And they say, "Hey, maybe, maybe we can run up the score there in ways nobody expected, ways we haven't seen before and we could pull a surprise in one of these blue [i.e., Democratic] states."[24]

Sure enough, the Trump campaign succeeded in several "blue states" (but not quite in Minnesota), apparently by mobilizing latent Republican voters—thereby changing the composition of state electorates that, in years past, had rejected Trump's party. As a result, it now seemed possible for a Republican, and not just Trump, to win in these states.

The takeaway is this: when deciding how to allocate resources, including visits, campaigns consider their party's relative strength in a given state and its strength among constituency groups within that state. To the extent that a campaign seeks to *mobilize* voters, it is likely to target its appeals within a particular state toward those groups that tend to favor the candidate's party. To the extent that it seeks to *persuade* voters, it is likely to target its appeal toward groups that tend to favor the opposing party or exhibit no clear partisan preference. Knowing how the party has performed within a given geographic area in the past, and the current population characteristics of that area with respect to partisan constituencies, makes it possible to estimate whether the strategic purpose of campaign resource allocations is to mobilize or persuade voters.

PARTISAN MOBILIZATION VERSUS PERSUASION

Candidates do not simply visit *states*; they visit specific cities, counties, and media markets within states. This presents the opportunity to select locations that align with a campaign's strategic objectives. As Damon M. Cann and Jeffrey Bryan Cole explain: "Candidates must zero in on the specific areas with large constituencies of either their core supporters, undecided voters, or both. In addition, they must target these groups within the states whose electoral votes are needed for victory."[25] In other words, campaign visits tell us not only which states a campaign is targeting, but which types of voters it is targeting there.

Previous studies have used campaign visits to make inferences about mobilization versus persuasion strategies. Huang and Shaw, for example, calculate the average number of visits that the 2008 presidential candidates, John McCain and Barack Obama, made to states classified by their campaigns as "battlegrounds" versus "leaning toward" or "safe" for either party. By far, McCain most often traveled to battleground states, and more often to Democratic- than to Republican-leaning or base states, thus indicating a persuasion strategy. Obama, for his part, visited Democratic-leaning states almost as often as battleground states, and base-Democratic states far more often than base-Republican states, thus indicating a mobilization strategy.[26]

As Lanhee J. Chen and Andrew Reeves point out: "States . . . are big and varied places. A candidate appearance in the panhandle of Florida reaches a very different audience—and results from different political and strategic motivations—than an appearance in Miami."[27] That is to say, state-level analyses provide limited insights into campaign strategy with respect to mobilization versus persuasion. Therefore, Chen and Reeves conducted a county-level analysis of campaign visits *within* battleground states to identify the local population characteristics associated with Democratic versus Republican campaign visits in 2008. Their analysis indicates that the Obama–Biden campaign pursued a persuasion, or "peripheral," strategy, by visiting counties that were more populous and faster-growing, while the McCain–Palin campaign pursued a mobilization, or "base," strategy, by visiting counties in which Republicans had performed better in past elections and had less population growth and fewer African Americans. In other words, Chen and Reeves assessed campaign strategy based on past party performance and the presence of party-affiliated social groups in those counties visited by the presidential and vice-presidential candidates.

Notably, these two studies of the 2008 election reach different conclusions regarding the strategies used by each campaign. Why? As is often the case in social science research, it comes down to methodological differences. First, as noted above, Huang and Shaw analyze campaign visits by state, whereas Chen and Reeves do so by county. That is to say, they use different units of analysis, which may yield different patterns of results. Second, Huang and Shaw characterize strategies based on mean comparisons—i.e., the average number of visits made by the candidates to one type of state versus another—whereas Chen and Reeves characterize strategies based on multivariate regression—i.e., by estimating the average effect of a specific cause (e.g., population growth, party vote in a previous election), or independent variable, on a specific outcome (number of visits per county, by party), or dependent variable, while statistically controlling for the simultaneous influence of other potential causes of that outcome. Among other things, this means that only Chen and Reeves's methodology accounts for multiple factors that might influence campaign visit allocations and estimates whether, and to what extent, the effects of each factor occur independent of others with which they might tend to coincide. This type of analysis more precisely estimates what *causes* allocation patterns to differ. Huang and Shaw's methodology, however, yields more intuitive results and avoids complex concerns about model specification that attend multivariate analyses.

The point of this discussion is twofold. First, it is to say that one must be very careful when designing and interpreting social science research. Often, one must choose between a number of credible methodologies and measurement strategies that may or may not lead to different substantive conclusions. This makes it important to weigh the pros and cons of such choices, and to be mindful of possible limitations when evaluating their results. In some cases, it may be wise to use multiple research methods and compare their results to see where they converge or diverge, thus warranting greater confidence or caution, respectively.

This leads to the second point. Both of the methodologies described above, mean comparisons and multivariate regression models, have their virtues—although I do believe the latter is better suited to this chapter's purposes, because it more precisely estimates causal relationships. Rather than simply choosing one methodology and discarding the other, however, in this chapter I use adaptations of both to evaluate whether candidates pursued strategies of mobilization versus persuasion via campaign visits. Specifically, I begin by calculating the average partisan preferences of counties visited by each of the 2008–2020 presidential and vice-presidential candidates to determine whether those counties differ, in favor of one party or the other, from the national popular vote. Then I estimate via multivariate regression models whether, and to what extent, partisan preferences influenced the number of times that a candidate visited a county, independent of other relevant political and demographic factors.

OTHER STRATEGIC MOTIVATIONS

Generally speaking, campaign visits provide a good indication of campaign strategy. However, given the concerns just stated with regard to research methodology, it is important to recognize that not all campaign visits should be interpreted as direct indicators of an effort to mobilize partisans or persuade undecided voters.

As Hillary Clinton's aversion to visiting Wisconsin in 2016 indicates, sometimes these decisions are designed to send, or avoid sending, signals to voters, the press, or an opponent about the state of the campaign. For example, campaign manager Robby Mook reportedly chose not to have then-President Barack Obama endorse Clinton in Pennsylvania or Michigan because Mook "was reluctant to give Trump a reason to think Hillary was worried about those states." Months later, the Clinton campaign continued to invest resources in Ohio and Iowa even though "the analytics suggested Hillary wasn't likely to win" there. Why? Because "the imperative to avoid signaling to the press and the public drove some of the decision making. That is, they kept real campaigns going in those states just to keep up the appearance that they were competitive."[28]

At other times, campaigns may schedule visits with the intention of diverting or "faking out" an opponent. For example, in 2016 Mook reportedly sent Clinton and her running mate, Tim Kaine, to some Republican-leaning states in hopes of distracting the Trump campaign from genuine battlegrounds. "Every day you make Trump go to Arizona, [Mook] liked to say, is a day he can't be someplace else."[29] This appears to be a common tactic—with campaign personnel attesting to using it in 1960, 1976, and 2000.[30] To cite just one authority on the matter, Shaw explains that "both [Bill] Clinton (in 1992 and 1996) and [George W.] Bush (in 2000) visited or bought television time in states that were not true battleground states in an effort to achieve publicity about the aggressiveness of the campaign and to draw the opposition into committing resources that were better spent elsewhere."[31] In that case, it would appear that the target audience for some visits is not the voter but rather the opposing campaign.

Candidates who expect to win the election also might use visits to enhance their power as president upon taking office. Specifically, they might try to expand their lead in the Electoral College or the popular vote in order to win more decisively and thereby claim a presidential mandate.[32] For example, Bill Clinton recounts that in 1996 his chief pollster "advised me that if I wanted to win a majority of the [national popular] votes, I needed to fly into the larger media markets in the big states and ask people to go to the polls. . . . On [the pollster's] advice we added a stop in Cleveland."[33] But Clinton did not win a popular vote majority, perhaps in part because—with his re-election all but assured—he mostly spent the last days of the campaign stumping for Democratic congressional candidates.

Finally, there are what Larry M. Bartels describes as "ornamental" campaign visits. "Much of what goes on [in campaigns] is intended not to win votes in any direct way," Bartels explains, "but to improve general public relations, preserve political traditions, or gratify individuals within the campaign organization." In other words, some visits are designed to keep up appearances or maintain good relationships between the candidate and his or her party, as opposed to "instrumental" visits, which are designed to directly influence presidential voters, particularly in battleground states. Bartels adds, "Each of these types of effort is (or at least may be) rational, in the sense that it contributes to the campaign goal of electoral victory; but any model of rationality based solely on the expected direct effect within states of instrumental allocations is bound to be misleading when applied to an effort that is actually ornamental in nature."[34]

In other words, any effort to discern campaign strategy based on campaign visits, particularly in terms of efforts to mobilize versus persuade voters, will inevitably be contaminated by some degree of measurement error because not all visits are designed to win votes, in any direct sense. Sometimes campaign visits serve a different purpose and they are intended for audiences other than local voters. As described above, their purpose may be to send (or avoid sending) a signal to the press or the opposition about the campaign's strategic intentions; to induce the opposition to divert its resources from battleground states; to enhance presidential power by securing a mandate or a (larger) party majority in Congress; or to fulfill "ornamental" goals aimed at maintaining good internal and external relationships.

The important question for this study is not whether campaign visits *ever* serve a purpose other than directly appealing to voters, in order to mobilize or persuade them, but whether visits intended for other purposes constitute the exception or the rule. It should be clear from the information presented throughout this book that those visits are the exception; trying to win votes directly, via campaign visits, is the rule. In that case, it is appropriate to make inferences about campaign strategy based on visit allocation patterns—even while recognizing that any empirical estimates will suffer from some (probably small) degree of measurement error due to the inclusion of some visits in the data that were meant for other purposes.

DISCUSSION

This section is designed to explain how political institutions influence campaign strategy and, more specifically, visit allocations, as a general matter and with respect to individual candidacies. First, the Electoral College—in combination with application of the unit rule in most states—incentivizes candidates to spend their time in competitive states, particularly those with a greater number of electoral votes. Second, political parties establish baseline levels of support and group-based coalitions that enable campaigns to allocate resources, including candidate visits, in service of mobilization or persuasion strategies. The preceding discussion prompts several hypotheses regarding campaign strategy and the allocation of campaign visits, which I propose and then test in the empirical sections that follow.

THE CAMPAIGN BATTLEGROUND

Given the incentive structure created by the Electoral College, as described above, I propose four hypotheses regarding campaign visits, in general. I test these hypotheses using data on the 2008–2020 presidential elections, from the Campaign Visits Database.

Hypothesis 1: In any given election, most states will *not* host a campaign visit. This is because campaigns must focus their resources on electorally competitive states, which, at least in recent elections, constitute a distinct minority; even if most states were competitive, the campaigns would have to prioritize those states that were most competitive and/or had the most electoral votes, so as not to spread their resources, including the candidates' time, too thin.

Hypothesis 2: It follows from the previous point that the number of campaign visits made by the candidates to a given state should be a function of that state's number of electoral votes *and* its competitiveness. Candidates should not travel to large states only: some small states may be competitive and some of the larger ones may not. Given that the overriding objective of a presidential campaign is to win an Electoral College majority, and most states allocate all of their electoral votes to the popular vote winner, candidates have an incentive to visit any state in which their presence can make the difference. However, they have greater incentive to visit competitive states with more electoral votes, because these states are most likely to secure them a majority in the Electoral College.

Hypothesis 3: The set of states that host (most) campaign visits should be relatively stable from one election to the next. In other words, we should not observe much fluctuation in terms of which battleground states candidates travel to, and which ones most frequently, in consecutive elections. Why? Because the incentives for visiting states mostly remain stable from one election to the next. Electoral votes are reallocated once every ten years, following the most recent census, and even then do not change for most states. Electoral competitiveness is primarily a function of partisan preferences and demographics, both of which—at the aggregate and, at least in some cases, the individual levels—may change over time, but usually not all of a sudden.

Hypothesis 4: The number of visits to each state made by the candidates should be highly correlated across parties. That is to say, generally both campaigns should agree on which states are battlegrounds, the relative importance of those battlegrounds, and the amount of resources required to win there. Why? Because both campaigns have access to similar information about the prospective outcome in each state, and a vested interest in accurately assessing that information and responding accordingly. While, as earlier examples demonstrate, campaigns sometimes reach different conclusions about which states are legitimate battlegrounds or resist allocating commensurate resources there, this should be the exception rather than the rule.

CAMPAIGN VISITS, BY STATE

Which states did candidates visit (most often) in recent presidential elections? Table 4.1 reports the total number of campaign visits per state made by the presidential and vice-presidential candidates from 2008 to 2020. Columns 1–4 disaggregate results by election year. Column 5 sums visits across all four elections. The states are listed in order, from most- to least-visited.

For ease of interpretation, figure 4.1 also presents the total number of visits by state, in graphical form. Specifically, this is a color-coded map, in which states range from white (no 2008–2020 visits) to black (the maximum number of recorded visits during that period). Figure 4.2 presents another color-coded map, this time indicating the number of elections in which each state hosted at least one campaign visit. States range from white (no visits in any election) to black (at least one visit in all four elections). While the same information can be gleaned from table 4.1, graphical depictions may render certain patterns of evidence more intuitive.

The results presented in table 4.1—some of which also are made visible in figures 4.1 and 4.2—tell us a great deal about how the Electoral College influences the geographical distribution of campaign visits. First, this evidence supports Hypothesis 1. In each of the four elections, most states did not host a single campaign visit—although nearly half of the fifty states, plus Washington, DC, did so in 2008 (twenty-five) and 2016 (twenty-four). In 2012 and 2020, about one-third of states—fifteen and eighteen, respectively—hosted a campaign visit. Over these four elections, the presidential and vice-presidential candidates visited thirty-three

TABLE 4.1 Presidential and Vice-Presidential Campaign Visits, by State (2008–2020)

State	2008	2012	2016	2020	Total
Ohio	94	110	53	16	273
Florida	59	62	64	36	221
Pennsylvania	66	7	43	53	169
North Carolina	23	4	55	33	115
Virginia	35	46	17	2	100
Colorado	27	33	15	0	75
Iowa	12	40	16	6	74
Wisconsin	15	32	9	17	73
Michigan	19	2	20	30	71
New Hampshire	14	22	24	3	63
Nevada	13	17	16	13	59
Missouri	26	1	2	0	29
Arizona	1	0	6	21	28
New Mexico	15	0	3	0	18
Minnesota	3	1	2	10	16
Indiana	11	0	2	1	14
Georgia	0	0	0	8	8
Maine	1	0	2	2	5
Texas	0	0	2	3	5
Illinois	0	2	2	0	4
Nebraska	1	0	1	1	3
New York	0	0	3	0	3
Alaska	2	0	0	0	2
District of Columbia	0	0	2	0	2
Utah	0	1	1	0	2
Alabama	0	0	1	0	1
California	1	0	0	0	1
Delaware	1	0	0	0	1
Montana	1	0	0	0	1
South Carolina	0	0	0	1	1
Tennessee	1	0	0	0	1

State	2008	2012	2016	2020	Total
Washington	1	0	0	0	1
West Virginia	1	0	0	0	1
Arkansas	0	0	0	0	0
Connecticut	0	0	0	0	0
Hawaii	0	0	0	0	0
Idaho	0	0	0	0	0
Kansas	0	0	0	0	0
Kentucky	0	0	0	0	0
Louisiana	0	0	0	0	0
Maryland	0	0	0	0	0
Massachusetts	0	0	0	0	0
Mississippi	0	0	0	0	0
New Jersey	0	0	0	0	0
North Dakota	0	0	0	0	0
Oklahoma	0	0	0	0	0
Oregon	0	0	0	0	0
Rhode Island	0	0	0	0	0
South Dakota	0	0	0	0	0
Vermont	0	0	0	0	0
Wyoming	0	0	0	0	0
TOTAL	443	380	361	256	1,440

states (including Washington, DC) and did not visit eighteen states even once.

Did the candidates ignore small states? Yes and no. It's true that candidates were particularly unlikely to visit less-populous states. Of the eighteen states that did not host any visits from 2008 to 2020, four had only the minimum number of electoral votes (three), and three had just above the minimum (four). On average, the unvisited states possessed 6.3 electoral votes (with New Jersey, at fourteen, having the most)—the lowest of any grouping depicted in figure 4.2.[35] But from there, it gets more complicated. States visited in only one or two elections possessed

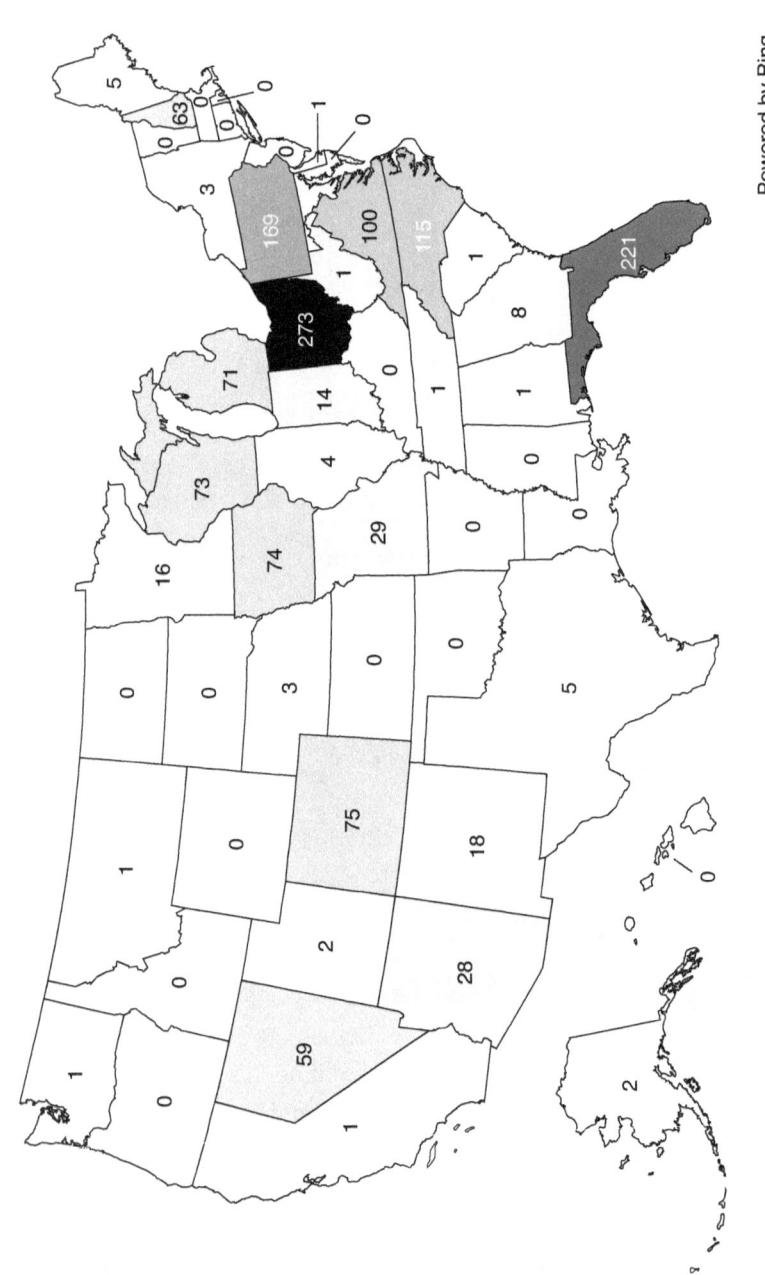

FIGURE 4.1 Total number of presidential campaign visits by state, 2008–2020

Source: Campaign Visits Database, available for download at christopherjdevine.com/data.html

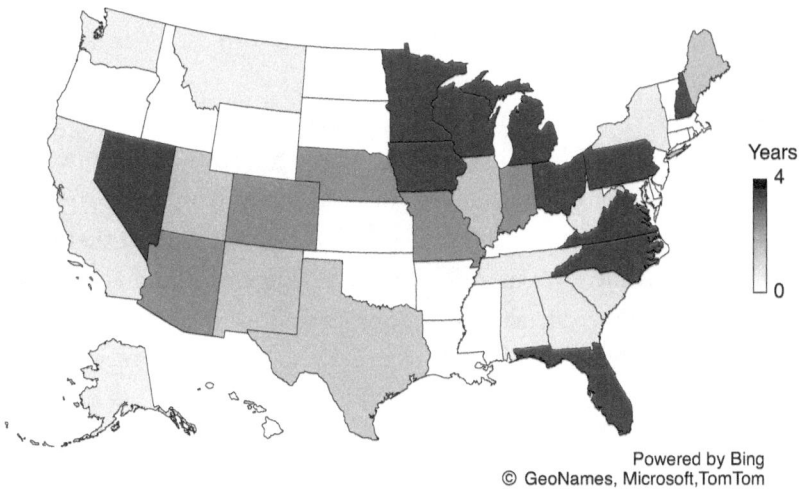

FIGURE 4.2 Number of elections with a campaign visit by state, 2008–2020

Source: Campaign Visits Database

many more electoral votes—13.2 and 17.3, respectively. But the former group includes two of the largest states, California (fifty-five electoral votes) and New York (twenty-nine), and the latter includes Texas (thirty-eight) and Illinois (twenty). And after this group, the average electoral vote count shrinks.

States that were visited in three or all four of the 2008–2020 elections possessed relatively few electoral votes—8.2 and 12.8, respectively, on average—including three states with just four electoral votes: Maine and Nebraska in the former group, and New Hampshire in the latter. In Maine and Nebraska, candidates were typically trying to win just a single electoral vote: Republicans in Maine's more conservative northern congressional district and Democrats in Nebraska's more liberal Omaha congressional district, as made possible by those states' unique allocation methods. Overall, candidates were less likely to visit small states with very few electoral votes—but in some cases, they did so regularly, while at the same time rarely visiting some of the largest states. Clearly, electoral vote counts matter, but they do not *determine* where candidates travel. As Hypothesis 2 predicts, campaigns also factor in a state's competitiveness.

Which states did the candidates visit most often? As figure 4.1 makes clear, Ohio (273) and Florida (221) attracted the most campaign visits, by far. Indeed, more than one-third of all visits from 2008 to 2020 (19.0 percent and 15.4 percent, respectively) took place in just these two states! Pennsylvania was the only other state to host more than one-tenth of the total number of visits during this period, with 169 (11.7 percent). With this, nearly half of all visits from 2008 to 2020 (46.1 percent) took place in just three states.

Ohio, Florida, and Pennsylvania consistently dominate in rankings of campaign visits by state, with one of them coming in first every year: Ohio in 2008 (21.2 percent of all visits that year) and 2012 (29.0 percent), immediately followed by Pennsylvania and Florida, respectively; Florida in 2016 (17.7 percent), followed by North Carolina, Ohio, and Pennsylvania; and Pennsylvania in 2020 (20.7 percent), followed by Florida. Florida ranks among the top three states in all four elections; Ohio in all but one (2020, ranking seventh); and Pennsylvania in two of four (ranking fourth in 2016 and ninth in 2012). This evidence indicates a remarkable degree of stability across elections, in terms of which states were treated as major battlegrounds. Indeed, of the ten most-visited states from 2008 to 2020, all but one—Colorado, which the candidates skipped in 2020—hosted a campaign visit in each election year. Together with the candidates' decisions *not* to visit eighteen states across all four elections, these results provide strong support for Hypothesis 3.

CAMPAIGN VISITS, BY PARTY

Do candidates from both parties agree on which states are battlegrounds and allocate visits accordingly? Theoretically, it's possible that some states consistently attract visits, but only from one party, or that the most-visited states attract far from more attention from one party than the other. To evaluate this possibility, table 4.2 presents a breakdown of visits in each year, by party. The first column reports the number of Republican visits to that state; the second column, Democratic visits; and the third column, the difference between party visits (calculated as Republican minus Democratic visits). If Hypothesis 4 is correct, we should find that, first, states typically attract visits from both parties in a given year, if at all; and second, that the difference between party visits is typically modest.

Judging by the evidence in table 4.2, it is somewhat common for only one party to visit a state in a given election year. This is the case for nearly half of all states visited in 2008 and 2016, but very few states in 2012 and 2020.[36] Nonetheless, most states visited by one party in a given election year (about 60 percent of them) also were visited by the other party. It is important to note that, of those states visited by only one party, none hosted more than three campaign visits and most just a single visit. In other words, I do not find any examples of one party treating a state as a major battleground, in terms of allocating campaign visits, and the other party ignoring it entirely. Nor do I find many examples of one party visiting a state far more often than the other party. The difference between party visits reaches double digits in just six cases, and in all but one of them (Colorado, 2016) both parties visited the state at least ten times each. Table 4.2 therefore provides strong support for Hypothesis 4.

To provide additional, more systematic evidence for this conclusion, I calculated the correlation between the number of campaign visits per state made by the candidates from both parties in each election year—first across all states, then only in those states that hosted at least one campaign visit. Figure 4.3 presents the results of this analysis. I find that the state-level correlation between party visits is extremely high in each case, at approximately 0.90. Indeed, these visits are so highly correlated that it would be impractical to use states as my units of analysis when comparing Democratic versus Republican campaign strategies in the next section of this chapter, or when testing the effect of campaign visits on vote choice and voter turnout in chapter 5. Instead, I use counties as my units of analysis. As shown in figure 4.3, interparty visits correlate fairly highly at the county level (approximately 0.60 within all states, and lower than 0.40 within visited states only). However, this is *far* below the

TABLE 4.2 Republican versus Democratic Presidential and Vice-Presidential Campaign Visits, by State (2008–2020)

State	2008			2012			2016			2020		
	Rep.	Dem.	Diff.	Rep.	Dem.	Diff.	Rep.	Dem.	Diff.	Rep.	Dem.	Diff.
Alabama	0	0	0	0	0	0	0	1	−1	0	0	0
Alaska	2	0	2	0	0	0	0	0	0	0	0	0
Arizona	1	0	1	0	0	0	3	3	0	10	11	−1
Arkansas	0	0	0	0	0	0	0	0	0	0	0	0
California	1	0	1	0	0	0	0	0	0	0	0	0
Colorado	15	12	3	21	12	9	13	2	11	0	0	0
Connecticut	0	0	0	0	0	0	0	0	0	0	0	0
Delaware	0	1	−1	0	0	0	0	0	0	0	0	0
District of Columbia	0	0	0	0	0	0	2	0	2	0	0	0
Florida	26	33	−7	30	32	−2	30	34	−4	17	19	−2
Georgia	0	0	0	0	0	0	0	0	0	3	5	−2
Hawaii	0	0	0	0	0	0	0	0	0	0	0	0
Idaho	0	0	0	0	0	0	0	0	0	0	0	0
Illinois	0	0	0	0	2	−2	1	1	0	0	0	0
Indiana	4	7	−3	0	0	0	2	0	2	1	0	1
Iowa	10	2	8	18	22	−4	10	6	4	5	1	4

State												
Kansas	0	0	0	0	0	0	0	0	0	0	0	0
Kentucky	0	0	0	0	0	0	0	0	0	0	0	0
Louisiana	0	0	0	0	0	0	0	0	0	0	0	0
Maine	1	0	1	0	0	0	2	2	2	0	0	2
Maryland	0	0	0	0	0	0	0	0	0	0	0	0
Massachusetts	0	0	0	0	0	0	0	0	0	0	0	0
Michigan	8	11	−3	1	1	0	14	6	8	12	18	−6
Minnesota	3	0	3	1	0	1	2	0	2	6	4	2
Mississippi	0	0	0	0	0	0	0	0	0	0	0	0
Missouri	12	14	−2	1	0	1	2	0	2	0	0	0
Montana	0	1	−1	0	0	0	0	0	0	0	0	0
Nebraska	1	0	1	1	0	0	1	0	1	1	0	1
Nevada	6	7	−1	8	9	−1	6	10	−4	7	6	1
New Hampshire	7	7	0	7	15	−8	15	9	6	3	0	3
New Jersey	0	0	0	0	0	0	0	0	0	0	0	0
New Mexico	10	5	5	0	0	0	3	0	3	0	0	0
New York	0	0	0	0	0	0	3	0	3	0	0	0
North Carolina	7	16	−9	2	2	0	30	25	5	21	12	9
North Dakota	0	0	0	0	0	0	0	0	0	0	0	0
Ohio	50	44	6	65	45	20	36	17	19	7	9	−2

(continued)

TABLE 4.2 Continued

State	2008			2012			2016			2020		
	Rep.	Dem.	Diff.	Rep.	Dem.	Diff.	Rep.	Dem.	Diff.	Rep.	Dem.	Diff.
Oklahoma	0	0	0	0	0	0	0	0	0	0	0	0
Oregon	0	0	0	0	0	0	0	0	0	0	0	0
Pennsylvania	40	26	14	5	2	3	24	19	5	23	30	-7
Rhode Island	0	0	0	0	0	0	0	0	0	0	0	0
South Carolina	0	0	0	0	0	0	0	0	0	1	0	1
South Dakota	0	0	0	0	0	0	0	0	0	0	0	0
Tennessee	1	0	1	0	0	0	0	0	0	0	0	0
Texas	0	0	0	0	0	0	0	2	-2	0	3	-3
Utah	0	0	0	1	0	1	1	0	1	0	0	0
Vermont	0	0	0	0	0	0	0	0	0	0	0	0
Virginia	12	23	-11	31	15	16	13	4	9	2	0	2
Washington	0	1	-1	0	0	0	0	0	0	0	0	0
West Virginia	0	1	-1	0	0	0	0	0	0	0	0	0
Wisconsin	10	5	5	12	20	-8	3	6	-3	12	5	7
Wyoming	0	0	0	0	0	0	0	0	0	0	0	0
TOTAL	227	216	11	203	177	26	216	145	71	133	123	10

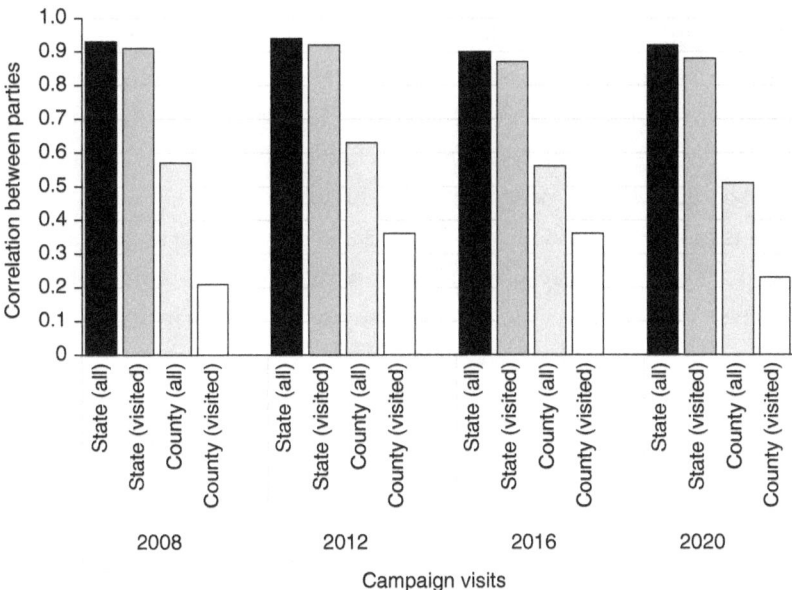

FIGURE 4.3 Correlation between Republican and Democratic campaign visits by state vs county, 2008–2020

Source: Campaign Visits Database

state-level correlations, and clearly indicates the feasibility of evaluating campaign visit strategies and their electoral effects at the county level.[37]

MOBILIZATION VERSUS PERSUASION CAMPAIGNS

Next, I analyze the strategic implications of campaign visits for individual candidates. Specifically, I evaluate whether certain candidates' visits were intended primarily to mobilize or to persuade voters. In doing so, I build upon a previous study from Chen and Reeves and one of my own that evaluate campaign strategy—in the 2008 and 2016 elections, respectively—based on the political and demographic characteristics of those counties visited by the presidential and vice-presidential candidates in a given election year.[38] I characterize campaign strategy according to the frequency with which a particular candidate visited counties whose political and/or demographic characteristics aligned (mobilization) or did not align (persuasion) with his or her partisan constituencies. This is in keeping with my previous discussion of parties as institutions; a party's performance in past elections provides a baseline whereby we may judge whether a particular geographic area is inclined to support or not support that party's candidate in the present election. To the extent that candidates seek out (un)favorable partisan constituencies, we may assume that their principal strategic objective is to mobilize (persuade) relevant segments of the electorate.

Before proceeding with this analysis, it is important to note that candidates do not always clearly pursue one strategy or another. For instance, Shaw, as well as Huang and Shaw, identify four campaign strategies, including "Offensive"—essentially, persuading voters in battleground states and states that slightly favor the opposing party—and "Defensive"—essentially, mobilizing voters in battleground states and states that slightly favor the candidate's party. Additionally, these studies describe a "Mixed" strategy in which candidates (such as Ronald Reagan in 1980) focus mostly on battleground states, but also states that lean toward one party or another, as well as a "Focused, high-risk" strategy entirely geared toward battleground states.[39] I characterize each campaign as strategically focused on "Mobilization" (i.e., "Defensive"), "Persuasion" (i.e., "Offensive" or "Focused, high-risk"), or "Mixed."

In contrast to the previous section, my consideration of institutional influences—in this case, political parties—does not call for a specific set of hypotheses. That is to say, belonging to a certain party, in and of itself, does not logically require a campaign strategy of mobilization versus persuasion. Rather, these strategies should be situational, or formulated in response to specific electoral conditions. In any given election, there may be a good argument to make in favor of one strategy or another; for example, these judgments may come down to whether one believes that independent or undecided voters constitute a relatively large versus small segment of the American electorate. But, to the extent that I can impose a general strategic logic on the campaigns, it is this: candidates who are on track to win an election should focus on consolidating their base of support, while candidates who are on track to lose an election should focus on expanding their base of support. This leads to *Hypothesis 5*: The candidate who is most likely to win a presidential election should use a mobilization strategy, and the candidate who is most likely to lose should use a persuasion strategy. After all, the former would seem to have enough support to win the election already, and the latter would seem to need greater support in order to win.

To judge which candidates were the frontrunners or the underdogs in a given election, I consult contemporaneous polling results. Specifically, I use the RealClearPolitics polling average from September 1 (the day on which I begin data collection for the Campaign Visits Database) to determine which party was ahead in the presidential race, at that time. In each case, from 2008 to 2020, the Democratic candidate led on September 1—and, indeed, would go on to win the national popular vote. Therefore, I hypothesize that the Democratic candidates—not because they were Democrats, but because they were the frontrunners—would allocate campaign visits according to a mobilization strategy, and Republican candidates according to a persuasion strategy.

At the same time, I am mindful that campaigns in general have gravitated more toward mobilization strategies since the early 2000s (see chapter 2). Since the logic of Hypothesis 5 requires an equal number of mobilization versus persuasion campaigns (one per election, depending on who was leading or trailing in the polls), I may very well be imposing a strategic balance that does not exist. To the extent that strategies tend toward imbalance, at least in recent elections, and the data do not fully align with Hypothesis 5, I expect the discrepancies to skew toward Republicans pursuing mobilization strategies.

To evaluate Hypothesis 5 and campaign strategies more generally in this part of the chapter, I analyze the geographical distribution of campaign visits, by candidate, from 2008 to 2020. Specifically, I analyze the political and demographic characteristics of those counties that were visited by each party's candidates. To the extent that candidates visited counties that were favorable to their parties, I classify them as pursuing a mobilization strategy; to the extent that candidates visited counties that were not favorable to their parties, I classify them as pursuing a persuasion strategy. Otherwise, I classify them as pursuing a mixed strategy.

It is important to explain, before going forward, that the subsequent results separate rather than combine visits by each party's presidential versus vice-presidential candidates. In other words, I calculate the political and demographic characteristics for those counties visited by each party's presidential versus vice-presidential candidates, separately. Why? Because these candidates often have different strengths relevant to mobilization versus persuasion strategies, and their campaign visits may be used, even if in a complementary sense, for distinct purposes. A memo written by Hamilton Jordan while serving as Jimmy Carter's campaign manager in 1976 provides anecdotal evidence of the campaigns taking such a complementary approach. In it, Jordan advised Carter and his running mate, Walter Mondale, to "play to their strengths" on the campaign trail. Specifically, "Mondale should work areas of the country where he is stronger than Carter and work with certain groups and elements of the party that he has special relationships with—liberals, labor unions, members of Congress, etc."[40]

By way of empirical evidence, Shaw finds that vice-presidential candidates in the 2000–2004 elections were typically used to reinforce the presidential candidate in states leaning toward one or the other party, rather than appearing in battleground states.[41] Furthermore, in 2016 Devine and Kopko find that the Republican vice-presidential candidate, Mike Pence, made visits to more conservative counties than did his presidential counterpart, Donald Trump, and the Democratic vice-presidential candidate, Tim Kaine, made visits to more moderate counties than did his presidential counterpart, Hillary Clinton—in both cases aligning with the running mate's ideological reputation.[42]

Also, according to Devine and Kopko, while the presidential and vice-presidential candidates from each party generally visited the same states, they tended to visit different counties within those states, with the Republican candidates' county-level visits correlating at 0.30 (versus 0.89 at the state level) and the Democratic candidates' county-level visits correlating at 0.46 (versus 0.94 at the state level). I find similar evidence in the present data. At the state level, the presidential and vice-presidential candidates' visits are nearly indistinguishable, with correlations ranging between 0.85 and 0.92 for all but one of the party tickets.[43] But at the county level, there is much greater variation between candidates, with intraparty correlations ranging from 0.02–0.51.

To overstate the case only slightly: presidential and vice-presidential candidates visit the same states, but go to different parts of them. Where they go within states is surely not random; in some cases, at least, it may reveal divergent—perhaps it is more accurate to say, complementary—strategies. Just as presidential candidates often try to "balance the ticket" when selecting a running mate, their campaign may try to exploit that balance by sending the respective candidates to different areas of a state in order to "play to their strengths."

MEAN COMPARISONS

Figure 4.4 provides the first, and perhaps the most direct, means of evaluating individual campaign strategy. Specifically, I compare each presidential and vice-presidential candidate in terms of whether, and to what extent, the counties that they visited had supported the Democratic presidential candidate in the previous election. To maximize comparability across election years, I use two-party vote share (i.e., excluding votes for minor party and independent candidates, so that the Republican and Democratic percentages total 100 percent).

To take one example, in 2008 Democratic presidential candidate Barack Obama visited counties that, on average, had given the previous Democratic nominee, John Kerry, 52.8 percent of the major-party presidential vote in 2004—significantly above the national average of 48.7 percent. Obama's vice-presidential running mate, Joe Biden, also visited counties that were more Democratic than the national average in 2004 (49.9 percent), but the difference is not statistically significant. Thus, Obama's visits seemed to be targeted toward mobilizing Democratic constituencies, while Biden's had no clear strategic intent. Among

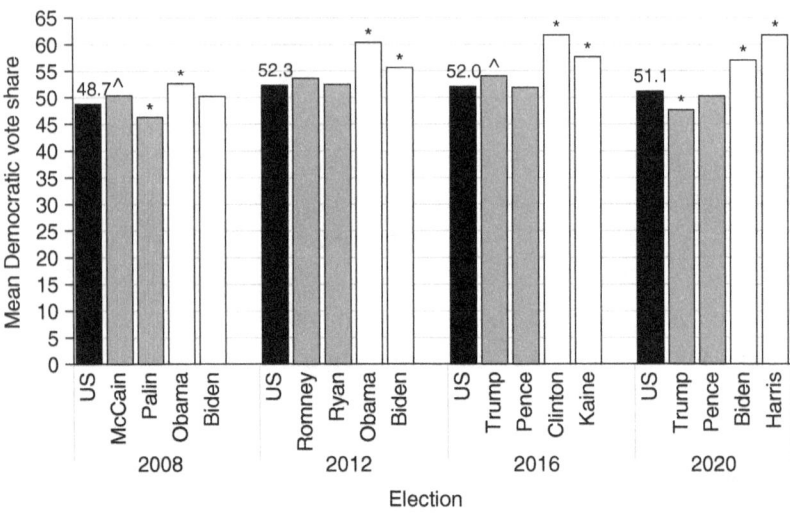

FIGURE 4.4 Mean Democratic vote share in the previous election for counties visited by 2008–2020 candidates

Sources: Campaign Visits Database; MIT Election Data and Science Lab

Note: T-tests for differences from national popular vote.

*p < 0.05; ^p < 0.10

Democratic candidates, only Biden in 2008 visited counties that were not significantly more Democratic than the national average in the previous election. In keeping with Hypothesis 5, this suggests that nearly all of the 2008–2020 Democratic candidates, each of whom led in national polling at the start of the fall campaign, prioritized mobilizing Democratic constituencies via campaign visits.

The results for Republican candidates are more varied. In 2008, Republican presidential candidate John McCain visited counties that were slightly more Democratic than the national average, suggesting a strategy of persuasion, while his running mate, Sarah Palin, visited counties that were significantly *less* Democratic than the national average, suggesting a strategy of mobilization. In subsequent elections, most of the Republican candidates visited counties that did not differ significantly from the national average in terms of Democratic vote share. The only exception was Donald Trump, who, as a presidential candidate, visited counties that were somewhat more Democratic (indicating a persuasion strategy) in 2016 and clearly less Democratic (indicating a strategy of mobilization) in 2020.

MULTIVARIATE REGRESSION

To provide a more comprehensive assessment of campaign strategy in the 2008–2020 elections, in tables 4.3–4.6, I present the results from a series of negative binomial regression models.[44] In each case, the dependent variable is the number of campaign visits per county made by a particular candidate, within battleground states.[45] The main independent variable in these models, indicating mobilization versus persuasion, is the Democratic Party's percentage of the two-party vote share in the last presidential election.[46] To the extent that Democrats (Republicans) pursued a strategy of mobilization (persuasion), I would expect this variable to be statistically significant and positively signed in the models from tables 4.3–4.6—indicating that the more a county favored Democrats, the more likely Democrats (Republicans) were to campaign there.

These models also include several control variables that might indicate mobilization versus persuasion of partisan constituencies. Specifically, these include median age; median household income; percent college-educated, Black, and Latino; population growth (percent change in county population from the previous year); and population density (county population, divided by square miles).[47] Additionally, to account for other aspects of partisan competition that might influence the allocation of campaign visits, I include control variables measuring electoral vote share (county percentage of the state population times electoral votes); campaign advertisements (number of Democratic minus Republican ads aired during the campaign); and the number of visits made to that county by each of the other presidential or vice-presidential candidates.[48] Finally, observations are clustered by media market.[49]

Given current partisan coalitions, if Democrats (Republicans) were pursuing a mobilization (persuasion) strategy, we might expect them to

TABLE 4.3 Predictors of County-Level Campaign Visits by Candidate, 2008

Parameter	McCain	Palin	Obama	Biden
Democratic Vote % in Previous Election	0.023^ (0.014)	−0.032** (0.012)	0.039*** (0.012)	0.028^ (0.016)
Median Age	−0.035 (0.022)	−0.230 (0.028)	−0.094* (0.047)	−0.036 (0.039)
Median Household Income ($1,000)	0.028* (0.013)	0.003 (0.011)	0.009 (0.016)	0.004 (0.016)
College Graduate %	0.027 (0.020)	0.045*** (0.013)	0.002 (0.024)	0.021 (0.021)
Black %	−0.015 (0.014)	−0.006 (0.012)	0.005 (0.010)	0.012 (0.013)
Latino %	0.017* (0.008)	−0.006 (0.009)	0.010 (0.008)	−0.012 (0.018)
Population Density	−0.000 (0.000)	0.000 (0.000)	−0.000 (0.000)	−0.000* (0.000)
Population Growth	−0.119 (0.132)	0.114 (0.116)	−0.006 (0.119)	0.064 (0.100)
Electoral Vote Share	0.994*** (0.273)	0.470* (0.202)	1.327** (0.418)	0.862* (0.361)
Campaign Ads (Dem.–Rep.)	−0.000 (0.000)	−0.000* (0.000)	−0.000 (0.000)	−0.000 (0.000)
McCain Visits	— —	0.475*** (0.075)	0.054 (0.205)	0.072 (0.334)
Palin Visits	0.635*** (0.163)	— —	0.578^ (0.336)	0.556* (0.268)
Obama Visits	0.305^ (0.166)	0.237 (0.145)	— —	0.301 (0.185)
Biden Visits	0.540** (0.210)	0.736*** (0.159)	0.484* (0.240)	— —
Constant	−4.697*** (1.070)	−1.624 (1.310)	−1.916 (1.723)	−3.484*** (1.523)
N	**1036**	**1036**	**1036**	**1036**
Log pseudolikelihood	**−229.905**	**−352.385**	**−349.681**	**−255.459**

Notes: Entries are negative binomial regression coefficients. Robust standard errors are in parentheses. The dependent variable in each model represents the number of presidential campaign visits per county, by candidate. Observations include every county in states that hosted at least five campaign visits in total. Observations are clustered by media market.
***p < 0.001; **p < 0.01; *p < 0.05; ^p < 0.10.

TABLE 4.4 Predictors of County-Level Campaign Visits by Candidate, 2012

Parameter	Romney	Ryan	Obama	Biden
Democratic Vote % in Previous Election	−0.021 (0.014)	−0.005 (0.013)	0.056*** (0.016)	0.057*** (0.014)
Median Age	−0.065* (0.030)	−0.076*** (0.022)	−0.094* (0.044)	−0.040 (0.035)
Median Household Income ($1,000)	0.002 (0.011)	−0.022^ (0.011)	0.004 (0.012)	−0.006 (0.011)
College Graduate %	0.036 (0.028)	0.030^ (0.016)	0.025 (0.023)	−0.008 (0.022)
Black %	0.020^ (0.011)	−0.007 (0.015)	0.007 (0.013)	−0.023^ (0.012)
Latino %	−0.017 (0.019)	−0.023 (0.015)	−0.007 (0.021)	−0.018 (0.015)
Population Density	0.000 (0.000)	−0.000 (0.000)	−0.000** (0.000)	−0.000^ (0.000)
Population Growth	0.010 (0.121)	0.246* (0.115)	0.192 (0.151)	0.440** (0.164)
Electoral Vote Share	0.962* (0.489)	0.997** (0.340)	0.865^ (0.479)	0.732^ (0.407)
Campaign Ads (Dem.–Rep.)	0.000 (0.000)	−0.000 (0.000)	−0.000 (0.000)	−0.000* (0.000)
Romney Visits	— —	0.581** (0.187)	0.666*** (0.180)	0.622^ (0.329)
Ryan Visits	0.248 (0.181)	— —	−0.021 (0.444)	0.414 (0.252)
Obama Visits	0.084 (0.122)	−0.389* (0.195)	— —	0.029 (0.268)
Biden Visits	0.287^ (0.159)	0.412** (0.155)	0.341^ (0.200)	— —
Constant	−0.077 (1.197)	1.405 (1.180)	−3.259 (2.065)	−2.807 (1.731)
N	**616**	**616**	**616**	**616**
Log pseudolikelihood	**−209.774**	**−223.997**	**−211.642**	**−221.034**

Notes: Entries are negative binomial regression coefficients. Robust standard errors are in parentheses. The dependent variable in each model represents the number of presidential campaign visits per county, by candidate. Observations include every county in states that hosted at least five campaign visits in total. Observations are clustered by media market.
***p < 0.001; **p < 0.01; *p < 0.05; ^p <0.10.

TABLE 4.5 Predictors of County-Level Campaign Visits by Candidate, 2016

Parameter	Trump	Pence	Clinton	Kaine
Democratic Vote % in Previous Election	0.004 (0.014)	0.004 (0.015)	0.062** (0.024)	0.038* (0.016)
Median Age	−0.031 (0.026)	−0.073* (0.032)	−0.018 (0.037)	−0.049 (0.032)
Median Household Income ($1,000)	0.007 (0.011)	−0.000 (0.010)	0.001 (0.017)	−0.020 (0.013)
College Graduate %	0.022 (0.016)	0.035^ (0.019)	0.027 (0.027)	0.054** (0.020)
Black %	0.016 (0.013)	−0.003 (0.008)	0.025 (0.016)	0.003 (0.011)
Latino %	−0.019 (0.023)	−0.016 (0.024)	−0.018 (0.017)	−0.017 (0.021)
Population Density	−0.000 (0.000)	−0.000 (0.000)	−0.000 (0.000)	0.000 (0.000)
Population Growth	0.221* (0.110)	0.029 (0.119)	0.327^ (0.185)	0.171 (0.178)
Electoral Vote Share	0.918 (1.014)	0.333* (0.157)	0.841* (0.415)	1.100 (0.761)
Campaign Ads (Dem.—Rep.)	0.000** (0.000)	0.000^ (0.000)	0.000** (0.000)	0.000** (0.000)
Trump Visits	— —	0.924*** (0.203)	0.337 (0.259)	0.284 (0.358)
Pence Visits	0.633*** (0.091)	— —	0.274 (0.178)	0.365 (0.257)
Clinton Visits	−0.173 (0.342)	−0.244 (0.303)	— —	−0.215 (0.275)
Kaine Visits	0.082 (0.218)	0.270 (0.158)	0.224 (0.251)	— —
Constant	−3.162^ (1.825)	−1.043 (1.374)	−8.243*** (2.385)	−4.139* (2.015)
N	814	814	814	814
Log pseudolikelihood	−229.593	−284.057	−107.315	−234.331

Notes: Entries are negative binomial regression coefficients. Robust standard errors are in parentheses. The dependent variable in each model represents the number of presidential campaign visits per county, by candidate. Observations include every county in states that hosted at least five campaign visits in total. Observations are clustered by media market.
***p < 0.001; **p < 0.01; *p < 0.05; ^p < 0.10.

TABLE 4.6 Predictors of County-Level Campaign Visits by Candidate, 2020

Parameter	Trump	Pence	Biden	Harris
Democratic Vote % in Previous Election	0.005 (0.015)	0.027 (0.020)	0.077*** (0.021)	0.032 (0.031)
Median Age	−0.009 (0.030)	−0.027 (0.028)	0.041 (0.025)	0.001 (0.047)
Median Household Income ($1,000)	−0.020 (0.019)	−0.029* (0.012)	−0.029 (0.023)	−0.027 (0.026)
College Graduate %	0.055* (0.023)	0.077** (0.026)	0.038 (0.030)	0.083** (0.032)
Black %	−0.000* (0.009)	−0.008 (0.014)	−0.014 (0.021)	0.037 (0.026)
Latino %	0.021 (0.009)	−0.019 (0.015)	−0.019 (0.024)	0.017 (0.029)
Population Density	0.000 (0.000)	−0.000 (0.000)	0.000 (0.000)	0.000 (0.000)
Population Growth	0.095 (0.119)	0.287 (0.218)	−0.201 (0.236)	−0.074 (0.278)
Electoral Vote Share	0.297 (0.358)	0.381 (0.305)	0.765^ (0.422)	1.102^ (0.626)
Campaign Ads (Dem.–Rep.)	0.000*** (0.000)	0.000^ (0.000)	0.000** (0.000)	0.000 (0.000)
Trump Visits	— —	1.004*** (0.248)	0.864** (0.290)	0.245 (0.343)
Pence Visits	0.519* (0.226)	— —	0.492 (0.393)	0.195 (0.284)
Biden Visits	0.263 (0.178)	0.119 (0.325)	— —	−0.102 (0.268)
Harris Visits	−0.265 (0.162)	−0.110 (0.282)	−0.255 (0.234)	— —
Constant	−3.239^ (1.657)	−3.712** (1.215)	−8.079*** (1.162)	−7.405*** 2.940
N	852	852	852	852
Log pseudolikelihood	−198.348	−192.574	−132.727	−146.789

Notes: Entries are negative binomial regression coefficients. Robust standard errors are in parentheses. The dependent variable in each model represents the number of presidential campaign visits per county, by candidate. Observations include every county in states that hosted at least five campaign visits in total. Observations are clustered by media market.
***$p < 0.001$; **$p < 0.01$; *$p < 0.05$; ^$p < 0.10$.

visit counties with a lower median age and median household income and higher percentages of college-educated, Black, and Latino residents, as well as greater population density. Also, following Chen and Reeves, one might interpret a positive association between population growth and campaign visits as indicative of persuasion for either party (i.e., appealing to new voters within that state).[50] The remaining variables constitute statistical controls: I assume that candidates are more likely to visit counties representing a greater proportion of the population in states with a greater number of electoral votes, those in which the campaign already is advertising more heavily, and those that attract visits by their partisan running mate and the opposition candidates.

What do the results from tables 4.3–4.6 tell us about campaign strategy? First, with respect to the Democratic candidates, I find strong evidence of mobilization via campaign visits, in accordance with Hypothesis 5. In all but one case (Kamala Harris, 2020), the Democratic candidates visited counties that, on average, had voted for the Democratic presidential candidate in the previous election at a higher rate than the nation as a whole. However, once again, the results for Republican candidates are more varied. Only in 2008 does past Democratic vote share predict Republican campaign visits by county, albeit in opposite directions; presidential candidate John McCain was somewhat more likely to visit counties that favored Democrats in the previous election, indicating a strategy of persuasion, while his running mate, Sarah Palin, was significantly more likely to visit counties that had favored Republicans in the previous election, indicating a strategy of mobilization. Palin also tended to campaign in counties where Republicans aired more television advertisements relative to Democrats. It is reasonable to conclude that McCain tended toward a persuasion strategy and Palin a mobilization strategy.

In 2012, past Democratic vote share was unrelated to Republican campaign visits, but presidential candidate Mitt Romney was significantly more likely to visit counties with a younger population and more Black residents. Meanwhile, his running mate, Paul Ryan, tended to visit counties that were younger, less wealthy, more college-educated, and had experienced greater population growth in the past year. Together, this provides modest evidence of a persuasion strategy among Republicans in 2012.

In 2016, Trump's and Pence's visits were unrelated to past Democratic vote share. However, Trump visited counties that were faster-growing and exposed to more Democratic advertisements, both of which are suggestive of a persuasion strategy. In 2020, Trump campaigned in counties that were more college-educated, more Latino, and aired more Democratic ads. While this provides some indication of a persuasion strategy, the data from figure 4.5 suggest that Trump campaigned in significantly less Democratic counties and in the multivariate model this variable is not statistically significant. Therefore, I cannot say with a great deal of confidence that Trump and Pence pursued a persuasion strategy in 2020; quite possibly, it was a mobilization strategy, but to be safe, I will call it mixed.

To summarize: the evidence indicates that all four Democratic campaigns—Obama-Biden in 2008 and 2012, Clinton-Kaine in 2016, and Biden-Harris in 2020—pursued mobilization strategies, as predicted by Hypothesis 5. However, none of the Republican campaigns clearly pursued one campaign strategy or the other. On balance, I would say that in 2008, McCain and Palin pursued a complementary strategy, with the former using campaign visits to persuade, and the latter to mobilize, voters; in 2012, Romney and Ryan pursued a mixed strategy, tending toward persuasion; in 2016, Trump and Pence did the same; and in 2020, Trump and Pence pursued a mixed strategy, with the former tending toward mobilization.

DISCUSSION

Parties, as institutions, do not dictate whether candidates should attempt to persuade versus mobilize voters in order to win elections. However, parties help to establish a baseline of support whereby candidates may judge whether winning an election requires consolidation (mobilization) or expansion (persuasion) of their existing electoral coalition. Once the campaign has decided upon a strategy, it may choose not just which states but which counties or other geographic areas within a state are most amenable to achieving its objectives. For instance, a campaign focused on mobilization should target visits toward those areas that have strongly supported its party in past elections, or whose population is skewed toward those demographic groups that traditionally align with the party. Meanwhile, a campaign focused on persuasion should do the opposite.

My analysis of the 2008–2020 elections suggests that candidates pursue different campaign strategies, seemingly in relation to their prospects of electoral victory. In each of these elections, Democrats were favored, and indeed, they won the national popular vote, if not always the majority of electoral votes. As predicted, these candidates also seemed to pursue a strategy of partisan mobilization. Republicans were not favored to win these elections, yet they did not consistently pursue persuasion strategies. In each case, Republicans' county-level visit allocations suggest a mixed strategy, but tending toward persuasion for McCain in 2008, Romney–Ryan in 2012, and Trump–Pence in 2016, versus mobilization for Palin in 2008 and Trump in 2020.

This chapter analyzes how institutional factors influence campaign strategy—specifically, in terms of campaign visit allocations—among candidates in general and individually. In particular, I examine the role that the electoral system—that is, the Electoral College, in combination with the unit rule in most states—and political parties play in shaping visit allocation patterns.

My analysis of the 2008–2020 elections confirms several hypotheses regarding campaign visits in general: most states do not host any campaign visits in a given election year; electoral votes *and* competitiveness influence whether, and how often, states attract campaign visits; the states that host visits (most often) are relatively stable from election to election; and both parties target the same states about equally. In short, campaigns respond rationally to the incentive structure created by the Electoral College.

Furthermore, with respect to individual campaigns, I find that some candidates' visits are intended to mobilize voters while others are intended to persuade. In keeping with my hypothesis, these patterns correspond at least somewhat to electoral prospects: the frontrunners—Democrats, as it happens, in each of the 2008–2020 elections—clearly pursued mobilization strategies, focused on engaging their partisan supporters; meanwhile, the apparent underdogs—Republicans, as it happens, in each of the 2008–2020 elections—pursued mixed strategies, in some cases tending toward persuasion (McCain 2008, Romney–Ryan 2012, Trump–Pence 2016), and in other cases tending toward mobilization (Palin 2008, Trump 2020).

This analysis of campaign strategy is a necessary precursor to the following chapter, in which I examine whether, and to what extent, candidate visits influence key electoral outcomes such as voter turnout and vote choice. While it is important to know, in a general sense, whether visits "mattered" in a given election, it is also important to know whether those visits were effective at achieving a campaign's objectives. Having established—on a systematic, empirical basis—what those strategic objectives have been in recent elections, I can determine whether a candidate's visits were, in fact, effective.

5

WHAT DIFFERENCE DO CAMPAIGN VISITS MAKE?

This chapter analyzes the effects of presidential campaign visits on voting behavior—specifically, in terms of people's decisions about whether (turnout) and for whom (vote choice) to cast a vote. I estimate these effects for each of the 2008–2020 presidential and vice-presidential candidates. Analyzing multiple elections, and multiple candidacies within each election—using the same data sources and empirical methods, throughout—allows me to draw reasonably general conclusions about the effects of campaign visits, while also recognizing that these effects may vary depending on a candidate's campaigning ability (see chapter 2) and campaign strategy (see chapter 4).

The purpose of this analysis is to determine not just whether (or, with respect to individual candidacies, when), but also *why* campaign visits sometimes influence voting behavior. That is to say, when such effects occur, what is the causal mechanism? Are campaign visits most effective at stimulating turnout among partisan supporters (mobilization), or winning over people who already intended to vote but had not decided on a candidate or favored an opponent (persuasion)? Might these effects vary systematically, in response to campaign strategy (see chapter 4)? For example, do candidates who pursue a mobilization strategy via campaign visits, such as Hillary Clinton in 2016, succeed in their efforts, or those pursuing a persuasion strategy, such as John McCain in 2008?

This chapter is divided into three parts. First, I conduct an aggregate-level analysis, estimating the effects of campaign visits on party vote share and voter turnout in U.S. counties. If the number of campaign visits per county made by a particular candidate is associated with an increase in party vote share *and* turnout, I interpret this as evidence of mobilization—i.e., gaining vote share by expanding the electorate. If a candidate's visits are associated with an increase in party vote share but *no change* in voter turnout, I interpret this as evidence of persuasion—-i.e., gaining vote share without changing the composition of the electorate. Also, because these effects might vary across political environments, I re-estimate the same vote choice and turnout models within counties that heavily favor ("safe"), slightly favor ("leaning"), or do not clearly favor ("swing") one party over the other. This provides a more nuanced estimate of campaign visit effects. Indeed, candidates who fail to gain votes or increase turnout overall nonetheless might prove effective among those segments of the electorate that are more favorably disposed toward their campaign strategy and message—for example, when trying to mobilize voters in safe counties or persuade voters in swing counties.

Second, I examine the same relationship at the individual level, using survey data. That is to say, I estimate the effects of exposure to campaign visits (by county of residence) on vote choice and voter turnout among survey respondents. As I explain in chapter 2, most previous studies of campaign visits rely exclusively on aggregate-level (e.g., state, county, or media market) data. However, this is problematic because decisions about whether and for whom to vote are made by people, not counties or other population aggregates. Using aggregate-level data to analyze individual-level decisions can yield misleading results and errors in ecological inference. Prior to recent elections, there was no practical way around this problem; while nationally representative surveys have existed since the 1930s, rarely have they included enough respondents per state or media market, let alone county, to reliably estimate the effects of local campaign visits on individuals' voting decisions in the electorate generally and especially within partisan subcategories. But that is no longer the case. Since 2006, the Cooperative Election Study (CES), previously known as the Cooperative Congressional Election Study (CCES), has fielded annual large-sample, nationally representative surveys based on interviews with respondents from nearly every county in the United States, and more than enough respondents living in counties hosting campaign visits to reliably estimate these effects. I use data from the 2008, 2012, and 2016 CCES, as well as the 2020 CES (hereafter referred to collectively as the CES), to estimate the effects of county-level visits by each candidate on vote choice and voter turnout among individual respondents. Here, too, I estimate these effects generally as well as within partisan subcategories—that is, among respondents who identify as Democrats, Republicans, independents leaning toward the Democratic or Republican party, or independents who do not lean toward either party—in order to characterize patterns of mobilization versus persuasion at the individual level. Generally speaking, for the reasons described above, I regard individual-level data as most appropriate for evaluating campaign visit effects. However, as I explain in greater detail below, it is quite valuable, from a scholarly perspective, to present evidence from both types of data sources and draw comparisons between them.

In the third and final section of this chapter, I address several questions that the preceding analyses might raise among readers. First, do large campaign *rallies* have a greater effect on voting behavior than campaign "visits," as I have more expansively defined them? Second, what difference would it make if media markets rather than counties were the units of analysis? Third, how can we account for the increasing number of early and absentee voters in an analysis such as this, given that so many campaign visits happen late in the campaign? Or is this even possible?

The results from each section point to the same fundamental conclusion: campaign visits usually do not influence voting behavior, but when they do, persuasion more often than mobilization is the cause.

FIRST, SOME PERSPECTIVE...

A comprehensive analysis of presidential campaign visits naturally culminates in what I present here: direct estimates of their relationship to voting behavior. For it is only by determining what difference campaign visits make, and under what conditions, that scholars and practitioners can properly assess their electoral value and the strategic implications thereof (as I discuss later). But to put these conclusions in their proper context, first it is important to review how we got here. Why should we care about the effects of campaign visits? Why might they influence voting behavior? And what results should we expect based on theory, past research, and this book's evaluation of recent campaign strategies? Before proceeding to the empirical sections of this chapter, I pause to briefly restate some of the major themes from previous chapters and to clarify expectations for the analyses that follow.

WHAT WE'VE LEARNED

Candidate visits are central—even defining—features of modern presidential campaigns. This has been the case at least since Harry Truman's legendary "whistle-stop" tour of 1948 (see chapter 1). Indeed, a candidate who does not engage in in-person campaigning (e.g., Joe Biden in spring of 2020) or engages only in a scaled-down version of it (e.g., Biden in summer and fall of 2020), risks being perceived as insufficiently committed to winning the presidency and thus not deserving of it (see Introduction). In that sense, campaign visits have significant implications for presidential legitimacy. Also, in practical terms, visits consume a great deal of a campaign's two most precious resources: time and money. Thus, it is important to evaluate the electoral significance of campaign visits and the conditions under which they are most likely to prove effective.

It is tempting to frame this study in binary terms, by asking: *Do campaign visits actually matter?* But, as I explain in chapter 2, that is not the right question. While it is clear from the political science literature that "fundamentals" such as national economic conditions and the incumbent president's popularity shape electoral outcomes, they are not entirely determinative. Elements of campaign strategy—including visits—can affect election outcomes, albeit typically at the margins, most of all in close races and when one candidate falls far short of the other in terms of resource allocation. Campaign visits, in particular, are most likely to influence (potential) voters via local media coverage, because relatively few people within the targeted city, county, or media market can attend in person, and those that do are already likely to be intent on voting for the visiting candidate. While the in-person audience might be mobilized as campaign volunteers, the people most likely to be persuaded by campaign visits are those who learn about it, perhaps only incidentally, via local news coverage.

A better question is this: *when* and *why* do campaign visits matter? That is to say, for whom and under what conditions do visits make a difference? The two principal mechanisms for achieving campaign effects are mobilization and persuasion—respectively, stimulating turnout among latent supporters versus changing preferences among existing voters. These mechanisms are not necessarily mutually exclusive; for instance, candidates might tailor their visits to different audiences, trying to mobilize some and persuade others, or change strategies at some point during the campaign. However, in recent years campaigns have tended to prioritize mobilization and most previous studies have cited this as the likeliest mechanism for influencing voters via campaign visits.

While I agree that campaign visits generally are more likely to mobilize than persuade voters, these effects might vary depending on campaign strategy. Previous studies find that some campaigns tend to allocate visits in states or counties already favorable to their party, thereby indicating a strategic emphasis on mobilization, while other campaigns tend to allocate visits in states or counties that favor neither party or favor the opposing party, indicating persuasion. I present such an analysis in chapter 4 and find a good deal of variation among candidates, even those on the same party ticket. Specifically, I find that each of the 2008–2020 Democratic presidential and vice-presidential candidates visited counties that were, on average, significantly more favorable to the Democratic Party than the nation as a whole in the preceding presidential election, thus indicating an emphasis on mobilization. Republican candidates were more varied. In 2008 presidential candidate John McCain seemed to pursue a persuasion strategy, while his vice-presidential running mate, Sarah Palin, who was more popular with the party's conservative base, seemed to pursue a mobilization strategy. The other Republican candidates seemed to pursue mixed strategies, based on campaign visit allocations alone, with some tending toward persuasion (Mitt Romney and Paul Ryan, 2012; Donald Trump and Mike Pence, 2016), and others mobilization (Trump, 2020) or neither (Pence, 2020).

Even if a candidate's visits do not appear to influence voters in general, they might be effective at influencing particular segments of the electorate that the campaign deems to be a strategic priority. This is one reason why it is important not just to estimate the overall effects of campaign visits, but also to distinguish their effects across partisan groups, with an eye toward identifying patterns of mobilization versus persuasion. Simply put, a candidate who is intent on mobilizing (persuading) voters via campaign visits should be judged successful if his or her visits appear to have mobilized (persuaded) voters, even if they had no discernible effect on the electorate as a whole.

What do previous studies tell us about the effects of campaign visits? In most cases, as detailed in chapter 2, they yield mixed results. Some studies find that one candidate's visits influenced vote choice and/or turnout in a given election year, while the opposing candidate's visits did not, or that these effects were evident in one election and not others. Whenever such effects are evident, however, they tend to be quite limited in magnitude and duration. In short, the available evidence suggests that campaign visits are unlikely to affect the outcome of a presidential election, and often have no discernible effect on voting behavior altogether. Yet overall estimates might obscure or underestimate visits' effectiveness among partisan or undecided voters. Unfortunately, relatively few studies provide direct or even indirect evidence of mobilization versus persuasion via campaign visits. Those that do typically yield mixed or inconclusive evidence, but point toward mobilization more often than persuasion.

Why do we need another study of campaign visits? Why isn't the existing evidence sufficient? Chapter 2 describes several important scholarly contributions to be made by this research. Briefly, my analysis of the 2008–2020 presidential elections is more generalizable than most previous studies that focus on one or two elections; it is updated to include the most recent elections, each of which took place following a general shift toward mobilization strategies in the early 2000s, and the 2020 election, which is unique in terms of the disparate size and scope of the Republican versus Democratic presidential candidates' visits; it evaluates the effectiveness of candidates' visits in relation to their campaign strategies of mobilization versus persuasion; and it uses aggregate- (county) as well as individual- (survey) level data to estimate the effects of campaign visits on voting behavior. Also, I use an original dataset, the Campaign Visits Database (CVD), to conduct this analysis (see chapter 3).

WHAT TO EXPECT

Given the preceding discussion, I do not expect to find that campaign visits always influence voting behavior or never do so. Nor do I expect to find that, when such effects occur, they are always attributable to mobilization or to persuasion. Rather, these effects should vary by candidate. But two general trends are to be expected, based on literature and theory. First, I expect that in most cases, campaign visits will have no discernible effect on voting behavior. Second, when such effects occur, I expect they will be attributable to mobilization more often than persuasion. The nature of these effects is likely to reflect campaign strategy. I would not hypothesize that candidates whose strategy it is to mobilize voters always succeed in doing so, nor those that seek to persuade; the evidence of campaign visits' effectiveness is too weak and inconsistent to warrant such faith in the candidates executing on their intentions. But when there is evidence that a candidate's visits mobilized or persuaded voters, it is reasonable to expect that these effects more often than not will align with the strategic intentions that brought the candidate to a certain geographic area or venue in the first place.

Specifically, based on the results from chapter 4, I expect that voters were more likely to be mobilized than persuaded by the campaign visits of Sarah Palin, Barack Obama, and Joe Biden in 2008; Obama and Biden in 2012; Hillary Clinton and Tim Kaine in 2016; and Donald Trump, Joe

Biden, and Kamala Harris in 2020. Conversely, I expect that voters were more likely to be persuaded than mobilized by the campaign visits of John McCain in 2008; Mitt Romney and Paul Ryan in 2012; and Trump and Pence in 2016. Chapter 4 yields no clear evidence of Pence's strategy in 2020, so I have no particular expectations in this case.

To help set expectations for the analyses that follow, three additional points of clarification are in order. First, the principal objective of this chapter is to estimate the effects of campaign visits—that is, to evaluate when and why they influence voting behavior. My objective is not to determine whether campaign visits decided the presidential election's outcome in a particular state or the nation as a whole. For present purposes, I am satisfied to establish the potential for such effects. Subsequent studies may build upon this analysis, perhaps using the same dataset or extending it into future elections, to explore the broader substantive significance of my research findings. For illustrative purposes, however, in many cases I present estimates of the substantive effects of campaign visits within counties or among individuals.

Second, empirically estimating the effects of campaign visits on voting behavior requires sophisticated methods of quantitative analysis. The details of such analyses are important, particularly for scholars who possess the relevant knowledge and skills to evaluate, critique, and build upon this research in future studies. But this book is intended to serve a wider audience than trained scholars alone. To that end, I address many of the methodological details in footnotes rather than in the main text. Also, when estimating multiple regression models, in this chapter's text I present only graphical depictions of the main effects—specifically, the effects of campaign visits (the independent variable) on vote choice or voter turnout (the dependent variable). Tables reporting the complete results for each model referenced in the text and, in some cases, the corresponding graphs may be found in appendix A.

Third, it is important to acknowledge that the following analyses are based on observational data. This limits my ability to determine whether campaign visits *caused* changes in voter turnout or vote choice. Ideally, for the purposes of this research, campaign visits would be randomly assigned, thus excluding any other systematic explanations for changes in voting behavior.[1] But the reality is that presidential campaign visits are not randomly assigned: candidates spend their time strategically in those states and counties where, in their judgment, campaign activity is most likely to make a difference in the Electoral College (see chapter 4). I try to account for such strategic considerations and activities in this chapter's empirical models by controlling for campaign advertisements and county-level demographic and political characteristics. This should help to isolate the independent effects of campaign visits. But it does not entirely exclude the influence of other factors. I think it is reasonable, under the circumstances, to frame the analyses that follow in terms of causal "effects." However, a more cautious approach would be to frame them in terms of empirical "relationships." For the sake of simplicity, I will use the former approach. But some readers may prefer to interpret these results in terms of the latter.

CAMPAIGN VISITS' EFFECTS AT THE COUNTY LEVEL

In the first empirical section of this chapter, I analyze the effects of presidential campaign visits in U.S. counties from 2008 to 2020. Specifically, I estimate whether, and to what extent, the number of visits per county made by each candidate is associated with an increase or decrease in Democratic vote share, as well as turnout, in that county. This allows me to determine not only whether but, if so, how a particular candidate's visits may have influenced voting behavior. If a candidate's visits increased his or her party's vote share while *also* increasing turnout, I interpret this as evidence of mobilization. If a candidate's visits increased his or her party's vote share *without* increasing turnout, I interpret this as evidence of persuasion. In essence, I am distinguishing between gains in vote share that are associated with an expanded electorate versus changing partisan preferences among the existing electorate.[2] Alternatively, many candidates—most of them, I expect—will be shown not to have gained votes via campaign visits.

However, as previously noted, overall estimates might obscure more nuanced effects among certain segments of the electorate. For instance, persuasion might be most evident in competitive "swing" counties and mobilization in more partisan "safe" counties. To identify such effects, I reestimate the vote choice and turnout models separately within five types of counties, based on their partisan vote share in the last presidential election: safely Republican, Republican-leaning, swing, Democratic-leaning, and safely Democratic.

RESEARCH METHODOLOGY

In the analyses that follow, I estimate a series of linear regression models predicting vote choice and voter turnout in counties located within battleground states, clustered by media market. The four main independent variables in these models represent the number of campaign visits per county made by each of the presidential and vice-presidential candidates in a given election year. The dependent variable for the vote choice model is the Democratic two-party vote share (i.e., the percentage of major-party presidential votes won by the Democratic candidate). The dependent variable for the turnout model is the percentage of eligible voters (specifically, citizens aged eighteen years or older) who cast a presidential vote.[3]

To isolate the unique effects of campaign visits, each model also includes several control variables that might be associated with vote choice and turnout. First, I control for a standard battery of county-level demographic characteristics, based on U.S. Census data: median age; median household income (in thousands of dollars); population growth (over the past year); and the percentages of Black, Latino, and college-educated residents.[4]

Second, I control for local political factors, including campaign advertising and partisan vote share in the last presidential election. The specific nature of these variables differs depending on the model, because vote choice is a partisan outcome and turnout is not. With respect to advertisements, in the vote choice model I control for the number of

Democratic minus Republican ads aired (essentially, the Democratic ad advantage) during the general election campaign and in the turnout model, the total number of ads aired. With respect to partisan vote share in the last presidential election, I divide counties into five groups: safely Republican (Democrats won 0–35 percent of the two-party vote); Republican-leaning (35–45 percent); swing (45–55 percent); Democratic-leaning (55–65 percent); and safely Democratic (65–100 percent). When separately estimating the effects of campaign visits on vote choice or turnout in different types of counties, I use this as a selection variable (i.e., estimating the model first in safely Republican counties only; then Republican-leaning counties only; and so forth). When estimating overall effects, I use this as a control variable. In the turnout models, I also control for county-level turnout in the last presidential election.[5]

Finally, in the turnout models, I control for weather conditions—specifically, the average temperature and inches of rainfall per county around the time of the election.[6] Past studies of campaign visits, and turnout more generally, demonstrate that it would be unwise to omit these variables.[7] However, there is no reason to believe that either variable is associated with *how* people vote. Therefore, I do not include them in the vote choice models.

OVERALL EFFECTS

Figures 5.1a and 5.1b graphically depict the effects of each candidate's campaign visits on vote choice and voter turnout, respectively, in the 2008–2020 elections. The top row in each figure reports these results for the Republican presidential (left) and vice-presidential candidates (right), by election year; the bottom row reports these results for the Democratic presidential (left) and vice-presidential candidates (right).

I have plotted the linear regression coefficient associated with a particular candidate's campaign visits, which appears as a dot in each figure. Each coefficient simply estimates the average change in the dependent variable associated with a one-unit increase in the independent variable—in this case, the change in Democratic vote share or voter turnout that we would expect if the candidate in question had visited a given county one more time. For example, in figure 5.1a (top left panel, first estimate), the dot (i.e., regression coefficient) associated with the Republican candidate in 2008, John McCain, lines up with a value of approximately −0.5 on the y-axis (representing the dependent variable, Democratic vote share). This indicates that an additional visit by McCain was associated, on average, with a 0.5 percentage point *decrease* in Democratic vote share per county—what we would expect, in fact, if McCain's visits were effective at winning votes, since he was the *Republican* candidate. If the coefficient were positive, it would indicate that McCain's visits were associated with an *increase* in Democratic vote share—in other words, that they were counterproductive and actually lost him votes. However, in many cases (for example, for each of the 2012–2020 vice-presidential candidates, in figure 5.1a) the dot associated with a particular candidate is located at or very near the horizontal line at the

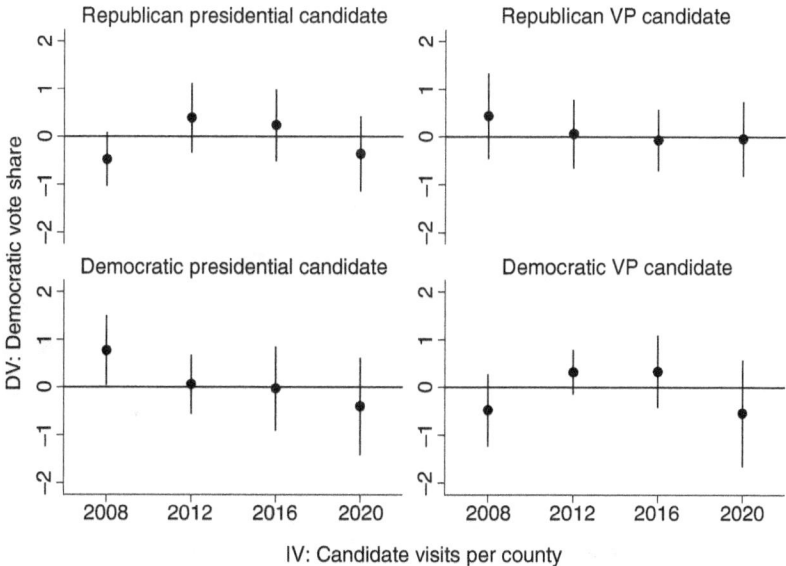

FIGURE 5.1A Effects of campaign visits on county Democratic vote share, 2008–2020

Sources: Campaign Visits Database, available for download at christopherjdevine.com/data.html; MIT Election Data and Science Lab

center of the graph, indicating a regression coefficient of zero. This means that, on average, an additional campaign visit by this candidate would have made no difference at all in terms of Democratic vote share or, in figure 5.1b, voter turnout.

Extending in both directions from each regression coefficient is a line representing the 95 percent confidence intervals. Essentially, these are indicators of how much confidence we can have in the estimated effect of the independent variable, as represented by its coefficient. If this line overlaps with zero (the center line in each figure) at any point, we cannot rule out that the actual effect of the candidate's visits is zero, on average. This does not necessarily mean that the candidate's visit actually had no effect, only that we lack sufficient confidence to say otherwise. If, however, the confidence intervals do not overlap with zero, we can have a high level of confidence that the candidate's visits *did* have an effect on the dependent variable, and in the direction indicated by the

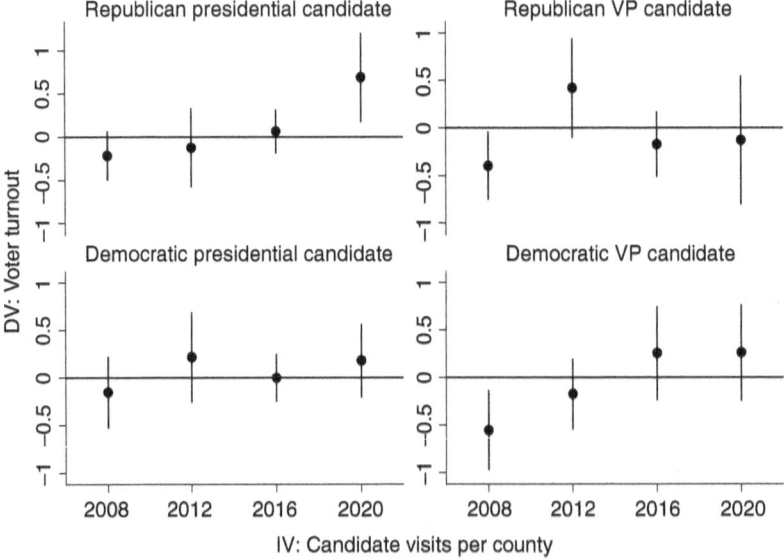

FIGURE 5.1B Effects of campaign visits on county turnout, 2008–2020

Sources: Campaign Visits Database; MIT Election Data and Science Lab; U.S. Census Bureau

regression coefficient. This is what it means to describe a variable as "statistically significant."

The effect of John McCain's campaign visits on Democratic vote share in 2008 is not statistically significant at conventional levels. The 95 percent confidence intervals for this estimate overlap with zero, albeit only slightly. Indeed, the p-value for this estimate is 0.098. This suggests that there is about a 10 percent chance that McCain's visits actually had no effect on Democratic vote share. Of course, this makes it (much) more likely than not that his visits actually did influence vote choice. But we do not have sufficient confidence to say, based on the present evidence, that this is the case.

Only McCain's opponent in 2008, Barack Obama, appears to have won votes via campaign visits. As figure 5.1a shows (bottom left panel, first estimate), the regression coefficient associated with Obama's visits is positive, and the 95 percent confidence intervals do not overlap with zero. Thus, the effect of his visits is statistically significant ($p = 0.039$). On average, each additional Obama visit in 2008 increased his share of the presidential vote in a given county by 0.77 percentage points. Notably, Obama's visits had no such effect when he was running for reelection in 2012. Nor did other candidates who are widely considered to have won (e.g., Trump 2016) or lost (e.g., Palin 2008) votes via their public appearances actually appear to have done so.

How did Obama win votes via campaign visits in 2008? Figure 5.1b suggests that it was by persuading, rather than mobilizing, voters. I say this because Obama's visits apparently were not associated with an increase in voter turnout. Thus, it would appear that he increased his vote share without changing the composition of the electorate—at least as a direct result of campaign visits. For the time being, absent more fine-grained, individual-level evidence, we can only assume this is because Obama's visits persuaded a significant number of voters to make up their minds in his favor or to switch from supporting McCain or a minor-party candidate to supporting him.

There is also evidence in figure 5.1b that Donald Trump's 2020 campaign visits increased voter turnout (by about 0.71 percentage points, on average). Conversely, visits by the 2008 vice-presidential candidates,

Sarah Palin and Joe Biden, appear to have caused decreases in voter turnout (by 0.40 and 0.55 percentage points, respectively). However, according to figure 5.1a, these candidates' visits generally did not influence partisan vote shares. In that case, it might be that their visits had relatively similar effects on turnout among both parties' supporters, since neither party clearly benefited from these expansions or contractions of the electorate.

EFFECTS, BY COUNTY PARTISANSHIP

While only one presidential or vice-presidential candidate (Obama, 2008) generally gained votes via campaign visits, according to the evidence from figure 5.1a, this does not mean that the other candidates' efforts were wholly ineffective. Indeed, their visits might have been effective only in certain types of counties, particularly ones that aligned with their strategic objectives. For instance, McCain (2008) might have succeeded at persuading voters in swing counties, where such a strategy would be most resonant, and Trump (2020) at mobilizing voters in safe or Republican-leaning counties. To provide a more nuanced analysis of campaign visits at the county level—specifically, with respect to candidates gaining vote share (vote choice models) and, if so, via mobilization versus persuasion (turnout models)—in this section I present further evidence obtained by re-estimating the models separately within five county subcategories, according to partisan vote share in the last presidential election: safely Republican, Republican-leaning, swing, Democratic-leaning, and safely Democratic.

For illustrative purposes, figures 5.2a (vote choice) and 5.2b (voter turnout) depict the model results from 2008 only. Corresponding graphs for 2012, 2016, and 2020 are presented in appendix B. The top row shows these effects for the Republican presidential (left) and vice-presidential (right) candidates, and the bottom row for the Democratic presidential (left) and vice-presidential (right) candidates. In each panel, the x-axis specifies county partisanship (safely Republican, Republican-leaning, swing, Democratic-leaning, safely Democratic) and the y-axis indicates

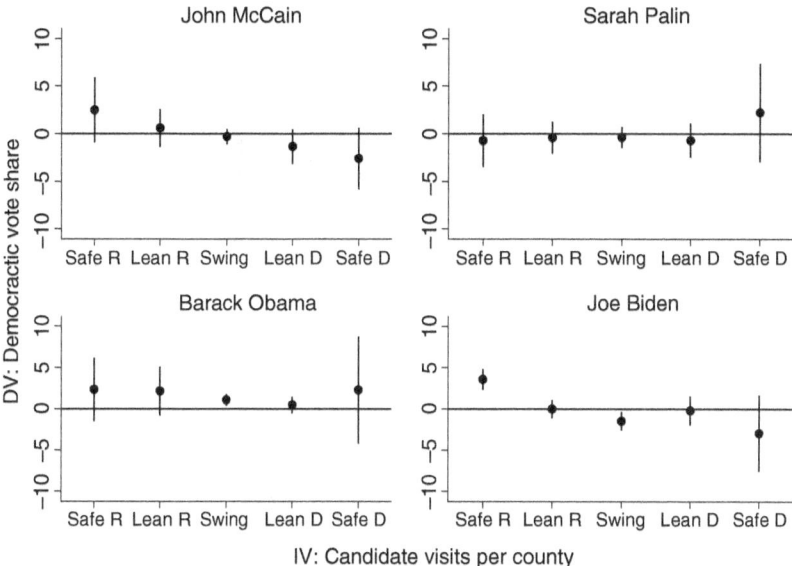

FIGURE 5.2A Effects of campaign visits on county Democratic vote share, 2008

Sources: Campaign Visits Database; MIT Election Data and Science Lab

the magnitude of the regression coefficient. Once again, individual coefficients are indicated by dots and their 95 percent confidence intervals by vertical lines extending in both directions. In short, figure 5.2 tells us whether a given candidate's visits had a statistically significant effect on voting behavior in each type of county in 2008.

I find some evidence—albeit, not overwhelming—of campaign visit effects. Out of eighty estimates from the 2008–2020 elections (sixteen candidates times five county categories), twelve reach conventional levels of statistical significance ($p > 0.05$), with a coefficient signed so as to indicate a gain in the candidate's party vote share. For example, I estimate that in 2008 Barack Obama increased the Democratic vote by about 1.07 percentage points per visit to swing counties. Obama's running mate, Joe Biden, likewise added 3.57 percentage points per visit to safely Republican counties. However, Biden's visits to swing counties are associated with a *decrease* in Democratic vote share of about 1.48 percentage

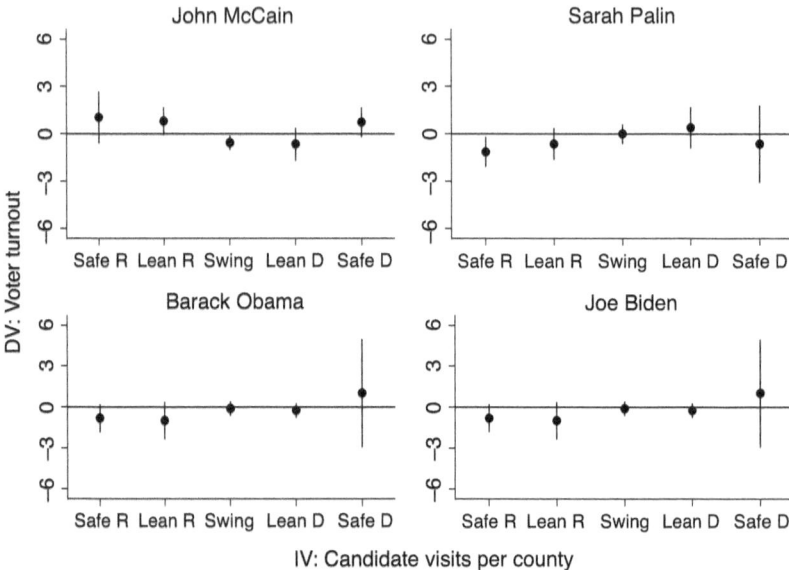

FIGURE 5.2B Effects of campaign visits on county turnout, 2008

Sources: Campaign Visits Database; MIT Election Data and Science Lab; U.S. Census Bureau

points—enough to offset Obama's gains. Donald Trump's visits to safely Republican counties in 2016 and Republican-leaning counties in 2020 also seem to have helped his opponents, increasing Democratic vote share by 2.91 and 2.26 percentage points per visit, respectively. The same is true for Mike Pence's visits to swing counties in 2016 (1.05 percentage points).

Negative effects are counterintuitive, but hardly unprecedented in the campaign visits literature.[8] It is unclear why such negative effects might occur, and the reasons probably vary depending on the candidate and circumstances in question.[9] For example, it might be the case that Trump alienated voters, particularly in Republican-leaning areas that were inclined to agree with his party's policies but disconcerted by the harsh rhetoric and negative local media coverage associated with his visits. However, I should stress, negative effects are rare. More often, we see evidence of positive effects—and more often than that, no discernible effect at all.

Who won votes via campaign visits, and where? In addition to their performance in 2008, as noted above, Obama and Biden proved effective in 2012, with both of them gaining vote share by visiting Republican-leaning counties and Biden by visiting safely Republican counties. Even more effective was the next Democratic presidential candidate, Hillary Clinton, in 2016; her visits were associated with increased Democratic vote share in safely Republican, Republican-leaning, *and* swing counties, by 8.78, 6.45, and 1.32 percentage points, respectively. This is especially noteworthy given Clinton's limited campaign schedule (see chapter 3) and lingering questions about whether she could have won the election by campaigning more aggressively.[10] Clinton's opponent in that election, Donald Trump, won votes in swing counties (decreasing Democratic vote share by 0.98 percentage points) via campaign visits—as he did in 2020 while also gaining votes in Democratic-leaning counties (by about 1.35 percentage points, in both cases). Trump's opponent in 2020, Joe Biden, also increased his vote share by 1.08 percentage points per visit to swing counties.

Indeed, the results from the turnout model suggest that campaign visits persuaded voters more often than it mobilized them. How do we know? Again, I assume that mobilization is at work when a candidate's visits are associated with an increase in party vote share *and* turnout. The only evidence of such an effect is for Barack Obama in 2012. Specifically, Obama's visits to swing counties increased Democratic vote share, albeit only at $p < 0.10$, while also increasing turnout, at $p < 0.05$. Otherwise, nearly every other time that a candidate's visits gained votes for his or her party, as described above, we observe no corresponding change in turnout—suggesting a process of persuasion rather than mobilization. The only other exception is in 2016, when Clinton's visits to Republican-leaning counties were associated with an increase in Democratic vote share but a *decrease* in turnout. Here, we cannot say that Clinton gained by expanding the electorate; if anything, she gained by convincing some voters to stay home. In effect, her visits seem to have *de*mobilized voters. Considering that Clinton's visits had a positive effect in safely Republican and swing counties, this result is particularly puzzling. One possibility is that Clinton's visits were effective at persuading voters in moderately Republican counties not to support Donald Trump, but failed to persuade them to vote for her. Instead, they might have abstained from voting altogether.

DISCUSSION

Are these results surprising? Yes and no. It is not surprising, in light of the expectations that I stated at the outset of this analysis, to find that campaign visits typically have no discernible effect on voting behavior. Only one candidate, Barack Obama in 2008, seems to have gained votes via campaign visits in counties generally. His opponent in that election, John McCain, is the only other candidate who came close to doing so. And only Donald Trump in 2020 apparently caused an increase in voter turnout. I find more evidence of such effects when analyzing counties separately, according to past partisanship. Half of the candidates included in this analysis—Obama and Biden in 2008 and 2012, Clinton in 2016, Trump in 2016 and 2020, and Biden in 2020—clearly appear to have gained votes in at least one type of county via campaign visits. But this is the exception, not the rule; sixty-two of eighty candidate–county estimates (77.5 percent) are statistically indistinguishable from zero, at conventional levels.

What *is* surprising about this analysis is that campaign visits seem to persuade, more often than mobilize, voters. In nearly every case that campaign visits are associated with an increase in party vote share, they are not associated with an increase in voter turnout, thereby suggesting that those gains came from changing preferences among the existing electorate. This is true for Barack Obama in 2008—in counties, generally, and swing counties, specifically—and for several other candidates. Only Obama in 2012 showed any evidence of mobilizing voters; in swing counties, ironically, his visits are associated with an increase in Democratic vote share *and* an increase in turnout. The other exception is Hillary Clinton, whose visits—by increasing Democratic vote share, while decreasing turnout—seemed to *de*mobilize voters in Republican-leaning counties.

This evidence, while compelling, has significant limitations. Most importantly, for present purposes, it uses aggregate-level (county) data to make inferences about individual-level decisions regarding vote choice ("Which candidate should I vote for?") and turnout ("Should I even vote?"). I explain in chapter 2 why such attempts at ecological inference are problematic. To give just one example, in the context of this evidence, consider the effect of Trump's visits to swing counties in 2020.

I estimate that Trump's 2020 visits to swing counties, on average, increased his vote share there by 1.36 percentage points, but did not cause an increase in turnout, thereby suggesting persuasion. It is a surprising finding, given the nature of Trump's campaign and the evidence in chapter 4 that he pursued a mobilization strategy. But let's imagine a different explanation: suppose Trump's visits did, in fact, motivate a large number of Republicans to go to the polls, but at the same time alienated about as many independents, who decided, in turn, not to cast a ballot. In this scenario, the mobilized Republicans and demobilized independents would essentially cancel each other out, so that we observe no net increase or decrease in overall turnout. But not so in terms of vote share: the mobilized Republicans would provide significant gains for Donald Trump, in comparison to the mixed preferences of those independents whom the Republicans replaced. There is no way to observe this based on county-level (or any other aggregate) data; we can only assume that a gain in Republican vote share, paired with no net change in turnout, is indicative of persuasion.

Individual-level data would allow us to observe such countervailing partisan trends within the electorate. Specifically, we could observe patterns of vote choice and turnout among Republicans *and* independents (as well as Democrats, and even strong versus weak partisans), to determine how the behavior of one group might offset or complement another. In the scenario just presented, we could observe that, while overall turnout remained unchanged, turnout increased among Republicans while decreasing among independents, thus revealing mobilization rather than persuasion as the causal mechanism behind Trump's vote gains.

Alternatively, we might find that turnout patterns did not vary among any partisan group, thus affirming that Trump's gains were attributable to persuasion rather than mobilization.

To be clear, I present this as an illustration of the potential benefits of using individual-level data, not to argue that such complex underlying patterns explain Trump's effectiveness in swing counties in 2020 or any other effects evident in the aggregate-level data. To the extent that individual-level data differ from the preceding analysis, perhaps this will require some reconsideration of the conclusions presented above. But, to the extent that individual-level data are consistent with the preceding analysis, we may have even greater confidence in those conclusions.

CAMPAIGN VISITS' EFFECTS AT THE INDIVIDUAL LEVEL

In the second empirical section of this chapter, I analyze the effects of presidential campaign visits on voting behavior among individuals who participated in the 2008–2020 Cooperative (Congressional) Election Studies (CES).[11] Specifically, I estimate whether the number of visits made by each candidate to a survey respondent's county is associated with changes in the respondent's likelihood of voting for the Democratic ticket or casting a vote in the first place. As in the previous section, at first I analyze these effects generally (that is, among all survey respondents), and then within partisan subcategories—in this case, separately among respondents who identify as Democrats, Republicans, independents, and independents who lean toward the Democratic or Republican parties.

CES data are ideal for the purposes of this analysis. Fielded annually since 2006, the CES is a nationally representative survey that includes an exceptionally large respondent sample: 32,800 respondents in 2008; 54,535 in 2012; 64,600 in 2016; and 61,000 in 2020. Most importantly, in the context of this analysis, it includes respondents from every state and the vast majority of U.S. counties: 81 percent of all counties in 2008 and

85 percent in 2012, 2016, and 2020. In fact, only four counties out of the 608 that hosted campaign visits from 2008 to 2020—one in 2008 and 2016, two in 2012—are not represented by respondents in the relevant CES dataset.[12] The 2008 CES features 8,532 respondents from counties that hosted campaign visits (21.3 percent of the overall sample) and 21,323 respondents from battleground states that hosted five or more visits (35.0 percent of the overall sample); the 2012 CES, 10,936 (20.1 percent) and 13,374 (24.6 percent); the 2016 CES, 19,577 (30.3 percent) and 22,973 (35.6 percent); and the 2020 CES, 12,948 (21.3 percent) and 21,323 (35.0 percent). The CES also validates voter turnout, based on public records. The 2008 CES includes 22,235 validated voters (67.8 percent of respondents overall), and 8,441 from battleground states (67.7 percent of respondents from those states); the 2012 CES, 36,402 (66.7 percent) and 9,293 (69.5 percent); the 2016 CES, 35,829 (55.5 percent) and 13,464 (58.6 percent); and the 2020 CES, 39,198 (64.3 percent) and 14,018 (65.7 percent). In short, CES data make it possible to estimate the effects of campaign visits among a large representative sample of survey respondents, as well as voters in all of the states and virtually all of the counties in which those visits occurred, in each of the 2008–2020 elections.

Before proceeding with this analysis, it is important to make two points of clarification. First, while I have argued that individual-level data are most appropriate for evaluating the effects of campaign visits on voting behavior, the purpose of this analysis is not simply to "check" results from the previous section. For example, if this analysis were to indicate that Barack Obama's campaign visits in 2008 did *not* have a positive effect on Democratic vote choice, in general or among independent (i.e., swing) voters, this would not somehow *disprove* the analogous county-level results from the previous section. After all, surveys are based on probabilistic samples of a given population, not the entirety of it. While applying survey weights, as I do in the analyses that follow, should help to mitigate such concerns, it does not obviate them altogether. Also, when it comes to vote choice, survey respondents might not provide accurate self-reports. In particular, past research suggests that respondents are more likely to misreport voting for the winning candidate.[13]

Furthermore, when it comes to analyzing visit effects among partisan subgroups, it is important to recognize that, when moving from county- to survey-level data, we are not quite comparing apples to apples. For example, swing counties, at the aggregate (county) level, are analogous to but certainly not equivalent to independent voters, at the individual (survey) level. Certainly, it is reasonable to assume that swing counties will contain a greater concentration of independent voters, in comparison to safely Democratic or safely Republican counties. But independent voters live in safe counties, too. Thus, it is possible that, say, John McCain's visits increased his vote share among independents, even if we observe no such effect within swing counties. Likewise, as indicated in the previous section, Donald Trump in 2020 might have increased his vote share in swing counties via campaign visits not by persuading independents, but by mobilizing Republicans. Aggregate-level data only suggest which voters might be responsible for such a result; individual-level data provide more direct evidence of visits' effects among voters belonging to particular partisan categories. In this sense, it is best to view the individual- versus aggregate-level data as complementary: that is to say, the former can help to make sense of patterns that we see within the latter.

Second, I am not presenting survey data as an ever-ready replacement for aggregate-level data when it comes to studying the effects of campaign visits on voting behavior. That is because, in addition to the limitations of survey data noted above, most election-related surveys do not include enough respondents, in total, or respondents from enough states or counties, in particular, to reliably estimate the effects of campaign visits. For example, the General Social Survey and the American National Election Studies, two of the most influential social and political science surveys, include samples of only two thousand to five thousand respondents in a typical election year. Indeed, to my knowledge, no survey other than the CES enables such a robust analysis of campaign visit effects as what I present here—and, prior to 2008, no survey does so across multiple elections. In that case, researchers analyzing campaign visit effects prior to 2008 may have to rely on aggregate-level data such as what I present in the previous section. This section's individual-level analysis cannot speak to the accuracy of studies from prior election years; however, by facilitating comparisons to the results from the preceding section, I hope to shed light on the implications of using aggregate-level data to draw conclusions about individual-level voting decisions.

RESEARCH METHODOLOGY

In the analysis that follows, I estimate a series of logistic regression models predicting vote choice and voter turnout among 2008–2020 CES respondents living within battleground states, clustered by media market.[14] Once more, the four main independent variables in these models represent the number of campaign visits per county made by each of the presidential and vice-presidential candidates in a given election year. The dependent variable for the vote choice model represents whether the respondent reported voting for the Democratic (1) versus Republican (0) candidate in that year's election (excluding votes for other candidates). The dependent variable for the turnout model represents whether the respondent was validated by CES as having voted (1) or not (0) in that year's election (excluding ineligible respondents, such as reported noncitizens).

To isolate the unique effects of campaign visits, each model also includes several control variables that might be associated with vote choice and turnout. To the extent practicable, I have tried to mirror those variables included in the aggregate-level analysis from the previous section. First, I control for a standard battery of individual-level demographic characteristics, including: age (by year); race (Black) and ethnicity (Latino); and college education.[15] To better capture the effects of economic interests on voting behavior, I control for perceptions of the national economy (in place of household income) and, in the turnout model, to better capture the effects of geographic mobility, I control for whether a respondent has moved in the past year (in place of population growth).[16] Also, I control for the respondent's gender.[17]

Second, I control for partisan factors, including campaign advertising and party identification. The advertising variable is the same as in the preceding analysis: I control for Democrats' relative (dis)advantage in campaign advertisements (i.e., the number of Democratic minus Republican ads aired) in the respondent's media market, in the vote choice model, and the total number of ads aired, in the turnout model. The party identification variable records whether the respondent identified as a Republican (1); an independent leaning toward the Republican Party (2); a pure independent, leaning toward neither party (3); an independent leaning toward the Democratic Party (4); or a Democrat (5). Similar to the preceding analysis, when separately analyzing the effects of campaign visits on vote choice or turnout among different groups of voters, I use this as a selection variable (i.e., estimating the model first among Republicans, then among Republican-leaning independents, and so forth). When estimating overall effects, I use this as a control variable. Also, in the turnout model, I control for the respondent's interest in politics, as an analog to past turnout at the county level (essentially, capturing predispositions to vote).[18] I do not control for weather conditions in the turnout model, because there is no practical individual-level measure of this available in the CES data.

OVERALL EFFECTS

Figures 5.3a and 5.3b graphically depict the effects of each candidate's campaign visits on vote choice and voter turnout, respectively, among 2008–2020 CES respondents. Each one reports these results for the Republican presidential and vice-presidential candidates, followed by the Democratic presidential and vice-presidential candidates, by election year.

I plot the logistic regression coefficient associated with the effect of a particular candidate's campaign visits, which appears as a dot in each figure. Extending in both directions from the regression coefficient is a line representing the 95 percent confidence intervals associated with each estimate. If this line overlaps with zero (the center line in each figure) at any point, we cannot rule out that the actual effect of a candidate's visits is zero, on average. If, however, the confidence intervals do not overlap

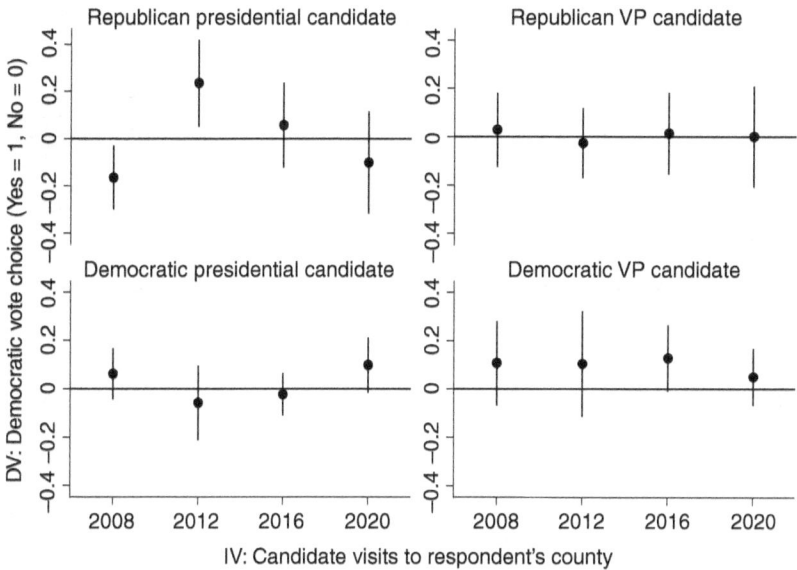

FIGURE 5.3A Effects of campaign visits on presidential vote, 2008–2020 CES

Sources: Campaign Visits Database; Cooperative (Congressional) Election Studies, 2008–2020

with zero, we can have a high level of confidence that the candidate's visits *did* have an effect on the dependent variable, and in the direction indicated by the regression coefficient.

What do we find? In short, about the same as in the previous analysis: there is very little evidence that campaign visits influence voting behavior. Only one candidate clearly gained votes via campaign visits, according to the evidence presented in figure 5.3a: John McCain in 2008 ($p = 0.017$). Two other candidates—Tim Kaine in 2016 ($p = 0.065$), and Joe Biden in 2020 ($p = 0.89$)—also seemed to influence vote choice in their favor, but only at marginal levels of statistical significance. Mitt Romney's visits in 2012 actually increased the probability of respondents voting for his Democratic opponent, Barack Obama ($p = 0.012$).

I find no evidence that campaign visits influenced voter turnout among survey respondents in general (see figure 5.3b). This includes McCain in 2008. Therefore, I conclude that McCain's visits generally

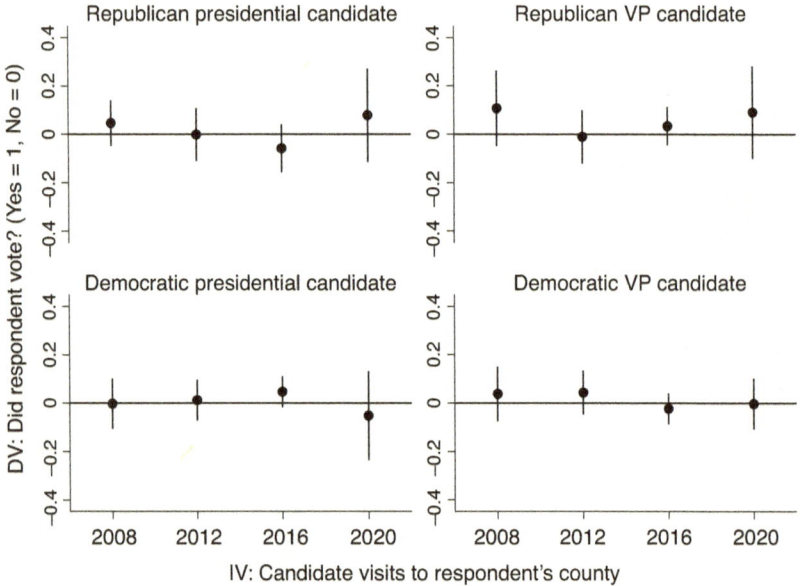

FIGURE 5.3B Effects of campaign visits on voter turnout, 2008–2020 CES

Sources: Campaign Visits Database; Cooperative (Congressional) Election Studies, 2008–2020

persuaded voters; he won additional support without bringing new voters to the polls. The same is true for Kaine in 2016 and Biden in 2020, although we cannot be as confident that their visits had an effect on vote choice in the first place. To the extent that Romney's visits in 2012 helped his opponent, it would appear to have been by persuading voters not to support him.

EFFECTS, BY PARTY IDENTIFICATION

To provide a more nuanced analysis of campaign visits at the individual level, in this section I present further evidence obtained by reestimating the vote choice and voter turnout models separately among five self-identified partisan subcategories of respondents: Republicans,

Republican-leaning independents, independents, Democratic-leaning independents, and Democrats. For illustrative purposes, figures 5.4a (vote choice) and 5.4b (turnout) depict the model results from 2008 only. Corresponding graphs for 2012, 2016, and 2020 may be found in appendix B.

I find very limited evidence that campaign visits influence vote choice among partisan subgroups. Only six estimates out of eighty in total (7.5 percent) are statistically significant at $p > 0.05$ and signed so as to indicate a gain in support for the visiting candidate.[19] Three other statistically significant estimates actually indicate a loss of votes for the visiting candidate: for Donald Trump and Hillary Clinton in 2016 among Republican-leaners, and Kamala Harris in 2020 among Republicans.

Who won votes via campaign visits, and among which groups of voters? Presidential candidates John McCain (2008) and Donald Trump (2020), as well as vice-presidential candidate Joe Biden (2012), each

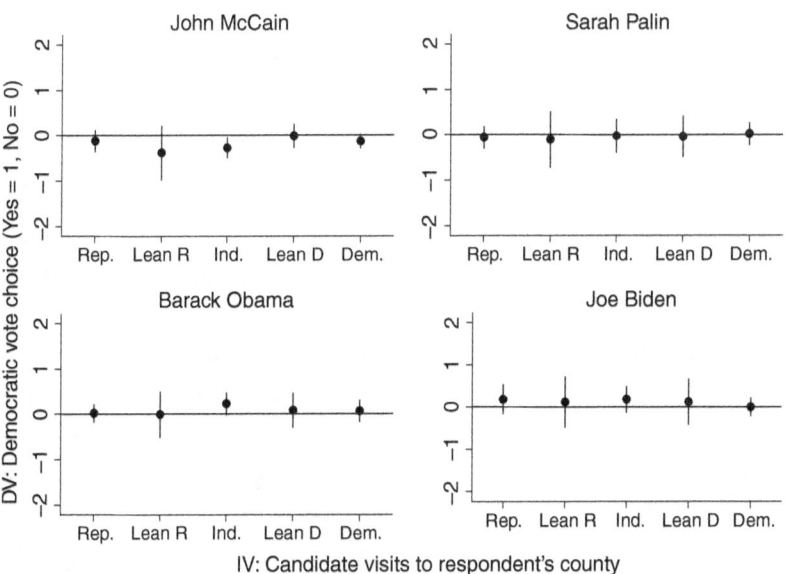

FIGURE 5.4A Effects of campaign visits on vote choice by party identification, 2008 CCES

Sources: Campaign Visits Database; Cooperative Congressional Election Study, 2008

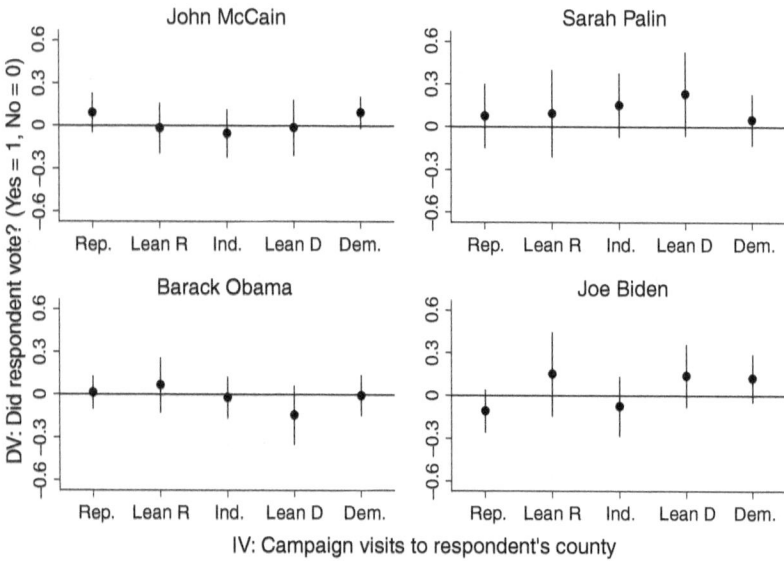

FIGURE 5.4B Effects of campaign visits on voter turnout by party identification, 2008 CCES

Sources: Campaign Visits Database; Cooperative Congressional Election Study, 2008

positively influenced vote choice among independents. Perhaps surprisingly, Trump's visits also gained him votes among Democrats in 2020. His running mate, Mike Pence, likewise gained votes among Republican-leaners in 2016 and Democratic-leaners in 2020.

The fact that most of these gains were made among independents or members of the opposing party suggests voter persuasion. To more fully evaluate the causal mechanism, however, we must again examine the effects of campaign visits on voter turnout. As figure 5.4b indicates, such effects are rare; indeed, only five of the eighty estimates (6.3 percent) from 2008 to 2020 are statistically significant at conventional levels. Specifically, Biden's visits increased the likelihood of voting among independents and Republican-leaners in 2012; Pence among Republicans and Clinton among Republican-leaners in 2016; and Trump among Democratic-leaners in 2020. Again, all but one of these effects occurred among independents or members of the opposing party. Of course, stimulating turnout among partisan opponents or even independents might not be indicative of success; perhaps they were alienated by the candidate's visit and mobilized to vote against his or her ticket. Or, a visit might persuade some partisan opponents in a candidate's favor while mobilizing others against him or her, so that turnout increases among that group but the overall effect on vote choice is statistically indistinguishable from zero. In that case, we must not analyze turnout effects in isolation, but in relation to the previously discussed effects on vote choice.

In most cases (five out of six, to be exact), candidates who positively influenced vote choice among a partisan subgroup via campaign visits had no corresponding effect on turnout. In other words, these visits appear to have changed respondents' minds about who they were voting for, but not whether to vote.[20] This suggests persuasion. Only Biden's visits in 2012 significantly influenced vote choice *and* turnout, among independents in that case. Such a pairing would seem to suggest mobilization. But, given that these are independents rather than members of Biden's party, it seems strange—perhaps even inappropriate—to apply that label here. Also, it is worth noting that Hillary Clinton's visits in 2016 made Republican-leaners more likely to vote but, at the same time, less likely to vote for her. This suggests that Clinton's visits actually might have mobilized Republicans to come out in support of Trump. But clearly, such effects are rare. In the vast majority of cases, campaign visits do not influence vote choice or voter turnout. When visits do influence vote choice, nearly every time it seems to be due to persuasion rather than mobilization.

DISCUSSION

How do these (survey-based) results compare to the results from the previous section? To facilitate comparison, I provide two tables indicating evidence of statistically significant effects in both datasets. Table 5.1 compares overall effects in the county versus survey data. Table 5.2

TABLE 5.1 Overall Effects of Campaign Visits in County vs. Survey Data, 2008–2020

	County Data		Survey Data	
	Vote Share	Turnout	Vote Choice	Turnout
2008				
John McCain	(✓)		✓	
Sarah Palin		X		
Barack Obama	✓			
Joe Biden		X		
2012				
Mitt Romney			X	
Paul Ryan				
Barack Obama				
Joe Biden				
2016				
Donald Trump				
Mike Pence				
Hillary Clinton				
Tim Kaine			(✓)	
2020				
Donald Trump		✓		
Mike Pence				
Joe Biden			(✓)	
Kamala Harris				

Note: A checkmark indicates that the candidate's visits had a positive effect on voting for their party, or increased voter turnout. An "X" indicates the opposite. The indicated effects are statistically significant at p < 0.05, if not in parentheses, or at p < 0.10, if in parentheses.

compares subgroup effects in the county versus survey data—respectively, based on county vote share in the previous election (safely Republican or Democratic, Republican- or Democratic-leaning, swing) versus respondents' partisan self-identification (Republican or Democrat, Republican- or Democratic-leaning, independent). A check mark in

TABLE 5.2 Party-Specific Effects of Campaign Visits in County vs. Survey Data, 2008–2020

	County Data		Survey Data	
	Vote Share	Turnout	Vote Choice	Turnout
2008				
John McCain		(✓)—Lean R, X—Swing	✓—Ind.	(✓)—Dem.
Sarah Palin		X—Safe R		
Barack Obama	✓—Swing		(✓)—Ind.	
Joe Biden	✓—Safe R, X—Swing	(X)—Lean R & Swing		
2012				
Mitt Romney	X—Lean R		(X)—Rep.	
Paul Ryan	(X)—Safe R	(✓)—Swing		
Barack Obama	✓—Lean R, (✓)—Swing	✓—Swing		(X)—Lean R
Joe Biden	✓—Safe R & Lean R	X—Safe D	✓—Ind.	✓—Lean R & Ind.
2016				
Donald Trump	X—Safe R, ✓—Swing	✓—Lean R	X—Lean R	(X)—Rep., (✓)—Ind.
Mike Pence	X—Swing, (✓)—Safe D	(✓)—Swing, X—Lean D	✓—Lean R	✓—Rep.
Hillary Clinton	✓—Safe R, Lean R, & Swing	X—Lean R, (X)—Lean D	X—Lean R	(✓)—Rep., ✓—Lean R
Tim Kaine				
2020				
Donald Trump	X—Lean R, ✓—Swing & Lean D		✓—Ind. & Dem.	✓—Lean D
Mike Pence	(X)—Safe R		(X)—Ind., ✓—Lean D	
Joe Biden	(X)—Safe R, ✓—Swing		(✓)—Rep.	
Kamala Harris	(✓)—Lean R	✓—Swing	X—Rep., (✓)—Ind.	

Notes: A checkmark indicates that the candidate's visits had a positive effect on voting for their party, or increased voter turnout. An "X" indicates the opposite. The indicated effects are statistically significant at $p < 0.05$, if not in parentheses, or at $p < 0.10$, if in parentheses. County-level subgroups are based on partisan voting in the last presidential election. These include Safely Republican or Safely Democratic, Leaning Republican or Leaning Democratic, and Swing counties. Individual-level subgroups are based on partisan self-identification. These include Republicans or Democrats, Republican Leaners or Democratic Leaners, and Independents.

these tables indicates that the candidate's visits had a statistically significant and positive effect on the dependent variable: that is to say, a Democratic (Republican) candidate's visits increased (decreased) Democratic vote share in the county data or the probability of Democratic vote choice in the survey data (vote choice models), or increased turnout (turnout models). An "x" in these tables indicates that the candidate's visit had a statistically significant but negative effect on the dependent variable, by costing his or her party votes or decreasing turnout. Effects are significant at conventional levels (p < 0.05), if not in parentheses, or at marginal levels (p < 0.10), if in parentheses. Table 5.2 also specifies those subgroups for which we observe significant effects.

Generally speaking, the results from both sets of analyses are very similar. First, I find that campaign visits typically do not influence voting behavior. Only one candidate's visits (McCain in 2008) significantly influenced vote choice in his favor among survey respondents in general, and none influenced turnout. In only six cases out of eighty do I find that a candidate's visits influenced vote choice in his or her favor among partisan subgroups, and voter turnout in five cases. Second, as in the previous section, what limited evidence of campaign visit effects that I find points mostly toward persuasion rather than mobilization as the causal mechanism. For example, McCain's visits generally made respondents more likely to vote for him in 2008, but did not make them more likely to cast a vote in the first place. In other words, he seemed to change the minds of people who were already going to vote. Also, when candidates' visits won them votes among partisan subgroups, in nearly every case it was among independents or members of the opposing party, without a corresponding increase in turnout.

However, the aggregate- versus individual-level results also differ in some important ways. Most notably, they sometimes yield different conclusions as to whether, and for whom, the candidates' visits influenced voting behavior. For example, whereas the county-level data indicate that Obama's visits in 2008 gained him votes and Trump's visits in 2020 increased voter turnout, the individual-level data indicate no such effects. Only for McCain in 2008 do I find similar evidence of an effect in both datasets—specifically, a positive effect on vote choice—but only at $p > 0.10$ at the county level, versus $p > 0.05$ at the individual level. Of course, it is important to remember that, in the vast majority of cases, the candidates' visits did not have a statistically significant effect on voting behavior in either dataset. In that case, the results are quite consistent.

Much the same can be said when estimating the effects of campaign visits across partisan subcategories, including counties distinguished by their past partisan vote share and survey respondents distinguished by their partisan self-identification. That is to say, in the vast majority of cases, we observe no effects at all, in either dataset. However, when such effects are evident in one dataset, we usually do not observe a corresponding effect in the other one. For example, in 2016 Clinton's visits appear to have increased her vote share in swing counties, but had no effect on vote choice among one roughly analogous group of survey respondents: self-identified independents. Likewise, in 2012 Biden's visits appear to have made independents more likely to vote for the Democratic ticket, but had no effect on vote share in swing counties. Only for Trump in 2020 do we see corresponding results in terms of statistical significance and direction; Trump's visits appear to have gained him votes in swing counties, as well as among independent voters. The same is true for Obama in 2008, except that his effect on independents is significant only at $p > 0.10$.

What should we make of such rare but notable discrepancies? It is difficult to say. As noted at the beginning of this section, while surveys in general—and the CES, in particular—are ideal for the purposes of analyzing the effects of campaign visits on individual-level decisions about whether to vote, and for whom, they have their limitations, too. For example, the dependent variable in the county-level vote choice model represents legally certified vote totals, whereas in the survey-based model it represents self-reported vote choice, which should be accurate in most cases but in others will surely be inaccurate. Thus, while from an inferential standpoint I would generally trust individual- over aggregate-level data, for an analysis such as this, it is important to recognize that both sources have their strengths and weaknesses. The most comprehensive approach is to use both types of datasets and compare their results. To the extent that they yield similar conclusions—such as the null results that I find in most cases, or affirmative evidence of McCain's effect on vote choice in 2008 and Trump's on swing counties/voters in 2020—we can have greater confidence that these are actual effects and not methodological artifacts.[21]

It is also worth reiterating that the aggregate- versus individual-level partisan subgroup analysis is not an entirely direct comparison. For example, swing counties—defined, for the purposes of this analysis, as those in which Democrats won 45–55 percent of the two-party vote share in the previous presidential election—are not exactly analogous to self-identified independent voters at the individual level. In that case, it is quite possible to conclude that a candidate's visits generally gained him or her votes among self-identified independents without significantly increasing his or her vote share in swing counties. Indeed, we observe this pattern of results for Joe Biden in 2012. Also, we observe that Biden's visits apparently increased Democratic vote share in safe Republican and Republican-leaning counties. Treating the two sets of results as complementary, rather than in competition with one another, might allow us to make sense of these results. For instance, while Biden's visits apparently appealed to independents in general, their effects might have been most pronounced in those Republican counties where independents tend to be surrounded by Republicans and exposed to more pro-Republican messaging. Biden's visits might have provided independents in those counties with a rare high-profile opportunity to hear from a member of the Democratic ticket and rally to his message—thereby changing the overall vote share in a way that we do not see in swing or Democratic counties, where such exposure is more common.

Whatever discrepancies there may be, the fundamental conclusion from both the aggregate- and the individual-level analyses is the same: campaign visits usually do not influence voting behavior, but when they do, it is more often attributable to persuasion rather than mobilization. The evidence confirms one of this chapter's hypotheses (that, in most cases, campaign visits have no discernible effect on voting behavior) while challenging another (that campaign visits typically mobilize rather than persuade voters).

At least, that is what the evidence presented thus far indicates. But are we missing something?

WHAT'S MISSING?

In social science research, definitive conclusions are hard to come by; often, we study concepts that cannot be measured objectively, and there is more than one way to credibly estimate the relationship between a particular set of variables. This is certainly true for campaign visits. Chapter 3 explains my approach to measurement when it comes to the question: "What is a campaign visit?" This chapter has already addressed one major methodological issue relevant to estimating the effects of campaign visits on voting behavior, by comparing results from aggregate- versus individual-level data on the 2008–2020 presidential elections. Both sets of results yield the same general conclusion: that campaign visits typically do not influence voting behavior, and persuade more often than mobilize voters. But there are plenty of other methodological issues to consider before accepting such a conclusion. I cannot address all of them here. I can, however, provide evidence addressing some methodological questions that strike me as particularly important—indeed, some of which readers may already be asking themselves.

First, do large campaign *rallies* have a greater effect on voting behavior than do campaign *visits*, as I have more expansively defined them? Second, do the effects of campaign visits vary as we zoom out from counties to larger geographic units such as media markets? In particular, as I suggest in chapter 2, do we see more evidence of persuasion in the latter? Third, how can an analysis such as this account for the increasing popularity of absentee, mail-in, and other early voting, considering that some campaign visits occur after many voters have already cast their ballots? Would the results look different if we focused on Election Day voters only, who were exposed to the full range of campaign visits?

This section addresses each question by presenting new evidence and comparing it to the previous results. For the sake of brevity, and to maintain a clear focus on this chapter's major takeaway points, I analyze the effects of each candidate's visits on voting behavior generally, and not by partisan subgroup. Tables presenting the model results described in this section may be found in appendix A.

CAMPAIGN VISITS—OR RALLIES?

In chapter 3, I define campaign visits as any public, in-person appearance apparently organized or initiated by the candidates or their campaign, for the purpose of appealing to a localized concentration of voters. This includes not only the large rallies at sports arenas or in public squares that first come to mind when picturing a "campaign visit," but also more intimate interactions such as an impromptu visit to a local business or the rare instance in which a candidate knocks on doors in a residential neighborhood. While most entrants in the Campaign Visits Database (CVD) that I use to conduct this analysis surely look more like the former, the inclusion of the latter could raise reasonable doubts about the precision of this chapter's estimates. A skeptic might argue: "The reason that you are not finding much evidence of campaign visit effects is because you've included too many small-scale events that didn't attract much media attention or involve much interaction with voters. By treating such minor 'visits' as equivalent to large campaign *rallies*—indeed, by including them at all—you've systematically underestimated the effects of campaign visits, properly defined, on voting behavior." In other words, my expansive definition of campaign visits might be biasing estimates of their effects toward zero. This is a perfectly plausible criticism that deserves to be addressed. But how to do so, exactly?

Ideally, I could estimate the effects of campaign rallies—events in which the candidate addresses a very large audience, thereby reaching many local voters directly while also attracting extensive local media coverage—by distinguishing visits based on crowd size. For example, I could treat "rallies" as those events that were attended by at least one thousand people and exclude from the dataset all events with fewer attendees. The problem is that there is no reliable way to estimate crowd sizes at campaign events. Based on my experience in building the CVD, I can attest that many news reports do not provide such estimates. Even when they do, it is all but impossible to gauge the accuracy of those estimates. For example, in chapter 3, I described Donald Trump's visit to the Harrisburg International Airport in September 2020. At that event, Trump bragged that the crowd numbered in the "tens of thousands . . . somebody said 17–18,000." But Secret Service agents' estimates differed: the airport hangar's capacity was only ten thousand to eleven thousand, they noted, and much of the available space was empty. A local reporter observed that only about two thousand seats around the podium were filled. *New York Times* reporters estimated that "perhaps a few thousand" supporters were in attendance.[22] Thus, even in those cases where crowd size estimates are publicly available, they are not reliable enough to employ a clear cutoff whereby we might distinguish large "rallies" from smaller "visits."

In that case, I propose using a reasonable proxy for crowd size: the type of venue in which a campaign visit took place (see chapter 3). Specifically, I isolate those visits taking place at venues that generally hold very large crowds (airports, arenas/convention centers, fairgrounds, public spaces, schools, theaters, and universities) versus those that do not (banquet and events centers, campaign offices, churches, government facilities, hotels/resorts/clubs, nonprofit facilities, places of business, private residences, and union offices).[23] I exclude the latter from this analysis and include only the former.[24] Specifically, I estimate the effects of campaign *rallies* on vote choice and voter turnout, at the aggregate and individual levels, using the same procedures as in the preceding analyses of campaign visits, broadly defined.

What difference does this make? Very little. With respect to vote choice, in most cases, I observe no meaningful differences from previous analyses of campaign *visits*. Much like the results depicted in figure 5.1a, I find that in 2008 Obama's rallies had a statistically significant and positive effect on county-level Democratic vote share (increasing it by 1.02 percentage points), while McCain's had a marginally significant and negative effect (decreasing it by 0.81 percentage points). In most other cases, mirroring my analysis of campaign visits, rallies' effects are not statistically significant. There are only two exceptions: in 2012 I find that Obama's rallies increased Democratic vote share by 0.61 percentage points, on average, albeit at marginal significance levels; whereas in 2020, at conventional significance levels, I find that Harris's rallies actually decreased Democratic vote share by 3.04 percentage points per visit.

With respect to voter turnout, the results are mostly the same; again, I find that Palin's and Biden's rallies in 2008 decreased turnout, while most other candidates' rallies had no effect. Trump's rallies in 2016 once more are associated with an increase in voter turnout, although the evidence is less certain in this case. The only clear departure from the previous results is for Harris in 2020, whose rallies are associated with a statistically significant increase in voter turnout, by 1.50 percentage points per visit. Also, there is weak evidence that Obama's rallies in 2008 actually had a negative effect on turnout.

The survey data also yield similar results. Most notably, I find—as in the preceding analysis of campaign visits—that McCain's rallies had a statistically significant and negative effect on the probability of a respondent's casting a vote for the Democratic ticket, and that Biden's 2020 rallies might have helped him gain votes. In 2012, again I find that Romney's rallies actually cost him votes. Each of these results is consistent with my survey-based analysis of campaign visits. And again, in most cases, campaign rallies had no apparent effect on vote choice or turnout. The two discrepant findings in terms of vote choice are for Paul Ryan in 2012, whose rallies might have helped his party win votes, and Tim Kaine in 2016, whose rallies had no apparent effect on vote choice. In all but two cases, the survey data also indicate that campaign rallies had no effect on voter turnout. The only exceptions are in 2016, when Trump's rallies appear to have decreased, and Mike Pence's rallies increased, the probability of survey respondents casting a vote.

In short, there is very little evidence that campaign "rallies" influence voting behavior any more than campaign "visits," as previously defined. In fifty-six of sixty-four cases (87.5 percent), there is no apparent difference, in terms of the statistical significance or direction of the estimated effect; I find no evidence of an effect in forty-eight cases and the same effect in eight cases. Only in eight other cases do I find a discrepancy, with rallies, but not visits, having a statistically significant effect on vote choice in one case and on turnout in three; a marginal effect on vote choice in two cases and turnout in one case; and no effect in one case, where it was marginally significant in the previous analysis.

This evidence indicates that my conclusions are not dependent on an expansive definition of campaign visits. Even when narrowing my focus to campaign rallies—based on a reasonable approximation thereof—I find very limited evidence of an effect on vote choice. And when those effects occur, the causal mechanism remains the same in each case: the candidate wins votes without affecting turnout (McCain and Obama 2008, in the county-level data; McCain 2008 and Biden 2020, in the survey data), thus indicating persuasion, or loses votes without increasing turnout (Romney 2012, in both datasets), which suggests demobilization. Of the two cases in which campaign rallies, but not visits, are associated with a gain in vote choice (Obama 2012, in the county-level data; Ryan 2012, in the survey data), I find no corresponding effect on turnout, thus indicating persuasion. Harris's rallies in 2020 appear to have cost her party votes while increasing turnout, thus indicating countermobilization of Republicans. However, given the way that I have defined campaign visits, and justified this approach in chapter 3, I am not inclined to treat these estimates of campaign rally effects as more credible than the initial estimates.

VISITS PER COUNTY—OR MEDIA MARKET?

The preceding analyses have focused on the effects of campaign visits within counties, in terms of vote share or vote choice among survey respondents living in a visited county. Previous studies of campaign visits also have used counties as their units of analysis.[25] But others have used media markets as their units of analysis—in other words, estimating the effects of campaign visits within a given media market on vote share (at the aggregate level) or vote choice (at the individual level).[26] Daron R. Shaw, for example, contends that the media market is "arguably the most appropriate unit of analysis" when analyzing the effects of campaign visits and ads. "Political communication is conducted at the level of the media market," he explains. "Most of the money in contemporary political campaigns . . . is dedicated to television advertising, while most of the candidate's time is wrapped up in visiting cities and towns in an effort to win local media coverage." Therefore, Shaw says, "We run the risk of mismeasurement if we ignore the point at which aggregate communication occurs."[27]

My analysis does not ignore the media market as a relevant point of aggregation: each empirical model clusters standard errors by media market to account for shared exposure, via local media coverage, to campaign visits and advertisements. I measure exposure to campaign visits at the county level, primarily in order to maximize the chances of detecting their effects on voting behavior. In essence, I assume that living in the county where a visit occurs is not equivalent to living in any other county within the same media market; building on the arguments presented in chapter 2, direct exposure via attendance (in-person audience) and indirect exposure via activism among those in attendance (downstream audience) should increase the likelihood of voter mobilization, especially in the immediate vicinity of the visit. However, it is entirely reasonable to suggest that these effects also will be detectable within the broader media market in which a visit takes place, and that the mechanisms for such effects might vary based on proximity to the visit in question. Specifically, I suggest that persuasion is more likely to occur at the media market versus county level, because the former is more likely to involve incidental rather than intentional exposure among voters who are not affiliated with a particular campaign or seeking to express support for it, but rather learn about a candidate's visit via local media coverage. This is not to say that I expect campaign visits to persuade voters at the media market level in most instances; rather, I expect to find more evidence of persuasion at the media market level than at the county level. But is that the case?

To address this issue, I recoded the CES survey data. Specifically, I switched the independent variables from the number of campaign visits to the survey respondent's *county*, to the number of visits to the respondent's *media market*. For example, in 2020 none of the presidential or vice-presidential candidates visited Navajo County, Arizona. But each of them visited the Phoenix media market that encompasses Navajo County: Trump, Pence, and Biden four times each and Harris five times. Therefore, while each of the independent (i.e., campaign visit) variables was coded zero for a 2020 CES respondent from Navajo County in the previous county-based analyses, in this market-based analysis, the same variables are coded four for the Republican presidential, Republican vice-presidential, and Democratic presidential candidates and five for the Democratic vice-presidential candidate. In other words, these respondents are treated as having been exposed to a substantial number of campaign visits rather than none at all. There is good reason to believe that this could lead to different results in terms of the estimated effects of campaign visits on vote choice and turnout.

Actually, it makes little difference. Once again, the models indicate that campaign visits—this time, to a respondent's media market—typically do not influence voting behavior. Only in 2012 do I find evidence that the number of visits per media market influences vote choice; Biden's visits significantly increase the probability of a Democratic vote, while Romney's visits—in stark contrast to previous evidence—significantly increase the probability of a Republican vote. In neither case is there a corresponding effect on voter turnout, thus indicating persuasion. In fact, campaign visits at the media market level usually do not influence turnout. Only Pence's market-level visits in 2020 are associated with a statistically significant increase in voter turnout. The effect of McCain's visits in 2008 reaches marginal levels of statistical significance, while Kaine's visits in 2016 have a statistically significant but negative effect on turnout.

This evidence indicates that my general conclusions are not dependent on the choice to measure campaign visits at the county rather than the media market level. While estimates relating to individual candidacies (in particular, for Mitt Romney in 2012) vary depending on the level at which campaign visits are aggregated, the major takeaway points remain the same. In both cases, I find that campaign visits typically do not influence voting behavior. Also, when a candidate's visits are associated with an increased probability of voting for his or her ticket, I find no corresponding increase in voter turnout. Thus, at both levels, whatever effects campaign visits have seem to be attributable to persuasion rather than mobilization. And, contrary to the argument that I present in chapter 2, persuasion does not seem to be more prevalent when campaign visits are measured at the media market versus county level.

WHAT TO DO ABOUT EARLY VOTING?

When it comes to estimating the effects of campaign visits on voting behavior, one significant and increasingly relevant problem is this: many campaign visits take place after voters in a given geographic area have already cast their ballots. Indeed, as chapter 3 shows, candidates campaign much more aggressively in the month just prior to an election, and particularly in the last several days. But in recent elections, Americans have become more likely to cast their vote prior to Election Day, as all but five states now allow in-person early or mail-in voting.[28] From 2008 to 2016, the share of votes cast on Election Day dropped from approximately 70 percent to 60 percent. In 2020, primarily due to public health concerns and policy changes relating to COVID-19, this plummeted to below 30 percent. Approximately the same percentage of voters cast early votes, while nearly half voted absentee and by mail.[29]

One way for researchers to account for this new reality, when using survey data, is to count only those visits taking place in the week or so before a respondent's interview. For example, James M. Snyder and Hasin Yousaf restrict their analysis to visits taking place within ten days prior to 2016 CCES respondents' preelection interviews.[30] This is a perfectly reasonable strategy, but it has drawbacks. First, when using interviews from CES's preelection waves, the dependent variable—except in those cases where state law already allows early voting, and the respondent has taken advantage by casting a vote—captures only the respondent's intended, rather than actual, vote choice. This is particularly concerning because, while nearly all respondents report that they intend to vote, actual turnout figures show that 30–45 percent of eligible voters in recent presidential elections do not. Second, Snyder and Yousaf's coding strategy excludes any consideration of visits that took place more than ten days prior to an interview. Thus, a candidate whose county or media market hosted a visit eleven days prior to the election, and perhaps several visits prior to that, would be coded as having been exposed to zero campaign visits—just like another respondent whose county or media market never hosted a visit during the general election campaign.

Ideally, when using survey data, we could code the number of campaign visits to a respondent's county or media market prior to the date on which he or she cast a vote. But while some surveys (including the CES) record whether a respondent voted early or on Election Day, I do not know of any survey that records the actual date on which an early vote was cast. This makes it impossible to determine, with any precision, the number of visits to which a respondent was exposed before casting a vote early, absentee, or by mail. The only respondents for whom we can determine the number of local campaign visits to which they were exposed prior to voting on a specific date are those who voted on Election Day. Since 2012, the CES has asked respondents when they cast their votes. But, again, many respondents say they voted when in fact they did not; for example, in 2020 more than 75 percent of CES respondents said they voted early or on Election Day, when in fact less than 67 percent of the eligible electorate did so. A more reliable means of estimation comes from the CES's validated voter records. Since 2012, the CES has used public records to document not only whether a respondent voted, but also whether he or she voted on Election Day or earlier.

To address concerns about how early voting might skew estimates of campaign visit effects, I reestimate the previous survey-based vote choice models while including only those respondents who were validated as having cast a vote on Election Day.[31] To be clear, Election Day voters are not necessarily representative of the electorate as a whole; particularly in 2020 there is reason to believe that they skewed toward Republicans. But, again, I cannot determine when verified early voters actually cast their ballots. And, while Snyder and Yousaf's use of the preelection interview date provides a clear cutoff point, it requires using intended rather than actual vote choice as the dependent variable, which inevitably includes many eventual nonvoters and excludes the possibility of voters changing their minds during the last month of the campaign (perhaps in response to campaign visits). In short, the strategy that I use here is far from perfect, but I believe it is the best practical option to address concerns about early voting.

When estimating the effects of campaign visits among Election Day voters only, once again the results barely differ from prior analyses. In the vast majority of cases, I find no evidence that campaign visits influenced vote choice. In one instance, I find generally consonant results: whereas Kaine's visits in 2016 had a positive but marginal effect on vote choice in the full-sample analysis from earlier, here the effect is statistically significant at conventional levels and positive. Only one other candidate's visits (Kamala Harris, 2020), had a marginally significant and positive effect on vote choice. In contrast to the full-sample analysis of CES data, I do not find that Romney's visits in 2012 or Biden's visits in 2020 significantly influenced vote choice. Because this analysis does not allow me to test the effects of campaign visits on voter turnout, I cannot say whether it is more indicative of mobilization or persuasion effects. But, given that only two candidates' visits reach even marginal levels of statistical significance in terms of their effects on vote choice, clearly there is little evidence of mobilization or persuasion among Election Day voters.

DISCUSSION

It is important, when conducting social science research, to consider how alternative measurements or model specifications might affect one's substantive conclusions. While there may be other legitimate concerns, this section addresses three particularly important methodological questions—specifically, relating to the implications of broadly defining campaign visits versus campaign rallies; counting visits at the county versus the media market level; and estimating the cumulative effect of campaign visits, even though many voters cast their ballots prior to Election Day. Addressing each of these issues yields somewhat different results with respect to individual candidacies, but the same fundamental conclusion: campaign visits typically do not influence voting behavior, and when they do, it is more often because of persuasion rather than mobilization.

At the beginning of this chapter, I proposed three hypotheses. First, I hypothesized that campaign visits usually do not influence voting behavior. Second, I hypothesized that when they do so, most often it is because of mobilization rather than persuasion. Third, I hypothesized that, when such effects occur, the causal mechanism will tend to align with campaign strategy (as measured in chapter 4): mobilization for each of the 2008–2020 Democratic candidates, as well as Sarah Palin in 2008 and Donald Trump in 2020; and persuasion for John McCain in 2008, Mitt Romney and Paul Ryan in 2012, and Trump and Pence in 2016.

The evidence presented in this chapter, based on aggregate- and individual-level data, supports some of these hypotheses but challenges others. First, campaign visits usually do not influence voting behavior. Indeed, in each of the full-sample analyses that I present in this chapter—including the overall county and survey data, as well as when accounting for campaign rallies, media market visits, and Election Day voters—no more than two or three of the sixteen presidential and vice-presidential candidates from 2008 to 2020 are shown to have had a statistically significant and positive effect on vote choice. Thus, in the vast majority of cases, we must conclude that the effect of campaign visits on voting behavior is statistically indistinguishable from zero. The clearest exception seems to be John McCain in 2008; there is evidence at the county and individual level that he won votes via campaign visits as well as campaign rallies, among independents in particular. The aggregate-level data also indicate that Barack Obama won votes via campaign visits (as well as rallies) in 2008, in general and among independents.

Second, it is *not* the case that campaign visits mobilize more often than persuade voters. The opposite seems to be true. In those exceptional cases where campaign visits influence voting behavior at the county or individual level, we usually do not see a corresponding increase in voter turnout. For example, McCain apparently won votes via campaign visits without affecting turnout. I argue that this is indicative of persuasion. Furthermore, most of the significant effects among partisan subgroups are indicative of persuasion; for example, at the county level, visits were far more likely to influence voting behavior in swing counties or in counties that leaned toward the opposing party, while at the individual level, they were more likely to do so among independents and members of the opposing party. In fact, I find only one, somewhat uncertain example of mobilization: in 2012 Obama's visits clearly increased turnout ($p < 0.05$) while perhaps increasing Democratic vote share ($p < 0.10$), as well. Also, in 2016 I find that Pence's visits had a positive effect on vote choice among Republican-leaning survey respondents, but that this does not correspond with an increase in turnout among the same respondents. To be clear, it is not the case that campaign visits generally tend to be persuasive; rather, *when they are effective at winning votes*, persuasion rather than mobilization is usually the cause.

Third, most candidates are not effective at executing their campaign strategy via campaign visits. This is because, first and foremost, most candidates' visits have no discernible effect on vote choice. The candidate whose visits most clearly seemed to have had such an effect, as noted above, is John McCain in 2008. In that case, McCain did appear to achieve his strategic objective by persuading voters in general and independents in particular. There is some rather limited evidence that Mitt Romney also persuaded voters; specifically, his visits in 2012 had a positive effect on vote choice, but no effect on turnout, at the media market level. But there is countervailing evidence, at the aggregate and individual levels, that Romney's visits actually cost his party votes. Donald Trump also showed evidence of persuading voters in 2016 by increasing Republican vote share in swing counties. This is consistent with his campaign strategy that year, according to the evidence from chapter 4. Trump's visits proved persuasive in 2020, as well, increasing his vote share in swing and Democratic-leaning counties, while also winning votes among independents and even Democrats. But chapter 4 suggests that in 2020 his visits were intended to mobilize more than persuade voters. Likewise, there is some indication that several of the Democratic candidates—namely, Clinton and Kaine in 2016 and Biden in 2020—persuaded voters via campaign visits, despite their apparent intent to mobilize, first and foremost. This points to something of a mismatch in the data: most candidates seem to pursue a mobilization strategy via campaign visits but—even when apparently intending to do so—they are more likely to persuade voters instead. Perhaps this suggests that presidential campaigns should focus more on persuasion in general, and particularly when it comes to making campaign visits.

How does this chapter add to the existing body of knowledge regarding campaign visits? First, it confirms what I would describe as the central finding in the relevant literature: that campaign visits have mixed, but mostly null effects on voting behavior. As I explain in chapter 2, most studies find that campaign visits influence presidential vote choice in some elections but not in others, or for one candidate in a given election but not another.[32] Likewise, many studies find mixed effects with respect to turnout or no effect at all.[33] However, this chapter provides unique evidence on both points, for the reasons that I allude to earlier in this chapter and describe in greater detail in chapter 2; specifically, it compares results based on aggregate- as well as individual-level data across multiple elections, including the most recent ones, for each of the presidential and vice-presidential candidates, based on an original dataset with clearly stated criteria for defining and counting campaign visits.

Second, this chapter provides unique evidence of the persuasive effects of campaign visits. As previously noted, relatively few studies directly test for the causal mechanism behind such effects. Some studies provide evidence that is more indicative of mobilization. For example, Jeffrey S. Hill, Elaine Rodriguez, and Amanda E. Wooden find that campaign visits are more effective in safe versus battleground states, and particularly in safe states that favor the visiting candidate's party.[34] Also, Boris Heersink and Brenton D. Peterson find that Harry Truman's visits in 1948 were effective in swing counties as well as safely Democratic ones, but more so in the latter. However, they also find that Truman's Republican opponent, Thomas Dewey, was most effective when visiting safely Democratic counties.[35] Shaw, for his part, finds evidence of mobilization and persuasion.[36] These studies, however, rely on aggregate-level data. Snyder and Yousaf, by contrast, use individual-level data (also from the CES) and find evidence of mobilization: specifically, that Trump's 2016 visits are associated with significant gains in intended vote choice *and* turnout.[37] They do not find evidence of persuasion. Clearly, I did not expect to find (much) evidence of persuasion, either. Not only are my findings at odds with the preponderance of the existing literature on campaign visits, but also with recent trends in campaign strategy and my assessment of campaign visit strategies in chapter 4.[38]

Yet these results clearly point toward persuasion as the most common causal mechanism for campaign visit effects. As it happens, this conclusion is consistent with the most comprehensive recent analysis of campaign advertisements—a presidential campaign's other major strategic resource, alongside visits—which also provides strong evidence of persuasion effects.[39] Perhaps, then, a reevaluation of the persuasive, versus mobilizing, potential of campaign activities is in order among scholars and practitioners alike. Indeed, in the next chapter, I close this book by discussing the substantive implications of my research findings.

CONCLUSION

This is not the first study to find that presidential campaign visits have very limited effects on voting behavior. Indeed, as chapter 2 explains, most previous studies also find little or no evidence that campaign visits influence vote choice and voter turnout across a wide range of elections. But this study is unique, in two respects.

First, my conclusions are based on an exceptionally comprehensive analysis of campaign visits, with respect to their effects on voting behavior. Specifically, I use an original dataset to estimate these effects for each of the presidential and vice-presidential candidates across the four most recent elections, using aggregate- *and* individual-level data. I also evaluate the causal mechanisms for these effects, when they occur, in relation to the campaign's apparent strategy to mobilize versus persuade voters. Previous studies include only some of these elements.[1] The fact that my most general conclusions align with those from previous studies should provide reassurance about the validity of both.

Second, I find that campaign visits are more likely to persuade than to mobilize voters. Most previous studies do not directly evaluate these causal mechanisms, and those that do tend to find more evidence of mobilization. Perhaps here the divergence from past studies should be disconcerting. But there is good reason to prefer the present findings on this point. Perhaps most important is that I use a multimethod approach, evaluating causal mechanisms first by comparing the effects of campaign visits on vote choice versus voter turnout, then by comparing their effects within partisan subgroups (e.g., swing counties at the aggregate level, independents at the individual level). The results are remarkably similar at the aggregate versus individual levels, using either methodological approach.[2] I also evaluate mobilization versus persuasion effects for sixteen candidates across four elections.

In short, this book provides strong evidence that campaign visits usually do not influence voting behavior, but can be effective at persuading undecided voters.

This raises an important question: *So what?* That is to say, what are the substantive implications of this research for the conduct and study of presidential campaigning? What difference, if any, should it make?

This chapter discusses how campaign practitioners and scholars alike might build upon my research findings in the future.

WHAT SHOULD CAMPAIGNS DO NEXT?

What should campaign practitioners—including strategists, party leaders, and even the candidates themselves—make of this book? What lessons should they learn from it? I would stress three points: first, don't stop campaigning; second, give persuasion a chance; third, get the most out of your vice-presidential candidate.

DON'T STOP CAMPAIGNING

If presidential campaign visits usually do not have any discernible effect on voting behavior, then why bother with them at all? Why not just stay home, or host fundraisers and conduct media interviews instead? Campaign personnel, who have a vested interest in conserving their most precious resources of time and money, might be particularly inclined to

CONCLUSION 211

ask such questions. Political scientists have wondered about the same. "Put succinctly, little hard evidence exists that would dissuade a skeptic from asking whether a candidate's time and energy might be better spent at home rather than on the road," write Daron Shaw and James Gimpel. Alan Abramowitz and Costas Panagopoulos concur: "Our findings suggest that whether or not presidential candidates are able to conduct traditional campaign events may have little impact on the behavior of the electorate."[3]

It is an interesting counterfactual, given evidence from past studies and the present one. But there is such a thing as overlearning a lesson. The fact that campaign visits usually do not influence voting behavior hardly means that they are irrelevant or dispensable. Why is that, exactly?

First, campaign visits sometimes *do* help to win votes. I find several examples of such effects, most notably for John McCain and Barack Obama in 2008. Mike Pence's visits in 2016 seem to have mobilized Republican leaners. Hillary Clinton's visits in 2016 (aggregate-level data only) and Donald Trump's in 2020 (aggregate- and individual-level data) seemed to persuade undecided voters. It is unclear exactly why these candidates' visits were effective at influencing vote choice in general or among specific groups of voters. What is clear is that they would have forfeited this advantage by staying home instead. I do not know how any candidate—at least, one who has a shot at winning the election in the first place—could accurately determine in advance that his or her campaign visits would prove to be ineffective or even counterproductive among voters in general and among partisan subgroups that could be targeted for in-person appeals. In that case, it is probably worth the candidate's time and the campaign's money—particularly given the relative cost efficiency of doing so (see chapter 2)—to at least try to win votes via campaign visits, if only because it is possible, though not very likely, that these visits will make a difference in the event of a close race.

Second, there is no way to know from the available data what the effects of campaign visits would be if one candidate made them and the other did not. Indeed, the evidence from chapter 3 indicates that candidates generally make a similar number of campaign visits and visit the same swing states in a given election year. Thus, the effects of their visits might cancel out or, in John Sides and Lynn Vavreck's terms, amount to something of a "tug-of-war."[4] We can only speculate as to what would happen if one candidate simply let go of the rope, and didn't campaign at all. Quite possibly, visits by the still-active candidate would prove more effective, because they would essentially go uncontested.[5] In that case—much as Sides and Vavreck find, with respect to campaign advertisements—the function of campaign visits might be more to maintain parity with one's opponent than to achieve a competitive advantage. This is another reason not to forgo them altogether.

Third, candidates who do not engage in in-person campaigning or do so to a lesser extent than usual risk being perceived by the public as insufficiently committed to winning the presidency. This could potentially undercut their legitimacy if elected. Joe Biden's 2020 presidential campaign, as I explain in the introductory chapter, raised precisely these concerns. In that case, staying home rather than engaging in extensive, in-person campaigning might make it less likely that a candidate will be elected, or that he or she will be successful as president. Candidates and their staff must consider such indirect effects, as well, when deciding whether, or to what extent, to engage in traditional, in-person campaigning.

GIVE PERSUASION A CHANCE

The evidence from chapter 4 indicates that most of the 2008–2020 presidential candidates, including each of the Democrats, pursued a strategy of mobilization via campaign visits. Panagopoulos also finds that presidential campaigns in general have shifted toward an emphasis on mobilization since the early 2000s.[6] Yet my analysis provides little evidence—at least, with respect to campaign visits—that mobilization strategies are effective. Rather, when campaign visits influence voting behavior, it is usually via persuasion rather than mobilization. Perhaps the most sophisticated recent analysis of campaign advertisements points toward the same conclusion.[7]

These findings suggest that campaigns should start focusing more on persuading undecided voters and less on mobilizing partisans. In many ways, that is counterintuitive: independents are few and far between these days, while partisanship is on the rise.[8] Indeed, I expected—and, at the beginning of chapter 5, hypothesized—otherwise. But the evidence is quite clear: I find *very* few examples of mobilization, and several more of persuasion. The choice, then, is to ignore the evidence or adapt.

But what would adaptation look like? Campaigns could build upon this evidence by targeting swing counties and independent voters when planning campaign visits. For example, they could make it a priority to schedule visits in counties that were more or less evenly divided in the previous election, rather than in partisan strongholds. Also, they could find ways to target independent or undecided voters, in particular. This might require some creativity. Perhaps, with respect to in-person attendees, they could reserve a certain number of tickets for self-described undecided voters or registered independents. And, to reach broader audiences, they could try to increase incidental exposure to a visit by conducting more interviews with local media outlets and engaging in more direct interactions with local residents. Finally, they could tailor their comments at an event to appeal more to undecided voters than to partisan sympathizers.

GET THE MOST OUT OF YOUR VICE-PRESIDENTIAL CANDIDATE

What about the vice-presidential candidates? Many previous studies of campaign visits do not include them in the data at all, or combine their visits with those of the presidential candidate, by party ticket.[9] However, vice-presidential candidates' visits sometimes serve a different, perhaps complementary, purpose in comparison to their presidential counterparts, and may prove more or less effective at winning votes than visits by the head of the ticket.[10]

This book separately considers the strategy and effectiveness of presidential versus vice-presidential candidates' visits. In terms of strategy,

I find some evidence of divergence; most notably, in 2008, John McCain's campaign visits seemed to be targeted toward persuasion, while those of his running mate, Sarah Palin, were targeted toward mobilization. In terms of effectiveness, I find many other discrepancies. For example, the aggregate-level data suggest that McCain's visits won him votes without increasing turnout, while Palin's visits decreased turnout without winning or losing votes. Other vice-presidential candidates seem to have won votes for their ticket via campaign visits. Joe Biden did so in safely Republican counties in 2008 and 2012, as well as in Republican-leaning counties and among independent voters in 2012. Mike Pence did so in safely Democratic counties in 2016, as well as among Republican-leaners and, in 2020, among Democratic-leaners. Pence, however, appears to have cost his ticket votes in swing counties in 2016, as did Biden in 2008 and Kamala Harris, Biden's 2020 running mate, among Republicans. Also, in 2016, I find weak evidence that Hillary Clinton's running mate, Tim Kaine, helped win support among voters in general via campaign visits.

Vice-presidential candidates clearly have the potential to influence vote choice and turnout via campaign visits. They may prove particularly effective among voters whom the presidential candidate struggles to reach. In that case, campaigns would be wise not to view the running mate's visits as redundant, or to banish him or her to the nether regions of the electoral battleground.[11] Instead, they should treat the running mate as an electoral asset—someone who can multiply the campaign's presence beyond that of the presidential candidate and expand its base of support among partisans (mobilization) or undecided voters (persuasion). As Dick Cheney put it when reflecting on his role as George W. Bush's running mate in 2000: "[W]e could double the territory we covered, hold twice as many rallies and town hall meetings, and generate twice the local press coverage."[12] This should be the vice-presidential candidate's role—to expand the campaign's reach and, in some cases, appeal to voters with whom he or she has a special rapport. In short, presidential campaigns should view the presidential *and* vice-presidential candidates' visits as electoral assets.

WHAT SHOULD POLITICAL SCIENTISTS DO NEXT?

Scholars who study presidential campaigns and voting behavior could also build upon this book's analysis in the future. To them, I would stress four key themes: causal inference, dependent variables, qualitative research, and data collection.

CAUSAL INFERENCE

How do I know whether campaign visits influenced voting behavior? Or whether those effects were due to mobilization versus persuasion? These are questions of causal inference—essentially, how to evaluate cause and effect. I address some key points relevant to making causal inferences in the fourth section of chapter 5, specifically concerning variable measurement (campaign visits versus campaign rallies) and units of analysis (counties versus media markets). In this section, I consider two additional points of concern: exposure to campaign visits and exposure to other campaign activities.

When it comes to evaluating the effects of campaign visits, in this book I have assumed that geographic proximity is equivalent to exposure: in other words, living in the county or media market in which a visit occurred means that the local population or a particular survey respondent knew about it and thus could respond to it. But there is no guarantee of this; some individuals, including voters, are not particularly interested in politics and might not be aware of important political events, even in their local area.[13] Indeed, Thomas Wood finds that many survey respondents do not know whether a candidate has recently visited their media market.[14]

There is no easy solution to this problem. Ideally, researchers could analyze survey data of appropriate size and scope, with respect to sampling, that asks respondents whether they were aware of a recent campaign visit. Respondents who reported being aware of such a visit (perhaps with additional information to indicate accurate recall) could be analyzed separately from other respondents who were unaware of it and therefore not "exposed" to the visit in any meaningful or direct way. This could give a more accurate indication of what effect exposure to a campaign visit has on voting behavior. The problem is that surveys, including the Cooperative Election Study, typically do not elicit such information.[15] And aggregate-level data are incapable of measuring such individual-level awareness. Thus, in order to address this problem, the necessary survey items must be added to the CES or another survey that includes a comparable number of respondents across most U.S. counties.

On a separate but related note, it is important to recognize that voters are exposed to campaign activities, including visits, by candidates for offices other than the presidency, such as governor or the U.S. Senate. Visits by these candidates have the potential to influence voting behavior, as well.[16] The same is true for presidential surrogates, including candidate spouses, former presidents, and political allies.[17] My analysis does not control for these visits or other non-presidential campaign activities such as advertisements and canvassing. Ideally, future analyses could account for the broader landscape of campaign activities in order to isolate the unique effects of presidential campaign visits.

DEPENDENT VARIABLES

This study focuses on the effects of campaign visits on voting behavior, specifically in terms of vote choice and turnout. These are the most direct behavioral outcomes—the ones that actually determine who wins and loses an election—but there are other, indirect factors that deserve scholarly attention. For example, some studies have analyzed the effects of campaign visits on campaign donations and on local media coverage.[18]

These and other election-related outcomes are worth exploring in future studies. For example, in chapter 2, I discuss how campaign visits might increase activism among the candidate's supporters, particularly those who attend in person. It would be easy to test this: many surveys, such as the CES or American National Election Study, include a battery of items measuring political activism, asking about things such as campaign donations, rally attendance, and working or volunteering for a campaign. One could estimate the effects of campaign visits on political activism in much the same way I do here, even using the same survey data, with one of these items or an index constructed from them swapped in as the dependent variable.

Or one could attempt to measure activism (e.g., donations, field office activity) at the aggregate level, perhaps in relation to other outcomes such as early voting or absentee ballot requests by party, in the states where this is practical. This would be one way to test for the "downstream effects" that I posit in chapter 2. Specifically, one might observe that campaign visits are associated with an increase in campaign activism locally and (after an appropriate time lag) an increase in early and absentee voting among members of the visiting candidate's party. Such evidence would indicate that campaign visits affect voters not only through direct exposure, via in-person attendance or media coverage, but also indirectly.

QUALITATIVE RESEARCH

Quantitative analysis is the norm when studying the effects of campaign visits; indeed, I do not know of any exceptions in the literature. For example, in chapter 5, I estimate logistic regression models to determine the average effect of exposure to campaign visits on vote choice and voter turnout and to gauge statistical significance. This may be the dominant method of evaluating campaign effects, but it is not the only one.

Political scientists and other scholars often use qualitative research methods to understand political phenomena with greater depth and nuance than quantitative methods allow. For example, I find that John McCain's campaign visits persuaded voters in general, and independents in particular, to support him. But why is that, exactly? Was it because of what McCain said at his events, or the media coverage of them? Did these events help to reinforce what voters already knew about McCain, or did they learn new information? Was it something about his personality or his policies that emerged from this event and won them over?

Quantitative analysis cannot easily answer these questions. But qualitative evidence, such as in-depth interviews with individuals or focus groups who attended an event or live within the city, county, or media market where a visit occurred, could provide answers. Participants could describe how they experienced the campaign visit and how it affected their voting behavior, in their own words. And researchers, rather than crunching numbers in a statistical software package (as I do here), could carefully review responses to look for patterns such as words or ideas that are commonly used to explain voters' reactions. This is painstaking work, and the results cannot easily be reduced to gratifying metrics such as percentages and p-values. But in some ways, at least, it could provide greater insight into people's perceptions and motivations than quantitative research methods allow.[19]

My original plan for this book was to supplement the quantitative analysis that you see here with a qualitative chapter, based on interviews with attendees at both parties' in-person campaign rallies. I would ask people why they were there, as well as whether they had already decided to vote, and for whom. Ideally, I would ask the same questions of people in the host community who had chosen not to attend the event. And I'd follow up with them in subsequent weeks to see what lasting effect the visit had on them, if any. But then—say it with me—COVID happened. Even if I had felt comfortable attending one presidential candidate's crowded, mostly maskless rallies, I could only make a strained comparison to the other candidate's much smaller, socially distanced events. It just wasn't the right time.

I hope that other scholars will take up this challenge—to investigate the same questions that animate this book, about when and why campaign visits matter, using qualitative (instead of or, preferably, in addition to quantitative) research methods. Following the logic presented in chapter 2, I expect that generally the in-person audience will be planning to vote already, and vote for the visiting candidate, but will become more active on behalf of that candidate following the event. Furthermore,

I expect that nonattendees will tend to learn about the visit through local media coverage, and persuasion will be most evident among those who live further away from the site of the event.

Perhaps the most useful part of this analysis would be finding out how nonattendees—who will always far outnumber the in-person attendees and may be more susceptible to persuasion—learned about the event, and what they learned from it. In essence, I wonder how a campaign visit comes to the attention of most voters, and what about this event, if anything, becomes relevant to their voting decision.

DATA COLLECTION

Finally, scholars ought to build upon this research by extending the Campaign Visits Database, using the definition and procedures spelled out in chapter 3, to include other presidential elections. I plan to update the CVD in future years, and to maintain it as a publicly available resource for other scholars. It is also possible to extend the dataset backward, to include presidential elections prior to 2008. I did not do so for this book for two reasons. First, the CES—to which I add campaign visits data in the individual-level analyses—only began in 2006. Second, I found it difficult, if not impossible, to reliably locate multiple online data sources for campaign visits in 2004, let alone earlier, because many of the relevant web pages are no longer active. Newspaper-based resources such as LexisNexis might make such an addition feasible. I leave it to others to undertake that endeavor.

As the CVD expands to include data from elections after 2020 (and, perhaps, before 2008), researchers may use the same empirical methods employed in this book to evaluate campaign strategy and the effects of campaign visits. If campaign strategies change in future elections, perhaps shifting from mobilization toward persuasion, and campaign visits have a greater or at least more consistent effect on voting behavior, we will need a common dataset—using the same methodology, throughout—to document these changes. The Campaign Visits Database makes that possible.

DO WE NEED CAMPAIGN VISITS?

Earlier in this chapter, I addressed the hypothetical that looms over this research subject: what if candidates just decided not to campaign (in person)? What difference would that make? Joe Biden, rather unfairly, was accused of doing this in 2020 (see Introduction). Other candidates, such as Richard Nixon in 1968 and Gerald Ford in 1976, toyed with the idea (see chapter 1). But no candidate, at least in modern times, has actually done it. And, whatever technological changes may come, I do not expect that any candidate ever will. Candidate visits appear to be an essential and permanent feature of presidential campaigning.

Why? Because there is something unique, and profoundly democratic, about a candidate taking the time to ask the people, in person, for their votes. It is not just that the candidate makes this effort, but that he or she comes *here*—of all places—to do so. Will it make a difference? Judging by the evidence that I've presented in this book, probably not. But the symbolism is important. By asking for our votes, the candidate acknowledges that we bestow or withhold the powers of the presidency. By coming to *this* city (or county or media market), the candidate signals the importance of *our* votes, specifically. It is an honor, and a responsibility, that any person or community would covet. Who would trade this in to become yet another audience member for a nationally broadcast advertisement or infomercial or livestream? Whatever the reality may be, that feels like giving away power—or prestige, at least. Even for those voters who do not live in swing states, the end of in-person campaigning would seem like a presumption, an affront to "the people" of whom we are all a part.

In that sense, I would argue, campaign visits have become not just familiar, but vital to American democracy. They help to define the relationship between candidates and the voters that empower them. They allow voters to feel present—not just in that moment but in memory, long afterward—in the political process. Indeed, one thing I have learned from writing a book about campaign visits is that everyone (or so it seems) has a story. People are only too eager to tell you about the time that a presidential candidate came to *their* town, to ask for *their* vote. It's as if this were the moment that history itself visited their lives.

I have my stories, too. I remember the time that Bill Clinton visited Springfield, Massachusetts (near where I grew up) late in the 1996 campaign, confident in his reelection and eager to help an incumbent senator from his party, John Kerry, win a close race. I wasn't there for the event, but I saw it on TV. Presidential candidates never came to my state, let alone my part of it. This was a big deal. Somehow, I—or really, "we"—felt important, in that moment. The memory has stayed with me, more than anything else from that entire presidential campaign. Years later, once I'd moved to the swing state of Ohio, campaign visits were not hard to come by. When my first child was six months old, Mitt Romney and Paul Ryan held a rally less than twenty minutes from our home. I hoisted my son on my shoulders at that event, because I wanted to know (even if it was incomprehensible to him) that he had witnessed history—that he'd seen the candidates for president and vice president of the United States in the flesh, and heard them ask for our votes. In that moment, the candidates were visible to us, and we were visible to them.

This is the power of campaign visits—to make voters feel that they are part of the political process, even if just a small part of it. What a privilege it is to hear a presidential candidate, a contestant for leader of the free world, say that he or she is *here* to ask for *your* vote. Is there any substitute for that?

APPENDIX A

TABLES

TABLE A.1A Effects of Campaign Visits on Democratic Vote Share in U.S. Counties, 2008–2020

Parameter	2008	2012	2016	2020
Rep. Presidential Candidate Visits	−0.472^	0.397	0.244	−0.357
	(0.283)	(0.364)	(0.377)	(0.394)
Rep. VP Candidate Visits	0.438	0.067	−0.064	−0.036
	(0.450)	(0.359)	(0.321)	(0.392)
Dem. Presidential Candidate Visits	0.772*	0.061	−0.025	−0.399
	(0.369)	(0.309)	(0.442)	(0.511)
Dem. VP Candidate Visits	−0.477	0.325	0.338	−0.537
	(0.380)	(0.234)	(0.379)	(0.560)
Partisanship (Past Dem. Vote)	9.498***	9.925***	7.923***	8.969***
	(0.284)	(0.209)	(0.245)	(0.327)
Campaign Ads (Dem.–Rep.)	0.001*	0.000	−0.000^	0.000***
	(0.000)	(0.000)	(0.000)	(0.000)
Median Age	−0.209***	−0.061	−0.027	0.024
	(0.047)	(0.059)	(0.031)	(0.051)
Median Household Income ($1,000)	0.036	−0.055^	−0.076***	0.019
	(0.028)	(0.029)	(0.020)	(0.031)
College Graduate %	0.070*	0.107**	0.532***	0.346***
	(0.029)	(0.032)	(0.030)	(0.033)
Black %	0.028	0.105***	0.284***	0.137***
	(0.026)	(0.015)	(0.019)	(0.036)
Latino %	0.059*	0.040*	0.161***	0.018
	(0.023)	(0.016)	(0.031)	(0.031)
Population Growth (Past Year)	−1.076***	−0.227	0.405*	−0.713*
	(0.227)	(0.139)	(0.162)	(0.279)
Constant	30.471***	19.122***	7.621***	8.997**
	(2.851)	(2.883)	(1.947)	(3.067)
N	1036	616	814	852
R-Squared	0.839	0.902	0.934	0.885

Notes: Entries are linear regression coefficients. Robust standard errors are in parentheses. ***p < 0.001; **p < 0.01; *p < 0.05; ^p < 0.10. The dependent variable is the percentage of major-party presidential votes won by the Democratic candidate in counties located within battleground states. Observations are clustered by media market.

TABLE A.1B Effects of Campaign Visits on Voter Turnout in U.S. Counties, 2008–2020

Parameter	2008	2012	2016	2020
Rep. Presidential Candidate Visits	−0.214	−0.122	0.066	0.689**
	(0.144)	(0.227)	(0.126)	(0.259)
Rep. VP Candidate Visits	−0.396*	0.421	−0.170	−0.126
	(0.180)	(0.261)	(0.172)	(0.339)
Dem. Presidential Candidate Visits	−0.152	0.217	0.000	0.180
	(0.188)	(0.237)	(0.125)	(0.194)
Dem. VP Candidate Visits	−0.552*	−0.172	0.256	0.262
	(0.210)	(0.185)	(0.248)	(0.254)
Turnout in Last Election	0.798***	0.836***	0.791***	0.760***
	(0.026)	(0.086)	(0.022)	(0.078)
Partisanship (Past Dem. Vote)	−0.443*	0.332^	−0.622***	−0.411
	(0.185)	(0.183)	(0.129)	(0.248)
Total Campaign Ads	−0.000	0.000	0.000	0.000
	(0.000)	(0.000)	(0.000)	(0.000)
Median Age	0.145***	0.164*	0.174***	0.262***
	(0.025)	(0.072)	(0.027)	(0.054)
Median Household Income ($1,000)	0.031*	0.077*	0.023	0.096***
	(0.016)	(0.036)	(0.015)	(0.026)
College Graduate %	0.180***	0.038	0.049*	0.050^
	(0.023)	(0.030)	(0.020)	(0.028)
Black %	0.183***	0.058**	−0.035**	0.048*
	(0.019)	(0.018)	(0.011)	(0.020)
Latino %	0.014	0.020	0.059^	−0.046
	(0.018)	(0.023)	(0.030)	(0.050)
Population Growth (Past Year)	−0.465***	0.179	0.450	0.965***
	(0.131)	(0.253)	(0.104)	(0.234)
Temperature	0.002	−0.134***	−0.014	−0.096***
	(0.032)	(0.028)	(0.018)	(0.026)
Precipitation	−0.192	−0.187	−0.029	0.107
	(0.128)	(0.135)	(0.052)	(0.079)
Constant	3.783^	3.837	6.257	8.864**
	(2.092)	(3.096)	(1.621)	(2.995)
N	1035	615	813	852
R-Squared	0.902	0.866	0.885	0.900

Notes: Entries are linear regression coefficients. Robust standard errors are in parentheses. ***p < 0.001; **p < 0.01; *p < 0.05; ^p < 0.10. The dependent variable is voter turnout among citizens of voting age in counties located within battleground states. Observations are clustered by media market.

TABLE A.2A Effects of Campaign Visits on Democratic Vote Share, by County Partisanship, 2008

Parameter	Safe R	Lean R	Swing	Lean D	Safe D
McCain Visits	2.479	0.586	−0.300	−1.330	−2.602
	(1.703)	(0.991)	(0.392)	(0.888)	(1.486)
Palin Visits	−0.721	−0.410	−0.375	−0.697	2.230
	(1.367)	(0.821)	(0.543)	(0.867)	(2.390)
Obama Visits	2.341	2.149	1.072**	0.476	2.276
	(1.913)	(1.473)	(0.344)	(0.493)	(2.983)
Biden Visits	3.568***	−0.012	−1.477**	−0.202	−2.936
	(0.622)	(0.553)	(0.559)	(0.861)	(2.130)
Campaign Ads (Dem.–Rep.)	0.001**	0.001**	0.000	−0.000	0.001
	(0.000)	(0.000)	(0.000)	(0.000)	(0.002)
Median Age	−0.147^	−0.185***	−0.197*	−0.237^	0.081
	(0.079)	(0.056)	(0.083)	(0.130)	(0.206)
Median Household Income ($1,000)	0.062	0.067	0.014	0.009	−0.327^
	(0.046)	(0.049)	(0.036)	(0.082)	(0.181)
College Graduate %	0.046	0.083	0.119**	0.045	0.318
	(0.079)	(0.060)	(0.041)	(0.080)	(0.257)
Black %	−0.073	0.001	0.042	0.061	0.051
	(0.080)	(0.033)	(0.039)	(0.036)	(0.118)
Latino %	−0.011	0.086***	0.073**	0.099**	−0.020
	(0.052)	(0.023)	(0.025)	(0.029)	(0.071)
Population Growth (Past Year)	−1.140***	−1.234***	−0.436	−0.719	−2.216
	(0.306)	(0.311)	(0.282)	(0.555)	(2.219)
Constant	36.426***	47.108***	58.522***	70.491***	77.672***
	(3.938)	(3.314)	(4.299)	(6.544)	(15.539)
N	285	367	287	71	26
R-Squared	0.174	0.241	0.250	0.313	0.518

Notes: Entries are linear regression coefficients. Robust standard errors are in parentheses. ***p < 0.001; **p < 0.01; *p < 0.05; ^p < 0.10. The dependent variable is the percentage of major-party presidential votes won by the Democratic candidate in counties located within battleground states. Observations are clustered by media market.

TABLE A.2B Effects of Campaign Visits on Voter Turnout, by County Partisanship, 2008

Parameter	Safe R	Lean R	Swing	Lean D	Safe D
McCain Visits	1.052	0.802^	−0.553*	−0.640	0.740
	(0.812)	(0.427)	(0.210)	(0.505)	(0.427)
Palin Visits	−1.138*	−0.631	0.006	0.405	−0.633
	(0.463)	(0.494)	(0.303)	(0.635)	(1.123)
Obama Visits	−0.798	−0.979	−0.096	−0.232	1.025
	(0.499)	(0.671)	(0.253)	(0.245)	(1.811)
Biden Visits	−0.142	−0.809^	−0.660^	−0.607	−1.086
	(0.545)	(0.446)	(0.371)	(0.734)	(1.205)
Turnout in Last Election	0.769***	0.849***	0.762***	0.705***	0.816***
	(0.049)	(0.025)	(0.036)	(0.068)	(0.073)
Total Campaign Ads	0.000	−0.000	−0.000	−0.000	−0.000^
	(0.000)	(0.000)	(0.000)	(0.000)	(0.000)
Median Age	0.231***	0.146***	0.098*	0.150*	0.050
	(0.051)	(0.043)	(0.044)	(0.059)	(0.186)
Median Household Income ($1,000)	0.051^	0.047*	0.033	0.010	−0.075
	(0.029)	(0.020)	(0.023)	(0.070)	(0.061)
College Graduate %	0.171**	0.193***	0.183***	0.158**	0.336*
	(0.055)	(0.027)	(0.036)	(0.053)	(0.137)
Black %	0.161**	0.196***	0.182***	0.153***	0.229***
	(0.053)	(0.029)	(0.019)	(0.044)	(0.047)
Latino %	−0.083*	0.019	0.038**	0.018	0.125**
	(0.033)	(0.021)	(0.014)	(0.025)	(0.042)
Population Growth (Past Year)	−0.407^	−0.569**	−0.292	−0.252	−0.897
	(0.233)	(0.182)	(0.209)	(0.317)	(1.050)
Temperature	0.060	0.003	−0.011	−0.059	−0.298
	(0.062)	(0.041)	(0.032)	(0.074)	(0.171)
Precipitation	0.087	−0.369*	−0.131	0.117	−0.959
	(0.275)	(0.175)	(0.167)	(0.501)	(1.353)
Constant	−2.925	−0.747	7.560*	12.733^	21.378
	(3.807)	(2.670)	(2.897)	(7.010)	(12.290)
N	285	367	287	70	26
R-Squared	0.911	0.910	0.898	0.874	0.983

Notes: Entries are linear regression coefficients. Robust standard errors are in parentheses. ***p < 0.001; **p < 0.01; *p < 0.05; ^p < 0.10. The dependent variable is voter turnout among citizens of voting age in counties located within battleground states. Observations are clustered by media market.

TABLE A.3A Effects of Campaign Visits on Democratic Vote Share, by County Partisanship, 2012

Parameter	Safe R	Lean R	Swing	Lean D	Safe D
Romney Visits	−0.003	2.967***	0.717	0.208	1.096
	(1.562)	(0.767)	(0.466)	(0.553)	(1.701)
Ryan Visits	2.837^	−0.566	0.535	0.319	0.829
	(1.526)	(0.728)	(0.505)	(0.912)	(1.526)
Obama Visits	–	2.231***	0.696^	−0.123	−1.675
	–	(0.630)	(0.410)	(0.462)	(1.912)
Biden Visits	5.707**	1.640*	0.284	0.326	−2.122
	(1.962)	(0.731)	(0.409)	(0.368)	(1.456)
Campaign Ads	−0.000	0.000	0.000	0.000*	−0.000
(Dem.–Rep.)	(0.000)	(0.000)	(0.000)	(0.000)	(0.000)
Median Age	0.370*	−0.014	−0.119^	−0.050	−0.225
	(0.178)	(0.098)	(0.066)	(0.076)	(0.377)
Median Household	0.062	0.007	−0.053	−0.056	−0.155
Income ($1,000)	(0.079)	(0.068)	(0.045)	(0.045)	(0.131)
College Graduate %	−0.073	0.021	0.151**	0.042	−0.019
	(0.163)	(0.079)	(0.053)	(0.040)	(0.309)
Black %	0.188*	0.114***	0.037^	0.089***	0.062
	(0.079)	(0.033)	(0.022)	(0.018)	(0.108)
Latino %	0.087	0.064	0.041	0.008	0.088
	(0.117)	(0.051)	(0.040)	(0.026)	(0.058)
Population Growth	−0.246	−0.357*	−0.673^	0.169	2.210
(Past Year)	(0.399)	(0.171)	(0.381)	(0.404)	(1.584)
Constant	7.518	35.767***	50.238***	59.444***	87.034***
	(8.139)	(6.218)	(4.280)	(3.307)	(19.916)
N	85	163	207	131	30
R-Squared	0.193	0.148	0.200	0.286	0.391

Notes: Entries are linear regression coefficients. Robust standard errors are in parentheses. ***p < 0.001; **p < 0.01; *p < 0.05; ^p < 0.10. The dependent variable is the percentage of major-party presidential votes won by the Democratic candidate in counties located within battleground states. Observations are clustered by media market. Blank cells indicate no observations.

TABLE A.3B Effects of Campaign Visits on Voter Turnout, by County Partisanship, 2012

Parameter	Safe R	Lean R	Swing	Lean D	Safe D
Romney Visits	0.349	−0.676	0.034	0.437	0.142
	(1.641)	(1.327)	(0.312)	(0.390)	(1.274)
Ryan Visits	−1.192	0.101	0.630^	0.365	0.885
	(1.060)	(0.467)	(0.353)	(0.417)	(0.937)
Obama Visits	−	0.456	0.645*	−0.279	0.875
	−	(0.881)	(0.249)	(0.296)	(1.418)
Biden Visits	−2.009	−0.235	−0.336	0.005	−1.826**
	(2.304)	(0.500)	(0.254)	(0.341)	(0.536)
Turnout in Last Election	0.747***	0.697***	0.893***	0.881***	0.800*
	(0.090)	(0.198)	(0.060)	(0.064)	(0.303)
Total Campaign Ads	−0.000	0.000	0.000	0.000	−0.000
	(0.000)	(0.000)	(0.000)	(0.000)	(0.000)
Median Age	−0.090	0.190	0.196*	0.235*	0.424
	(0.188)	(0.270)	(0.074)	(0.088)	(0.259)
Median Household Income ($1,000)	−0.034	0.176*	0.074*	0.020	−0.033
	(0.078)	(0.081)	(0.035)	(0.032)	(0.060)
College Graduate %	0.490*	0.069	0.002	−0.007	0.046
	(0.210)	(0.063)	(0.066)	(0.044)	(0.164)
Black %	−0.193	0.043	0.089**	0.055**	−0.022
	(0.164)	(0.042)	(0.029)	(0.019)	(0.049)
Latino %	−0.125	−0.034	0.021	0.054^	−0.005
	(0.103)	(0.058)	(0.032)	(0.027)	(0.065)
Population Growth (Past Year)	−1.231*	0.292	0.384	0.725*	1.972^
	(0.554)	(0.480)	(0.329)	(0.342)	(1.079)
Temperature	0.003	−0.072	−0.188***	−0.195***	0.102
	(0.099)	(0.060)	(0.037)	(0.041)	(0.112)
Precipitation	−0.600	−0.294	−0.134	−0.193	−0.244
	(0.549)	(0.185)	(0.171)	(0.198)	(0.434)
Constant	14.790	3.233	2.994	6.139	−4.562
	(11.080)	(4.508)	(3.426)	(4.711)	(10.911)
N	**85**	**163**	**207**	**130**	**30**
R-Squared	**0.871**	**0.865**	**0.900**	**0.862**	**0.937**

Notes: Entries are linear regression coefficients. Robust standard errors are in parentheses. ***p < 0.001; **p < 0.01; *p < 0.05; ^p < 0.10. The dependent variable is voter turnout among citizens of voting age in counties located within battleground states. Observations are clustered by media market. Blank cells indicate no observations.

TABLE A.4A Effects of Campaign Visits on Democratic Vote Share, by County Partisanship, 2016

Parameter	Safe R	Lean R	Swing	Lean D	Safe D
Trump Visits	2.913*	0.051	−0.977*	0.467	2.784
	(1.143)	(0.714)	(0.422)	(0.573)	(1.778)
Pence Visits	0.634	−0.481	1.054*	−0.558	−2.893^
	(1.629)	(0.644)	(0.512)	(0.588)	(1.562)
Clinton Visits	8.780***	6.447***	1.325*	−0.405	0.584
	(2.006)	(1.540)	(0.549)	(0.412)	(1.061)
Kaine Visits	–	−0.185	0.830	−0.053	−1.910
	–	(0.743)	(0.747)	(0.449)	(2.397)
Campaign Ads (Dem.–Rep.)	0.000	−0.000^	−0.000^	−0.000	−0.000
	(0.000)	(0.000)	(0.000)	(0.000)	(0.000)
Median Age	0.240*	0.012	−0.078	−0.064	−0.502^
	(0.114)	(0.051)	(0.050)	(0.067)	(0.276)
Median Household Income ($1,000)	−0.026	−0.082**	−0.042	−0.045	−0.050
	(0.048)	(0.031)	(0.033)	(0.031)	(0.072)
College Graduate %	0.403***	0.502***	0.586***	0.506***	0.378*
	(0.107)	(0.054)	(0.041)	(0.056)	(0.152)
Black %	0.302***	0.276***	0.287***	0.288***	0.256**
	(0.082)	(0.029)	(0.020)	(0.027)	(0.083)
Latino %	0.103	0.207***	0.163***	0.162***	0.149*
	(0.068)	(0.055)	(0.028)	(0.033)	(0.056)
Population Growth (Past Year)	0.294	0.371	0.039	0.144	1.241
	(0.386)	(0.247)	(0.249)	(0.424)	(0.894)
Constant	3.028	23.311***	30.282***	39.624	71.976***
	(6.280)	(3.291)	(2.883)	(3.163)	(15.225)
N	158	250	246	117	43
R-Squared	0.497	0.709	0.812	0.832	0.681

Notes: Entries are linear regression coefficients. Robust standard errors are in parentheses. ***p < 0.001; **p < 0.01; *p < 0.05; ^p < 0.10. The dependent variable is the percentage of major-party presidential votes won by the Democratic candidate in counties located within battleground states. Observations are clustered by media market. Blank cells indicate no observations.

TABLE A.4B Effects of Campaign Visits on Voter Turnout, by County Partisanship, 2016

Parameter	Safe R	Lean R	Swing	Lean D	Safe D
Trump Visits	−0.480	0.851*	−0.111	0.053	1.052
	(0.509)	(0.366)	(0.266)	(0.407)	(0.844)
Pence Visits	−0.599	0.070	0.580^	−0.337	−1.602*
	(0.848)	(0.278)	(0.293)	(0.386)	(0.699)
Clinton Visits	−0.287	−2.927*	−0.179	−0.403^	0.162
	(2.155)	(1.244)	(0.346)	(0.222)	(0.449)
Kaine Visits	−	0.416	−0.153	0.359	−0.273
	−	(0.465)	(0.353)	(0.296)	(1.255)
Turnout in Last Election	0.849***	0.770***	0.716***	0.758***	0.853***
	(0.029)	(0.035)	(0.043)	(0.055)	(0.065)
Total Campaign Ads	−0.000	−0.000	0.000	0.000	0.000
	(0.000)	(0.000)	(0.000)	(0.000)	(0.000)
Median Age	0.060	0.290***	0.203***	0.346***	0.113
	(0.122)	(0.060)	(0.032)	(0.063)	(0.107)
Median Household Income ($1,000)	0.015	0.036	0.075	−0.032	−0.083
	(0.033)	(0.022)	(0.047)	(0.038)	(0.048)
College Graduate %	−0.008	0.031	0.039	0.156***	0.124^
	(0.061)	(0.039)	(0.039)	(0.030)	(0.060)
Black %	−0.079	−0.085**	−0.040*	−0.018	−0.104***
	(0.063)	(0.031)	(0.017)	(0.022)	(0.026)
Latino %	0.072	0.059*	0.107^	0.044*	−0.020
	(0.080)	(0.028)	(0.061)	(0.018)	(0.034)
Population Growth (Past Year)	0.749***	0.501**	0.329^	0.642	−0.434
	(0.172)	(0.177)	(0.167)	(0.433)	(0.593)
Temperature	−0.048	0.023	0.047^	−0.082^	0.269**
	(0.039)	(0.046)	(0.026)	(0.046)	(0.090)
Precipitation	−0.006	−0.002	−0.053	−0.037	−0.055
	(0.136)	(0.085)	(0.067)	(0.117)	(0.119)
Constant	11.076^	−0.882	1.960	2.544	−9.691
	(5.829)	(3.809)	(2.420)	(4.501)	(8.246)
N	158	250	246	116	43
R-Squared	0.894	0.901	0.903	0.856	0.958

Notes: Entries are linear regression coefficients. Robust standard errors are in parentheses. ***p < 0.001; **p < 0.01; *p < 0.05; ^p < 0.10. The dependent variable is voter turnout among citizens of voting age in counties located within battleground states. Observations are clustered by media market. Blank cells indicate no observations.

TABLE A.5A Effects of Campaign Visits on Democratic Vote Share, by County Partisanship, 2020

Parameter	Safe R	Lean R	Swing	Lean D	Safe D
Trump Visits	−0.244	2.255*	−1.364**	−1.345*	−3.594
	(1.288)	(0.975)	(0.474)	(0.553)	(2.576)
Pence Visits	3.479^	0.301	0.139	−0.262	−1.890
	(1.871)	(1.044)	(0.565)	(0.560)	(2.329)
Biden Visits	−2.267^	−0.135	1.084***	0.227	−2.059
	(1.253)	(0.835)	(0.314)	(0.439)	(1.185)
Harris Visits	–	1.794^	−0.018	0.074	1.248
	–	(1.051)	(0.385)	(0.534)	(1.187)
Campaign Ads (Dem.–Rep.)	0.000***	0.000*	0.000	−0.000	0.000
	(0.000)	(0.000)	(0.000)	(0.000)	(0.000)
Median Age	0.166*	−0.101^	−0.154	−0.049	−1.048**
	(0.080)	(0.053)	(0.097)	(0.129)	(0.295)
Median Household Income ($1,000)	0.032	−0.023	0.062	0.027	0.370
	(0.043)	(0.025)	(0.039)	(0.078)	(0.297)
College Graduate %	0.527***	0.248***	0.244***	0.237**	−0.376
	(0.084)	(0.035)	(0.048)	(0.069)	(0.293)
Black %	0.222***	0.077**	0.081**	0.084**	0.107
	(0.058)	(0.025)	(0.030)	(0.030)	(0.096)
Latino %	0.080	−0.016	−0.061	0.071^	−0.031
	(0.055)	(0.029)	(0.041)	(0.040)	(0.069)
Population Growth (Past Year)	−1.478***	−0.043	0.787	−1.086	3.635^
	(0.353)	(0.286)	(0.570)	(0.717)	(2.061)
Constant	6.482	38.809***	45.407***	50.783***	100.630***
	(4.302)	(3.418)	(3.459)	(5.297)	(12.824)
N	439	232	101	53	27
R-Squared	0.375	0.359	0.541	0.434	0.658

Notes: Entries are linear regression coefficients. Robust standard errors are in parentheses. ***p < 0.001; **p < 0.01; *p < 0.05; ^p < 0.10. The dependent variable is the percentage of major-party presidential votes won by the Democratic candidate in counties located within battleground states. Observations are clustered by media market. Blank cells indicate no observations.

TABLE A.5B **Effects of Campaign Visits on Voter Turnout, by County Partisanship, 2020**

Parameter	Safe R	Lean R	Swing	Lean D	Safe D
Trump Visits	0.970	0.956	0.430	0.679	0.080
	(0.932)	(0.909)	(0.344)	(0.931)	(0.842)
Pence Visits	−2.251	−0.648	0.084	−0.778	0.341
	(1.714)	(0.596)	(0.495)	(0.693)	(0.827)
Biden Visits	1.236	0.607	0.373	−0.118	0.768
	(1.119)	(0.703)	(0.301)	(0.356)	(0.827)
Harris Visits	–	−0.866	0.544*	−0.027	−0.462
	–	(0.525)	(0.236)	(0.936)	(0.619)
Turnout in Last Election	0.777***	0.748***	0.898***	0.671***	0.657***
	(0.095)	(0.083)	(0.072)	(0.158)	(0.171)
Total Campaign Ads	0.000	0.000*	0.000	0.000	−0.000
	(0.000)	(0.000)	(0.000)	(0.000)	(0.000)
Median Age	0.243**	0.229***	0.295***	0.416***	0.156
	(0.077)	(0.065)	(0.068)	(0.104)	(0.172)
Median Household Income ($1,000)	0.118*	0.009	0.101***	0.206*	0.194
	(0.046)	(0.024)	(0.027)	(0.088)	(0.153)
College Graduate %	0.010	0.156**	−0.025	0.042	−0.048
	(0.040)	(0.047)	(0.050)	(0.093)	(0.097)
Black %	0.078*	0.072*	0.076**	−0.021	0.021
	(0.037)	(0.030)	(0.024)	(0.083)	(0.064)
Latino %	−0.107^	−0.119	0.083*	−0.106	0.079
	(0.059)	(0.089)	(0.039)	(0.122)	(0.063)
Population Growth (Past Year)	1.056***	1.221*	0.332	0.595	1.180
	(0.206)	(0.548)	(0.370)	(0.866)	(0.844)
Temperature	−0.103*	−0.138***	−0.100**	0.056	−0.082
	(0.041)	(0.024)	(0.037)	(0.091)	(0.175)
Precipitation	0.199^	0.041	0.228	−0.451*	−0.121
	(0.110)	(0.125)	(0.153)	(0.218)	(0.296)
Constant	8.064*	15.359**	−2.278	−4.432	14.853
	(3.791)	(5.051)	(3.910)	(8.710)	(9.455)
N	439	232	101	53	27
R-Squared	0.908	0.897	0.955	0.886	0.968

Notes: Entries are linear regression coefficients. Robust standard errors are in parentheses. ***p < 0.001; **p < 0.01; *p < 0.05; ^p < 0.10. The dependent variable is voter turnout among citizens of voting age in counties located within battleground states. Observations are clustered by media market. Blank cells indicate no observations.

TABLE A.6A Effects of Campaign Visits on Presidential Vote Choice, 2008–2020 CES

Parameter	2008	2012	2016	2020
Rep. Presidential Candidate Visits	−0.164* (0.069)	0.235* (0.093)	0.057 (0.091)	−0.100 (0.110)
Rep. VP Candidate Visits	0.029 (0.077)	−0.026 (0.073)	0.015 (0.085)	0.001 (0.106)
Dem. Presidential Candidate Visits	0.062 (0.054)	−0.058 (0.078)	−0.022 (0.044)	0.099^ (0.058)
Dem. VP Candidate Visits	0.107 (0.088)	0.104 (0.111)	0.129^ (0.070)	0.051 (0.060)
Party Identification	1.278*** (0.035)	1.476*** (0.071)	1.247*** (0.042)	1.625*** (0.055)
Campaign Ads (Dem.–Rep.)	0.000 (0.000)	0.000* (0.000)	−0.000 (0.000)	0.000 (0.000)
Age	−0.014*** (0.004)	−0.009 (0.005)	−0.015*** (0.004)	−0.017*** (0.003)
Evaluation of National Economy	−1.028*** (0.107)	1.670*** (0.121)	1.407*** (0.097)	−1.128*** (0.054)
Education	0.104*** (0.029)	−0.081 (0.059)	0.195*** (0.048)	0.209*** (0.043)
Black	2.536*** (0.521)	1.589*** (0.279)	1.928*** (0.391)	1.618*** (0.226)
Latino	0.620* (0.314)	0.001 (0.527)	0.617^ (0.326)	0.490* (0.241)
Female	−0.114 (0.111)	0.223 (0.207)	0.504*** (0.120)	0.230* (0.103)
Constant	−2.218*** (0.286)	−8.649*** (0.682)	−8.343*** (0.429)	−2.730 (0.291)
N	7212	7504	10951	12383
Log pseudolikelihood	−1797.007	−1277.111	−2450.232	−2106.205

Notes: Entries are logistic regression coefficients. Robust standard errors are in parentheses. ***p < 0.001; **p < 0.01; *p < 0.05; ^p < 0.10. The dependent variable is self-reported presidential vote choice among validated voters. It is coded one for a Democratic vote, zero for a Republican vote, and missing otherwise. Observations are clustered by media market.

TABLE A.6B Effects of Campaign Visits on Voter Turnout, 2008–2020 CES

Parameter	2008	2012	2016	2020
Rep. Presidential Candidate Visits	0.046 (0.048)	−0.001 (0.055)	−0.058 (0.050)	0.079 (0.098)
Rep. VP Candidate Visits	0.107 (0.079)	−0.010 (0.056)	0.034 (0.040)	0.091 (0.097)
Dem. Presidential Candidate Visits	−0.002 (0.052)	0.012 (0.042)	0.046 (0.033)	−0.052 (0.093)
Dem. VP Candidate Visits	0.038 (0.057)	0.043 (0.046)	−0.023 (0.032)	−0.002 (0.053)
Political Interest	0.436*** (0.041)	0.399*** (0.038)	0.338*** (0.028)	0.454*** (0.042)
Party Identification	0.004 (0.015)	−0.062** (0.024)	−0.052*** (0.014)	0.046 (0.034)
Total Campaign Ads	0.000 (0.000)	0.000 (0.000)	−0.000 (0.000)	0.000^ (0.000)
Age	0.011*** (0.002)	0.020*** (0.002)	0.023*** (0.002)	0.030*** (0.003)
Evaluation of National Economy	0.072* (0.035)	0.119* (0.050)	0.106*** (0.025)	−0.020 (0.055)
Education	0.106** (0.035)	0.214*** (0.028)	0.062*** (0.016)	0.312*** (0.044)
Black	−0.239 (0.212)	0.365** (0.124)	−0.328** (0.110)	−0.872*** (0.155)
Latino	0.129 (0.150)	−0.328** (0.106)	−0.404*** (0.121)	−0.235 (0.176)
Female	0.341*** (0.051)	0.225*** (0.065)	0.159*** (0.049)	−0.032 (0.100)
Moved in Past Year	−0.528*** (0.080)	−0.253** (0.096)	−0.181* (0.081)	−0.032 (0.179)
Constant	−1.982*** (0.195)	−2.429*** (0.246)	−2.101*** (0.142)	−1.505*** (0.316)
N	12246	10737	18879	13720
Log pseudolikelihood	−7390.2	−6284.055	−11916.3	−3389.56

Notes: Entries are logistic regression coefficients. Robust standard errors are in parentheses. ***p < 0.001; **p < 0.01; *p < 0.05; ^p < 0.10. The dependent variable is validated voter turnout in the specified election. It is coded one for voting, zero for not voting, and missing if ineligible to vote. Observations are clustered by media market.

TABLE A.7A Effects of Campaign Visits on Presidential Vote Choice, by Party Identification, 2008 CES

Parameter	Republican	Leans Rep.	Independent	Leans Dem.	Democrat
McCain Visits	−0.121	−0.383	−0.279*	−0.017	−0.131
	(0.124)	(0.304)	(0.115)	(0.133)	(0.080)
Palin Visits	−0.058	−0.106	−0.025	−0.039	0.022
	(0.127)	(0.317)	(0.189)	(0.234)	(0.126)
Obama Visits	0.021	−0.009	0.226^	−0.080	0.065
	(0.100)	(0.256)	(0.127)	(0.194)	(0.123)
Biden Visits	0.187	0.120	0.184	−0.121	0.004
	(0.181)	(0.307)	(0.159)	(0.278)	(0.111)
Campaign Ads (Dem.–Rep.)	0.000	−0.000	−0.000	0.000	0.000
	(0.000)	(0.000)	(0.000)	(0.000)	(0.000)
Age	−0.006	−0.026	−0.003	−0.008	−0.021***
	(0.006)	(0.017)	(0.008)	(0.009)	(0.005)
Evaluation of National Economy	−1.165***	−0.941**	−0.668***	−0.572*	−1.237***
	(0.333)	(0.340)	(0.209)	(0.225)	(0.251)
Education	0.054	0.204	−0.022	0.047	0.189***
	(0.075)	(0.131)	(0.086)	(0.077)	(0.038)
Black	2.616***	−	1.415^	−	−
	(0.706)	−	(0.792)	−	−
Latino	0.899	−0.508	0.822^	0.392	0.649
	(0.582)	(1.508)	(0.439)	(0.766)	(0.436)
Female	−0.276	0.597^	0.119	−0.619^	−0.226
	(0.196)	(0.345)	(0.228)	(0.333)	(0.203)
Constant	−0.747	−0.760	0.992^	3.731	4.323***
	(0.636)	(1.282)	(0.566)	(0.734)	(0.521)
N	2649	674	550	633	2389
Log pseudolikelihood	−447.181	−107.273	−341.557	−143.818	−639.017

Notes: Entries are logistic regression coefficients. Robust standard errors are in parentheses. ***p < 0.001; **p < 0.01; *p < 0.05; ^p < 0.10. The dependent variable is self-reported presidential vote choice among validated voters. It is coded one for a Democratic vote, zero for a Republican vote, and missing otherwise. Observations are clustered by media market. Blank cells indicate observations were dropped due to lack of variation in the dependent variable.

TABLE A.7B Effects of Campaign Visits on Voter Turnout, by Party Identification, 2008 CES

Parameter	Republican	Leans Rep.	Independent	Leans Dem.	Democrat
McCain Visits	0.093	−0.016	−0.052	−0.011	0.096^
	(0.070)	(0.089)	(0.086)	(0.100)	(0.057)
Palin Visits	0.077	0.094	0.154	0.233	0.051
	(0.114)	(0.155)	(0.114)	(0.150)	(0.091)
Obama Visits	0.015	0.067	−0.020	−0.141	−0.004
	(0.058)	(0.098)	(0.073)	(0.104)	(0.072)
Biden Visits	−0.106	0.154	−0.073	0.141	0.124
	(0.076)	(0.150)	(0.106)	(0.112)	(0.085)
Political Interest	0.128	0.306**	0.609	0.320**	0.262***
	(0.080)	(0.115)	(0.073)	(0.110)	(0.070)
Total Campaign Ads	0.000	−0.000	−0.000***	0.000	0.000
	(0.000)	(0.000)	(0.000)	(0.000)	(0.000)
Age	0.015***	0.005	0.005	0.018***	0.010**
	(0.003)	(0.006)	(0.005)	(0.005)	(0.003)
Evaluation of National Economy	0.151*	0.177^	0.004	0.120	−0.065
	(0.065)	(0.102)	(0.098)	(0.167)	(0.078)
Education	0.019	0.053	0.269***	0.134*	0.086*
	(0.048)	(0.074)	(0.055)	(0.064)	(0.040)
Black	−0.474	−1.205*	0.112	−0.358	−0.394
	(0.372)	(0.551)	(0.374)	(0.291)	(0.254)
Latino	−0.136	−0.170	−0.203	0.485	0.162
	(0.213)	(0.522)	(0.368)	(0.397)	(0.192)
Female	0.376***	0.477**	0.182	0.316^	0.290***
	(0.104)	(0.157)	(0.126)	(0.169)	(0.080)
Moved in Past Year	−0.619***	−0.776***	−0.157	−0.362	−0.629***
	(0.124)	(0.212)	(0.205)	(0.229)	(0.120)
Constant	−0.710	−1.178*	−3.082***	−2.248***	−0.924**
	(0.333)	(0.531)	(0.335)	(0.597)	(0.317)
N	**4100**	**1167**	**1466**	**1166**	**4347**
Log pseudolikelihood	**−1925.322**	**−584.408**	**−1055.013**	**−731.116**	**−2837.601**

Notes: Entries are logistic regression coefficients. Robust standard errors are in parentheses. ***p < 0.001; **p < 0.01; *p < 0.05; ^p < 0.10. The dependent variable is validated voter turnout in the specified election. It is coded one for voting, zero for not voting, and missing if ineligible to vote. Observations are clustered by media market.

TABLE A.8A Effects of Campaign Visits on Presidential Vote Choice, by Party Identification, 2012 CES

Parameter	Republican	Leans Rep.	Independent	Leans Dem.	Democrat
Romney Visits	0.272^	0.239	0.219	0.512	0.026
	(0.149)	(0.283)	(0.179)	(0.474)	(0.241)
Ryan Visits	−0.068	0.047	−0.046	0.075	0.178
	(0.160)	(0.262)	(0.079)	(0.373)	(0.168)
Obama Visits	−0.103	−0.267	−0.079	0.383	−0.103
	(0.097)	(0.204)	(0.080)	(0.293)	(0.103)
Biden Visits	0.074	−0.003	0.225*	−0.320	−0.126
	(0.190)	(0.174)	(0.114)	(0.244)	(0.174)
Campaign Ads	0.000	0.000	−0.000	0.000^	0.000
(Dem.–Rep.)	(0.000)	(0.000)	(0.000)	(0.000)	(0.000)
Age	0.015	0.029	−0.024^	−0.028	−0.024*
	(0.011)	(0.018)	(0.013)	(0.017)	(0.011)
Evaluation of	2.032***	1.537***	1.500***	1.849***	1.807***
National Economy	(0.332)	(0.268)	(0.168)	(0.339)	−0.167
Education	−0.146	−0.065	−0.233**	0.016	0.088
	(0.116)	(0.185)	(0.088)	(0.173)	(0.098)
Black	1.761**	–	2.543^	−1.256*	3.943***
	(0.606)	–	(1.493)	(0.610)	(1.082)
Latino	0.464	1.797*	0.495	–	−0.413
	(0.986)	(0.762)	(0.397)	–	(0.574)
Female	0.675*	0.021	−0.002	−0.278	0.620^
	(0.340)	(0.374)	(0.272)	(0.618)	(0.342)
Constant	−9.350***	−8.756***	−2.029^	−1.191	−2.262**
	(1.408)	(1.383)	(1.050)	(1.486)	(0.760)
N	2427	994	643	706	2680
Log pseudolikelihood	−270.788	−89.08	−312.281	−125.897	−298.821

Notes: Entries are logistic regression coefficients. Robust standard errors are in parentheses. ***p < 0.001; **p < 0.01; *p < 0.05; ^p < 0.10. The dependent variable is self-reported presidential vote choice among validated voters. It is coded one for a Democratic vote, zero for a Republican vote, and missing otherwise. Observations are clustered by media market. Blank cells indicate observations were dropped due to lack of variation in the dependent variable.

TABLE A.8B Effects of Campaign Visits on Voter Turnout, by Party Identification, 2012 CES

Parameter	Republican	Leans Rep.	Independent	Leans Dem.	Democrat
Romney Visits	−0.017	0.224	−0.124	0.024	0.002
	(0.071)	(0.151)	(0.131)	(0.182)	(0.091)
Ryan Visits	−0.049	−0.013	−0.061	0.085	0.002
	(0.066)	(0.163)	(0.118)	(0.123)	(0.066)
Obama Visits	0.056	−0.225^	0.081	−0.015	0.017
	(0.053)	(0.130)	(0.062)	(0.079)	(0.059)
Biden Visits	−0.013	0.293**	0.226*	0.023	−0.033
	(0.099)	(0.105)	(0.097)	(0.184)	(0.062)
Political Interest	0.461***	0.381***	0.421***	0.290*	0.261***
	(0.067)	(0.120)	(0.078)	(0.119)	(0.064)
Total Campaign Ads	−0.000	−0.000	−0.000	0.000	0.000
	(0.000)	(0.000)	(0.000)	(0.000)	(0.000)
Age	0.007	0.028***	0.017*	0.034***	0.022***
	(0.005)	(0.007)	(0.008)	(0.007)	(0.004)
Evaluation of National Economy	−0.030	0.276*	0.003	0.051	0.290***
	(0.080)	(0.135)	(0.121)	(0.162)	(0.052)
Education	0.265***	0.141^	0.324***	0.200**	0.154**
	(0.055)	(0.084)	(0.075)	(0.077)	(0.050)
Black	0.038	1.474	0.241	0.160	0.267
	(0.596)	(1.054)	(0.256)	(0.400)	(0.165)
Latino	−0.139	−0.260	−1.010***	−0.510	−0.147
	(0.198)	(0.275)	(0.248)	(0.348)	(0.161)
Female	0.227*	0.002	0.129	0.188	0.288**
	(0.113)	(0.192)	(0.176)	(0.205)	(0.097)
Moved in Past Year	−0.461*	−0.180	−0.114	0.007	−0.433^
	(0.208)	(0.297)	(0.280)	(0.287)	(0.242)
Constant	−1.664***	−2.765***	−2.987***	−3.024***	−2.645***
	(0.453)	(0.839)	(0.765)	(0.785)	(0.354)
N	3165	1383	1481	1040	3668
Log pseudolikelihood	−1697.992	−566.284	−941.088	−1007.500	−1914.100

Notes: Entries are logistic regression coefficients. Robust standard errors are in parentheses. ***p < 0.001; **p < 0.01; *p < 0.05; ^p < 0.10. The dependent variable is validated voter turnout in the specified election. It is coded one for voting, zero for not voting, and missing if ineligible to vote. Observations are clustered by media market.

TABLE A.9A Effects of Campaign Visits on Presidential Vote Choice, by Party Identification, 2016 CES

Parameter	Republican	Leans Rep.	Independent	Leans Dem.	Democrat
Trump Visits	0.054	0.509**	0.060	−0.169	0.146
	(0.178)	(0.192)	(0.158)	(0.167)	(0.155)
Pence Visits	0.059	−0.462***	−0.014	0.177	0.079
	(0.146)	(0.136)	(0.146)	(0.179)	(0.159)
Clinton Visits	−0.066	−0.210*	−0.015	−0.062	0.068
	(0.078)	(0.092)	(0.103)	(0.097)	(0.090)
Kaine Visits	0.072	−0.143	0.110	0.216	0.114
	(0.110)	(0.166)	(0.159)	(0.180)	(0.158)
Campaign Ads (Dem.–Rep.)	0.000	−0.000	−0.000	−0.000***	0.000
	(0.000)	(0.000)	(0.000)	(0.000)	(0.000)
Age	−0.017*	−0.034^	−0.014*	−0.002	−0.008
	(0.008)	(0.020)	(0.006)	(0.012)	(0.007)
Evaluation of National Economy	1.462***	1.356^	1.356***	1.215***	1.329***
	(0.189)	(0.733)	(0.145)	(0.214)	(0.117)
Education	0.164*	0.127	0.132^	0.202	0.311**
	(0.073)	(0.127)	(0.069)	(0.152)	(0.116)
Black	2.071***	2.447**	2.569***	1.635^	1.751**
	(0.601)	(0.789)	(0.705)	(0.937)	(0.618)
Latino	0.944	0.678	0.293	−0.744	0.698
	(0.677)	(0.931)	(0.543)	(0.607)	(0.536)
Female	0.312	0.600	0.472**	0.024	0.792***
	(0.203)	(0.536)	(0.182)	(0.372)	(0.226)
Constant	−6.806***	−5.273	−4.389***	−1.191	−3.242***
	(0.841)	(3.570)	(0.699)	(0.872)	(0.561)
N	3275	1021	1264	1059	4332
Log pseudolikelihood	−625.185	−194.011	−576.002	−170.087	−759.314

Notes: Entries are logistic regression coefficients. Robust standard errors are in parentheses. ***p < 0.001; **p < 0.01; *p < 0.05; ^p < 0.10. The dependent variable is self-reported presidential vote choice among validated voters. It is coded one for a Democratic vote, zero for a Republican vote, and missing otherwise. Observations are clustered by media market.

TABLE A.9B Effects of Campaign Visits on Voter Turnout, by Party Identification, 2016 CES

Parameter	Republican	Leans Rep.	Independent	Leans Dem.	Democrat
Trump Visits	−0.101^	−0.132	0.113^	−0.061	−0.113
	(0.060)	(0.119)	(0.064)	(0.109)	(0.069)
Pence Visits	0.107*	0.099	−0.080	0.104	0.029
	(0.050)	(0.121)	(0.054)	(0.096)	(0.055)
Clinton Visits	0.043^	0.218**	0.007	−0.046	0.054
	(0.024)	(0.077)	(0.044)	(0.065)	(0.040)
Kaine Visits	0.010	−0.217	−0.095	0.052	−0.017
	(0.049)	(0.139)	(0.076)	(0.096)	(0.046)
Political Interest	0.215***	0.443***	0.449***	0.172	0.217***
	(0.051)	(0.113)	(0.058)	(0.117)	(0.053)
Total Campaign Ads	−0.000*	0.000	−0.000	−0.000*	0.000
	(0.000)	(0.000)	(0.000)	(0.000)	(0.000)
Age	0.019***	0.021***	0.016***	0.021***	0.029***
	(0.004)	(0.006)	(0.004)	(0.006)	(0.004)
Evaluation of National Economy	0.019	0.072	−0.050	0.262*	0.184***
	(0.053)	(0.099)	(0.046)	(0.109)	(0.050)
Education	−0.042	0.057	0.180***	0.121*	0.073**
	(0.031)	(0.065)	(0.037)	(0.060)	(0.024)
Black	−0.167	−0.153	−0.357	−0.934***	−0.351**
	(0.378)	(0.463)	(0.327)	(0.225)	(0.123)
Latino	−0.173	−0.705	−0.574**	0.123	−0.548***
	(0.217)	(0.440)	(0.186)	(0.307)	(0.152)
Female	0.031	0.018	0.020	−0.069	0.364***
	(0.081)	(0.168)	(0.114)	(0.137)	(0.096)
Moved in Past Year	−0.346*	0.142	−0.212	−0.140	−0.096
	(0.150)	(0.357)	(0.149)	(0.205)	(0.117)
Constant	−0.792*	−2.463***	−2.624***	−2.022***	−2.592***
	(0.332)	(0.623)	(0.317)	(0.569)	(0.237)
N	5026	1720	3511	1797	6825
Log pseudolikelihood	−3370.996	−1103.875	−2077.826	−1058.516	−4057.175

Notes: Entries are logistic regression coefficients. Robust standard errors are in parentheses. ***p < 0.001; **p < 0.01; *p < 0.05; ^p < 0.10. The dependent variable is validated voter turnout in the specified election. It is coded one for voting, zero for not voting, and missing if ineligible to vote. Observations are clustered by media market.

TABLE A.10A Effects of Campaign Visits on Presidential Vote Choice, by Party Identification, 2020 CES

Parameter	Republican	Leans Rep.	Independent	Leans Dem.	Democrat
Trump Visits	0.206	−0.038	−0.673***	0.134	−0.309*
	(0.179)	(0.240)	(0.177)	(0.381)	(0.134)
Pence Visits	0.150	−0.071	0.303^	−0.999*	−0.107
	(0.184)	(0.259)	(0.181)	(0.423)	(0.127)
Biden Visits	0.197^	−0.190	0.110	0.430	−0.008
	(0.105)	(0.265)	(0.092)	(0.371)	(0.084)
Harris Visits	−0.221*	0.126	0.203^	0.481	0.086
	(0.097)	(0.256)	(0.117)	(0.393)	(0.076)
Campaign Ads (Dem.–Rep.)	0.000	0.000	0.000	−0.000	−0.000
	(0.000)	(0.000)	(0.000)	(0.000)	(0.000)
Age	−0.006	−0.044***	−0.017**	−0.004	−0.027***
	(0.004)	(0.009)	(0.006)	(0.010)	(0.006)
Evaluation of National Economy	−0.977***	−1.212***	−1.384***	−1.252***	−1.156***
	(0.115)	(0.153)	(0.103)	(0.288)	(0.075)
Education	0.357***	0.355***	0.124*	0.245**	0.128^
	(0.085)	(0.110)	(0.055)	(0.091)	(0.065)
Black	0.585	2.444***	2.201***	0.888	1.884***
	(0.563)	(0.524)	(0.398)	(0.685)	(0.533)
Latino	1.036**	−0.003	−0.219	1.190	1.614***
	(0.369)	(0.536)	(0.511)	(1.246)	(0.371)
Female	0.125	0.225	0.314	0.446	−0.020
	(0.173)	(0.306)	(0.211)	(0.533)	(0.211)
Constant	−2.101***	0.475	2.582***	4.580***	6.668***
	(0.347)	(0.704)	(0.482)	(0.947)	(0.559)
N	3732	1092	1216	1325	5018
Log pseudolikelihood	−647.528	−182.85	−497.804	−156.204	−446.179

Notes: Entries are logistic regression coefficients. Robust standard errors are in parentheses. ***p < 0.001; **p < 0.01; *p < 0.05; ^p < 0.10. The dependent variable is self-reported presidential vote choice among validated voters. It is coded one for a Democratic vote, zero for a Republican vote, and missing otherwise. Observations are clustered by media market.

TABLE A.10B Effects of Campaign Visits on Voter Turnout, by Party Identification, 2020 CES

Parameter	Republican	Leans Rep.	Independent	Leans Dem.	Democrat
Trump Visits	0.0122	0.382	−0.050	0.543*	0.056
	(0.197)	(0.374)	(0.167)	(0.146)	(0.144)
Pence Visits	0.247	0.216	0.067	−0.146	0.094
	(0.202)	(0.360)	(0.098)	(0.212)	(0.134)
Biden Visits	−0.178	−0.066	0.051	0.099	−0.072
	(0.145)	(0.255)	(0.131)	(0.216)	(0.120)
Harris Visits	−0.055	0.008	−0.076	−0.097	0.049
	(0.091)	(0.202)	(0.088)	(0.144)	(0.090)
Political Interest	0.482***	0.653***	0.303**	0.376^	0.332***
	(0.086)	(0.147)	(0.098)	(0.194)	(0.078)
Total Campaign Ads	−0.000	0.000	0.000^	0.000	0.000*
	(0.000)	(0.000)	(0.000)	(0.000)	(0.000)
Age	0.033***	0.024*	0.024***	0.036***	0.025***
	(0.007)	(0.009)	(0.006)	(0.011)	(0.006)
Evaluation of	0.007	0.062	0.081	0.007	−0.300**
National Economy	(0.076)	(0.167)	(0.105)	(0.190)	(0.105)
Education	0.220**	0.260	0.504***	0.294*	0.329***
	(0.077)	(0.189)	(0.076)	(0.120)	(0.051)
Black	−1.739***	−1.080	−0.948**	−0.905^	−0.614**
	(0.336)	(0.892)	(0.309)	(0.499)	(0.223)
Latino	−0.127	0.127	0.046	−0.212	−0.440
	(0.347)	(0.595)	(0.448)	(0.581)	(0.299)
Female	0.105	−0.572	−0.179	0.298	−0.197
	(0.207)	(0.390)	(0.175)	(0.382)	(0.249)
Moved in Past Year	−0.112	−1.299*	−0.137	0.826^	−0.405
	(0.399)	(0.596)	(0.440)	(0.497)	(0.336)
Constant	−1.055^	−1.389	−2.362***	−1.562	−0.206
	(0.541)	(0.910)	(0.499)	(0.977)	(0.446)
N	4039	1210	1704	1438	5329
Log pseudolikelihood	−998.201	−265.987	−637.705	−292.089	−1072.736

Notes: Entries are logistic regression coefficients. Robust standard errors are in parentheses. ***p < 0.001; **p < 0.01; *p < 0.05; ^p < 0.10. The dependent variable is validated voter turnout in the specified election. It is coded one for voting, zero for not voting, and missing if ineligible to vote. Observations are clustered by media market.

TABLE A.11A Effects of Campaign Rallies on Democratic Vote Share by County, 2008–2020

Parameter	2008	2012	2016	2020
Rep. Presidential Candidate Rallies	−0.814^ (0.465)	−0.481 (0.468)	0.199 (0.459)	−0.058 (0.439)
Rep. VP Candidate Rallies	0.482 (0.440)	0.707 (0.548)	0.631 (0.535)	0.095 (0.519)
Dem. Presidential Candidate Rallies	1.020* (0.428)	0.605^ (0.334)	−0.123 (0.569)	−0.574 (0.693)
Dem. VP Candidate Rallies	−0.379 (0.479)	0.430 (0.479)	0.277 (0.598)	−3.036** (1.137)
Partisanship (Past Dem. Vote)	9.502*** (0.282)	9.920*** (0.207)	7.942*** (0.245)	9.015*** (0.332)
Campaign Ads (Dem.–Rep.)	0.001* (0.000)	0.000 (0.000)	−0.000 (0.000)	0.000*** (0.000)
Median Age	−0.207*** (0.047)	−0.061 (0.059)	−0.025 (0.031)	0.028 (0.050)
Median Household Income ($1,000)	0.038 (0.028)	−0.053^ (0.029)	−0.075*** (0.020)	0.020 (0.030)
College Graduate %	0.069* (0.028)	0.107** (0.032)	0.531*** (0.031)	0.346*** (0.033)
Black %	0.027 (0.026)	0.107*** (0.014)	0.285*** (0.019)	0.137*** (0.035)
Latino %	0.058* (0.024)	0.042* (0.016)	0.163*** (0.031)	0.030 (0.026)
Population Growth (Past Year)	−1.064*** (0.225)	−0.227 (0.138)	0.410* (0.163)	−0.729** (0.275)
Constant	30.260*** (2.845)	19.022*** (2.897)	7.447*** (1.940)	8.614** (2.989)
N	1036	616	814	852
R-Squared	0.839	0.902	0.934	0.886

Notes: Entries are linear regression coefficients. Robust standard errors are in parentheses. ***p < 0.001; **p < 0.01; *p < 0.05; ^p < 0.10. The dependent variable is the percentage of major-party presidential votes won by the Democratic candidate in counties located within battleground states. Observations are clustered by media market.

TABLE A.11B Effects of Campaign Rallies on Voter Turnout by County, 2008–2020

Parameter	2008	2012	2016	2020
Rep. Presidential Candidate Rallies	−0.343 (0.213)	−0.107 (0.282)	−0.044 (0.189)	0.476^ (0.243)
Rep. VP Candidate Rallies	−0.445^ (0.234)	0.404 (0.374)	−0.348 (0.281)	0.071 (0.607)
Dem. Presidential Candidate Rallies	−0.450^ (0.268)	0.287 (0.406)	0.108 (0.142)	0.151 (0.374)
Dem. VP Candidate Rallies	−0.531* (0.238)	−0.089 (0.383)	0.380 (0.307)	1.497* (0.623)
Turnout in Last Election	0.797*** (0.026)	0.837*** (0.086)	0.790*** (0.021)	0.758*** (0.079)
Partisanship (Past Dem. Vote)	−0.437* (0.186)	0.327^ (0.183)	−0.623*** (0.127)	−0.425^ (0.242)
Total Campaign Ads	−0.000 (0.000)	0.000 (0.000)	0.000 (0.000)	0.000 (0.000)
Median Age	0.145*** (0.025)	0.163* (0.072)	0.174*** (0.027)	0.262*** (0.054)
Median Household Income ($1,000)	0.032* (0.016)	0.076* (0.036)	0.023 (0.015)	0.096*** (0.026)
College Graduate %	0.180*** (0.023)	0.038 (0.030)	0.049* (0.020)	0.050^ (0.028)
Black %	0.182*** (0.019)	0.059** (0.018)	−0.035** (0.011)	0.048* (0.020)
Latino %	0.015 (0.018)	0.021 (0.023)	0.059^ (0.030)	−0.050 (0.051)
Population Growth (Past Year)	−0.461*** (0.133)	0.180 (0.253)	−0.104 (0.104)	0.970*** (0.234)
Temperature	0.003 (0.032)	−0.136 (0.029)	−0.014 (0.018)	−0.097*** (0.027)
Precipitation	−0.212^ (0.127)	−0.188 (0.135)	−0.030 (0.053)	0.094 (0.073)
Constant	3.829^ (2.061)	3.968 (3.111)	6.279*** (1.623)	9.054** (3.004)
N	1035	615	813	852
R-Squared	0.901	0.865	0.885	0.900

Notes: Entries are linear regression coefficients. Robust standard errors are in parentheses. ***p < 0.001; **p < 0.01; *p < 0.05; ^p < 0.10. The dependent variable is voter turnout among citizens of voting age in counties located within battleground states. Observations are clustered by media market.

TABLE A.12A Effects of Campaign Rallies on Presidential Vote Choice, 2008–2020 CES

Parameter	2008	2012	2016	2020
Rep. Presidential Candidate Rallies	−0.230* (0.092)	0.502*** (0.137)	−0.082 (0.112)	0.039 (0.163)
Rep. VP Candidate Rallies	0.115 (0.092)	−0.230^ (0.122)	0.305 (0.207)	−0.076 (0.198)
Dem. Presidential Candidate Rallies	−0.015 (0.066)	0.001 (0.085)	0.066 (0.049)	0.147^ (0.083)
Dem. VP Candidate Rallies	0.144 (0.104)	−0.122 (0.144)	0.058 (0.096)	0.028 (0.107)
Party Identification	1.280*** (0.034)	1.482*** (0.069)	1.249*** (0.043)	1.623*** (0.055)
Campaign Ads (Dem.–Rep.)	0.000 (0.000)	0.000** (0.000)	−0.000 (0.000)	0.000^ (0.000)
Age	−0.014*** (0.004)	−0.008^ (0.005)	−0.014*** (0.004)	−0.017*** (0.003)
Evaluation of National Economy	−1.025*** (0.107)	1.689*** (0.117)	1.419*** (0.096)	−1.127*** (0.054)
Education	0.104*** (0.029)	−0.078 (0.060)	0.193*** (0.048)	0.217*** (0.044)
Black	2.520*** (0.527)	1.614*** (0.284)	1.895*** (0.362)	1.651*** (0.211)
Latino	0.603^ (0.324)	−0.061 (0.537)	0.736* (0.324)	0.515* (0.236)
Female	−0.117 (0.109)	0.243 (0.202)	0.501*** (0.119)	0.231* (0.103)
Constant	−2.215*** (0.282)	−8.706*** (0.660)	−8.398 (0.422)	−2.747*** (0.303)
N	7212	7504	10951	12383
Log pseudolikelihood	−1797.63	−1269.909	−2446.29	−2109.98

Notes: Entries are logistic regression coefficients. Robust standard errors are in parentheses. ***p < 0.001; **p < 0.01; *p < 0.05; ^p < 0.10. The dependent variable is self-reported presidential vote choice among validated voters. It is coded one for a Democratic vote, zero for a Republican vote, and missing otherwise. Observations are clustered by media market.

TABLE A.12B Effects of Campaign Rallies on Voter Turnout, 2008–2020 CES

Parameter	2008	2012	2016	2020
Rep. Presidential Candidate Rallies	0.085 (0.064)	−0.039 (0.064)	−0.081** (0.027)	0.168 (0.169)
Rep. VP Candidate Rallies	0.124 (0.112)	0.027 (0.086)	0.143* (0.066)	−0.052 (0.205)
Dem. Presidential Candidate Rallies	0.021 (0.078)	0.017 (0.051)	0.037 (0.039)	−0.072 (0.134)
Dem. VP Candidate Rallies	0.016 (0.083)	0.032 (0.099)	−0.014 (0.044)	−0.028 (0.074)
Political Interest	0.438*** (0.040)	0.398*** (0.038)	0.337*** (0.028)	0.453*** (0.043)
Party Identification	0.006 (0.016)	−0.062* (0.024)	−0.051*** (0.014)	0.045 (0.034)
Total Campaign Ads	0.000 (0.000)	0.000 (0.000)	−0.000 (0.000)	0.000^ (0.000)
Age	0.011*** (0.002)	0.020*** (0.002)	0.023*** (0.002)	0.030*** (0.003)
Evaluation of National Economy	0.073* (0.035)	0.119* (0.050)	0.106*** (0.025)	−0.025 (0.056)
Education	0.107** (0.034)	0.214*** (0.029)	0.061*** (0.016)	0.314*** (0.044)
Black	−0.208 (0.210)	0.374** (0.121)	−0.321** (0.111)	−0.867*** (0.157)
Latino	0.123 (0.142)	−0.307** (0.100)	−0.371** (0.121)	−0.186 (0.158)
Female	0.342*** (0.051)	0.223*** (0.065)	0.155** (0.050)	−0.029 (0.100)
Moved in Past Year	−0.536*** (0.081)	−0.255** (0.096)	−0.178* (0.081)	−0.263 (0.182)
Constant	−1.995*** (0.202)	−2.430*** (0.252)	−2.115*** (0.142)	−1.479*** (0.321)
N	12246	10737	18879	13720
Log pseudolikelihood	−7396.620	−6285.216	−11911.158	−3390.390

Notes: Entries are logistic regression coefficients. Robust standard errors are in parentheses. ***p < 0.001; **p < 0.01; *p < 0.05; ^p < 0.10. The dependent variable is validated voter turnout in the specified election. It is coded one for voting, zero for not voting, and missing if ineligible to vote. Observations are clustered by media market.

TABLE A.13A Effects of Media Market Visits on Presidential Vote Choice, 2008–2020 CES

Parameter	2008	2012	2016	2020
Rep. Presidential Candidate Visits	−0.018 (0.033)	−0.087* (0.038)	0.037 (0.046)	0.029 (0.065)
Rep. VP Candidate Visits	0.043 (0.049)	−0.042 (0.042)	0.034 (0.037)	−0.020 (0.036)
Dem. Presidential Candidate Visits	0.036 (0.037)	0.001 (0.043)	−0.037 (0.028)	0.020 (0.042)
Dem. VP Candidate Visits	−0.033 (0.039)	0.243*** (0.040)	0.001 (0.045)	0.003 (0.025)
Party Identification	1.274*** (0.036)	1.491*** (0.071)	1.249*** (0.043)	1.625*** (0.055)
Campaign Ads (Dem.–Rep.)	0.000 (0.000)	0.000^ (0.000)	−0.000 (0.000)	0.000 (0.000)
Age	−0.014*** (0.003)	−0.009^ (0.005)	−0.015*** (0.004)	−0.017*** (0.003)
Evaluation of National Economy	−1.028*** (0.105)	1.698*** (0.112)	1.409*** (0.098)	−1.129*** (0.054)
Education	0.098*** (0.030)	−0.064 (0.059)	0.195*** (0.047)	0.215*** (0.043)
Black	2.496*** 0.508	1.753*** (0.291)	1.938*** (0.386)	1.654*** (0.217)
Latino	0.450 (0.366)	0.086 (0.536)	0.784* (0.317)	0.518* (0.233)
Female	−0.118 (0.109)	0.227 (0.203)	0.492*** (0.121)	0.231* (0.104)
Constant	−2.256*** (0.277)	8.921*** (0.613)	−8.367*** (0.434)	−2.774*** (0.301)
N	7212	7504	10951	12383
Log pseudolikelihood	−1803.486	−1265.941	−2453.123	−2110.825

Notes: Entries are logistic regression coefficients. Robust standard errors are in parentheses. ***p < 0.001; **p < 0.01; *p < 0.05; ^p < 0.10. The dependent variable is self-reported presidential vote choice among validated voters. It is coded one for a Democratic vote, zero for a Republican vote, and missing otherwise. Observations are clustered by media market.

TABLE A.13B Effects of Media Market Visits on Voter Turnout, 2008–2020 CES

Parameter	2008	2012	2016	2020
Rep. Presidential Candidate Visits	0.205^	0.030	−0.018	−0.007
	(0.108)	(0.026)	(0.019)	(0.072)
Rep. VP Candidate Visits	−0.117	0.002	0.029	0.132*
	(0.076)	(0.029)	(0.021)	(0.059)
Dem. Presidential Candidate Visits	−0.054	−0.010	−0.002	0.044
	(0.055)	(0.037)	(0.021)	(0.046)
Dem. VP Candidate Visits	−0.145	0.018	−0.052*	−0.031
	(0.116)	(0.038)	(0.024)	(0.026)
Political Interest	0.444***	0.401***	0.336***	0.451***
	(0.038)	(0.039)	(0.028)	(0.043)
Party Identification	−0.001	−0.063*	−0.049***	0.039
	(0.015)	(0.024)	(0.014)	(0.034)
Total Campaign Ads	0.000	−0.000	0.000	0.000
	(0.000)	(0.000)	(0.000)	(0.000)
Age	0.011***	0.020***	0.023***	0.030***
	(0.002)	(0.002)	(0.002)	(0.003)
Evaluation of National Economy	0.068*	0.121*	0.108***	−0.017
	(0.034)	(0.050)	(0.025)	(0.056)
Education	0.108***	0.216***	0.066***	0.310***
	(0.032)	(0.029)	(0.016)	(0.045)
Black	−0.126	0.367***	−0.307**	−0.833***
	(0.187)	(0.110)	(0.110)	(0.151)
Latino	−0.005	−0.290**	−0.360**	−0.176
	(0.169)	(0.102)	(0.119)	(0.164)
Female	0.346***	0.225***	0.153**	−0.031
	(0.050)	(0.065)	(0.050)	(0.104)
Moved in Past Year	−0.539***	−0.249**	−0.185*	−0.252
	(0.080)	(0.096)	(0.082)	(0.186)
Constant	−1.808***	−2.462***	−2.099***	−1.478***
	(0.234)	(0.258)	(0.151)	(0.325)
N	12246	10737	18879	13720
Log pseudolikelihood	−7327.055	−6280.904	−11910.29	−3381.265

Notes: Entries are logistic regression coefficients. Robust standard errors are in parentheses. ***p < 0.001; **p < 0.01; *p < 0.05; ^p < 0.10. The dependent variable is validated voter turnout in the specified election. It is coded one for voting, zero for not voting, and missing if ineligible to vote. Observations are clustered by media market.

TABLE A.14 Effects of Campaign Visits on Vote Choice for Election Day Voters, 2012–2020 CES

Parameter	2012	2016	2020
Rep. Presidential Candidate Visits	0.108	0.116	−0.013
	(0.149)	(0.128)	(0.261)
Rep. VP Candidate Visits	0.010	−0.063	−0.161
	(0.121)	(0.100)	(0.199)
Dem. Presidential Candidate Visits	−0.042	−0.045	0.117
	(0.107)	(0.052)	(0.086)
Dem. VP candidate visits	0.127	0.192*	0.149^
	(0.166)	(0.088)	(0.080)
Party Identification	1.433***	1.198***	1.481***
	(0.106)	(0.061)	(0.129)
Campaign Ads (Dem.–Rep.)	0.000*	−0.000	0.000*
	(0.000)	(0.000)	(0.000)
Age	−0.017*	−0.021***	−0.031***
	(0.008)	(0.006)	(0.006)
Evaluation of National Economy	1.537***	1.303***	−1.015***
	(0.165)	(0.131)	(0.130)
Education	−0.157***	0.160*	0.228***
	(0.046)	(0.069)	(0.054)
Black	1.680**	2.727***	1.894
	(0.610)	(0.213)	(0.371)
Latino	−0.429	0.696	0.321
	(0.811)	(0.737)	(0.482)
Female	0.270	0.415**	−0.043
	(0.283)	(0.158)	(0.204)
Constant	−7.508***	−7.536***	−2.870***
	(0.824)	(0.716)	(0.581)
N	**3441**	**4632**	**2420**
Log pseudolikelihood	**−682.293**	**−1172.606**	**−478.617**

Notes: Entries are logistic regression coefficients. Robust standard errors are in parentheses. ***p < 0.001; **p < 0.01; *p < 0.05; ^p < 0.10. The dependent variable is self-reported presidential vote choice among validated voters. It is coded one for a Democratic vote, zero for a Republican vote, and missing otherwise. Observations are clustered by media market.

APPENDIX B

FIGURES

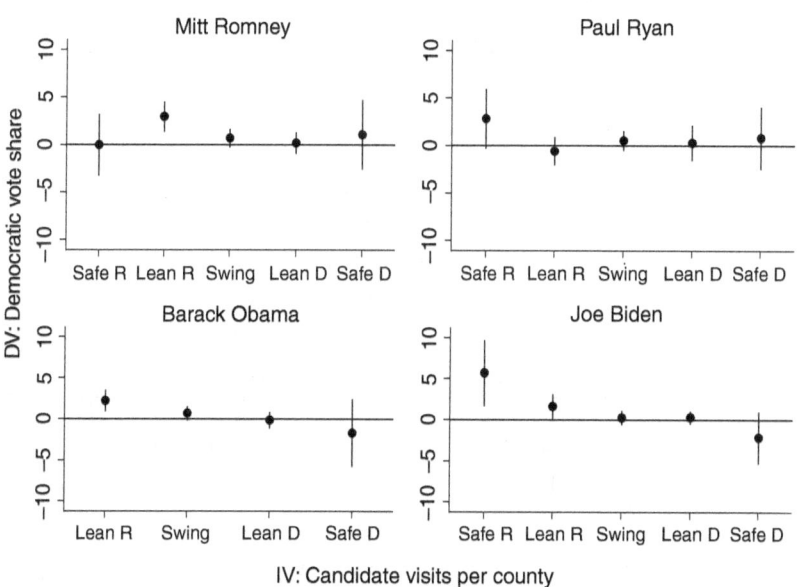

FIGURE A.1A Effects of campaign visits on county Democratic vote share, 2012

Sources: Campaign Visits Database, available for download at christopherjdevine.com/data.html; MIT Election Data and Science Lab

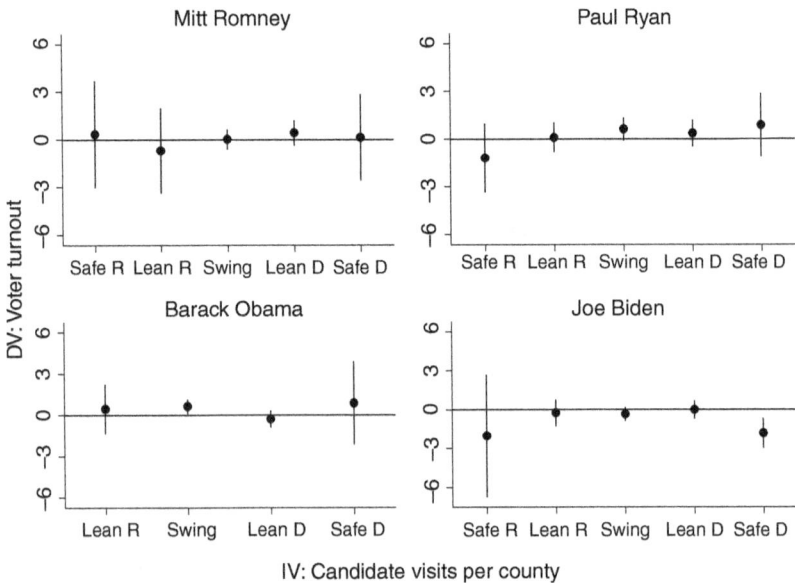

FIGURE A.1B Effects of campaign visits on county turnout, 2012

Sources: Campaign Visits Database; MIT Election Data and Science Lab; U.S. Census Bureau

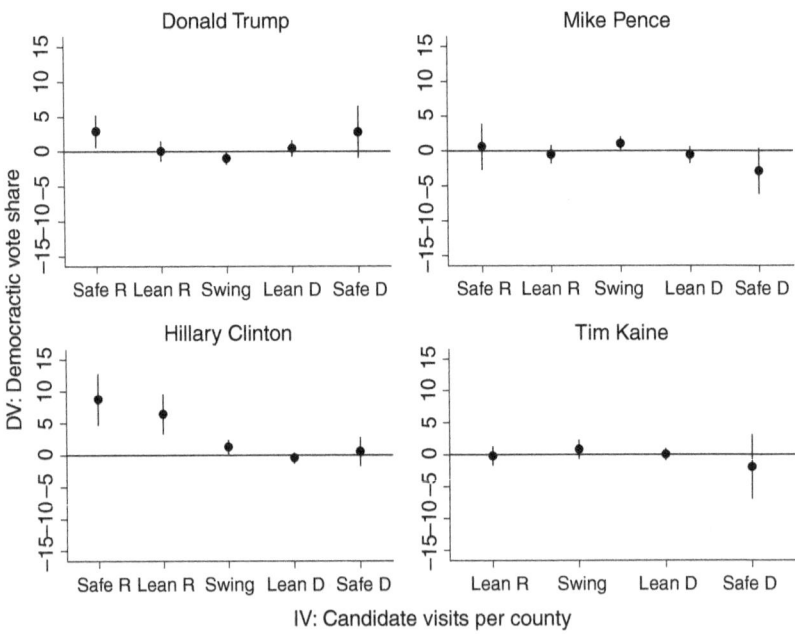

FIGURE A.2A Effects of campaign visits on county Democratic vote share, 2016

Sources: Campaign Visits Database; MIT Election Data and Science Lab

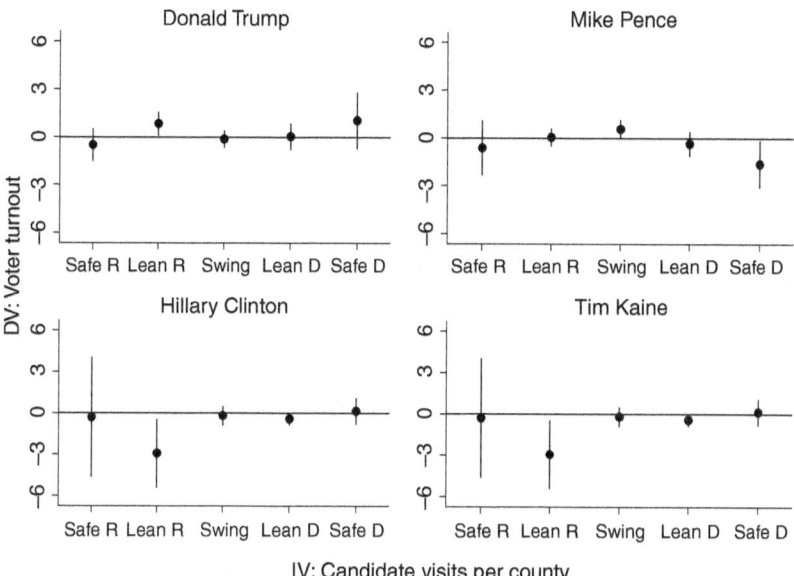

FIGURE A.2B Effects of campaign visits on county turnout, 2016

Sources: Campaign Visits Database; MIT Election Data and Science Lab; U.S. Census Bureau

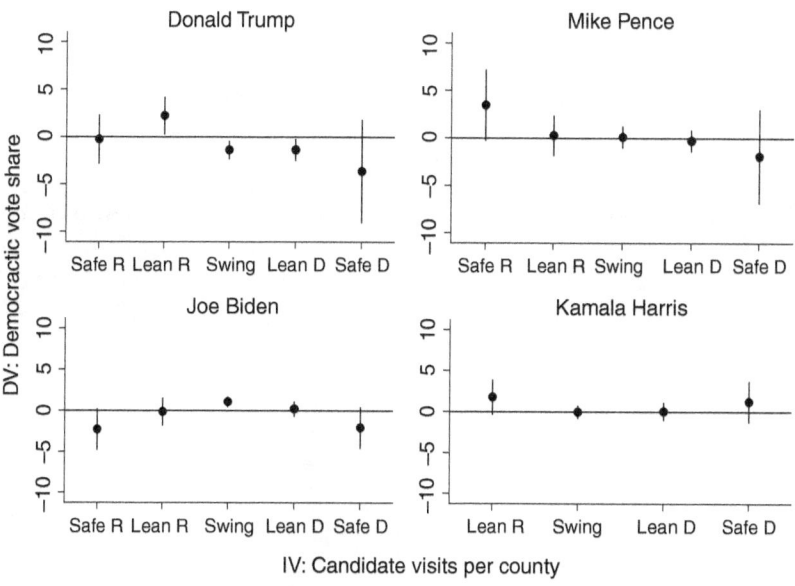

FIGURE A.3A Effects of campaign visits on county Democratic vote share, 2020

Sources: Campaign Visits Database; MIT Election Data and Science Lab

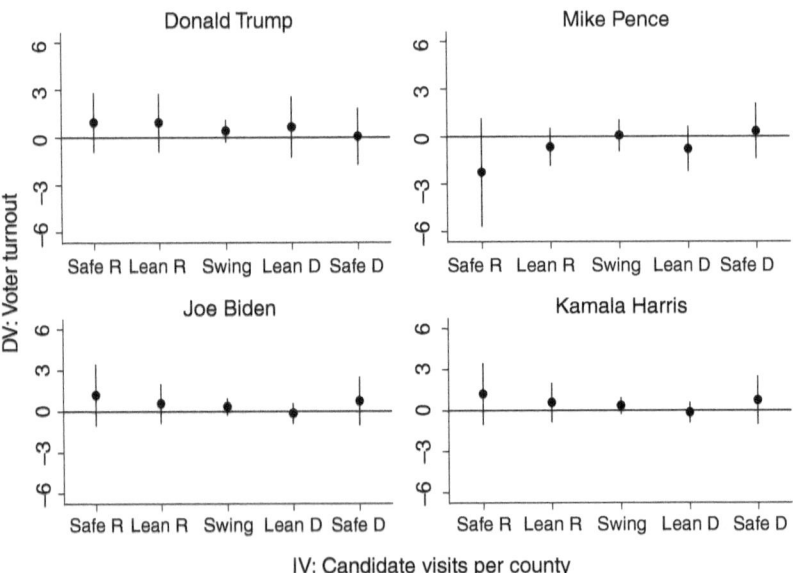

FIGURE A.3B Effects of campaign visits on county turnout, 2020

Sources: Campaign Visits Database; MIT Election Data and Science Lab; U.S. Census Bureau

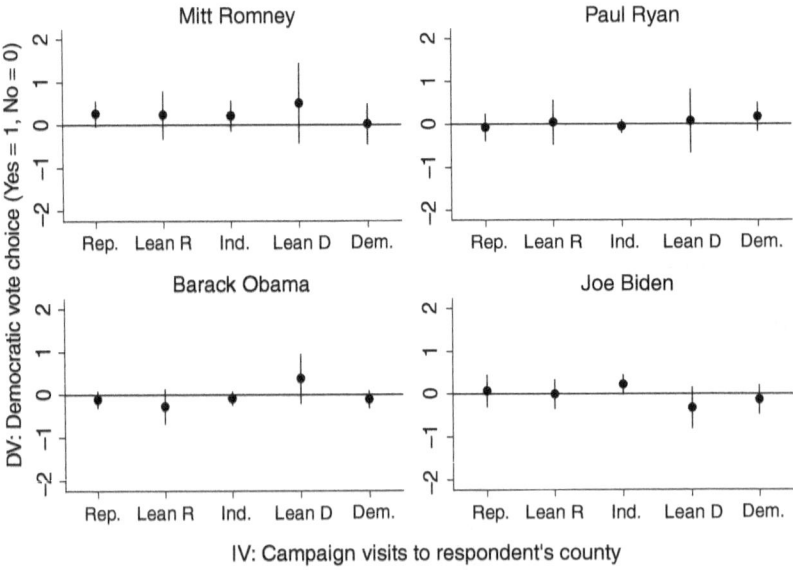

FIGURE A.4A Effects of campaign visits on vote choice by party identification, 2012 CCES

Sources: Campaign Visits Database; Cooperative Congressional Election Study, 2012

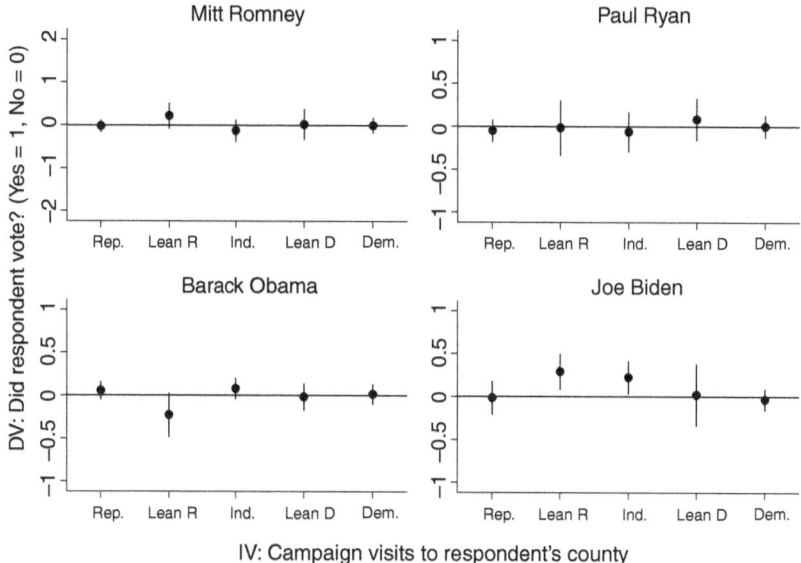

FIGURE A.4B Effects of campaign visits on turnout by party identification, 2012 CCES

Sources: Campaign Visits Database; Cooperative Congressional Election Study, 2012

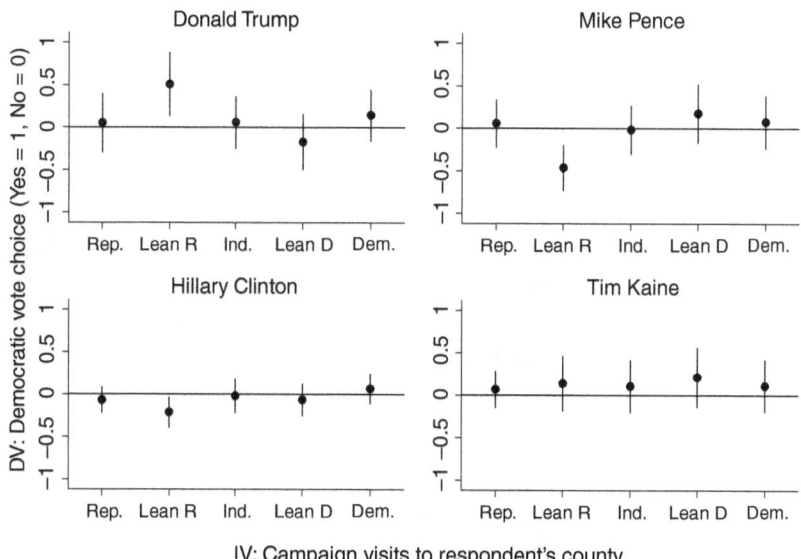

FIGURE A.5A Effects of campaign visits on vote choice by party identification, 2016 CCES

Sources: Campaign Visits Database; Cooperative Congressional Election Study, 2016

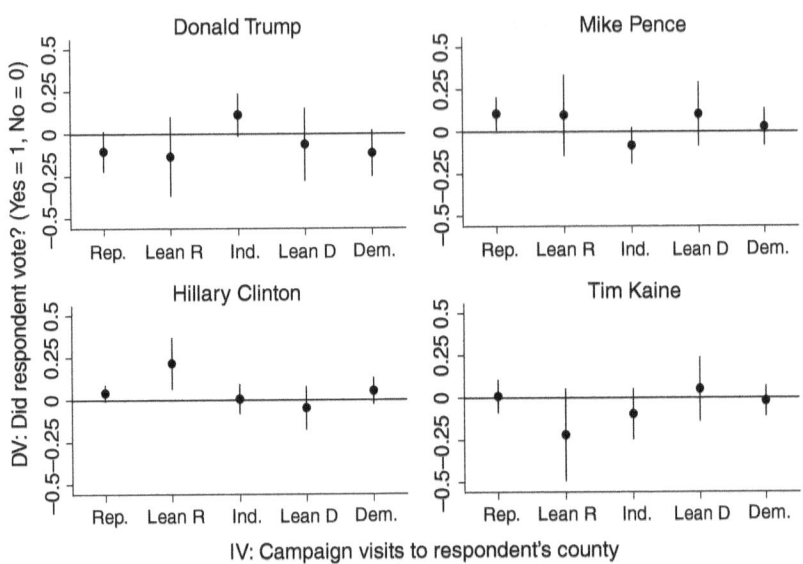

FIGURE A.5B Effects of campaign visits on turnout by party identification, 2016 CCES

Sources: Campaign Visits Database; Cooperative Congressional Election Study, 2016

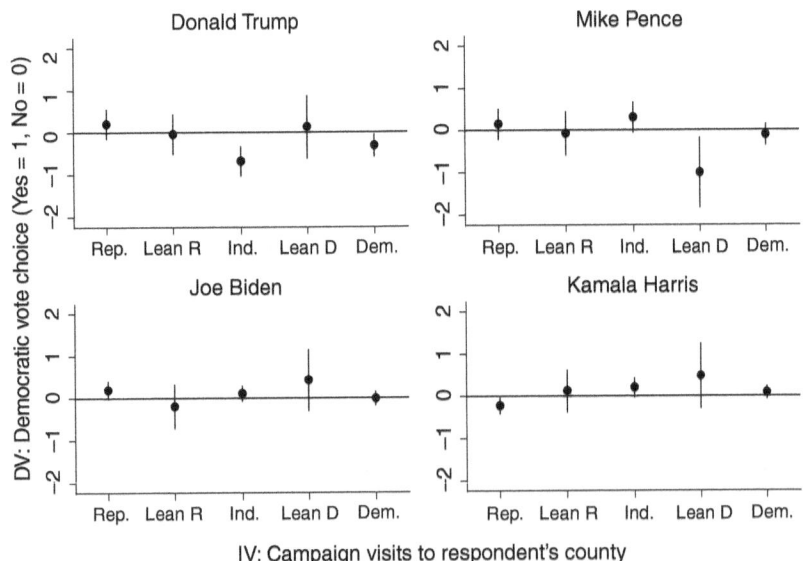

FIGURE A.6A Effects of campaign visits on vote choice by party identification, 2020 CES

Sources: Campaign Visits Database; Cooperative Election Study, 2020

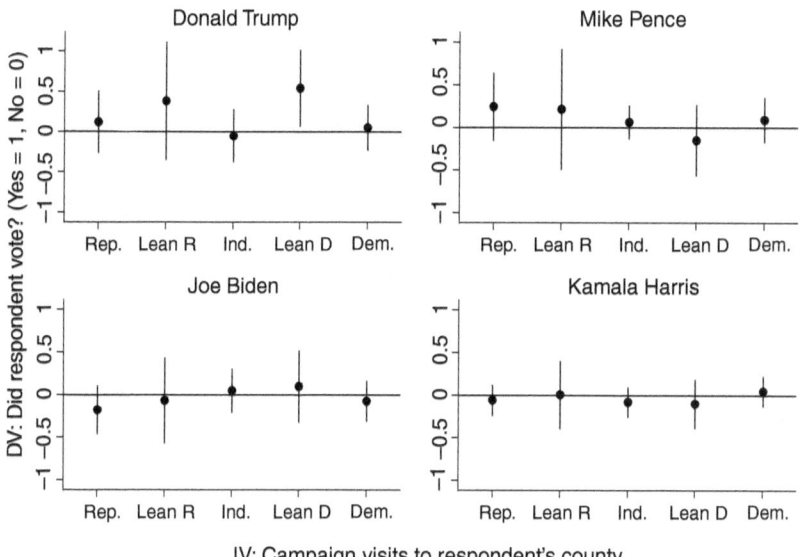

FIGURE A.6B Effects of campaign visits on turnout by party identification, 2020 CES

Sources: Campaign Visits Database; Cooperative Election Study, 2020

NOTES

INTRODUCTION

1. "Joe Biden Holds Virtual Rally for Tampa, Florida," 10 Tampa Bay (CBS affiliate), accessed December 10, 2022, www.youtube.com/watch?v=ABEE2PEfbb8.
2. Nearly every speech, including Biden's, was plagued by unstable audio and video. For several minutes during Congressman Charlie Crist's speech, the video cut out entirely. And several speakers, like Biden, went seconds or even minutes without realizing that they were on screen. As one reporter put it, "Their feeds were visibly delayed as if they were transmitting from Afghanistan, not Tampa Bay." Kirby Wilson, "Joe Biden Hosted a Virtual Campaign Rally in Tampa. It Didn't Go Great," *Tampa Bay Times*, May 7, 2020, www.tampabay.com/florida-politics/buzz/2020/05/07/joe-biden-hosted-a-virtual-campaign-rally-in-tampa-it-didnt-go-great/.
3. Andrew Ferguson, "Biden's Virtual Campaign Is a Disaster," *The Atlantic*, May 5, 2020, www.theatlantic.com/ideas/archive/2020/05/bidens-virtual-campaign-disaster/611698.
4. See Christopher J. Devine, "What If Hillary Clinton *Had* Gone to Wisconsin? Presidential Campaign Visits in the 2016 Election," *Forum* 16, no. 2 (2018): 211–34.
5. See Sydney Ember, Annie Karni, and Maggie Haberman, "Sanders and Biden Cancel Events as Coronavirus Fears Upend Primary," *New York Times*, March 10, 2020, www.nytimes.com/2020/03/10/us/politics/sanders-biden-rally-coronavirus.html; Seth Richardson, "Joe Biden Cancels Cleveland Rally Over Coronavirus Concerns," *Cleveland Plain Dealer*, March 10, 2020, www.cleveland.com/open/2020/03/joe-biden-cancels-cleveland-rally-over-coronavirus-concerns.html.
6. Daniel Strauss and Lauren Gambino, "#WhereIsJoe: Biden Campaign Tries to Stay Relevant amid Coronavirus," *The Guardian*, March 28, 2020, www.theguardian.com/us-news/2020/mar/28/joe-biden-campaign-coronavirus.

7. Ferguson, "Biden's Virtual Campaign"; Marianna Sotomayor and Mike Memoli, "Biden Is Forced to Find New Ways to Connect, One Year into the Campaign," NBC, April 25, 2020, www.nbcnews.com/politics/2020-election/biden-forced-find-new-ways-connect-one-year-campaign-n1192176.
8. Asma Khalid and Tamara Keith, "Trump and Biden Wage an Uneven Virtual Campaign," NPR, May 21, 2020, www.npr.org/2020/05/21/859932268/trump-and-biden-wage-an-uneven-virtual-campaign.
9. See, for example, "40 Times Trump Said the Coronavirus Would Go Away," *Washington Post*, November 2, 2020, www.washingtonpost.com/video/politics/40-times-trump-said-the-coronavirus-would-go-away/2020/04/30/d2593312-9593-4ec2-aff7-72c1438fca0e_video.html.
10. Zeke Miller, "Trump Knocks Biden for Campaigning from Basement amid Virus," Associated Press, May 8, 2020, www.wsls.com/news/politics/2020/05/08/trump-offers-biden-rapid-covid-19-test-to-resume-travel.
11. Jonathan Allen and Amy Parnes, *Shattered: Inside Hillary Clinton's Doomed Campaign* (New York: Crown, 2017), 451.
12. Marc Caputo and Christopher Cadelago, "Dems Warm to Biden's Bunker Strategy," *Politico*, June 24, 2020, www.politico.com/news/2020/06/24/dems-warm-to-bidens-bunker-strategy-338853.
13. Oliver Willis, "Fox News Falsely Claimed Biden Was 'In His Basement' 322 Times in 2 Months," The American Independent, August 14, 2020, americanindependent.com/fox-news-joe-biden-basement-lies-322-times-coronavirus-2020-election.
14. Glenn Kessler, "Trump Campaign Ad Manipulates Three Images to Put Biden in a 'Basement,'" *Washington Post*, August 7, 2020, www.washingtonpost.com/politics/2020/08/07/trump-campaign-ad-manipulates-three-images-put-biden-basement.
15. Trevor Hunnicutt, Elizabeth Culliford, and James Oliphant, "As Trump Returns to the Road, Some Democrats Want to Bust Biden Out of His Basement," Reuters, May 8, 2020, www.usnews.com/news/top-news/articles/2020-05-08/as-trump-returns-to-the-road-some-democrats-want-to-bust-biden-out-of-his-basement.
16. "Basement-Bound Biden Campaign Worries Democrats," Associated Press, June 16, 2020, bangordailynews.com/2020/05/13/news/basement-bound-biden-campaign-worries-democrats-2.
17. David Axelrod and David Plouffe, "What Joe Biden Needs to Do to Beat Trump," *New York Times*, May 4, 2020, www.nytimes.com/2020/05/04/opinion/axelrod-plouffe-joe-biden.html.
18. "Joe Biden Calls Trump's COVID-19 Response 'Incompetent,'" *Good Morning America*, May 12, 2020, www.goodmorningamerica.com/news/video/joe-biden-calls-trumps-covid-19-response-incompetent-70632338.
19. See Katie Glueck, "Biden's Caution: Wise Campaign Tactic or Misguided Gamble?," *New York Times*, October 28, 2020, www.nytimes.com/2020/10/28/us/politics/joe-biden-virus.html.
20. See Alan I. Abramowitz, "It's the Pandemic, Stupid! A Simplified Model for Forecasting the 2020 Presidential Election," *Sabato's Crystal Ball*, UVA Center for Politics,

August 4, 2020, centerforpolitics.org/crystalball/articles/its-the-pandemic-stupid-a-simplified-model-for-forecasting-the-2020-presidential-election; "Public Approval of President Trump's Handling of the Coronavirus," RealClearPolitics.com, 2021, www.realclearpolitics.com/epolls/other/public_approval_of_president_trumps_handling_of_the_coronavirus-7088.html#polls.

21. See Gil Troy, *See How They Ran: The Changing Role of the Presidential Candidate* (New York: Free Press, 1991).

22. Perhaps the best example comes from a press conference that Biden held in Delaware on July 28. "All this stuff about hiding in the basement?" he scoffed. "Well, over 340 million people have watched what we've done like this on television. That's as big as the American population. So I'm learning that the way people are viewing the news and absorbing the news these days is totally different than it was before." Naftali Bendavid, "Joe Biden Takes a Non-Virtual Moment to Muse on His Basement, Apocalyptic Ads and Being Trump's 'Antithesis,' " *Washington Post*, July 29, 2020, www.washingtonpost.com/politics/joe-biden-takes-a-non-virtual-moment-to-muse-on-his-basement-apocalyptic-ads-and-being-trumps-antithesis/2020/07/29/801405f2-d133-11ea-8c55-61e7fa5e82ab_story.html. In other words, Biden implied, campaigning can and perhaps should be defined by *how many people one reaches*, not how one reaches them—particularly given recent technological changes and behavioral adaptations to them among the general public. As the next chapter demonstrates, this is not the first time that a candidate has suggested technology might be making in-person campaigning less important, perhaps even superfluous.

23. "Joe Biden Calls Trump's COVID-19 Response 'Incompetent.' "

24. Willis, "Fox News."

25. Lisa Lerer, "What Joe Biden's Event Was Like," *New York Times*, June 17, 2020, www.nytimes.com/2020/06/17/us/politics/joe-biden-campaign-event.html.

26. J. Edward Moreno, "Trump Mocks Biden Event That Practiced Social Distancing," *The Hill*, June 19, 2020, thehill.com/homenews/campaign/503647-trump-mocks-biden-event-that-practiced-social-distancing. Trump's June 17 rally in Tulsa, Oklahoma, did not go well; he spoke to a half-empty arena, and Tulsa experienced a surge in COVID cases following the visit. Kay Jones and Brian Ries, "Tulsa Sees Covid-19 Surge in the Wake of Trump's June Rally," CNN, July 9, 2020, www.cnn.com/2020/07/08/us/tulsa-covid-trump-rally-contact-tracers-trnd/index.html. Trump would not hold another in-person rally for two months, until August 17. In the meantime, the president—much like Biden, whose virtual campaign events he spent months ridiculing—got creative. On July 17, for example, Trump held a "tele-rally"—essentially a conference call with supporters, who dialed in to hear the President deliver a twenty-three-minute speech. For the time being, Trump explained, "it's going to be tough to have those big massive rallies, so I'm doing telephone rallies, and we'll call them the Trump rallies, but we'll do it by telephone." Donald Judd, "Donald Trump Holds 'Tele-Rally' in Campaign First amid Coronavirus Pandemic," CNN, July 18, 2020, www.cnn.com/2020/07/18/politics/donald-trump-telerally-campaign-event/index.html. By this standard, Biden's more technologically sophisticated virtual

rallies surely should have counted as campaign rallies and, indeed, as campaigning.

27. Tom Davidson, "Joe Biden Makes Campaign Stop in Pittsburgh, Says He's Not Banning Fracking," *Pittsburgh Tribune-Review*, August 31, 2020, triblive.com/news/politics-election/joe-biden-makes-campaign-stop-in-pittsburgh-says-hes-not-banning-fracking.

28. Josh Dawsey, Michael Scherer, and Annie Linskey, "Campaign of Contrasts: Trump's Raucous Crowds vs Biden's Distanced Gatherings," *Washington Post*, September 9, 2020, www.washingtonpost.com/politics/campaign-of-contrasts-trumps-raucous-crowds-vs-bidens-distanced-gatherings/2020/09/08/8633e69a-f1dc-11ea-b796-2dd09962649c_story.html.

29. Jason Lanning and Dale Greenstein, "Biden Gets Rained Out at the Florida State Fairgrounds Hours after Trump's Raymond James Rally," Spectrum News, October 30, 2020, www.baynews9.com/fl/tampa/news/2020/10/28/dueling-rallies--president-trump--biden-both-to-hit-tampa-thursday.

30. Will Weissert, Alexandra Jaffe, and Alan Fram, "Biden's Low-Key Campaign Style Worries Some Democrats," Associated Press, September 25, 2020, apnews.com/article/election-2020-virus-outbreak-ruth-bader-ginsburg-delaware-elections-9282e7a189e965b124f1fc31c857903e. The campaign tried to squeeze all the publicity it could out of these visits. According to this article, "Biden's swing state visits often seem tailor-made for a television package: A small, socially distanced roundtable or town hall, always with fewer than 25 people; occasionally a stop at a local business or a visit with first responders; and then hours of back-to-back local media interviews."

31. As Weissert et al. noted in late September: "Biden maintains a vigorous schedule even when he's not traveling, doing many events online. His campaign has become a fundraising powerhouse through largely virtual events. He raised a record $364 million in August that has allowed him to blanket the airwaves across the country and outspend Trump." Weissert et al., "Low-Key." In fact, after trailing far behind Trump (who, unlike Biden, did not face a competitive primary) in spring 2020, by late October Biden had more than four times as much money on hand as his opponent and he more than doubled Trump's spending in the first two weeks of that month. Jennifer Epstein and Tyler Pager, "Biden Picking Up Campaign Pace as Trump Blitzes Battlegrounds," Bloomberg, October 26, 2020, www.bloomberg.com/news/articles/2020-10-26/biden-keeps-light-schedule-amid-pandemic-as-trump-travels-widely.

32. Angelo Fichera, "Biden Hasn't Suspended In-Person Campaigning," FactCheck.org, October 26, 2020, www.factcheck.org/2020/10/biden-hasnt-suspended-in-person-campaigning.

33. "Presidential Debate: 'We Can't Lock Ourselves Up in a Basement Like Joe Does,' Says Trump on Coronavirus Lockdowns," Global News, accessed December 10, 2022, globalnews.ca/video/7415028/presidential-debate-we-cant-lock-ourselves-up-in-a-basement-like-joe-does-says-trump-on-coronavirus-lockdowns.

34. An op-ed in *The Hill* by conservative journalist Sharyl Attkisson captures these sentiments well. Contrasting Biden's "low-key, understated events" unfavorably with

Trump's "all-out rallies"—at which, she marvels, "he never seems to go shorter than an hour; it's often closer to two"—Attkisson observes that Biden "doesn't even seem to be trying" and "hasn't even been showing up." She concludes: "Whether Biden isn't trying very hard or is simply unable to try harder, if he doesn't get in the game soon, there's a growing feeling that he could squander what some thought and hoped would be a slam-dunk election." In other words, Attkisson suggests, Biden is not making a legitimate effort to win the election—isn't *earning* it—and thus may not, probably should not, be rewarded with the presidency. Sharyl Attkisson, "When Will 'Basement Biden' Get in the Game?," *The Hill*, September 26, 2020, thehill.com/opinion/campaign/518180-when-will-basement-biden-get-in-the-game.
35. Dawsey et al., "Campaign of Contrasts." Emphasis added.
36. Jonathan Easley, "Biden Defends Light Campaign Schedule During Unscheduled Pennsylvania Stop," *The Hill*, October 26, 2020, thehill.com/homenews/campaign/522844-biden-defends-light-campaign-schedule-during-pennsylvania-stop.
37. Biden also held two drive-in rallies in Michigan with former president Barack Obama on the day of this tweet.
38. The U.S. Secret Service estimated that 771 people attended the rally, in 375 cars. Janice Yu, "Joe Biden Hosts Drive-In Campaign Event in Atlanta," Fox 5 Atlanta, October 27, 2020, www.fox5atlanta.com/news/joe-biden-hosts-drive-in-campaign-event-in-atlanta.
39. Joe Biden (@JoeBiden), Twitter post, October 31, 2020, twitter.com/joebiden/status/1322569017412997122?lang=en.
40. Richard J. Ellis and Mark Dedrick, "The Presidential Candidate, Then and Now," *Perspectives on Political Science* 26, no. 4 (1997): 208–16; Troy, *See How They Ran*.
41. Jay Wendland, *Campaigns That Matter: The Importance of Campaign Visits in Presidential Nominating Contests* (Lanham, MD: Lexington Books, 2017).
42. Daron R. Shaw, *The Race to 270: The Electoral College and the Campaign Strategies of 2000 and 2004* (Chicago: University of Chicago Press, 2006).

1. A BRIEF HISTORY OF PRESIDENTIAL CAMPAIGN VISITS

1. H. R. Haldeman, "Campaign '68," box 33, folder 14, White House Special Files Collection, Richard Nixon Presidential Library, 1968, 4.
2. Haldeman, "Campaign '68," 2–3.
3. Haldeman, "Campaign '68," 2.
4. Haldeman, "Campaign '68," 3.
5. Qtd. in Gil Troy, *See How They Ran: The Changing Role of the Presidential Candidate* (New York: Free Press, 1991), 224.
6. According to author Rick Perlstein, Nixon typically held only one rally per day—versus many more for Humphrey—at or near an airport so that news footage could be immediately dispatched to New York City for inclusion in that evening's national

television news broadcasts. Nixon's relative inactivity would not be apparent to TV audiences because "Eager to be fair, the networks would always show one clip of the Democrat and one clip of the Republican." Rick Perlstein, *Nixonland: The Rise of a President and the Fracturing of America* (New York: Scribner, 2008), 329.

7. Perlstein, *Nixonland*, 347.
8. Campaign adviser William Galvin wrote a memo elaborating on this point: "LBJ [President Johnson] puts great store in his 'pressing the flesh,' establishing physical contact with as many thousands as he can. It probably works; what we've got to devise is *a workable substitute, that can accomplish the same thing wholesale that he does more or less retail.* The film is one device" for accomplishing this, because "The physical presence of someone close to the candidate can bridge the space between the screen and the audience." Joe McGinniss, *The Selling of the President 1968* (New York: Trident, 1969), 214. Emphasis added.
9. McGinniss, *Selling*, 66.
10. Troy, *See How They Ran*, 194.
11. Theodore H. White, *The Making of the President 1972* (New York: Atheneum, 1973), 283.
12. Ford's Democratic opponent, Jimmy Carter, ridiculed this strategy, using language eerily reminiscent of Donald Trump's attacks on Joe Biden more than forty years later. "Mr. Ford is in hiding," Carter sneered at a campaign rally. "He comes out of the Rose Garden, memorizes a 90-second speech, and goes back into hiding." Martin Schram, *Running for President 1976: The Carter Campaign* (New York: Stein and Day, 1977), 324.
13. Troy, *See How They Ran*, 261.
14. Liz Smith, "How Joe Biden Can Defeat Trump from His Basement," *New York Times*, May 7, 2020, www.nytimes.com/2020/05/07/opinion/joe-biden-trump-2020.html.
15. Troy, *See How They Ran*, 178–79.
16. Troy, *See How They Ran*, 179.
17. Richard J. Ellis and Mark Dedrick, "The Presidential Candidate, Then and Now," *Perspectives on Political Science* 26, no. 4 (1997): 208–16, 208.
18. Ellis and Dedrick rightly caution against assuming uniformity in nineteenth-century campaigns or a linear progression from "standing" to "running" for president over the course of U.S. history. They write: "In nineteenth-century presidential campaigns, there was no single norm, no constitutional 'old way,' but rather contested, rival norms derived from divergent political cultures." Ellis and Dedrick, "Presidential Candidate," 3.
19. Ellis and Dedrick, "Presidential Candidate," 547–48.
20. Harlow Giles Unger, *John Quincy Adams* (Boston: Da Capo, 2012), 223; Paul C. Nagler, *John Quincy Adams: A Public Life, A Private Life* (Cambridge, MA: Harvard University Press, 1997), 246.
21. Walter R. Borneman, *Polk: The Man Who Transformed the Presidency and America* (New York: Random House, 2008), 114.

1. A BRIEF HISTORY OF PRESIDENTIAL CAMPAIGN VISITS 265

22. Stephen W. Sears, *George B. McClellan: The Young Napoleon* (New York: Ticknor & Fields, 1988), 366.
23. Allan Nevins, ed., *Letters of Grover Cleveland, 1850–1908* (New York: Da Capo, 1970), 35.
24. Richard J. Ellis, *Old Tip vs. the Sly Fox: The 1840 Election and the Making of a Partisan Nation* (Lawrence: University Press of Kansas, 2020), 179.
25. Jon Meacham, *Thomas Jefferson: The Art of Power* (New York: Random House, 2012), 302; David McCullough, *John Adams* (New York: Simon & Schuster, 2001), 536.
26. Troy, *See How They Ran*, 16.
27. Ellis and Dedrick, "Presidential Candidate," 209.
28. Mark R. Cheathem, *The Coming of Democracy: Presidential Campaigning in the Age of Jackson* (Baltimore: Johns Hopkins University Press, 2018), 29.
29. Cheathem, *Coming of Democracy*, 29.
30. Benjamin T. Arrington, *The Last Lincoln Republican: The Presidential Election of 1880* (Lawrence: University Press of Kansas, 2020), 139. In 1852, Franklin Pierce became the first presidential candidate to be formally notified of his nomination in person, when a delegation from the recently concluded Democratic convention arrived at his home in New Hampshire. Troy, *See How They Ran*, 56. The "notification ceremony" soon became a major campaign event, often including an acceptance speech from the candidate. In 1892, Grover Cleveland became the first presidential candidate to accept his nomination not at home or an executive residence, but at a campaign rally, in this case before twenty thousand people at Madison Square Garden in New York City. Allan Nevins, *Grover Cleveland: A Study in Courage* (New York: Dodd, Mead, 1933), 503. In 1932, Franklin Roosevelt set a new standard by flying to the Democratic Party's convention in Chicago to accept its nomination in person. The last notification ceremony took place in 1940 in Wendell Willkie's hometown of Elwood, Indiana. Troy, *See How They Ran*, 175.
31. Robert M. Alexander, *Representation and the Electoral College* (Oxford: Oxford University Press, 2019), 58; Michael F. Holt, *The Rise and Fall of the American Whig Party: Jacksonian Politics and the Onset of the Civil War* (New York: Oxford University Press, 1999), 8.
32. Cheathem, *Coming of Democracy*, 7, 36.
33. Historians and journalists, past and present, have differed over which candidate truly conducted the first in-person presidential campaign. I concur with Cheathem's judgment that "Harrison's overt campaigning" in 1836 was "a first for a presidential candidate." Cheathem, *Coming of Democracy*, 103; see also Ellis, *Old Tip*, chapter 4. Harrison's 1840 campaign more often is recognized as "the first presidential speaking tour." Jeffrey Norman Bourdon, *From Garfield to Harding: The Success of Midwestern Front Porch Campaigns* (Kent, OH: Kent State University Press, 2019), 42. But this, to say nothing of the 1836 campaign, has been dismissed by other historians as not substantive enough to qualify as a real political campaign. See, e.g., Troy, *See How They Ran*, 21. Ellis (*Old Tip*, 186–98) clearly refutes this argument. Indeed, differences in historical interpretation often come down to whether the candidate in question

openly engaged in political campaigning or merely conducted a ceremonial tour; that is why, for example, some historians cite Stephen Douglas in 1860 or Horace Greeley in 1872 as the first candidate to conduct a presidential campaign. See, e.g., Marvin R. Weisbord, *Campaigning for President: A New Look at the Road to the White House* (Washington, DC: Public Affairs, 1964), 4; William E. Rickert, "Horace Greeley on the Stump: Presidential Campaign of 1872," *Western Journal of Communication* 39, no. 3 (1975): 175. Similar disagreements can be found in contemporary news accounts. For example, in 1852, the *Nashville Union* declared, in reference to Winfield Scott: "Here, for the first time in the history of our republic, is a presidential candidate, seen taking the stump." Troy, *See How They Ran*, 53. Twenty years later, in 1872, the *Hartford Courant* made nearly the same pronouncement about Horace Greeley: "For the first time in the history of the country a prominent candidate for the presidency has found it necessary to take the stump on his own behalf." Troy, *See How They Ran*, 76.

34. Cheathem, *Coming of Democracy*, 102.
35. Ellis, *Old Tip*, 91.
36. Cheathem, *Coming of Democracy*, 102.
37. Cheathem, *Coming of Democracy*, 103.
38. Ellis, *Old Tip*, 182.
39. Troy, *See How They Ran*, 25.
40. Ellis, *Old Tip*, 187–88.
41. Ellis, *Old Tip*, 188.
42. Ellis, *Old Tip*, 187–97.
43. Ellis, *Old Tip*, 191, 197. Many attendees would travel long distances, even across state lines, to attend these events. "Thanks to the new railroads and the new roads Whig speakers were able to move rapidly from one rally to another and large crowds of listeners were able to travel to hear them." Donald B. Cole, *Martin Van Buren and the American Political System* (Princeton, NJ: Princeton University Press, 1984), 369.
44. Ellis, *Old Tip*, 197; Holt, *Whig Party*, 110.
45. Troy, *See How They Ran*, 25.
46. Troy, *See How They Ran*, 55.
47. Charles Winslow Elliott, *Winfield Scott: The Soldier and the Man* (New York: Macmillan, 1937), 637.
48. Robert W. Johannsen, "Stephen A. Douglas' New England Campaign, 1860," *New England Quarterly* 35, no. 2 (1962): 162–86; 171, 173.
49. Johnson, "Stephen A. Douglas'," 437, 438. Emphasis added.
50. Troy, *See How They Ran*, 71.
51. Robert C. Williams, *Horace Greeley: Champion of American Freedom* (New York: New York University Press, 2006), 302–4.
52. Mark D. Hirsch, "Election of 1884," in *History of American Presidential Elections, 1789–1968*, vol. 2, ed. Arthur M. Schlesinger Jr. and Fred L. Israel (New York: Chelsea House, 1971), 1577.
53. President Ulysses Grant summarized the reigning logic well in an 1872 letter to a political ally, explaining why he would not stump for reelection that year: "It has been

1. A BRIEF HISTORY OF PRESIDENTIAL CAMPAIGN VISITS   267

done, so far as I remember, by but two presidential candidates [Douglas in 1860 and Seymour in 1868] heretofore, and both of them were public speakers and both of them were beaten. I am no speaker and I don't want to be beaten." Troy, *See How They Ran*, 73.

54. Qtd. in Johannsen, "Stephen A. Douglas," 164.
55. Troy, *See How They Ran*, 65.
56. Douglas R. Egerton, *Year of Meteors: Stephen Douglas, Abraham Lincoln, and the Election That Brought on the Civil War* (New York: Bloomsbury, 2010), 205.
57. Hirsch, "Election of 1884," 1606, 1578.
58. Troy, *See How They Ran*, 95.
59. Arrington, *Last Lincoln Republican*, 129.
60. Bourdon, *From Garfield to Harding*, 11.
61. Bourdon, *From Garfield to Harding*, 1; Ellis and Dedrick, "Presidential Candidate," 211.
62. Robert W. Merry, *President McKinley: Architect of the American Century* (New York: Simon & Schuster, 2017), 140.
63. Margaret Leech, *In the Days of McKinley* (New York: Harper & Brothers, 1959), 92–93.
64. Michael Kazin, *A Godly Hero: The Life of William Jennings Bryan* (New York: Anchor, 2006), 66.
65. Leech, *In the Days of McKinley*, 88.
66. Bourdon, *From Garfield to Harding*, 72, 2.
67. R. Hal Williams, *Realigning America: McKinley, Bryan, and the Remarkable Election of 1896* (Lawrence: University Press of Kansas, 2010), 99, 98.
68. Troy, *See How They Ran*, 103.
69. Qtd. in Merry, *President McKinley*, 138.
70. Kazin, *A Godly Hero*, 106.
71. Troy, *See How They Ran*, 121.
72. Ellis and Dedrick, "Presidential Candidate," 214; Troy, *See How They Ran*, 137.
73. Jean Edward Smith, *FDR* (New York: Random House, 2007), 181; Weisbord, *Campaigning for President*, 85.
74. Troy, *See How They Ran*, 155.
75. Ellis and Dedrick, "Presidential Candidate," 215.
76. Eugene Lyons, *Herbert Hoover: A Biography* (Garden City, NY: Doubleday, 1964), 292; Richard Norton Smith, *An Uncommon Man: The Triumph of Herbert Hoover* (New York: Simon & Schuster, 1984), 148.
77. Smith, *FDR*, 369–70.
78. Troy, *See How They Ran*, 192.
79. David McCullough, *Truman* (New York: Simon & Schuster, 1992), 627.
80. Harry S. Truman, *Memoirs*, Vol. 2: *Years of Trial and Hope* (Garden City, NY: Doubleday, 1956), 178.
81. John Dickerson, *Whistlestop: My Favorite Stories from Presidential Campaign History* (New York: Twelve, 2016), 54.
82. McCullough, *Truman*, 662; Dickerson, *Whistlestop*, 47–48.

83. Dickerson, *Whistlestop*, 209.
84. McCullough, *Truman*, 53.
85. Truman, *Memoirs*, 219.
86. McCullough, *Truman*, 624, 628, 626, 679.
87. See, e.g., McCullough, *Truman*, 713 and Thomas M. Holbrook, "Did the Whistle-Stop Campaign Matter?," *PS: Political Science and Politics* 35, no. 1 (2002): 59–66, 64.
88. Troy, *See How They Ran*, 195.
89. Weisbord, *Campaigning for President*, 155.
90. John A. Farrell, *Richard Nixon: The Life* (New York: Doubleday, 2017), 282.
91. White, *Making of the President 1972*, 330. By contrast, one might think of earlier (i.e., pre-television) campaigns as being targeted toward a narrower geographic unit: the town, city, or county in which a visit took place. As A. Scott Berg explains in regard to one such campaign: "All media in 1912 was local. The way to ignite an entire nation was by setting small fires across the country. That meant giving a speech in a major city and making shorter talks from the back of a train at the smaller whistle-stops en route to the next city. Regional press would report what was said, but word of mouth remained the best publicity." A. Scott Berg, *Wilson* (New York: Putnam, 2013), 237.
92. Daron R. Shaw, *The Race to 270: The Electoral College and the Campaign Strategies of 2000 and 2004* (Chicago: University of Chicago Press, 2006), 59.
93. Troy, *See How They Ran*, 231.
94. Peter Goldman, Tom Mathews, et al., *The Quest for the Presidency: The 1988 Campaign* (New York: Simon & Schuster, 1989), 367.
95. McCullough, *Truman*, 685, 667, 669.
96. Troy, *See How They Ran*, 177.
97. Geoffrey Perret, *Eisenhower* (Holbrook, MA: Adams Media Corporation, 1999), 411.
98. Weisbord, *Campaigning for President*, 159–160.
99. Richard M. Nixon, *The Memoirs of Richard Nixon* (New York: Grosset & Dunlap, 1978), 111; John A. Farrell, *Richard Nixon: The Life* (New York: Doubleday, 2017), 244.
100. Weisbord, *Campaigning for President*, 5–6, 184.
101. Theodore H. White, *The Making of the President 1960* (New York: Atheneum, 1961), 251–52.
102. Air travel does, however, make it difficult for candidates to visit more remote and rural areas that do not have airports capable of accommodating large jets. As Gil Troy notes, this has encouraged presidential candidates to restrict their visits to major urban centers. Troy, *See How They Ran*, 197, 231.
103. John McCain and Mark Salter, *The Restless Wave: Good Times, Just Causes, Great Fights, and Other Appreciations* (New York: Simon & Schuster, 2018), 65.
104. Bill Clinton, *My Life* (New York: Alfred A. Knopf, 2004), 422.
105. Clinton, *My Life*, 442.
106. David C. King and David Morehouse, "Moving Voters in the 2000 Presidential Campaign: Local Visits, Local Media," in *Lights, Camera, Campaign! Media, Politics, and Political Advertising*, ed. David A. Schultz (New York: Peter Lang, 2004), 301–17.

107. Theodore H. White, *The Making of the President 1968* (New York: Atheneum, 1969), 435.
108. This dynamic is even more apparent when it comes to air travel, which transports candidates across vast geographic spaces without any visual or cultural markers—only the relentless uniformity of the sky—to fill their passages in between. As a result, much like touring musicians, candidates often cannot even remember where they are speaking, let alone identify with the people there. Dick Cheney's recollection of the 2004 campaign illustrates this point well: "In order to avoid the obvious disaster, a staff member was assigned to tape a piece of paper just inside the airplane door, so as I disembarked I would see 'Portland, Oregon' or 'Everett, Washington' or 'Las Vegas, Nevada' and know for sure where we had landed and where I could say I was glad to be." Dick Cheney with Liz Cheney, *In My Time: A Personal and Political Memoir* (New York: Threshold Editions, 2011), 285.
109. Cheney, *In My Time*, 276.
110. Shaw, *Race to 270*, 9–10, 69.
111. Jeffrey S. Hill, Elaine Rodriguez, and Amanda E. Wooden, "Stump Speeches and Road Trips: The Impact of State Campaign Appearances in Presidential Elections," *PS: Political Science & Politics* 43, no. 2 (2010): 243–54, 245; Scott L. Althaus, Peter F. Nardulli, and Daron R. Shaw, "Candidate Appearances in Presidential Elections, 1972–2000," *Political Communication* 19, no. 1 (2002): 49–72, 50; Taofang Huang and Daron R. Shaw, "Beyond the Battlegrounds? Electoral College Strategies in the 2008 Presidential Election," *Journal of Political Marketing* 8, no. 4 (2009): 272–91, 277.

2. WHEN AND WHY DO CAMPAIGN VISITS MATTER?

1. Presidential candidates from both parties have used the same line, or close approximations thereof, for many years. In 1960, John F. Kennedy greeted a boisterous crowd in Waterbury, Connecticut, by proclaiming: "My name is Kennedy and I have come to ask for your support." Marvin R. Weisbord, *Campaigning for President: A New Look at the Road to the White House* (Washington, DC: Public Affairs, 1964), 172. Barack Obama closed out his 2012 reelection campaign by announcing: "I've come back to Iowa one more time to ask for your vote." Mark Halperin and John Heilemann, *Double Down: Game Change 2012* (New York: Penguin, 2013), 462. And in 2020, leading candidates for the Democratic presidential nomination—including Elizabeth Warren and Pete Buttigieg—also advertised their deference to democratic tradition by assuring rallygoers, as if there were any doubt: "I'm here to ask for your vote." Jamie Dupree, "Warren Slams Bloomberg, Presses for Money in 2020 Race," *Atlanta Journal-Constitution*, February 13, 2020, www.ajc.com/blog/jamie-dupree/warren-slams-bloomberg-presses-for-money-2020-race/wQpYKo4ZaGOX7PNRsRsBkM; "Buttigieg Rallies on Scott Hall Lawn," *New Hampshire*, November 1, 2020, tnhdigital.com/2019/11/01/buttigieg.

2. "Remarks in Cuyahoga Falls, Ohio," Government Publishing Office, accessed December 10, 2022, www.govinfo.gov/content/pkg/WCPD-2004-10-11/html/WCPD-2004-10-11-Pg2235.htm; "President's Remarks in Tampa, Florida," White House Archives, accessed December 10, 2022, georgewbush-whitehouse.archives.gov/news/releases/2004/10/text/20041031-3.html; "Remarks in Alamogordo, New Mexico," American Presidency Project, accessed December 10, 2022, www.presidency.ucsb.edu/documents/remarks-alamogordo-new-mexico.

3. Alison Mitchell, "In a Style Change, Bush Talks More Directly to the Voters," *New York Times*, September 9, 2000, www.nytimes.com/2000/09/09/us/2000-campaign-texas-governor-style-change-bush-talks-more-directly-voters.html.

4. Richard Johnston, Michael G. Hagen, and Kathleen Hall Jamieson, *The 2000 Presidential Election and the Foundations of Party Politics* (Cambridge: Cambridge University Press, 2004), 75–76. Campaigns spend much more on advertisements than on visits, but in large part this is because visits are more cost-efficient. As David C. King and David Morehouse note: "on a dollars-per-vote basis, candidate trips to key regions are very often a more effective way to move voters than blanketing an area with television advertisements." "Moving Voters in the 2000 Presidential Campaign: Local Visits, Local Media," in *Lights, Camera, Campaign! Media, Politics, and Political Advertising*, ed. David A. Schultz (New York: Peter Lang, 2004), 301–17, 302. More succinctly: "Compared to running advertisements, visits are cheap." Jay Wendland, *Campaigns That Matter: The Importance of Campaign Visits in Presidential Nominating Contests* (Lanham, MD: Lexington, 2017), 4. By way of example, in 2000, Al Gore's presidential campaign spent approximately $10.7 million on travel (versus $44.6 million on ads), and in the early stages of the 2016 Democratic primaries Bernie Sanders's campaign spent $5 million on travel (versus approximately $45 million on ads), with two-thirds going to pay for transportation and one-third for venues. King and Morehouse, "Moving Voters," 203; Wendland, *Campaigns That Matter*, 54. Even in 1976, when Gerald Ford famously (but not entirely) ran for president from the White House's Rose Garden, his campaign spent more than 10 percent of its overall budget on travel—by Ford, as well as incumbent vice president Nelson Rockefeller, running mate Bob Dole, the Ford family, and other surrogates. Martin Schram, *Running for President 1976: The Carter Campaign* (New York: Stein and Day, 1977), 267.

5. See this book's introduction.

6. Christopher J. Devine and Kyle C. Kopko, *Do Running Mates Matter? The Influence of Vice Presidential Candidates in Presidential Elections* (Lawrence: University Press of Kansas, 2020); Jody C. Baumgartner and Peter L. Francia, *Conventional Wisdom and American Elections: Exploding Myths, Exploring Misconceptions* (Lanham, MD: Rowman & Littlefield, 2019), chapter 8; John Sides and Lynn Vavreck, *The Gamble: Choice and Chance in the 2012 Presidential Election* (Princeton, NJ: Princeton University Press, 2013).

7. See, e.g., Alan I. Abramowitz, "Will Time for Change Mean Time for Trump?," *PS: Political Science & Politics* 49, no. 4 (2016): 659–60; Ruth Dassonneville and Charles

Tien, "Introduction to Forecasting the 2020 US Elections," *PS: Political Science & Politics* 54, no. 1 (2021): 47–51.

8. See, e.g., Sides and Vavreck, *The Gamble*, chapter 7; John Sides, Michael Tesler, and Lynn Vavreck, *Identity Crisis: The 2016 Presidential Campaign and the Battle for the Meaning of America* (Princeton, NJ: Princeton University Press, 2018), chapter 8.

9. Costas Panagopoulos, *Bases Loaded: How US Presidential Campaigns Are Changing and Why It Matters* (Oxford: Oxford University Press, 2020), 37–41.

10. As Henry E. Brady, Richard Johnston, and John Sides point out in "The Study of Political Campaigns," in *Capturing Campaign Effects*, eds. Henry E. Brady and Richard Johnston (Ann Arbor: University of Michigan Press, 2006), the works of the "Columbia School"—e.g., Paul F. Lazarsfeld, Bernard Berelson, and Hazel Gaudet, *The People's Choice: How the Voter Makes Up His Mind in a Presidential Campaign* (New York: Columbia University Press, 1948); Bernard R. Berelson, Paul F. Lazarsfeld, and William N. McPhee, *Voting: A Study of Opinion Formation in a Presidential Campaign* (Chicago: University of Chicago Press, 1954)—have often been mischaracterized on this point. Lazarsfeld et al. affirm the importance of campaigns in discouraging partisan defection, and find that 8 percent of voters in Erie County, Ohio, did switch their vote intentions over the course of the 1940 campaign. Also, Berelson et al. determine that Harry Truman's 1948 campaign was particularly effective at persuading Catholics and union members in Elmira, New York, to support him. Findings such as these, Brady et al. note (p. 5), are "largely overlooked and not consonant with a minimal effects characterization."

11. Taofang Huang and Daron R. Shaw, "Beyond the Battlegrounds? Electoral College Strategies in the 2008 Presidential Election," *Journal of Political Marketing* 8, no. 4 (2009): 273; Brady et al., "Study of Political Campaigns," 7.

12. Larry M. Bartels, "Messages Received: The Political Impact of Media Exposure," *American Political Science Review* 87, no. 2 (1993): 267–85; Steven E. Finkel, "Re-Examining the 'Minimal Effects' Model in Recent Presidential Elections," *Journal of Politics* 55, no. 1 (1993): 1–21; Andrew Gelman and Gary King, "Why Are American Presidential Election Polls So Variable When Votes Are So Predictable?," *British Journal of Political Science* 23, no. 4 (1993): 409–51.

13. James Campbell, *The American Campaign* (College Station: Texas A&M Press, 2000), 188.

14. Thomas M. Holbrook, "Campaigns, National Conditions, and U.S. Presidential Election," *American Journal of Political Science* 38, no. 4 (1994): 973–98, 977.

15. See Robert S. Erikson and Christopher Wleizen, *The Timeline of Presidential Elections: How Campaigns Do (and Do Not) Matter* (Chicago: University of Chicago Press, 2012); Thomas M. Holbrook, *Do Campaigns Matter?* (Thousand Oaks, CA: Sage, 1996).

16. Brady et al., "Study of Political Campaigns," 12.

17. Gary C. Jacobson, "How Do Campaigns Matter?," *Annual Review of Political Science* 18 (2015): 32.

18. Gelman and King, "Why Are American."

19. Johnston et al., *2000 Presidential Election*.

20. Larry M. Bartels, "Priming and Persuasion in Presidential Campaigns," in *Capturing Campaign Effects*, ed. Henry E. Brady and Richard Johnston (Ann Arbor: University of Michigan Press, 2006), 79–80.
21. John R. Zaller, *The Nature and Origins of Mass Opinion* (Cambridge: Cambridge University Press, 1992).
22. Daron Shaw states: "At the theoretical level, presidential campaigns provide the most demanding test of whether campaign effects exist. Arguably, presidential elections are the least susceptible to campaign effects because election laws create approximate financial equity between the two major parties' candidates." "The Impact of News Media Favorability and Candidate Events in Presidential Campaigns," *Political Communication* 16, no. 2 (1999): 186.
23. Sides and Vavreck, *Gamble*, 9.
24. Daron R. Shaw, *The Race to 270: The Electoral College and the Campaign Strategies of 2000 and 2004* (Chicago: University of Chicago Press, 2006), 166.
25. Marjorie Randon Hershey, *Party Politics in America*, 17th ed. (New York: Routledge, 2017), chapter 11.
26. Panagopoulos, *Bases Loaded*.
27. Thomas M. Holbrook, "Did the Whistle-Stop Campaign Matter?," *PS: Political Science and Politics* 35, no. 1 (2002): 60.
28. Daron R. Shaw and James G. Gimpel, "What If We Randomize the Governor's Schedule? Evidence on Campaign Appearance Effects from a Texas Field Experiment," *Political Communication* 29, no. 2 (2012): 141.
29. However, as Thomas Wood explains, most campaign officials believe that traveling together between events provides the candidate and his or her staff with valuable opportunities to develop constructive relationships with influential national journalists, which may affect the tone and content of their coverage. Thomas Wood, "What the Heck Are We Doing in Ottumwa, Anyway? Presidential Candidate Visits and Their Political Consequence," *Annals of the American Academy of Political and Social Science* 667, no. 1 (2016): 111. Also, he describes the events themselves as "a valuable service provided for TV journalists," redounding to the campaign's benefit "in a tacit exchange for positive coverage." Wood elaborates: "[C]ampaign visits are a vital source of TV footage, and a campaign's failure to have visits would be a slight to the press" (p. 113).
30. Shaw and Gimpel, "What If," 156.
31. Scott L. Althaus, Peter F. Nardulli, and Daron R. Shaw, "Candidate Appearances in Presidential Elections, 1972–2000," *Political Communication* 19, no. 1 (2002): 52.
32. King and Morehouse, "Moving Voters," 304.
33. King and Morehouse, "Moving Voters," 305.
34. Wood, "What the Heck," 114.
35. One famous example came in late 1999, when George W. Bush—then running for the Republican Party's presidential nomination—flunked a Boston reporter's "pop quiz" on foreign affairs. Scott Shepard, "Gore Chides Bush for Missing Names of Foreign Leaders," *Greensboro News & Record*, November 5, 1999, greensboro.com/gore-chides

-bush-for-missing-names-of-foreign-leaders-a-bush-aide-says-the-presidential/article_4e3c2402-bfac-5441-b865-8a2bf7f6b9b8.html.
36. See, e.g., Marion R. Just, Ann N. Crigler, Dean E. Alger, Timothy E. Cook, Montague Kern, and Darrell M. West, *Crosstalk: Citizens, Candidates, and the Media in a Presidential Campaign* (Cambridge: Cambridge University Press, 1996).
37. Shaw and Gimpel, "What If," 143.
38. Jeffrey M. Jones, "Does Bringing Out the Candidate Bring Out the Votes? The Effects of Nominee Campaigning in Presidential Elections," *American Politics Quarterly* 26, no. 4 (1998): 397.
39. John McCain and Mark Salter, *The Restless Wave: Good Times, Just Causes, Great Fights, and Other Appreciations* (New York: Simon & Schuster, 2018), 38–39.
40. Theodore H. White, *The Making of the President 1972* (New York: Atheneum, 1973), 228–29.
41. Jimmy Carter, *White House Diary* (New York: Farrar, Straus and Giroux, 2010), 459–60.
42. J. Paul Herr, "The Impact of Campaign Appearances in the 1996 Election," *Journal of Politics* 64, no. 3 (2002): 912; see also Jones, "Does Bringing," 395.
43. Thomas M. Holbrook and Scott D. McClurg, "The Mobilization of Core Supporters: Campaigns, Turnout, and Electoral Composition in United States Presidential Elections," *American Journal of Political Science* 49, no. 4 (2005): 689, 692.
44. Herr, "Impact," 905; see also Althaus et al., "Candidate Appearances"; Jones, "Does Bringing."
45. Holbrook and McClurg, "Mobilization," 689, 691.
46. Huang and Shaw, "Beyond the Battlegrounds"; Shaw, *Race to 270*.
47. Lanhee J. Chen and Andrew Reeves, "Turning Out the Base or Appealing to the Periphery? An Analysis of County-Level Candidate Appearances in the 2008 Presidential Campaign," *American Politics Research* 39, no. 3 (2011): 534–56; Christopher J. Devine, "Oh, the Places They'll Go: The Geography and Political Strategy of Presidential Campaign Visits in 2016," in *Studies of Communication in the 2016 Presidential Campaign*, ed. Robert E. Denton Jr. (Lanham, MD: Lexington, 2018), 45–68.
48. For example, in Hillary Clinton's 2016 campaign, an "elemental split" over whether to engage in efforts at persuasion "hung over nearly every internal skirmish over strategy and targets—from . . . the development of her message to where she held rallies." Jonathan Allen and Amy Parnes, *Shattered: Inside Hillary Clinton's Doomed Campaign* (New York: Crown, 2017), 398.
49. See, e.g., Chen and Reeves, "Turning out," on Barack Obama's 2008 campaign.
50. Theodore H. White, *The Making of the President 1960* (New York: Atheneum, 1961), 254–55.
51. Shaw and Gimpel, "What If," 142.
52. King and Morehouse, "Moving Voters," 303.
53. See Introduction.
54. Holbrook and McClurg, "Mobilization," 692; see also chapter 1.

55. King and Morehouse, "Moving Voters," 303.
56. Jones, "Does Bringing," 397. Emphasis added.
57. Wood, "What the Heck," 116.
58. Jay Wendland, "Rallying Votes? A Multilevel Approach to Understanding Voter Decision-Making in the 2016 Presidential Nominating Contests," *Journal of Political Marketing* 18, no. 1-2 (2018): 92–118, 8. Emphases added. See also Wendland, *Campaigns That Matter*, 79–80, 143.
59. See Panagopoulos, *Bases Loaded*.
60. Here, I review only studies of campaign visit effects in U.S. presidential elections, during the general election period. This excludes studies of visit effects in non-presidential races (e.g., Shaw and Gimpel, "What If"), presidential primaries (e.g., Lynn Vavreck, Constantine J. Spiliotes, and Linda L. Fowler, "The Effects of Retail Politics in the New Hampshire Primary," *American Journal of Political Science* 46, no. 3 (2002): 595–610; Wendland, *Campaigns That Matter*; Wendland, "Rallying Votes"), and elections outside the U.S. (e.g., Joy Langston and Guillermo Rosas, "Risky Business: Where Do Presidential Campaigns Visit?," *Electoral Studies* 55 (2018): 120–30; Alia Middleton, "The Effectiveness of Leader Visits During the 2010 British General Election Campaign," *British Journal of Politics and International Relations* 17, no. 2 (2015): 244–59). Also, I consider only studies that directly estimate the effects of campaign visits, as distinguished from studies of "campaign events" that typically include some visits but also, if not mostly, other planned and unplanned events that do not meet my definition of "campaign visits" (see chapter 3). For example, Holbrook ("Campaigns, National Conditions," 981) defines campaign events, for the purposes of his analysis, in such a manner as to include scheduled rallies or speeches, the vice-presidential announcement, and "events that 'happen' to campaigns—such as staff shake-ups, accusations about one of the candidates, or a major campaign blunder." See also Daron R. Shaw, "A Study of Presidential Campaign Event Effects from 1952 to 1992," *Journal of Politics* 61, no. 2 (1999): 387–422; Shaw, "Impact of News"). I take no issue with this approach to studying campaign events; I would only distinguish it from studying campaign *visits*, specifically.
61. Boris Heersink and Brenton D. Peterson, "Truman Defeats Dewey: The Effect of Campaign Visits on Election Outcomes," *Electoral Studies* 49 (2017): 49.
62. *Influence*: King and Morehouse, "Moving Voters"; Daron R. Shaw, "The Effect of TV Ads and Candidate Appearances on Statewide Presidential Votes, 1988–96," *American Political Science Review* 93, no. 2 (1999): 345–61. *Do not influence*: Christopher J. Devine, "What If Hillary Clinton *Had* Gone to Wisconsin? Presidential Campaign Visits in the 2016 Election," *Forum* 16, no. 2 (2018): 211–34; Christopher J. Devine and Aaron C. Weinschenk, "Surrogate-in-Chief: Did Bill Clinton's Campaign Visits Help (or Hurt) Hillary Clinton in 2016?," *Forum* 18, no. 2 (2020): 177–95; Holbrook and McClurg, "Mobilization"; Johnston et al., *2000 Presidential Election*.
63. *1948*: Heersink and Peterson, "Truman Defeats Dewey"; Holbrook, "Whistle-Stop." *1980–1988*: Jones, "Does Bringing." *1996*: Herr, "Impact." *2000*: Charles Franklin, "Pre-Election Polls in Nation and State: A Dynamic Bayesian Hierarchical Model," paper

presented at the annual meeting of the American Political Science Association, San Francisco, 2001. *2000–2004*: Shaw, *Race to 270*. *2000–2008*: Jeffrey S. Hill, Elaine Rodriguez, and Amanda E. Wooden, "Stump Speeches and Road Trips: The Impact of State Campaign Appearances in Presidential Elections," *PS: Political Science & Politics* 43, no. 2 (2010): 243–54. *2012*: Wood, "What the Heck." *2008–2016*: James M. Snyder Jr. and Hasin Yousaf, "Making Rallies Great Again: The Effects of Presidential Campaign Rallies on Voter Behavior, 2008–2016," Working paper (2020), www.nber.org/papers/w28043. Many of these studies estimate campaign visit effects in multiple contexts. To keep this summary as straightforward as possible, I characterize each study's findings only in the most general sense. For example, I say that my 2018 study ("What If Hillary") finds no evidence of visit effects in the 2016 election. This is true of the overall effects for each candidate, across states. However, my analysis also indicates that Hillary Clinton's visits had a statistically significant effect on vote choice in one state, Pennsylvania. My description reflects only the former, more general conclusion.

64. Holbrook, "Whistle-Stop"; Heersink and Peterson, "Truman Defeats Dewey."
65. Heersink and Peterson, "Truman Defeats Dewey," 52–53.
66. Herr, "Impact."
67. Snyder and Yousaf, "Making Rallies" (but see Devine, "What If Hillary"); Devine and Weinschenk, "Surrogate-in-Chief."
68. *Good times/bad times*: Herr "Impact," 911. *Partisan asymmetries*: Jones, "Does Bringing," 407 (but see Shaw, "Effect of TV," 357). *Campaign visit imbalances*: Holbrook, "Whistle-Stop," 65 (see also Shaw, "Effect of TV").
69. See Erikson and Wleizen, *Timeline*; Sides and Vavreck, *The Gamble*.
70. Snyder and Yousaf, "Making Rallies," 16.
71. Wood, "What the Heck," 123.
72. Herr, "Impact."
73. Jones, "Does Bringing."
74. Snyder and Yousaf, "Making Rallies," table 8.
75. Heersink and Peterson, "Truman Defeats Dewey."
76. *≤0.5 point*: Herr, "Impact"; Hill et al., "Stump Speeches"; Holbrook, "Whistle-Stop"; Shaw, *Race to 270*. *One point*: Shaw, "Effect of TV." *Three points*: Jones, "Does Bringing."
77. *One point*: Devine, "What If Hillary"; Devine and Weinschenk, "Surrogate-in-Chief"; *Three points*: Heersink and Peterson, "Truman Defeats Dewey."
78. Indeed, Shaw's simulation suggests that a net advantage of three campaign visits across all states would have gained Republicans an average of sixty-four electoral votes and Democrats eighty-seven in the 1988–1996 elections. Shaw, "Effect of TV."
79. The 1948 campaign met each of these conditions: Truman was effective at campaigning, while Dewey was not; Truman made many more campaign visits than Dewey; and the fundamentals dictated a naturally competitive electoral environment. Indeed, both Holbrook and Heersink and Peterson conclude that Truman's visits made the difference in winning the key battleground states of California, Illinois, and

Ohio—and with them, the election. Holbrook, "Whistle-Stop"; Heersink and Peterson, "Truman Defeats Dewey."
80. Wood, "What the Heck," 118.
81. Jones, "Does Bringing."
82. Snyder and Yousaf, "Making Rallies."
83. *Increase*: Damon M. Cann and Jeffrey Bryan Cole, "Strategic Campaigning, Closeness, and Voter Mobilization in U.S. Presidential Elections," *Electoral Studies* 30, no. 2 (2011): 344–52. *Do not increase*: Herr, "Impact"; Holbrook and McClurg, "Mobilization."
84. Wood, "What the Heck," 119.
85. Snyder and Yousaf, "Making Rallies."
86. Snyder and Yousaf, "Making Rallies."
87. Boris Heersink, Brenton D. Peterson, and Jordan Carr Peterson, "Mobilization and Countermobilization: The Effect of Candidate Visits on Campaign Donations in the 2016 Presidential Election," *The Journal of Politics* 83, no. 4 (2021): 1878–83.
88. Holbrook, "Whistle-Stop."
89. Moreover, we should not expect these effects to be uniform across all states or all areas within a given state. Rather, a candidate's visits may be more effective in some geographic areas than in others, perhaps due to more or less personally favorable political conditions. Devine, "What If Hillary"; Devine and Weinschenk, "Surrogate-in-Chief"; Hill et al., "Stump Speeches."
90. Jones ("Does Bringing," 397–98) makes this point well: "[O]ne candidate's visits may successfully mobilize and persuade a bloc of voters, but his or her opponent may also visit and likewise persuade another set of voters. Depending on the size of the group involved, the campaign visit's impact may appear small or negligible in the aggregate, even if the absolute effect is sizable." See also Heersink et al., "Mobilization," 4. Moreover, Shaw and Gimpel provide direct evidence of such an effect in their study of the 2010 Texas gubernatorial campaign. They find that Governor Rick Perry's campaign visits gained him support among Republicans and independents, but this was nearly matched by increased opposition among Democrats. "This countermobilization meant that the net effect of a Perry appearance on voter preferences was oftentimes close to zero." Shaw and Gimpel, "What If," 153.
91. See Holbrook and McClurg, "Mobilization," for a critique.
92. Heersink and Peterson, "Truman Defeats Dewey."
93. Hill et al., "Stump Speeches."
94. Cann and Cole, "Strategic Campaigning."
95. Shaw, "Effect of TV."
96. Shaw, *Race to 270*, 141.
97. Holbrook and McClurg, "Mobilization."
98. Snyder and Yousaf, "Making Rallies."
99. Cann and Cole, "Strategic Campaigning"; Hill et al., "Stump Speeches"; Holbrook and McClurg, "Mobilization"; Jones, "Does Bringing"; Shaw, "Effect of TV"; Shaw, *Race to 270*; Snyder and Yousaf, "Making Rallies."

100. Devine, "What If Hillary"; Devine and Weinschenk, "Surrogate-in-Chief"; Franklin, "Pre-election Polls"; Heersink and Peterson, "Truman Defeats Dewey"; Heersink et al., "Mobilization"; Herr, "Impact"; Holbrook, "Whistle-Stop"; Johnston et al., *2000 Presidential Election*; King and Morehouse, "Moving Voters"; Wood, "What the Heck." Shaw and Gimpel, in a somewhat different context, cite this as one of their concerns about the existing literature. They note: "Much of what we know of campaign effects comes from analyses of one or two presidential elections. This raises obvious questions about generalizability." Shaw and Gimpel, "What If," 139.
101. Shaw, *Race to 270*, 11–12.
102. Panagopoulos, *Bases Loaded*.
103. Shaw, *Race to 270*, 39.
104. Shaw, *Race to 270*, 23–24.
105. Wood, "What the Heck," 124.
106. Althaus et al., "Candidate Appearances," 70.
107. Shaw and Gimpel, "What If," 138.
108. Alan I. Abramowitz and Costas Panagopoulos, "Trump on the Trail: Assessing the Impact of Presidential Campaign Visits on Voting Behavior in the 2018 Midterm Elections," *Presidential Studies Quarterly* 50, no. 3 (2020): 504.
109. Joshua P. Darr, "In 2020, the Ground Game is All Trump," *Mischiefs of Faction*, October 9, 2020, www.mischiefsoffaction.com/post/2020-ground-game.
110. Johnston et al., *2000 Presidential Election*; Snyder and Yousaf, "Making Rallies"; Wood, "What the Heck."
111. Snyder and Yousaf, "Making Rallies."
112. See, e.g., Chen and Reeves, "Turning out"; Devine, "Oh, the Places."

3. PRESIDENTIAL CAMPAIGN VISITS, BY THE NUMBERS

1. The dataset is available for download at christopherjdevine.com/data.html.
2. Josh Dawsey and Colby Itkowitz, "Trump Says He and First Lady Have Tested Positive for the Coronavirus," *Washington Post*, October 2, 2020, www.washingtonpost.com/politics/hope-hicks-close-trump-aide-tests-positive-for-coronavirus/2020/10/01/af238f7c-0444-11eb-897d-3a6201d6643f_story.html.
3. Caitlin Oprysko and Gabby Orr, "Trump Campaign Says In-Person Events Will Be Made Virtual or Postponed," *Politico*, October 2, 2020, www.politico.com/news/2020/10/02/bill-stepien-trump-campaign-staffers-quarantine-425165.
4. Nancy Cook, "Trump's 2020 Cure-All: Rallies, Rallies and More Rallies," *Politico*, October 21, 2020, www.politico.com/news/2020/10/21/trumps-2020-cure-all-rallies-430552.
5. Dawsey and Itkowitz, "Trump Says."
6. Colin Kinniburgh, "In Pennsylvania, Trump Fans Cheer His 'Excellent Choice' for the Supreme Court," *France24*, September 27, 2020, www.france24.com/en/20200927

-in-pennsylvania-trump-fans-cheer-his-excellent-choice-for-the-supreme-court; Michael D. Shear and Michael Crowley, "In Critical Swing State, Trump Again Stokes Doubt on Election Process," *New York Times*, September 26, 2020, www.nytimes.com /2020/09/26/us/politics/trump-rally-middletown-pa.html; Candy Woodall, "Trump Rally in Middletown, Pa.: Takeaways After the President Nominates Amy Coney Barrett," *York Daily Record*, September 26, 2020, www.ydr.com/story/news/politics /elections/2020/09/26/trump-holds-rally-middletown-pa-after-naming-supreme -court-pick/3529047001.

7. Sabrina Eaton, "Trump Shows Off Lordstown Motors Pickup Truck at White House on the Eve of Cleveland Presidential Debate," Cleveland.com, September 28, 2020, www.cleveland.com/open/2020/09/trump-shows-off-lordstown-motors-pickup-truck -at-white-house-on-the-eve-of-cleveland-presidential-debate.html.
8. Dawsey and Itkowitz, "Trump Says."
9. CBS News, "Trump Rallies Supporters in Minnesota," CBS News, September 30, 2020, www.cbsnews.com/news/watch-live-stream-trump-rallies-supporters-in-minnesota -today-09-30-2020; Patrick Condon, "Guest Says Minn. Fundraiser with Trump 'Very Safely Done,'" *Star Tribune*, October 3, 2020, www.startribune.com/trump-s-minn -fundraiser-was-very-safely-done-guest-says/572626631.
10. CBS News, "Trump Rallies"; Nancy Cook and Matthew Choi, "Trump Basks in Cheers of Minnesota Rally, Far from Debate Criticism," *Politico*, September 30, 2020, www .politico.com/news/2020/09/30/trump-debate-minnesota-rally-424308; Dan Kraker and Brian Bakst, "Trump Rakes in Money, Stirs up Supporters in Minnesota Trip," MPR News, September 30, 2020, www.mprnews.org/story/2020/09/30/trump-returns -to-minnesota-for-postdebate-rally-fundraiser.
11. Carol Leonnig and Philip Rucker, *I Alone Can Fix It: Donald J. Trump's Catastrophic Final Year* (New York: Penguin Press, 2021).
12. Dawsey and Itkowitz, "Trump Says"; Paul P. Murphy, "Trump Took Photos, Had Roundtable with Donors at Bedminster Fundraiser Hours before Announcing Covid Diagnosis," CNN, October 4, 2020, www.cnn.com/2020/10/03/politics/bedminister -trump-fundraiser-coronavirus/index.html; Olivia Rubin, Matthew Mosk, Soo Rin Kim, and Will Steakin, "Day After Seeing Trump at Bedminster Fundraiser, Guests 'Flabbergasted' to Learn He Was Stricken," ABC News, October 3, 2020, abcnews.go .com/Politics/day-trump-bedminster-fundraiser-guests-flabbergasted-learn -stricken/story?id=73394174; Riley Yates, "As Many as 300 Attended Trump Fundraiser at Bedminster, Attendee Says," NJ.com, October 2, 2020, www.nj.com /coronavirus/2020/10/as-many-as-300-attended-trump-fundraiser-at-bedminster -attendee-says.html.
13. Dawsey and Itkowitz, "Trump Says"; Leonnig and Rucker, *I Alone*.
14. Daron R. Shaw, "A Study of Presidential Campaign Event Effects from 1952 to 1992," *The Journal of Politics* 61, no. 2 (1999): 390; see also Thomas M. Holbrook, "Campaigns, National Conditions, and U.S. Presidential Elections," *American Journal of Political Science* 38, no. 4 (1994): 973–98; Daron R. Shaw and Brian E. Roberts, "Campaign

Events, the Media and the Prospects of Victory: The 1992 and 1996 US Presidential Elections," *British Journal of Political Science* 30, no. 2 (2000): 259–89.

15. Take presidential debates, for example. While both campaigns, working with the Commission on Presidential Debates, participate in a planning process that includes selecting a host city and venue, this is a collective decision and thus not comparable to other, more traditional "campaign visits" in which the candidates and their campaign staff independently decide where to allocate their time. Also, while the debates should be especially salient to voters in and around the host city, they attract a great deal of attention nationwide; thus, their effects are likely to be general rather than localized. Finally, because both candidates participate in debates, there is no reason to expect that one candidate would make greater gains locally from such an event than the other; essentially, they should cancel out.

16. Visits to campaign offices—which *are* included in my data—might seem analogous, in that candidates do not go there to win votes in any direct sense; presumably, anyone volunteering their time to work on a campaign is already planning to vote for that candidate. However, these visits are distinguishable from fundraisers on the points raised above. Whatever effect visits to campaign offices might have on volunteers— to encourage them to volunteer more and recruit others, one would assume—should have indirect effects on the local community. That is to say, volunteers are not dispersing across the country like campaign funds; typically they live and volunteer in their local community. Also, visits to campaign offices are usually covered by local media. Thus, it is quite reasonable to think that, unlike fundraisers, visits to campaign offices might have indirect effects on a localized concentration of voters, via increased volunteer activity and media coverage.

17. "Clinton Makes Surprise Visits to UNCG, NC A&T Homecoming," Fox8, October 27, 2016, myfox8.com/news/you-decide-2016/clinton-makes-surprise-visits-to-uncg-nc-at-homecoming.

18. *Advance announcement*: Charles Franklin, "Pre-Election Polls in Nation and State: A Dynamic Bayesian Hierarchical Model," Paper presented at the annual meeting of the American Political Science Association, San Francisco, 2001, 5. *Campaign itineraries*: See, e.g., J. Paul Herr, "The Impact of Campaign Appearances in the 1996 Election," *Journal of Politics* 64, no. 3 (2002): 904–13. *Online resources*: See, e.g., "94% of 2016 Presidential Campaign Was in Just 12 Closely Divided States," National Popular Vote, accessed January 25, 2023, www.nationalpopularvote.com/campaign-events-2016. FairVote's definition of campaign visits does not explicitly exclude unannounced events, as described above, but such visits are not included in its dataset.

19. Jay Wendland, *Campaigns That Matter: The Importance of Campaign Visits in Presidential Nominating Contests* (Lanham, MD: Lexington, 2017), 137.

20. Scott L. Althaus, Peter F. Nardulli, and Daron R. Shaw, "Candidate Appearances in Presidential Elections, 1972–2000," *Political Communication* 19, no. 1 (2002): 53.

21. See, e.g., Boris Heersink and Brenton D. Peterson, "Truman Defeats Dewey: The Effect of Campaign Visits on Election Outcomes," *Electoral Studies* 49 (2017): 49–64; Thomas

Wood, "What the Heck Are We Doing in Ottumwa, Anyway? Presidential Candidate Visits and Their Political Consequence," *Annals of the American Academy of Political and Social Science* 667, no. 1 (2016): 110–25.

22. For studies, see, e.g., James M. Snyder Jr. and Hasin Yousaf, "Making Rallies Great Again: The Effects of Presidential Campaign Rallies on Voter Behavior, 2008–2016," Working paper (2020), www.nber.org/papers/w28043; Wood, "What the Heck." "Candidate Travels—Rationale, Methodology and Limitations," Democracy in Action, accessed January 25, 2023, www.democracyinaction.us/2020/chrnfall/candidatetravels.html.

23. Jay Wendland, "Rallying Votes? A Multilevel Approach to Understanding Voter Decision-Making in the 2016 Presidential Nominating Contests," *Journal of Political Marketing* 18, no. 1–2 (2018): 7; Boris Heersink, Brenton D. Peterson, and Jordan Carr Peterson, "Mobilization and Countermobilization: The Effect of Candidate Visits on Campaign Donations in the 2016 Presidential Election," *Journal of Politics* 83, no. 4 (2021): 6.

24. Steven J. Brams and Morton D. Davis, "The 3/2's Rule in Presidential Campaigning," *American Political Science Review* 68, no. 1 (1974): 124; see also Althaus et al., "Candidate Appearances," 56.

25. See also Christopher J. Devine, "What If Hillary Clinton *Had* Gone to Wisconsin? Presidential Campaign Visits in the 2016 Election," *Forum* 16, no. 2 (2018): 211–34; Christopher J. Devine, "Oh, the Places They'll Go: The Geography and Political Strategy of Presidential Campaign Visits in 2016," in *Studies of Communication in the 2016 Presidential Campaign*, ed. Robert E. Denton Jr., 45–68 (Lanham, MD: Lexington, 2018); Christopher J. Devine, "Voter Mobilization 101: Presidential Campaign Visits to Colleges and Universities in the 2016 Election," *PS: Political Science & Politics* 52, no. 2 (2019): 261–66; Christopher J. Devine and Kyle C. Kopko, "Split Tickets? On the Strategic Allocation of Presidential versus Vice Presidential Campaign Visits in 2016," *SAGE Open* July–September (2018): 1–12; Christopher J. Devine and Aaron C. Weinschenk, "Surrogate-in-Chief: Did Bill Clinton's Campaign Visits Help (or Hurt) Hillary Clinton in 2016?," *Forum* 18, no. 2 (2020): 177–95.

26. "President Obama and Vice President Biden Campaign Rally in Dayton, Ohio," C-SPAN, October 23, 2012, accessed December 10, 2022, www.c-span.org/video/?308993-1/president-obama-vice-president-biden-campaign-rally-dayton-ohio#!

27. Andrew Kurtz, "Biden Continues Ohio Campaign on UT Campus," UT:10 News, October 24, 2012, accessed December 10, 2022, www.ut10news.com/election-2012.html; "VP Joe Biden Speaks at UT," WTOL, October 18, 2012, accessed December 10, 2022, www.wtol.com/amp/article/news/vp-joe-biden-speaks-at-ut/512-a415a115-6a33-47ca-baef-ff497dccffee.

28. "Biden Makes Stop at Schmucker's Restaurant," *The Blade*, October 23, 2012, accessed December 10, 2022, www.toledoblade.com/local/2012/10/23/Biden-makes-stop-at-Schmucker-s-Restaurant/stories/20121023136; Hunter Walker, "Joe Biden Gets a Side Order of Negativity on His Lunch Break," *Observer*, October 23, 2012, accessed

December 10, 2022, observer.com/2012/10/joe-biden-spends-lunch-break-with-man-who-tells-him-to-prepare-to-lose.

29. Jennifer Bendery, "Joe Biden Makes Surprise Stop At Ohio Campaign Office, Women Swoon," *HuffPost*, October 24, 2012, accessed December 10, 2022, www.huffpost.com/entry/joe-biden-ohio-campaign-office-women-swoon_n_2007603; Donovan Slack, "Biden: 'I'm a Pizza Guy!'" *Politico*, October 23, 2012, accessed December 10, 2022, www.politico.com/blogs/politico44/2012/10/biden-im-a-pizza-guy-139410.

30. Damon M. Cann and Jeffrey Bryan Cole, "Strategic Campaigning, Closeness, and Voter Mobilization in U.S. Presidential Elections," *Electoral Studies* 30, no. 2 (2011): 344–52; Heersink and Peterson, "Truman Defeats Dewey"; Herr, "Impact of Campaign"; Thomas M. Holbrook, "Did the Whistle-Stop Campaign Matter?," *PS: Political Science and Politics* 35, no. 1 (2002): 59–66; Thomas M. Holbrook and Scott D. McClurg, "The Mobilization of Core Supporters: Campaigns, Turnout, and Electoral Composition in United States Presidential Elections," *American Journal of Political Science* 49, no. 4 (2005): 689–703; Jeffrey M. Jones, "Does Bringing Out the Candidate Bring Out the Votes? The Effects of Nominee Campaigning in Presidential Elections," *American Politics Quarterly* 26, no. 4 (1998): 395–419; Daron R. Shaw, "The Effect of TV Ads and Candidate Appearances on Statewide Presidential Votes, 1988–96," *American Political Science Review* 93, no. 2 (1999): 345–61; Snyder and Yousaf, "Making Rallies Great"; see also Althaus et al., "Candidate Appearances," for the 1972–1996 elections.

31. *By party*: Brams and Davis, "The 3/2's Rule"; Lanhee J. Chen and Andrew Reeves, "Turning Out the Base or Appealing to the Periphery? An Analysis of County-Level Candidate Appearances in the 2008 Presidential Campaign," *American Politics Research* 39, no. 3 (2011): 534–56; Devine, "Oh, the Places"; Franklin, "Pre-Election Polls"; Taofang Huang and Daron R. Shaw, "Beyond the Battlegrounds? Electoral College Strategies in the 2008 Presidential Election," *Journal of Political Marketing* 8, no. 4 (2009): 272–91; Richard Johnston, Michael G. Hagen, and Kathleen Hall Jamieson, *The 2000 Presidential Election and the Foundations of Party Politics* (Cambridge: Cambridge University Press, 2004); Wood, "What the Heck"; see also, Althaus et al., "Candidate Appearances," for the 2000 election. *By candidate*: Devine, "What If Hillary"; Devine and Kopko, "Split Tickets?"; Heersink et al., "Mobilization and Countermobilization"; Jeffrey S. Hill, Elaine Rodriguez, and Amanda E. Wooden, "Stump Speeches and Road Trips: The Impact of State Campaign Appearances in Presidential Elections," *PS: Political Science & Politics* 43, no. 2 (2010): 243–54; Daron R. Shaw, *The Race to 270: The Electoral College and the Campaign Strategies of 2000 and 2004* (Chicago: University of Chicago Press, 2006); Darrell M. West, "Constituencies and Travel Allocations in the 1980 Presidential Campaign," *American Journal of Political Science* 27, no. 3 (1983): 515–29.

32. *Spouses only*: Susan A. MacManus and Andrew F. Quecan, "Spouses as Campaign Surrogates: Strategic Appearances by Presidential and Vice Presidential Candidates' Wives in the 2004 Election," *PS: Political Science & Politics* 41, no. 2 (2008): 337–48. Spouses and candidates: Devine and Weinschenk, "Surrogate-in-Chief."

33. Christopher J. Devine and Kyle C. Kopko, *Do Running Mates Matter? The Influence of Vice Presidential Candidates in Presidential Elections* (Lawrence: University Press of Kansas, 2020).
34. Shaw, *Race to 270*; Hill et al., "Stump Speeches."
35. Heersink et al., "Mobilization and Countermobilization."
36. Devine, "What If Hillary."
37. Devine and Kopko, *Do Running Mates Matter?*
38. Steve Gorman, "Palin-Biden Debate Sets TV Ratings Record," Reuters, October 3, 2008, accessed December 10, 2022, www.reuters.com/article/us-usa-politics-ratings/palin-biden-debate-sets-tv-ratings-record-idUSTRE4927XF20081004.
39. Jones, "Does Bringing"; Daron R. Shaw, "The Impact of News Media Favorability and Candidate Events in Presidential Campaigns," *Political Communication* 16, no. 2 (1999): 183–202; Wendland, *Campaigns That Matter*.
40. Jones, "Does Bringing," 401.
41. Shaw, *Race to 270*, 77.
42. See, e.g., Althaus et al., "Candidate Appearances"; Herr, "Impact of Campaign"; Holbrook, "Did the Whistle-Stop"; Shaw, *Race to 270*; Jay Wendland, "Rallying Votes? A Multilevel Approach to Understanding Voter Decision-Making in the 2016 Presidential Nominating Contests," *Journal of Political Marketing* 18, no. 1–2 (2018): 92–118; West, "Constituencies and Travel."
43. Shaw, *Race to 270*, 77.
44. West, "Constituencies and Travel," 519.
45. Maria Gavrilovic, "Obama's Philadelphia Campaign Blitz," CBS News, October 11, 2008, www.cbsnews.com/news/obamas-philadelphia-campaign-blitz.
46. *September 1*: Althaus et al., "Candidate Appearances"; Steven J. Brams and Morton D. Davis, "The 3/2's Rule in Presidential Campaigning," *American Political Science Review* 68, no. 1 (1974): 113–34; Shaw, "Effect of TV Ads"; West, "Constituencies and Travel." *After September 1*: Chen and Reeves, "Turning out the Base"; Holbrook, "Whistle-Stop"; Johnston et al., *2000 Presidential Election*; Shaw, *Race to 270*; Wood, "What the Heck."
47. Shaw, "Effect of TV Ads," 349.
48. See, e.g., Devine, "What If Hillary."
49. Althaus et al., "Candidate Appearances," 55.
50. Amy Gwaltney, "Palin Speaks in Salem Monday," *The Breeze*, October 30, 2008, www.breezejmu.org/palin-speaks-in-salem-monday/article_dadca26f-3b70-5d26-9c40-2244f42754f6.html.
51. Some cases were more difficult because the visit took place at a specific location within a larger complex that contains multiple addresses. For example, Palin's visit to Salem, Virginia, referenced above, took place at Salem High School's football stadium, called Salem Stadium. Searching for "Salem High School" versus "Salem Stadium" yields two different addresses. I always use the most specific address available (e.g., for Salem Stadium). This issue comes up most often for visits held at universities—usually sprawling sites with many different buildings and outdoor spaces—or airports, where

visits usually take place at one of the various on-site hangars. In those cases where I cannot determine a more specific location, I use the complex's main address.

52. "8:15 a.m.—A Very Presidential Saturday," *Albuquerque Journal*, October 24, 2008, www.abqjournal.com/21632/815 a.m.-a-very-presidential-saturday.html.
53. Accounting for differences in election dates does not change this rank ordering; on average, Obama and Palin (2008) made 1.8 visits per day, McCain (2008) and Trump (2016), 1.7.
54. In fairness, Harris was quite active in other ways that fall, including doing many virtual "visits" and fundraisers.
55. I do not do the same for vice-presidential candidates, in the interest of space.
56. Trump's days spent off the campaign trail due to COVID-19 are not relevant here; the numerator is the candidate's total number of campaign visits and the denominator is the number of days on which he or she made a campaign visit.
57. John McCain and Mark Salter, *The Restless Wave: Good Times, Just Causes, Great Fights, and Other Appreciations* (New York: Simon & Schuster, 2018).
58. Devine, "Voter Mobilization 101." West's 1983 analysis is very similar, but not quite the same, in that he analyzes the type of audience, or constituencies (e.g., Republican, Black, Catholic, agricultural, college student), for primary and general election campaign visits in 1980. He finds that most visits were targeted toward a general audience, but when specific groups were targeted, it was most likely to be partisans, college students, or businesspeople. Also, Susan A. MacManus and Andrew F. Quecan ("Spouses as Campaign Surrogates: Strategic Appearances by Presidential and Vice Presidential Candidates' Wives in the 2004 Election," *PS: Political Science & Politics* 41, no. 2 [2008]: 337–48) classify the types of events and audiences for campaign visits by the 2004 presidential and vice-presidential candidates' spouses. Again, they find that most visits were targeted toward a general audience, followed by partisan and college audiences.
59. Devine, "Voter Mobilization 101," 263; West, "Constituencies and Travel," 520.
60. I also count within this category most visits that take place outside of a building or facility that would otherwise qualify for a different category. For instance, many events take place just outside of a government facility such as a city hall or state capitol. I count this as a "Public Space." But if the event were held inside that building, I would count it as a "Government Facility." These are difficult cases, but, building on a point from above, my goal is to capture the environment in which the host site is embedded. Speaking outside of a place of business is different, in this respect. In some cases, candidates speak from the stairs or a sidewalk just outside of a place of business—for example, in the present data, at the Cheesecake Factory or a famous restaurant and hotel owned by U.S. Senator Rob Portman's family in Lebanon, Ohio, called the Golden Lamb. See, for example, Mayhill Fowler, "Palin (and McCain) Say Little and Fire up Faithful in Ohio," *HuffPost*, October 11, 2008, www.huffpost.com/entry/palin-and-mccain-fire-up_b_125282. While much of the crowd for these events fills a public space nearby (e.g., street, town square), the candidates are clearly speaking from this spot with the permission of the business owner(s)—indeed, Portman

spoke at both events in the dataset held at the Golden Lamb—and thus associating themselves with that business, quite possibly to communicate a message to voters about their support for the specific establishment or businesses generally. Another example is the one I mention earlier, about Joe Biden speaking outside his campaign office in Fort Lauderdale, Florida; I assume the choice of a campaign office isn't random and may have been intended to reward and energize volunteers. Classifying this venue as a public space ignores that context, which would have been apparent to those in attendance or observing the associated media coverage.

61. It is to be expected that these percentages would differ from my 2019 article, as here I use a different time frame for analysis.

4. WHERE DO THE CANDIDATES GO—AND WHY?

1. But see David C. King and David Morehouse, "Moving Voters in the 2000 Presidential Campaign: Local Visits, Local Media," in *Lights, Camera, Campaign! Media, Politics, and Political Advertising*, ed. David A. Schultz (New York: Peter Lang, 2004), 301–17; Daron R. Shaw, *The Race to 270: The Electoral College and the Campaign Strategies of 2000 and 2004* (Chicago: University of Chicago Press, 2006); Thomas Wood, "What the Heck Are We Doing in Ottumwa, Anyway? Presidential Candidate Visits and Their Political Consequence," *Annals of the American Academy of Political and Social Science* 667, no. 1 (2016): 110–25.

2. As Shaw, who worked on two presidential campaigns, states: "[D]escribing the distribution of resources"—specifically, campaign ads and visits—"is critical to assessing campaign strategies and, ultimately, shifts in voters' preferences." Shaw, *Race to 270*, 72; see also Scott L. Althaus, Peter F. Nardulli, and Daron R. Shaw, "Candidate Appearances in Presidential Elections, 1972–2000," *Political Communication* 19, no. 1 (2002): 50; Lanhee J. Chen and Andrew Reeves, "Turning Out the Base or Appealing to the Periphery? An Analysis of County-Level Candidate Appearances in the 2008 Presidential Campaign," *American Politics Research* 39, no. 3 (2011): 549.

3. See, e.g., King and Morehouse, "Moving Voters," 303; Shaw, *Race to 270*, 102.

4. Taofang Huang and Daron R. Shaw, "Beyond the Battlegrounds? Electoral College Strategies in the 2008 Presidential Election," *Journal of Political Marketing* 8, no. 4 (2009): 277. The scholarly consensus on this point is striking, given the range of resources available to campaigns and the uncertain effects of campaign visits. For example: "No resource in a presidential campaign is more valuable than the candidate's time" (Chen and Reeves, "Turning Out," 539); "A candidate's time is the most precious commodity in presidential campaigns" (King and Morehouse, "Moving Voters," 302); and "Many textbooks and primers state that the candidate's time is the most valuable resource to a campaign" (Daron R. Shaw and James G. Gimpel, "What If We Randomize the Governor's Schedule? Evidence on Campaign Appearance Effects from a Texas Field Experiment," *Political Communication* 29, no. 2 [2012]: 137).

5. Dick Cheney with Liz Cheney, *In My Time: A Personal and Political Memoir* (New York: Threshold Editions, 2011), 285; Institute of Politics, *Campaign for President: The Managers Look at 2004* (Lanham, MD: Rowman & Littlefield, 2006).
6. Christopher J. Devine and Kyle C. Kopko, "Split Tickets? On the Strategic Allocation of Presidential versus Vice Presidential Campaign Visits in 2016," *SAGE Open* July–September 2018: 2.
7. Steven J. Brams and Morton D. Davis, "The 3/2's Rule in Presidential Campaigning," *American Political Science Review* 68, no. 1 (1974): 124.
8. Darrell M. West, "Constituencies and Travel Allocations in the 1980 Presidential Campaign," *American Journal of Political Science* 27, no. 3 (1983): 517.
9. Christopher Galdieri captures the point well: "Candidate time is a zero-sum commodity: Any time spent on a safe state is time not spent in Florida or Pennsylvania or New Hampshire or an emerging swing state." Christopher J. Galdieri, *Donald Trump and New Hampshire Politics* (Cham, Switzerland: Palgrave Macmillan, 2020), 59.
10. "Address Accepting the Presidential Nomination at the Republican National Convention in Chicago," American Presidency Project, accessed December 10, 2022, www.presidency.ucsb.edu/documents/address-accepting-the-presidential-nomination-the-republican-national-convention-chicago.
11. The Twenty-Third Amendment also gives Washington, DC, three electoral votes.
12. Huang and Shaw, "Beyond the Battlegrounds?"; Shaw, *Race to 270*.
13. Huang and Shaw, "Beyond the Battlegrounds?"
14. Brams and Davis, "3/2's Rule."
15. Althaus et al., "Candidate Appearances," 59.
16. Benjamin Oestericher, "America's Winner-Take-All System Gives Attention to the Few at the Expense of the Many," FairVote, October 14, 2020, www.fairvote.org/america_s_winner_take_all_system_gives_attention_to_the_few_at_the_expense_of_the_many.
17. George C. Edwards III, *Why the Electoral College Is Bad for America* (New Haven, CT: Yale University Press, 2004), 107. Emphasis added.
18. Jimmy Carter's campaign manager, Hamilton Jordan, provided a stark illustration of this strategy. In an August 1976 memo, Jordan outlined a point system to determine, in systematic fashion, where the campaign should invest its resources and, in terms of campaign visits, which candidate or surrogate should travel to a given state and for how long. Jordan's formula for deciding where to allocate resources included three weighted variables: "the *size* of the state" (50 percent); "the *Democratic potential* of a state" (25 percent); and "the *need* we have to mount an effective campaign" (25 percent). This system explicitly considered electoral votes *and* competitiveness when deciding how to allocate campaign resources, but assigned twice as much weight to the former. Martin Schram, *Running for President 1976: The Carter Campaign* (New York: Stein and Day, 1977), 246.
19. See Thomas M. Holbrook, "Did the Whistle-Stop Campaign Matter?," *PS: Political Science and Politics* 35, no. 1 (2002): 59–66.

20. Marty Cohen, David Karol, Hans Noel, and John Zaller, *The Party Decides: Presidential Nominations Before and After Reform* (Chicago: University of Chicago Press, 2008), 6.
21. See, for example, Marjorie Randon Hershey, *Party Politics in America*, 17th ed. (New York: Routledge, 2017), 157–58.
22. Angus Campbell, Philip E. Converse, Warren E. Miller, and Donald E. Stokes, *The American Voter* (Chicago: University of Chicago Press, 1960); Michael S. Lewis-Beck, William G. Jacoby, Helmut Norpoth, and Herbert F. Weisberg, *The American Voter Revisited* (Ann Arbor: University of Michigan Press, 2008); Lilliana Mason, *Uncivil Agreement: How Politics Became Our Identity* (Chicago: University of Chicago Press, 2018).
23. Trump visited all three states in 2016, even though they had not voted for a Republican presidential candidate since at least the 1980s. Clinton visited Michigan only four times from September 1 to Election Day, and never visited Minnesota or Wisconsin.
24. *Hardball with Chris Matthews*, Transcript 11/6/2016, MSNBC, accessed December 10, 2022, www.msnbc.com/transcripts/hardball/2016-11-06-msna924066.
25. Damon M. Cann and Jeffrey Bryan Cole, "Strategic Campaigning, Closeness, and Voter Mobilization in U.S. Presidential Elections," *Electoral Studies* 30, no. 2 (2011): 346.
26. Huang and Shaw, "Beyond the Battlegrounds?"
27. Chen and Reeves, "Turning out," 535.
28. Jonathan Allen and Amy Parnes, *Shattered: Inside Hillary Clinton's Doomed Campaign* (New York: Crown, 2017), 245, 312.
29. Allen and Parnes, *Shattered*, 238.
30. 1960: Theodore H. White, *The Making of the President 1960* (New York: Atheneum, 1961), 272. 1976: Schram, *Running for President*, 247. 2000: Shaw, *Race to 270*, 159.
31. Shaw, *Race to 270*, 69.
32. Julia R. Azari, *Delivering the People's Message: The Changing Politics of the Presidential Mandate* (Ithaca, NY: Cornell University Press, 2014).
33. Bill Clinton, *My Life* (New York: Alfred A. Knopf, 2004), 731–32.
34. Larry M. Bartels, "Resource Allocation in a Presidential Campaign," *Journal of Politics* 47, no. 3 (1985): 932.
35. Here, I am using the number of electoral votes from the 2012–2020 elections, apportioned in accordance with the 2010 U.S. Census. Some states had slightly fewer or more electoral votes in the 2008 election. To account for this in the accompanying text would confuse more than clarify, since it does not change the relevant substantive conclusions.
36. A plausible explanation for this disparity is that candidates campaign more widely in open-seat elections, such as in 2008 and 2016, exploring the possibility of new electoral coalitions, and narrow their focus when an incumbent is running for reelection, as in 2012 and 2020.
37. The presidential and vice-presidential candidates visited 306 counties from 2008 to 2020, or about 10 percent of all U.S. counties. They visited 185 counties in 2008

(5.9 percent), 156 in 2012 (5.0 percent), 158 in 2016 (5.0 percent), and 109 in 2020 (3.5 percent).
38. Chen and Reeves, "Turning out"; Christopher J. Devine, "What If Hillary Clinton *Had* Gone to Wisconsin? Presidential Campaign Visits in the 2016 Election," *Forum* 16, no. 2 (2018): 211–34.
39. Shaw, *Race to 270*; Huang and Shaw, "Beyond the Battlegrounds?"
40. Schram, *Running for President*, 247–48.
41. Shaw, *Race to 270*, 105.
42. Devine and Kopko, "Split Tickets?"
43. The exception is the 2020 Democratic ticket: Joe Biden and Kamala Harris's state-level visits correlate at 0.69, which is still high.
44. Negative binomial regression is most appropriate for this analysis, given concerns about overdispersion in the data. See Jay Wendland, *Campaigns That Matter: The Importance of Campaign Visits in Presidential Nominating Contests* (Lanham, MD: Lexington, 2017), 57. Similar studies use Poisson regression models: Chen and Reeves, "Turning out"; Christopher J. Devine, "Oh, the Places They'll Go: The Geography and Political Strategy of Presidential Campaign Visits in 2016," in *Studies of Communication in the 2016 Presidential Campaign*, ed. Robert E. Denton Jr. (Lanham, MD: Lexington, 2018), 45–68. However, Chen and Reeves also ran a negative binomial regression model and found similar results (see their footnote 16).
45. For the purposes of this analysis, I define battleground states as those that hosted five or more campaign visits in total in a given election year. Previous studies use similar standards. Specifically, Chen and Reeves restrict their analysis to battleground states, as defined by the *New York Times* and RealClearPolitics.com, while I restrict my analysis to states that attracted ten or more campaign visits in 2016. Chen and Reeves, "Turning out"; Devine, "Oh, the Places." As Langston and Rosas explain: "[I]ncluding *all* non-visited [units of analysis] would swamp our dataset with an inordinate number of zeroes that would likely bias our estimates downward." Joy Langston and Guillermo Rosas, "Risky Business: Where Do Presidential Campaigns Visit?," *Electoral Studies* 55 (2018): 124.
46. County-level vote totals come from the MIT Election Data and Science Lab, "County Presidential Election Returns 2000–2020," doi.org/10.7910/DVN/VOQCHQ, Harvard Dataverse, V10; countypres_2000-2020.tab [fileName], UNF:6:pVAMya52q7VM1Pl7EZMWoQ== [fileUNF], 2018.
47. Census data for median age, income per household, and college graduate percentage, in 2008 to 2020, as well as Black and Latino percentages in 2020, were obtained from the Federal Reserve Bank of St. Louis's GeoFRED website (geofred.stlouisfed.org/map, accessed June 1, 2022). Black and Latino percentages for 2008 (www.census.gov/data/datasets/time-series/demo/popest/intercensal-2000-2010-counties.html), 2012, and 2016 (www.census.gov/data/tables/time-series/demo/popest/2010s-counties-detail.html), were derived from state-level population estimates made available on the Census Bureau website. Specifically, I calculated each percentage as follows: 100 × (number of persons per state identifying as Black or Latino ÷ number of persons per state). Population growth was also calculated based on state-level population

estimates made available on the Census Bureau website, for 2008 (www.census.gov/data/datasets/time-series/demo/popest/intercensal-2000-2010-counties.html), 2012, 2016 (www.census.gov/data/tables/time-series/demo/popest/2010s-counties-detail.html), and 2020 (www.census.gov/programs-surveys/popest/technical-documentation/research/evaluation-estimates/2020-evaluation-estimates/2010s-counties-total.html). Specifically, I calculated population growth as follows: 100 × ((Population$_T$ − Population$_{T-1}$) ÷ Population$_{T-1}$). Data on square miles per county were obtained from Sage's Data Planet (dataplanet.sagepub.com, accessed June 1, 2022).

48. Campaign advertising data for 2008 come from Kenneth Goldstein, Sarah Niebler, Jacob Neiheisel, and Matthew Holleque, "Presidential, Congressional, and Gubernatorial Advertising, 2008," Combined File [dataset], initial release, Madison: University of Wisconsin Advertising Project, Department of Political Science at the University of Wisconsin–Madison, 2011. The 2016 and 2020 data were obtained from Dropbox files linked to Wesleyan Media Project's figure 3 and table 4, respectively. The 2012 data were obtained from the *Washington Post* and based on research by Kantar Media/CMAG. "Mad Money: TV Ads in the 2012 Presidential Campaign," *Washington Post*, November 14, 2012, www.washingtonpost.com/wp-srv/special/politics/track-presidential-campaign-ads-2012. In each case, the data include all ads sponsored by the presidential campaigns or their supporters (e.g., national parties, political action committees).

49. Clustering is appropriate because counties within the same media market are exposed to the same campaign advertisements, as well as local coverage of campaign visits, and therefore cannot be treated as independent observations. See Devine, "What If Hillary"; Shaw and Gimpel, "What If We"; John Sides, Lynn Vavreck, and Christopher Warshaw, "The Effect of Television Advertising in United States Elections," *American Political Science Review* 116, no. 2 (2022): 702–18; James M. Snyder Jr. and Hasin Yousaf, "Making Rallies Great Again: The Effects of Presidential Campaign Rallies on Voter Behavior, 2008–2016," Working paper (2020), www.nber.org/papers/w28043. The vast majority of counties are associated with one media market and only rarely change markets from one year to the next. Media market designations, for this study, are based on maps produced by Jorg L. Spenkuch and David Toniatti, "Political Advertising and Election Results: Appendix Materials," 2018, for 2008, and Nielsen for the closest available year to the 2012 (www.iamanedgecutter.com/resources/DMA_Maps/2013_Nielsen_DMA_Geographical.pdf), 2016 (www.iamanedgecutter.com/resources/DMA_Maps/2016_Nielsen_DMA_Geographical.pdf), and 2020 (thevab.com/storage/app/media/Toolkit/DMA_Map_2019.pdf) elections.

50. Chen and Reeves, "Turning out."

5. WHAT DIFFERENCE DO CAMPAIGN VISITS MAKE?

1. See Daron R. Shaw and James G. Gimpel, "What If We Randomize the Governor's Schedule? Evidence on Campaign Appearance Effects from a Texas Field Experiment," *Political Communication* 29, no. 2 (2012): 137–59.

2. This logic is consistent with previous studies of campaign visits and other studies of aggregate voting behavior. See, for example, Christopher J. Devine and Kyle C. Kopko, "Presidential versus Vice Presidential Home State Advantage: A Comparative Analysis of Electoral Significance, Causes, and Processes, 1884–2008," *Presidential Studies Quarterly* 43, no. 4 (2013): 814–38; J. Paul Herr, "The Impact of Campaign Appearances in the 1996 Election," *Journal of Politics* 64, no. 3 (2002): 912; John Sides, Lynn Vavreck, and Christopher Warshaw, "The Effect of Television Advertising in United States Elections," *American Political Science Review* 116, no. 2 (2022): 702–18.
3. I would prefer a more robust eligibility measure that also accounts for those residents who are excluded from voting because (depending on state law) they are currently incarcerated, on probation, or on parole, or who have committed a felony—essentially, the Voting Eligible Population statistic used by Michael McDonald (see the United States Election Project, electproject.org). But, to my knowledge, such data are not available at the county level for the 2008–2020 presidential elections. The U.S. Census Bureau's website, however, provides annual estimates of the Citizen Voting Age Population (CVAP) from 2009 to 2020, based on the American Community Surveys. I use the 2009 estimates for 2008. To calculate turnout rates, I divide each county's CVAP by the total number of votes cast for president (any candidate) in a given year, and multiply by one hundred.
4. See chapter 4 for details on variable measurement.
5. I was unable to find Census Bureau CVAP estimates prior to 2009. Therefore, when controlling for past turnout in the 2008 model (i.e, turnout in the 2004 presidential election), I had to impute county-level CVAP based on its relationship to overall population in the earliest available (2009) data. The numerator when calculating 2004 turnout, however, is the actual vote total per county.
6. Data were obtained from the National Oceanic and Atmospheric Administration (NOAA) website, as monthly averages. I use the average for October rather than November because Election Day is in early November. Also, particularly in recent elections, weather conditions might have influenced decisions about early voting during October in those states that allowed it. See here: www.ncei.noaa.gov/access/monitoring/climate-at-a-glance/county/mapping/110/tavg/202010/1/mean. Accessed June 1, 2022.
7. See, e.g., Jeffrey M. Jones, "Does Bringing Out the Candidate Bring Out the Votes? The Effects of Nominee Campaigning in Presidential Elections," *American Politics Quarterly* 26, no. 4 (1998): 395–419.
8. Alan I. Abramowitz and Costas Panagopoulos, "Trump on the Trail: Assessing the Impact of Presidential Campaign Visits on Voting Behavior in the 2018 Midterm Elections," *Presidential Studies Quarterly* 50, no. 3 (2020): 496–506; Christopher J. Devine and Aaron C. Weinschenk, "Surrogate-in-Chief: Did Bill Clinton's Campaign Visits Help (or Hurt) Hillary Clinton in 2016?," *Forum* 18, no. 2 (2020): 177–95; Richard Johnston, Michael G. Hagen, and Kathleen Hall Jamieson, *The 2000 Presidential Election and the Foundations of Party Politics* (Cambridge: Cambridge University Press, 2004); Jeffrey S. Hill, Elaine Rodriguez, and Amanda E. Wooden, "Stump Speeches and Road Trips: The Impact of State Campaign Appearances in

Presidential Elections," *PS: Political Science & Politics* 43, no. 2 (2010): 243–54; Daron R. Shaw, *The Race to 270: The Electoral College and the Campaign Strategies of 2000 and 2004* (Chicago: University of Chicago Press, 2006).

9. Hill et al., "Stump Speeches," 249, for one, speculates that such negative effects might be caused by sending a candidate to an area where the opposing party is dominant or has recently gained in the polls. Faced with similar results, other scholars have essentially thrown up their hands. Johnston et al., *The 2000 Presidential Election*, 82.

10. See Christopher J. Devine, "What If Hillary Clinton *Had* Gone to Wisconsin? Presidential Campaign Visits in the 2016 Election," *Forum* 16, no. 2 (2018): 211–34.

11. Stephen Ansolabehere, "Cooperative Congressional Election Study, 2008: Common Content," Release 4, July 15, 2011; Stephen Ansolabehere, "Cooperative Congressional Election Study, 2012: Common Content," Release 1, April 15, 2013; Stephen Ansolabehere and Brian F. Schaffner, "Cooperative Congressional Election Study, 2016: Common Content," Release 2, August 4, 2017; Stephen Ansolabehere, Brian F. Schaffner, and Sam Luks, "Cooperative Election Study, 2020: Common Content," Release 2, August 4, 2021, all available via cces.gov.harvard.edu.

12. Technically, the missing "counties" are actually independent cities in Virginia: Fairfax in 2008 and 2012, Lexington in 2012, and Williamsburg in 2016. Only Fairfax in 2008 hosted more than one campaign visit (two).

13. Lonna Rae Atkeson, "'Sure I Voted for the Winner!' Overreport of the Primary Vote for the Party Nominee in the National Elections," *Political Behavior* 21, no. 3 (1999): 197–215; Gerald C. Wright, "Misreports of Vote Choice in the 1988 NES Senate Election Study," *Legislative Studies Quarterly* 15, no. 4 (1990): 543–63.

14. I use CES's "vvweight"—indicating that a respondent "answered both waves and [was] matched to a registration record"—in models based on 2012–2020 survey data. In 2008, only a preelection wave weight is available. I define battleground states as those that hosted five or more campaign visits in a given election year. I assigned respondents to a media market based on their county of residence, as reported in the preelection survey. Media market boundaries were determined in the same way as described in chapter 4.

15. *Age*: I subtract the respondent's reported birth year from the year in which the survey was conducted. *Race*: The CES asks: "Which racial or ethnic group best describes you?" Respondents are coded one if they chose "Black or African American," and zero otherwise. *Ethnicity*: The 2008 CES asked: "Which racial or ethnic group best describes you?" Respondents are coded one if they chose "Hispanic" and zero otherwise. Respondents to the 2012–2020 CES were asked, as a follow-up to the question about race, "Are you Spanish, Latino, or Hispanic origin or descent?" Respondents are coded one if they chose "Yes," and zero for "No." *College education*: The CES asks respondents to state the highest level of education they have completed, ranging from: no high school (1); high school graduate (2); some college (3); two-year college degree (4); four-year college degree (5); to post-graduate degree (6).

16. *Economy*: Respondents are coded from rating the national economy over the past year as having "Gotten much worse" (1), "Gotten worse" (2), "Stayed about the same" or

"Not sure" (3), "Gotten better" (4), to "Gotten much better" (5). *Residence*: The CES asks: "How long have you lived at your present address?" Respondents who answered with less than one year ("Less than one month," "1 to 6 months," or "7 to 11 months") are coded one, and those who answered with one year or more ("1 to 2 years," "3 to 4 years," or "5 or more years") are coded zero.

17. The CES asks: "Are you male or female?" Respondents who answered "female" are coded one, and those who answered "male" are coded zero.
18. The CES does ask whether, and for whom, respondents voted in the last presidential election. However, self-reported turnout in past, as well as present, elections is far too high to be treated as a reliable measure for the purposes of this analysis. In that case, it is better to ask about a respondent's level of interest in politics—assuming that those who are more interested in politics, and follow it regularly, are more predisposed to vote. The CES presents the question as follows: "Some people seem to follow what's going on in government and public affairs most of the time, whether there's an election going on or not. Others aren't that interested. Would you say you follow what's going on in government and public affairs?" Respondents are categorized as follows: "Hardly at all" or "Don't know" (1); "Only now and then" (2); "Some of the time" (3); "Most of the time" (4); Skipped or not asked (missing).
19. Three other estimates are significant only at $p < 0.10$, but signed so as to indicate a positive effect on vote choice: for Barack Obama among independents in 2008; Joe Biden among Republicans in 2020; and Kamala Harris among independents in 2020.
20. The same is true for those three candidates whose visits had a marginally significant effect on vote choice, in their party's favor; in each case, the corresponding effect on turnout was not statistically significant even at $p < 0.10$.
21. Gary Jacobson makes much the same point in reference to campaign effects generally: "No single survey or study can be other than suggestive, but when multiple sources and studies converge on a conclusion, we can have some confidence that it approximates reality." Gary C. Jacobson, "How Do Campaigns Matter?," *Annual Review of Political Science* 18 (2015): 43.
22. Colin Kinniburgh, "In Pennsylvania, Trump Fans Cheer His 'Excellent Choice' for the Supreme Court," France24, September 27, 2020, www.france24.com/en/20200927-in-pennsylvania-trump-fans-cheer-his-excellent-choice-for-the-supreme-court; Candy Woodall, "Trump Rally in Middletown, Pa.: Takeaways After the President Nominates Amy Coney Barrett," *York Daily Record*, September 26, 2020, www.ydr.com/story/news/politics/elections/2020/09/26/trump-holds-rally-middletown-pa-after-naming-supreme-court-pick/3529047001; Michael D. Shear and Michael Crowley, "In Critical Swing State, Trump Again Stokes Doubt on Election Process," *New York Times*, September 26, 2020, www.nytimes.com/2020/09/26/us/politics/trump-rally-middletown-pa.html.
23. This classification scheme hardly guarantees accuracy. For example, in 2008 John McCain and Sarah Palin spoke to a very large crowd in Lebanon, Ohio, from the balcony of a restaurant and hotel called the Golden Lamb. Although most attendees were standing outside on public sidewalks or in the streets, for reasons that I describe

at length in Chapter 3, I code this visit as being held at a "Place of Business," thus disqualifying it from the present analysis of campaign rallies. Also, while visits occurring at "Private Residences" typically could not be described as campaign rallies—such as Joe Biden's participation in several small 2020 gatherings in supporters' backyards, as a precaution against spreading COVID-19—there are exceptions. For example, in 2012 Mitt Romney addressed 1,200 attendees in a speech at a family farm in Iowa. Emily Schultheis, "Romney Goes Rural," *Politico*, October 9, 2012, www.politico.com/story/2012/10/romney-goes-rural-082199. Conversely, there is no guarantee that a candidate who holds an event at a sports arena or university will attract a large crowd. Again, without reliable attendance estimates across all visits, I can only make general assumptions about crowd size—and thus, "campaign rally" status—based on venue type. This is a reasonable, but imperfect, method of approximation.

24. On average, 63.1 percent of campaign visits also qualify as campaign rallies. The distinction generally tracks with common perceptions of individual candidacies. Trump in 2020 (81.3 percent) and 2016 (76.1 percent), had the highest percentage of rallies out of total visits, and Biden (36.4 percent) in 2020, the lowest.

25. Devine, "What If Hillary"; Devine and Weinschenk, "Surrogate-in-Chief"; Boris Heersink and Brenton D. Peterson, "Truman Defeats Dewey: The Effect of Campaign Visits on Election Outcomes," *Electoral Studies* 49 (2017): 49–64.

26. Johnston et al., *The 2000 Presidential Election*; Jones, "Does Bringing"; David C. King and David Morehouse, "Moving Voters in the 2000 Presidential Campaign: Local Visits, Local Media," in *Lights, Camera, Campaign! Media, Politics, and Political Advertising*, ed. David A. Schultz (New York: Peter Lang, 2004), 301–17; Shaw, *Race to 270*; James M. Snyder Jr. and Hasin Yousaf, "Making Rallies Great Again: The Effects of Presidential Campaign Rallies on Voter Behavior, 2008–2016," Working paper (2020), www.nber.org/papers/w28043; Thomas Wood, "What the Heck Are We Doing in Ottumwa, Anyway? Presidential Candidate Visits and Their Political Consequence," *Annals of the American Academy of Political and Social Science* 667, no. 1 (2016): 110–25.

27. Shaw, *Race to 270*, 59, 4.

28. National Conference of State Legislatures, "Early In-Person Voting," NCSL.org, March 23, 2022, www.ncsl.org/research/elections-and-campaigns/early-voting-in-state-elections.aspx.

29. "Voting by Mail and Absentee Voting," MIT Election Data and Science Lab, March 16, 2021, electionlab.mit.edu/research/voting-mail-and-absentee-voting.

30. Snyder and Yousaf, "Making Rallies."

31. Specifically, I code respondents as Election Day voters if CES validates them as voting via "polling" rather than "absentee," "early vote," "mail," or "unknown." I do not replicate the voter turnout models because, by definition, Election Day voters turned out to vote; thus, there can be no variation in the dependent variable.

32. Charles Franklin, "Pre-Election Polls in Nation and State: A Dynamic Bayesian Hierarchical Model," Paper presented at the annual meeting of the American Political

Science Association, San Francisco, 2001; Heersink and Peterson, "Truman Defeats Dewey"; J. Paul Herr, "The Impact of Campaign Appearances in the 1996 Election," *Journal of Politics* 64, no. 3 (2002): 904–13; Hill et al., "Stump Speeches"; Thomas M. Holbrook, "Did the Whistle-Stop Campaign Matter?," *PS: Political Science and Politics* 35, no. 1 (2002): 59–66; Jones, "Does Bringing"; Shaw, *Race to 270*; Snyder and Yousaf, "Making Rallies"; Wood, "What the Heck."

33. *Mixed effects*: Jones, "Does Bringing"; Snyder and Yousaf, "Making Rallies." *No effect*: Herr, "1996 Election"; Thomas M. Holbrook and Scott D. McClurg, "The Mobilization of Core Supporters: Campaigns, Turnout, and Electoral Composition in United States Presidential Elections," *American Journal of Political Science* 49, no. 4 (2005): 689–703; but see Damon M. Cann and Jeffrey Bryan Cole, "Strategic Campaigning, Closeness, and Voter Mobilization in U.S. Presidential Elections," *Electoral Studies* 30, no. 2 (2011): 344–52.
34. Hill et al., "Stump Speeches."
35. Heersink and Peterson, "Truman Defeats Dewey."
36. Daron R. Shaw, "A Study of Presidential Campaign Event Effects from 1952 to 1992," *Journal of Politics* 61, no. 2 (1999): 387–422.
37. Snyder and Yousaf, "Making Rallies."
38. See Costas Panagopoulos, *Bases Loaded: How US Presidential Campaigns Are Changing and Why It Matters* (Oxford: Oxford University Press, 2020).
39. Sides et al., "Effect of Television."

CONCLUSION

1. James M. Snyder and Hasin Yousaf's work is particularly noteworthy here. They analyze the effects of campaign visits on voting behavior in three presidential elections (2008–2016), using survey data from the Cooperative Congressional Election Study, and, for Donald Trump in 2016, test for mobilization versus persuasion effects. However, as I explain in chapter 5, their estimates rely on survey data alone, and a measure of intended rather than actual vote choice. Also, they estimate mobilization versus persuasion effects for Trump only, do not include vice-presidential candidates' visits in their data, and do not statistically control for the effects of visits by an opposing candidate (see chapter 2 for more on these points). Yet their analysis is more comprehensive than mine in other respects. For example, moving beyond the direct effects of campaign visits on voting behavior, Snyder and Yousaf estimate their effects on local media coverage, campaign advertising, and campaign donations. They also estimate the duration of campaign visit effects and quantify their impact on election outcomes. Indeed, theirs is a remarkable and comprehensive analysis in its own right, which anyone interested in evaluating campaign visit effects must consult. James M. Snyder Jr. and Hasin Yousaf, "Making Rallies Great Again: The Effects of Presidential Campaign Rallies on Voter Behavior, 2008–2016," Working paper (October 2020), www.nber.org/papers/w28043.

2. Only in two instances do I find any direct evidence of mobilization via campaign visits—for Barack Obama in swing counties in 2012 (aggregate-level data) and for Mike Pence among Republican-leaning voters in 2016 (individual-level data). Most of the other cases in which a candidate's visits are associated with changes in vote choice suggest persuasion as the causal mechanism. For instance, in 2008, there is evidence that John McCain and Barack Obama gained votes via campaign visits but did not influence turnout; the same pattern is evident for McCain among independent voters and Obama in swing counties.
3. Daron R. Shaw and James G. Gimpel, "What If We Randomize the Governor's Schedule? Evidence on Campaign Appearance Effects from a Texas Field Experiment," *Political Communication* 29, no. 2 (2012): 138; Alan I. Abramowitz and Costas Panagopoulos, "Trump on the Trail: Assessing the Impact of Presidential Campaign Visits on Voting Behavior in the 2018 Midterm Elections," *Presidential Studies Quarterly* 50, no. 3 (2020): 504.
4. John Sides and Lynn Vavreck, *The Gamble: Choice and Chance in the 2012 Presidential Election* (Princeton, NJ: Princeton University Press, 2013), 9.
5. John R. Zaller, *The Nature and Origins of Mass Opinion* (Cambridge: Cambridge University Press, 1992).
6. Costas Panagopoulos, *Bases Loaded: How US Presidential Campaigns Are Changing and Why It Matters* (Oxford: Oxford University Press, 2020).
7. John Sides, Lynn Vavreck, and Christopher Warshaw, "The Effect of Television Advertising in United States Elections," *American Political Science Review* 116, no. 2 (2022): 702–18.
8. Alan I. Abramowitz and Steven W. Webster, "Negative Partisanship: Why Americans Dislike Parties but Behave Like Rabid Partisans," *Advances in Political Psychology* 39, no. 1 (2018): 119–35; Julia R. Azari, *Delivering the People's Message: The Changing Politics of the Presidential Mandate* (Ithaca, NY: Cornell University Press, 2014); Samara Klar and Yanna Krupnikov, *Independent Politics: How American Disdain for Parties Leads to Political Inaction* (Cambridge: Cambridge University Press, 2016).
9. *Vice presidents not included*: Thomas M. Holbrook and Scott D. McClurg, "The Mobilization of Core Supporters: Campaigns, Turnout, and Electoral Composition in United States Presidential Elections," *American Journal of Political Science* 49, no. 4 (2005): 689–703; Snyder and Yousaf, "Making Rallies." *Combined with presidential data*: Lanhee J. Chen and Andrew Reeves, "Turning Out the Base or Appealing to the Periphery? An Analysis of County-Level Candidate Appearances in the 2008 Presidential Campaign," *American Politics Research* 39, no. 3 (2011): 534–56; Richard Johnston, Michael G. Hagen, and Kathleen Hall Jamieson, *The 2000 Presidential Election and the Foundations of Party Politics* (Cambridge: Cambridge University Press, 2004); Charles Franklin, "Pre-Election Polls in Nation and State: A Dynamic Bayesian Hierarchical Model," Paper presented at the annual meeting of the American Political Science Association, San Francisco, 2001; Thomas Wood, "What the Heck Are We Doing in Ottumwa, Anyway? Presidential Candidate Visits and Their

Political Consequence," *Annals of the American Academy of Political and Social Science* 667, no. 1 (2016): 110–25.
10. *Different purpose*: See Christopher J. Devine and Kyle C. Kopko, "Split Tickets? On the Strategic Allocation of Presidential versus Vice Presidential Campaign Visits in 2016," *SAGE Open* (July–September 2018): 1–12; see also chapter 4 of this book. *More effective*: Jeffrey S. Hill, Elaine Rodriguez, and Amanda E. Wooden, "Stump Speeches and Road Trips: The Impact of State Campaign Appearances in Presidential Elections," *PS: Political Science & Politics* 43, no. 2 (2010): 243–54. *Less effective*: Daron R. Shaw, *The Race to 270: The Electoral College and the Campaign Strategies of 2000 and 2004* (Chicago: University of Chicago Press, 2006).
11. See, for example, Charles J. Holden, Zach Messitte, and Jerald Podair, *Republican Populist: Spiro Agnew and the Origins of Donald Trump's America* (Charlottesville: University of Virginia Press, 2019), 133; Ashley Parker and Michael Barbaro, "Caution, Not Flash, as Romney Seeks His No. 2," *New York Times*, July 17, 2012, www.nytimes.com/2012/07/18/us/politics/romney-vice-presidential-search-began-months-ago.html.
12. Dick Cheney with Liz Cheney, *In My Time: A Personal and Political Memoir* (New York: Threshold Editions, 2011), 272.
13. Yanna Krupnikov and John Barry Ryan, *The Other Divide: Polarization and Disengagement in American Politics* (Cambridge: Cambridge University Press, 2022).
14. Wood, "What the Heck."
15. Some surveys, such as the American National Election Study, ask respondents whether they have "attend[ed]a rally or speech" recently. However, there is no way to know whether respondents answering yes to this question attended an event having to do with the presidential election and, if so, for which campaign.
16. Shaw and Gimpel, "What If We."
17. Christopher J. Devine and Aaron C. Weinschenk, "Surrogate-in-Chief: Did Bill Clinton's Campaign Visits Help (or Hurt) Hillary Clinton in 2016?," *Forum* 18, no. 2 (2020): 177–95.
18. *Donations*: Boris Heersink, Brenton D. Peterson, and Jordan Carr Peterson, "Mobilization and Countermobilization: The Effect of Candidate Visits on Campaign Donations in the 2016 Presidential Election," *Journal of Politics* 83, no. 4 (2021): 1878–83; Snyder and Yousaf, "Making Rallies." *Media Coverage*: Snyder and Yousaf, "Making Rallies;" Wood, "What the Heck."
19. See, for example, Katherine J. Cramer, *The Politics of Resentment: Rural Consciousness in Wisconsin and the Rise of Scott Walker* (Chicago: University of Chicago Press, 2016).

BIBLIOGRAPHY

Abramowitz, Alan. "It's the Pandemic, Stupid! A Simplified Model for Forecasting the 2020 Presidential Election." *Sabato's Crystal Ball*, UVA Center for Politics, August 4, 2020. centerforpolitics.org/crystalball/articles/its-the-pandemic-stupid-a-simplified-model-for-forecasting-the-2020-presidential-election. Accessed December 10, 2022.

Abramowitz, Alan I. "Will Time for Change Mean Time for Trump?" *PS: Political Science & Politics* 49, no. 4 (2016): 659–60.

Abramowitz, Alan I., and Costas Panagopoulos. "Trump on the Trail: Assessing the Impact of Presidential Campaign Visits on Voting Behavior in the 2018 Midterm Elections." *Presidential Studies Quarterly* 50, no. 3 (2020): 496–506.

Abramowitz, Alan I., and Steven W. Webster. "Negative Partisanship: Why Americans Dislike Parties but Behave Like Rabid Partisans." *Advances in Political Psychology* 39, no. 1 (2018): 119–35.

Alexander, Robert M. *Representation and the Electoral College*. Oxford: Oxford University Press, 2019.

Allen, Jonathan, and Amy Parnes. *Lucky: How Joe Biden Barely Won the Presidency*. New York: Crown, 2021.

Allen, Jonathan, and Amy Parnes. *Shattered: Inside Hillary Clinton's Doomed Campaign*. New York: Crown, 2017.

Althaus, Scott L., Peter F. Nardulli, and Daron R. Shaw. "Candidate Appearances in Presidential Elections, 1972–2000." *Political Communication* 19, no. 1 (2002): 49–72.

Ansolabehere, Stephen. "Cooperative Congressional Election Study, 2008: Common Content." Release 4, July 15, 2011. Cambridge, MA: Harvard University. cces.gov.harvard.edu. Accessed June 1, 2022.

Ansolabehere, Stephen. "Cooperative Congressional Election Study, 2012: Common Content." Release 1, April 15, 2013. Cambridge, MA: Harvard University. cces.gov.harvard.edu. Accessed June 1, 2022.

Ansolabehere, Stephen, and Brian F. Schaffner. "Cooperative Congressional Election Study, 2016: Common Content." Release 2, August 4, 2017. Cambridge, MA: Harvard University. cces.gov.harvard.edu. Accessed June 1, 2022.

Ansolabehere, Stephen, Brian F. Schaffner, and Sam Luks. "Cooperative Election Study, 2020: Common Content." Release 2, August 4, 2021. Cambridge, MA: Harvard University. cces.gov.harvard.edu. Accessed June 1, 2022.

Arrington, Benjamin T. *The Last Lincoln Republican: The Presidential Election of 1880*. Lawrence: University Press of Kansas, 2020.

"As Trump Returns to the Road, Some Democrats Want to Bust Biden Out of His Basement." Reuters, May 8, 2020. www.usnews.com/news/top-news/articles/2020-05-08/as-trump-returns-to-the-road-some-democrats-want-to-bust-biden-out-of-his-basement. Accessed December 10, 2022.

Atkeson, Lonna Rae. "'Sure I Voted for the Winner!' Overreport of the Primary Vote for the Party Nominee in the National Elections." *Political Behavior* 21, no. 3 (1999): 197–215.

Attkisson, Sharyl. "When Will 'Basement Biden' Get in the Game?" *The Hill*, September 26, 2020. thehill.com/opinion/campaign/518180-when-will-basement-biden-get-in-the-game. Accessed December 10, 2022.

Axelrod, David, and David Plouffe. "What Joe Biden Needs to Do to Beat Trump." *New York Times*, May 4, 2020. www.nytimes.com/2020/05/04/opinion/axelrod-plouffe-joe-biden.html. Accessed December 10, 2022.

Azari, Julia. "Weak Parties and Strong Partisanship Are a Bad Combination." *Vox*, November 3, 2016. vox.com/mischiefs-of-faction/2016/11/3/13512362/weak-parties-strong-partisanship-bad-combination. Accessed December 10, 2022.

Azari, Julia R. *Delivering the People's Message: The Changing Politics of the Presidential Mandate*. Ithaca, NY: Cornell University Press, 2014.

Bartels, Larry M. "Messages Received: The Political Impact of Media Exposure." *American Political Science Review* 87, no. 2 (1993): 267–85.

Bartels, Larry M. "Priming and Persuasion in Presidential Campaigns." In *Capturing Campaign Effects*, ed. Henry E. Brady and Richard Johnston, 78–113. Ann Arbor: University of Michigan Press, 2006.

Bartels, Larry M. "Resource Allocation in a Presidential Campaign." *Journal of Politics* 47, no. 3 (1985): 928–36.

"Basement-Bound Biden Campaign Worries Democrats." Associated Press, June 16, 2020. bangordailynews.com/2020/05/13/news/basement-bound-biden-campaign-worries-democrats-2. Accessed December 10, 2022.

Baumgartner, Jody C., and Peter L. Francia. *Conventional Wisdom and American Elections: Exploding Myths, Exploring Misconceptions*. Lanham, MD: Rowman & Littlefield, 2019.

Bendavid, Naftali. "Joe Biden Takes a Non-Virtual Moment to Muse on His Basement, Apocalyptic Ads and Being Trump's 'Antithesis.'" *Washington Post*, July 29, 2020. www.washingtonpost.com/politics/joe-biden-takes-a-non-virtual-moment-to-muse-on-his-basement-apocalyptic-ads-and-being-trumps-antithesis/2020/07/29/801405f2-d133-11ea-8c55-61e7fa5e82ab_story.html. Accessed December 10, 2022.

Bendery, Jennifer. "Joe Biden Makes Surprise Stop at Ohio Campaign Office, Women Swoon." *HuffPost*, October 24, 2012. www.huffpost.com/entry/joe-biden-ohio-campaign-office-women-swoon_n_2007603. Accessed December 10, 2022.

Berelson, Bernard R., Paul F. Lazarsfeld, and William N. McPhee. *Voting: A Study of Opinion Formation in a Presidential Campaign*. Chicago: University of Chicago Press, 1954.

Berg, A. Scott. *Wilson*. New York: Putnam, 2013.

"Biden Makes Stop at Schmucker's Restaurant." *The Blade*, October 23, 2012. www.toledoblade.com/local/2012/10/23/Biden-makes-stop-at-Schmucker-s-Restaurant/stories/20121023136. Accessed December 10, 2022.

Borneman, Walter R. *Polk: The Man Who Transformed the Presidency and America*. New York: Random House, 2008.

Bourdon, Jeffrey Norman. *From Garfield to Harding: The Success of Midwestern Front Porch Campaigns*. Kent, OH: Kent State University Press, 2019.

Brady, Henry E., Richard Johnston, and John Sides. "The Study of Political Campaigns." In *Capturing Campaign Effects*, ed. Henry E. Brady and Richard Johnston, 1–26. Ann Arbor: University of Michigan Press, 2006.

Brams, Steven J., and Morton D. Davis. "The 3/2's Rule in Presidential Campaigning." *American Political Science Review* 68, no. 1 (1974): 113–34.

"Buttigieg Rallies on Scott Hall Lawn." *New Hampshire*, November 1, 2020. tnhdigital.com/2019/11/01/buttigieg. Accessed December 10, 2022.

Campbell, Angus, Philip E. Converse, Warren E. Miller, and Donald E. Stokes. *The American Voter*. Chicago: University of Chicago Press, 1960.

Campbell, James. *The American Campaign*. College Station: Texas A&M Press, 2000.

Cann, Damon M., and Jeffrey Bryan Cole. "Strategic Campaigning, Closeness, and Voter Mobilization in U.S. Presidential Elections." *Electoral Studies* 30, no. 2 (2011): 344–52.

Caputo, Marc, and Christopher Cadelago. "Dems Warm to Biden's Bunker Strategy." *Politico*, June 24, 2020. www.politico.com/news/2020/06/24/dems-warm-to-bidens-bunker-strategy-338853. Accessed December 10, 2022.

Carter, Jimmy. *White House Diary*. New York: Farrar, Straus and Giroux, 2010.

Cheathem, Mark R. *The Coming of Democracy: Presidential Campaigning in the Age of Jackson*. Baltimore: Johns Hopkins University Press, 2018.

Chen, Lanhee J., and Andrew Reeves. "Turning Out the Base or Appealing to the Periphery? An Analysis of County-Level Candidate Appearances in the 2008 Presidential Campaign." *American Politics Research* 39, no. 3 (2011): 534–56.

Cheney, Dick, with Liz Cheney. *In My Time: A Personal and Political Memoir*. New York: Threshold Editions, 2011.

Chernow, Ron. *Washington: A Life*. New York: Penguin Press, 2010.

Clinton, Bill. *My Life*. New York: Alfred A. Knopf, 2004.

"Clinton Makes Surprise Visits to UNCG, NC A&T Homecoming." Fox8, October 27, 2016. myfox8.com/news/you-decide-2016/clinton-makes-surprise-visits-to-uncg-nc-at-homecoming. Accessed December 10, 2022.

Cohen, Marty, David Karol, Hans Noel, and John Zaller. *The Party Decides: Presidential Nominations Before and After Reform*. Chicago: University of Chicago Press, 2008.

Cole, Donald B. *Martin Van Buren and the American Political System*. Princeton, NJ: Princeton University Press, 1984.
Condon, Patrick. "Guest Says Minn. Fundraiser with Trump 'Very Safely Done.'" *Star Tribune*, October 3, 2020. www.startribune.com/trump-s-minn-fundraiser-was-very-safely-done-guest-says/572626631. Accessed December 10, 2022.
Cook, Nancy. "Trump's 2020 Cure-All: Rallies, Rallies and More Rallies." *Politico*, October 21, 2020. www.politico.com/news/2020/10/21/trumps-2020-cure-all-rallies-430552. Accessed December 10, 2022.
Cook, Nancy, and Matthew Choi. "Trump Basks in Cheers of Minnesota Rally, Far from Debate Criticism." *Politico*, September 30, 2020. www.politico.com/news/2020/09/30/trump-debate-minnesota-rally-424308. Accessed December 10, 2022.
Cramer, Katherine J. *The Politics of Resentment: Rural Consciousness in Wisconsin and the Rise of Scott Walker*. Chicago: University of Chicago Press, 2016.
Darr, Joshua P. "In 2020, the Ground Game Is All Trump." Mischiefs of Faction, October 9, 2020. www.mischiefsoffaction.com/post/2020-ground-game. Accessed December 10, 2022.
Dassonneville, Ruth, and Charles Tien. "Introduction to Forecasting the 2020 US Elections." *PS: Political Science & Politics* 54, no. 1 (2021): 47–51.
Davidson, Tom. "Joe Biden Makes Campaign Stop in Pittsburgh, Says He's Not Banning Fracking." *Pittsburgh Tribune-Review*, August 31, 2020. triblive.com/news/politics-election/joe-biden-makes-campaign-stop-in-pittsburgh-says-hes-not-banning-fracking. Accessed December 10, 2022.
Dawsey, Josh, and Colby Itkowitz. "Trump Says He and First Lady Have Tested Positive for the Coronavirus." *Washington Post*, October 2, 2020. www.washingtonpost.com/politics/hope-hicks-close-trump-aide-tests-positive-for-coronavirus/2020/10/01/af238f7c-0444-11eb-897d-3a6201d6643f_story.html. Accessed December 10, 2022.
Dawsey, Josh, Michael Scherer, and Annie Linskey. "Campaign of Contrasts: Trump's Raucous Crowds vs. Biden's Distanced Gatherings." *Washington Post*, September 9, 2020. www.washingtonpost.com/politics/campaign-of-contrasts-trumps-raucous-crowds-vs-bidens-distanced-gatherings/2020/09/08/8633e69a-f1dc-11ea-b796-2dd09962649c_story.html. Accessed December 10, 2022.
Devine, Christopher J. "Oh, the Places They'll Go: The Geography and Political Strategy of Presidential Campaign Visits in 2016." In *Studies of Communication in the 2016 Presidential Campaign*, ed. Robert E. Denton Jr., 45–68. Lanham, MD: Lexington, 2018.
Devine, Christopher J. "Voter Mobilization 101: Presidential Campaign Visits to Colleges and Universities in the 2016 Election." *PS: Political Science & Politics* 52, no. 2 (2019): 261–66.
Devine, Christopher J. "What If Hillary Clinton *Had* Gone to Wisconsin? Presidential Campaign Visits in the 2016 Election." *Forum* 16, no. 2 (2018): 211–34.
Devine, Christopher J., and Kyle C. Kopko. *Do Running Mates Matter? The Influence of Vice Presidential Candidates in Presidential Elections*. Lawrence: University Press of Kansas, 2020.

Devine, Christopher J., and Kyle C. Kopko. "Presidential versus Vice Presidential Home State Advantage: A Comparative Analysis of Electoral Significance, Causes, and Processes, 1884–2008." *Presidential Studies Quarterly* 43, no. 4 (2013): 814–38.

Devine, Christopher J., and Kyle C. Kopko. "Split Tickets? On the Strategic Allocation of Presidential versus Vice Presidential Campaign Visits in 2016." *SAGE Open* July-September (2018): 1–12.

Devine, Christopher J. and Aaron C. Weinschenk. "Surrogate-in-Chief: Did Bill Clinton's Campaign Visits Help (or Hurt) Hillary Clinton in 2016?" *Forum* 18, no. 2 (2020): 177–95.

Dickerson, John. *Whistlestop: My Favorite Stories from Presidential Campaign History*. New York: Twelve, 2016.

Dupree, Jamie. "Warren Slams Bloomberg, Presses for Money in 2020 Race." *Atlanta Journal-Constitution*, February 13, 2020. www.ajc.com/blog/jamie-dupree/warren-slams-bloomberg-presses-for-money-2020-race/wQpYK04ZaGOX7PNRsRsBkM. Accessed December 10, 2022.

"Early In-Person Voting." National Conference of State Legislatures, March 23, 2022. www.ncsl.org/research/elections-and-campaigns/early-voting-in-state-elections.aspx. Accessed December 10, 2022.

Easley, Jonathan. "Biden Defends Light Campaign Schedule During Unscheduled Pennsylvania Stop." *The Hill*, October 26, 2020. thehill.com/homenews/campaign/522844-biden-defends-light-campaign-schedule-during-pennsylvania-stop. Accessed December 10, 2022.

Eaton, Sabrina. "Trump Shows Off Lordstown Motors Pickup Truck at White House on the Eve of Cleveland Presidential Debate." Cleveland.com, September 28, 2020. www.cleveland.com/open/2020/09/trump-shows-off-lordstown-motors-pickup-truck-at-white-house-on-the-eve-of-cleveland-presidential-debate.html. Accessed December 10, 2022.

Edwards, George C., III. *Why the Electoral College Is Bad for America*. New Haven, CT: Yale University Press, 2004.

Egerton, Douglas R. *Year of Meteors: Stephen Douglas, Abraham Lincoln, and the Election That Brought on the Civil War*. New York: Bloomsbury, 2010.

"8:15 a.m.—A Very Presidential Saturday." *Albuquerque Journal*, October 24, 2008. www.abqjournal.com/21632/815 a.m.-a-very-presidential-saturday.html. Accessed December 10, 2022.

Elliott, Charles Winslow. *Winfield Scott: The Soldier and the Man*. New York: Macmillan, 1937.

Ellis, Richard J. *Old Tip vs. the Sly Fox: The 1840 Election and the Making of a Partisan Nation*. Lawrence: University Press of Kansas, 2020.

Ellis, Richard J., and Mark Dedrick. "The Presidential Candidate, Then and Now." *Perspectives on Political Science* 26, no. 4 (1997): 208–16.

Ember, Sydney, Annie Karni, and Maggie Haberman. "Sanders and Biden Cancel Events as Coronavirus Fears Upend Primary." *New York Times*, March 10, 2020. www.nytimes.com/2020/03/10/us/politics/sanders-biden-rally-coronavirus.html. Accessed December 10, 2022.

Epstein, Jennifer, and Tyler Pager. "Biden Picking Up Campaign Pace as Trump Blitzes Battlegrounds." *Bloomberg*, October 26, 2020. www.bloomberg.com/news/articles/2020-10-26/biden-keeps-light-schedule-amid-pandemic-as-trump-travels-widely. Accessed December 10, 2022.

Erikson, Robert S., and Christopher Wleizen. *The Timeline of Presidential Elections: How Campaigns Do (and Do Not) Matter*. Chicago: University of Chicago Press, 2012.

Farrell, John A. *Richard Nixon: The Life*. New York: Doubleday, 2017.

Ferguson, Andrew. "Biden's Virtual Campaign Is a Disaster." *The Atlantic*, May 15, 2020. www.theatlantic.com/ideas/archive/2020/05/bidens-virtual-campaign-disaster/611698. Accessed December 10, 2022.

Fichera, Angelo. "Biden Hasn't Suspended In-Person Campaigning." FactCheck.org, October 26, 2020. www.factcheck.org/2020/10/biden-hasnt-suspended-in-person-campaigning. Accessed December 10, 2022.

Finkel, Steven E. "Re-Examining the 'Minimal Effects' Model in Recent Presidential Elections." *Journal of Politics* 55, no. 1 (1993): 1–21.

"40 Times Trump Said the Coronavirus Would Go Away." *Washington Post*, November 2, 2020. www.washingtonpost.com/video/politics/40-times-trump-said-the-coronavirus-would-go-away/2020/04/30/d2593312-9593-4ec2-aff7-72c1438fca0e_video.html. Accessed December 10, 2022.

Fowler, Mayhill. "Palin (and McCain) Say Little and Fire Up Faithful in Ohio." *HuffPost*, October 11, 2008. www.huffpost.com/entry/palin-and-mccain-fire-up_b_125282. Accessed December 10, 2022.

Franklin, Charles. "Pre-Election Polls in Nation and State: A Dynamic Bayesian Hierarchical Model." Paper presented at the annual meeting of the American Political Science Association, San Francisco, 2001.

Galdieri, Christopher J. *Donald Trump and New Hampshire Politics*. Cham, Switzerland: Palgrave Macmillan, 2020.

Gavrilovic, Maria. "Obama's Philadelphia Campaign Blitz." CBS News, October 11, 2008. www.cbsnews.com/news/obamas-philadelphia-campaign-blitz. Accessed December 10, 2022.

Gelman, Andrew, and Gary King. "Why Are American Presidential Election Polls So Variable When Votes Are So Predictable?" *British Journal of Political Science* 23, no. 4 (1993): 409–51.

Glueck, Katie. "Biden's Caution: Wise Campaign Tactic or Misguided Gamble?" *New York Times*, October 28, 2020. www.nytimes.com/2020/10/28/us/politics/joe-biden-virus.html. Accessed December 10, 2022.

Goldman, Peter, and Tom Mathews, with Lucille Beachy, Thomas M. DeFrank, Shawn Doherty, Vern E. Smith, Bill Turque, Anne Underwood, and Lauren Picker. *The Quest for the Presidency: The 1988 Campaign*. New York: Simon & Schuster, 1989.

Goldstein, Kenneth, Sarah Niebler, Jacob Neiheisel, and Matthew Holleque. "Presidential, Congressional, and Gubernatorial Advertising, 2008." Combined File [dataset]. Initial release. Madison: University of Wisconsin Advertising Project, Department of Political Science at the University of Wisconsin–Madison, 2011.

Gomez, Henry J. "President Obama, Vice President Joe Biden Greet Crowds in Dayton, Tout Their Successes." Cleveland.com, October 23, 2012. www.cleveland.com/open/2012/10/obama_biden_greet_crowds_in_da.html. Accessed December 10, 2022.

Gorman, Steve. "Palin-Biden Debate Sets TV Ratings Record." Reuters, October 3, 2008. www.reuters.com/article/us-usa-politics-ratings/palin-biden-debate-sets-tv-ratings-record-idUSTRE4927XF20081004. Accessed December 10, 2022.

Haldeman, H.R. "Campaign '68." Box 33, Folder 14, White House Special Files Collection, Richard Nixon Presidential Library, 1968. www.nixonlibrary.gov/sites/default/files/virtuallibrary/documents/whsfreturned/WHSF_Box_33/WHSF33-14.pdf. Accessed December 10, 2022.

Halperin, Mark, and John Heilemann. *Double Down: Game Change 2012*. New York: Penguin, 2013.

Heersink, Boris, and Brenton D. Peterson. "Truman Defeats Dewey: The Effect of Campaign Visits on Election Outcomes." *Electoral Studies* 49 (2017): 49–64.

Heersink, Boris, Brenton D. Peterson, and Jordan Carr Peterson. "Mobilization and Countermobilization: The Effect of Candidate Visits on Campaign Donations in the 2016 Presidential Election." *Journal of Politics* 83, no. 4 (2021): 1878–83.

Herr, J. Paul. "The Impact of Campaign Appearances in the 1996 Election." *Journal of Politics* 64, no. 3 (2002): 904–13.

Hershey, Marjorie Randon. *Party Politics in America*, 17th ed. New York: Routledge, 2017.

Hill, Jeffrey S., Elaine Rodriguez, and Amanda E. Wooden. "Stump Speeches and Road Trips: The Impact of State Campaign Appearances in Presidential Elections." *PS: Political Science & Politics* 43, no. 2 (2010): 243–54.

Hirsch, Mark D. "Election of 1884." In *History of American Presidential Elections, 1789–1968*, Vol. 2, ed. Arthur M. Schlesinger Jr. and Fred L. Israel, 1559–611. New York: Chelsea House, 1971.

Holbrook, Thomas M. "Campaigns, National Conditions, and U.S. Presidential Elections." *American Journal of Political Science* 38, no. 4 (1994): 973–98.

Holbrook, Thomas M. "Did the Whistle-Stop Campaign Matter?" *PS: Political Science and Politics* 35, no. 1 (2002): 59–66.

Holbrook, Thomas M. *Do Campaigns Matter?* Thousand Oaks, CA: Sage, 1996.

Holbrook, Thomas M., and Scott D. McClurg. "The Mobilization of Core Supporters: Campaigns, Turnout, and Electoral Composition in United States Presidential Elections." *American Journal of Political Science* 49, no. 4 (2005): 689–703.

Holden, Charles J., Zach Messitte, and Jerald Podair. *Republican Populist: Spiro Agnew and the Origins of Donald Trump's America*. Charlottesville: University of Virginia Press, 2019.

Holt, Michael F. *The Rise and Fall of the American Whig Party: Jacksonian Politics and the Onset of the Civil War*. New York: Oxford University Press, 1999.

Huang, Taofang, and Daron R. Shaw. "Beyond the Battlegrounds? Electoral College Strategies in the 2008 Presidential Election." *Journal of Political Marketing* 8, no. 4 (2009): 272–91.

Institute of Politics. *Campaign for President: The Managers Look at 2004*. Lanham, MD: Rowman & Littlefield, 2006.

Jacobson, Gary C. "How Do Campaigns Matter?" *Annual Review of Political Science* 18 (2015): 31–47.

"Joe Biden Calls Trump's COVID-19 Response 'Incompetent.'" *Good Morning America*, May 12, 2020. www.goodmorningamerica.com/news/video/joe-biden-calls-trumps-covid-19-response-incompetent-70632338. Accessed December 10, 2022.

Johannsen, Robert W. "Stephen A. Douglas' New England Campaign, 1860." *New England Quarterly* 35, no. 2 (1962): 162–86.

Johnson, Allen. *Stephen A. Douglas: A Study in American Politics*. New York: Da Capo, 1970.

Johnston, Richard, Michael G. Hagen, and Kathleen Hall Jamieson. *The 2000 Presidential Election and the Foundations of Party Politics*. Cambridge: Cambridge University Press, 2004.

Jones, Jeffrey M. "Does Bringing Out the Candidate Bring Out the Votes? The Effects of Nominee Campaigning in Presidential Elections." *American Politics Quarterly* 26, no. 4 (1998): 395–419.

Jones, Kay, and Brian Ries. "Tulsa Sees Covid-19 Surge in the Wake of Trump's June Rally." CNN, July 9, 2020. www.cnn.com/2020/07/08/us/tulsa-covid-trump-rally-contact-tracers-trnd/index.html. Accessed December 10, 2022.

Judd, Donald. "Donald Trump Holds 'Tele-Rally' in Campaign First amid Coronavirus Pandemic." CNN, July 18, 2020. www.cnn.com/2020/07/18/politics/donald-trump-telerally-campaign-event/index.html. Accessed December 10, 2022.

Just, Marion R., Ann N. Crigler, Dean E. Alger, Timothy E. Cook, Montague Kern, and Darrell M. West. *Crosstalk: Citizens, Candidates, and the Media in a Presidential Campaign*. Cambridge: Cambridge University Press, 1996.

Kazin, Michael. *A Godly Hero: The Life of William Jennings Bryan*. New York: Anchor, 2006.

Kessler, Glenn. "Trump Campaign Ad Manipulates Three Images to Put Biden in a 'Basement.'" *Washington Post*, August 7, 2020. www.washingtonpost.com/politics/2020/08/07/trump-campaign-ad-manipulates-three-images-put-biden-basement. Accessed December 10, 2022.

Khalid, Asma, and Tamara Keith. "Trump and Biden Wage an Uneven Virtual Campaign." National Public Radio, May 21, 2020. www.npr.org/2020/05/21/859932268/trump-and-biden-wage-an-uneven-virtual-campaign. Accessed December 10, 2022.

King, David C., and David Morehouse. "Moving Voters in the 2000 Presidential Campaign: Local Visits, Local Media." In *Lights, Camera, Campaign! Media, Politics, and Political Advertising*, ed. David A. Schultz, 301–17. New York: Peter Lang, 2004.

Kinniburgh, Colin. "In Pennsylvania, Trump Fans Cheer His 'Excellent Choice' for the Supreme Court." France24, September 27, 2020. www.france24.com/en/20200927-in-pennsylvania-trump-fans-cheer-his-excellent-choice-for-the-supreme-court. Accessed December 10, 2022.

Klar, Samara, and Yanna Krupnikov. *Independent Politics: How American Disdain for Parties Leads to Political Inaction*. Cambridge: Cambridge University Press, 2016.

Kraker, Dan, and Brian Bakst. "Trump Rakes in Money, Stirs up Supporters in Minnesota Trip." MPR News, September 30, 2020. www.mprnews.org/story/2020/09/30/trump-returns-to-minnesota-for-postdebate-rally-fundraiser. Accessed December 10, 2022.

Krupnikov, Yanna, and John Barry Ryan. *The Other Divide: Polarization and Disengagement in American Politics*. Cambridge: Cambridge University Press, 2022.

Kurtz, Andrew. "Biden Continues Ohio Campaign on UT Campus." *UT:10 News*, October 24, 2012. www.ut10news.com/election-2012.html. Accessed December 10, 2022.

Langston, Joy, and Guillermo Rosas. "Risky Business: Where Do Presidential Campaigns Visit?" *Electoral Studies* 55 (2018): 120–30.

Lanning, Jason, and Dale Greenstein. "Biden Gets Rained Out at the Florida State Fairgrounds Hours after Trump's Raymond James Rally." Spectrum News, October 30, 2020. www.baynews9.com/fl/tampa/news/2020/10/28/dueling-rallies--president-trump--biden-both-to-hit-tampa-thursday. Accessed December 10, 2022.

Lazarsfeld, Paul F., Bernard Berelson, and Hazel Gaudet. *The People's Choice: How the Voter Makes Up His Mind in a Presidential Campaign*. New York: Columbia University Press, 1948.

Leech, Margaret. *In the Days of McKinley*. New York: Harper & Brothers, 1959.

Leonnig, Carol, and Philip Rucker. *I Alone Can Fix It: Donald J. Trump's Catastrophic Final Year*. New York: Penguin Press, 2021.

Lerer, Lisa. "What Joe Biden's Event Was Like." *New York Times*, June 17, 2020. www.nytimes.com/2020/06/17/us/politics/joe-biden-campaign-event.html. Accessed December 10, 2022.

Lewis-Beck, Michael S., William G. Jacoby, Helmut Norpoth, and Herbert F. Weisberg. *The American Voter Revisited*. Ann Arbor: University of Michigan Press, 2008.

Lyons, Eugene. *Herbert Hoover: A Biography*. Garden City, NY: Doubleday, 1964.

MacManus, Susan A., and Andrew F. Quecan. "Spouses as Campaign Surrogates: Strategic Appearances by Presidential and Vice Presidential Candidates' Wives in the 2004 Election." *PS: Political Science & Politics* 41, no. 2 (2008): 337–48.

"Mad Money: TV Ads in the 2012 Presidential Campaign." *Washington Post*, November 14, 2012. www.washingtonpost.com/wp-srv/special/politics/track-presidential-campaign-ads-2012. Accessed December 10, 2022.

Mason, Lilliana. *Uncivil Agreement: How Politics Became Our Identity*. Chicago: University of Chicago Press, 2018.

McCain, John, and Mark Salter. *The Restless Wave: Good Times, Just Causes, Great Fights, and Other Appreciations*. New York: Simon & Schuster, 2018.

McCullough, David. *John Adams*. New York: Simon & Schuster, 2001.

McCullough, David. *Truman*. New York: Simon & Schuster, 1992.

McGinniss, Joe. *The Selling of the President 1968*. New York: Trident Press, 1969.

Meacham, Jon. *Thomas Jefferson: The Art of Power*. New York: Random House, 2012.

Merry, Robert W. *President McKinley: Architect of the American Century*. New York: Simon & Schuster, 2017.

Middleton, Alia. "The Effectiveness of Leader Visits During the 2010 British General Election Campaign." *British Journal of Politics and International Relations* 17, no. 2 (2015): 244–59.

Miller, Zeke. "Trump Knocks Biden for Campaigning from Basement amid Virus." Associated Press, May 8, 2020. www.wsls.com/news/politics/2020/05/08/trump-offers-biden-rapid-covid-19-test-to-resume-travel. Accessed December 10, 2022.

Mitchell, Alison. "In a Style Change, Bush Talks More Directly to the Voters." *New York Times*, September 9, 2000. www.nytimes.com/2000/09/09/us/2000-campaign-texas-governor-style-change-bush-talks-more-directly-voters.html. Accessed December 10, 2022.

MIT Election Data and Science Lab. "County Presidential Election Returns 2000–2020." doi.org/10.7910/DVN/VOQCHQ, Harvard Dataverse, V10; countypres_2000-2020.tab [fileName], UNF:6:pVAMya52q7VM1Pl7EZMWoQ== [fileUNF], 2018.

Moreno, J. Edward. "Trump Mocks Biden Event That Practiced Social Distancing." *The Hill*, June 19, 2020. thehill.com/homenews/campaign/503647-trump-mocks-biden-event-that-practiced-social-distancing. Accessed December 10, 2022.

Murphy, Paul P. "Trump Took Photos, Had Roundtable with Donors at Bedminster Fundraiser Hours before Announcing Covid Diagnosis." CNN, October 4, 2020. www.cnn.com/2020/10/03/politics/bedminster-trump-fundraiser-coronavirus/index.html. Accessed December 10, 2022.

Nagler, Paul C. *John Quincy Adams: A Public Life, A Private Life*. Cambridge, MA: Harvard University Press, 1997.

Nevins, Allan. *Grover Cleveland: A Study in Courage*. New York: Dodd, Mead, 1933.

Nevins, Allan, ed. *Letters of Grover Cleveland, 1850–1908*. New York: Da Capo, 1970.

Nixon, Richard. 1978. *The Memoirs of Richard Nixon*. New York: Grosset & Dunlap, 1978.

Oestericher, Benjamin. "America's Winner-Take-All System Gives Attention to the Few at the Expense of the Many." FairVote, October 14, 2020. www.fairvote.org/america_s_winner_take_all_system_gives_attention_to_the_few_at_the_expense_of_the_many. Accessed December 10, 2022.

Oprysko, Caitlin, and Gabby Orr. "Trump Campaign Says In-Person Events Will Be Made Virtual or Postponed." *Politico*, October 2, 2020. www.politico.com/news/2020/10/02/bill-stepien-trump-campaign-staffers-quarantine-425165. Accessed December 10, 2022.

"Palin Speaks in Salem Monday." *The Breeze*, October 30, 2008. www.breezejmu.org/palin-speaks-in-salem-monday/article_dadca26f-3b70-5d26-9c40-2244f42754f6.html. Accessed December 10, 2022.

Panagopoulos, Costas. *Bases Loaded: How US Presidential Campaigns Are Changing and Why It Matters*. Oxford: Oxford University Press, 2020.

Parker, Ashley, and Michael Barbaro. "Caution, Not Flash, as Romney Seeks His No. 2." *New York Times*, July 17, 2012. www.nytimes.com/2012/07/18/us/politics/romney-vice-presidential-search-began-months-ago.html. Accessed December 10, 2022.

Perlstein, Rick. *Nixonland: The Rise of a President and the Fracturing of America*. New York: Scribner, 2008.

Perret, Geoffrey. *Eisenhower*. Holbrook, MA: Adams Media Corporation, 1999.

"Presidential General Election Ad Spending Tops $1.5 Billion." Wesleyan Media Project, October 29, 2020. mediaproject.wesleyan.edu/releases-102920. Accessed December 10, 2022.

"President Obama and Vice President Biden Campaign Rally in Dayton, Ohio." C-SPAN, October 23, 2012. www.c-span.org/video/?308993-1/president-obama-vice-president-biden-campaign-rally-dayton-ohio#!. Accessed December 10, 2022.

"Public Approval of President Trump's Handling of the Coronavirus." RealClearPolitics.com, 2021. www.realclearpolitics.com/epolls/other/public_approval_of_president_trumps_handling_of_the_coronavirus-7088.html#polls. Accessed December 10, 2022.

Richardson, Seth. "Joe Biden Cancels Cleveland Rally over Coronavirus Concerns." *Cleveland Plain Dealer*, March 10, 2020. www.cleveland.com/open/2020/03/joe-biden-cancels-cleveland-rally-over-coronavirus-concerns.html. Accessed December 10, 2022.

Rickert, William E. "Horace Greeley on the Stump: Presidential Campaign of 1872." *Western Journal of Communication* 39, no. 3 (1975): 175–83.

Rubin, Olivia, Matthew Mosk, Soo Rin Kim, and Will Steakin. "Day After Seeing Trump at Bedminster Fundraiser, Guests 'Flabbergasted' to Learn He Was Stricken." ABC News, October 3, 2020. abcnews.go.com/Politics/day-trump-bedminster-fundraiser-guests-flabbergasted-learn-stricken/story?id=73394174. Accessed December 10, 2022.

Schram, Martin. *Running for President 1976: The Carter Campaign*. New York: Stein and Day, 1977.

Schultheis, Emily. "Romney Goes Rural." *Politico*, October 9, 2012. www.politico.com/story/2012/10/romney-goes-rural-082199. Accessed December 10, 2022.

Sears, Stephen W. *George B. McClellan: The Young Napoleon*. New York: Ticknor & Fields, 1988.

Shaw, Daron R. "The Effect of TV Ads and Candidate Appearances on Statewide Presidential Votes, 1988–96." *American Political Science Review* 93, no. 2 (1999): 345–61.

Shaw, Daron R. "The Impact of News Media Favorability and Candidate Events in Presidential Campaigns." *Political Communication* 16, no. 2 (1999): 183–202.

Shaw, Daron R. *The Race to 270: The Electoral College and the Campaign Strategies of 2000 and 2004*. Chicago: University of Chicago Press, 2006.

Shaw, Daron R. "A Study of Presidential Campaign Event Effects from 1952 to 1992." *Journal of Politics* 61, no. 2 (1999): 387–422.

Shaw, Daron R., and James G. Gimpel. "What If We Randomize the Governor's Schedule? Evidence on Campaign Appearance Effects from a Texas Field Experiment." *Political Communication* 29, no. 2 (2012): 137–59.

Shaw, Daron R., and Brian E. Roberts. "Campaign Events, the Media and the Prospects of Victory: The 1992 and 1996 US Presidential Elections." *British Journal of Political Science* 30, no. 2 (2000): 259–89.

Shear, Michael D., and Michael Crowley. "In Critical Swing State, Trump Again Stokes Doubt on Election Process." *New York Times*, September 26, 2020. www.nytimes.com/2020/09/26/us/politics/trump-rally-middletown-pa.html. Accessed December 10, 2022.

Shepard, Scott. "Gore Chides Bush for Missing Names of Foreign Leaders." *Greensboro News & Record*, November 5, 1999. greensboro.com/gore-chides-bush-for-missing-names-of-foreign-leaders-a-bush-aide-says-the-presidential/article_4e3c2402-bfac-5441-b865-8a2bf7f6b9b8.html. Accessed December 10, 2022.

Sides, John, Michael Tesler, and Lynn Vavreck. *Identity Crisis: The 2016 Presidential Campaign and the Battle for the Meaning of America*. Princeton, NJ: Princeton University Press, 2018.

Sides, John, and Lynn Vavreck. *The Gamble: Choice and Chance in the 2012 Presidential Election.* Princeton, NJ: Princeton University Press, 2013.

Sides, John, Lynn Vavreck, and Christopher Warshaw. "The Effect of Television Advertising in United States Elections." *American Political Science Review* 116, no. 2 (2022): 702–18.

Slack, Donovan. "Biden: 'I'm a Pizza Guy!' " *Politico*, October 23, 2012. www.politico.com/blogs/politico44/2012/10/biden-im-a-pizza-guy-139410. Accessed December 10, 2022.

Smith, Jean Edward. *FDR.* New York: Random House, 2007.

Smith, Liz. "How Joe Biden Can Defeat Trump from His Basement." *New York Times*, May 7, 2020. www.nytimes.com/2020/05/07/opinion/joe-biden-trump-2020.html. Accessed December 10, 2022.

Smith, Richard Norton. *An Uncommon Man: The Triumph of Herbert Hoover.* New York: Simon & Schuster, 1984.

Snyder, James M. Jr., and Hasin Yousaf. "Making Rallies Great Again: The Effects of Presidential Campaign Rallies on Voter Behavior, 2008–2016." Working paper, 2020. www.nber.org/papers/w28043. Accessed December 22, 2021.

Sotomayor, Marianna, and Mike Memoli. "Biden Is Forced to Find New Ways to Connect, One Year into the Campaign." NBC, April 25, 2020. www.nbcnews.com/politics/2020-election/biden-forced-find-new-ways-connect-one-year-campaign-n1192176. Accessed December 10, 2022.

Spenkuch, Jorg L., and David Toniatti. "Political Advertising and Election Results: Appendix Materials." 2018. web.archive.org/web/20180325000318/https://www.kellogg.northwestern.edu/faculty/spenkuch/research/advertising_appendix.pdf. Accessed January 25, 2023.

Strauss, Daniel, and Lauren Gambino. "#WhereIsJoe: Biden Campaign Tries to Stay Relevant amid Coronavirus." *The Guardian*, March 28, 2020. www.theguardian.com/us-news/2020/mar/28/joe-biden-campaign-coronavirus. Accessed December 10, 2022.

Troy, Gil. *See How They Ran: The Changing Role of the Presidential Candidate.* New York: Free Press, 1991.

Truman, Harry S. *Memoirs of Harry S. Truman.* Volume 2: *Years of Trial and Hope.* Garden City, NY: Doubleday, 1956.

"Trump Rallies Supporters in Minnesota." CBS News, September 30, 2020. https://www.cbsnews.com/news/watch-live-stream-trump-rallies-supporters-in-minnesota-today-09-30-2020. Accessed December 10, 2022.

"2016 Election Study Published." Wesleyan Media Project, March 6, 2017. mediaproject.wesleyan.edu/2016-election-study-published. Accessed December 22, 2021.

Unger, Harlow Giles. *John Quincy Adams.* Boston: Da Capo, 2012.

Vavreck, Lynn, Constantine J. Spiliotes, and Linda L. Fowler. "The Effects of Retail Politics in the New Hampshire Primary." *American Journal of Political Science* 46, no. 3 (2002): 595–610.

"Voting by Mail and Absentee Voting." MIT Election Data and Science Lab, March 16, 2021. electionlab.mit.edu/research/voting-mail-and-absentee-voting. Accessed December 10, 2022.

"VP Joe Biden Speaks at UT." WTOL, October 18, 2012. www.wtol.com/amp/article/news/vp-joe-biden-speaks-at-ut/512-a415a115-6a33-47ca-baef-ff497dccffee. Accessed December 10, 2022.

Walker, Hunter. "Joe Biden Gets a Side Order of Negativity on His Lunch Break." *Observer*, October 23, 2012. observer.com/2012/10/joe-biden-spends-lunch-break-with-man-who-tells-him-to-prepare-to-lose. Accessed December 10, 2022.

Weisbord, Marvin R. *Campaigning for President: A New Look at the Road to the White House*. Washington, DC: Public Affairs, 1964.

Weissert, Will, Alexandra Jaffe, and Alan Fram. "Biden's Low-Key Campaign Style Worries Some Democrats." Associated Press, September 25, 2020. apnews.com/article/election-2020-virus-outbreak-ruth-bader-ginsburg-delaware-elections-9282e7a189e965b124f1fc31c857903e. Accessed December 10, 2022.

Wendland, Jay. *Campaigns That Matter: The Importance of Campaign Visits in Presidential Nominating Contests*. Lanham, MD: Lexington Books, 2017.

Wendland, Jay. "Rallying Votes? A Multilevel Approach to Understanding Voter Decision-Making in the 2016 Presidential Nominating Contests." *Journal of Political Marketing* 18, no. 1–2 (2018): 92–118.

West, Darrell M. "Constituencies and Travel Allocations in the 1980 Presidential Campaign." *American Journal of Political Science* 27, no. 3 (1983): 515–29.

White, Theodore H. *The Making of the President 1960*. New York: Atheneum, 1961.

White, Theodore H. *The Making of the President 1968*. New York: Atheneum, 1969.

White, Theodore H. *The Making of the President 1972*. New York: Atheneum, 1973.

Williams, R. Hal. *Realigning America: McKinley, Bryan, and the Remarkable Election of 1896*. Lawrence: University Press of Kansas, 2010.

Williams, Robert C. *Horace Greeley: Champion of American Freedom*. New York: New York University Press, 2006.

Willis, Oliver. "Fox News Falsely Claimed Biden Was 'In His Basement' 322 Times in 2 Months." American Independent, August 14, 2020. americanindependent.com/fox-news-joe-biden-basement-lies-322-times-coronavirus-2020-election. Accessed December 10, 2022.

Wilson, Kirby. "Joe Biden Hosted a Virtual Campaign Rally in Tampa. It Didn't Go Great." *Tampa Bay Times*, May 7, 2020. www.tampabay.com/florida-politics/buzz/2020/05/07/joe-biden-hosted-a-virtual-campaign-rally-in-tampa-it-didnt-go-great. Accessed December 10, 2022.

Wood, Thomas. "What the Heck Are We Doing in Ottumwa, Anyway? Presidential Candidate Visits and Their Political Consequence." *Annals of the American Academy of Political and Social Science* 667, no. 1 (2016): 110–25.

Woodall, Candy. "Trump Rally in Middletown, Pa.: Takeaways After the President Nominates Amy Coney Barrett." *York Daily Record*, September 26, 2020. www.ydr.com/story/news/politics/elections/2020/09/26/trump-holds-rally-middletown-pa-after-naming-supreme-court-pick/3529047001. Accessed December 10, 2022.

Wright, Gerald C. "Misreports of Vote Choice in the 1988 NES Senate Election Study." *Legislative Studies Quarterly* 15, no. 4 (1990): 543–63.

Yates, Riley. "As Many as 300 Attended Trump Fundraiser at Bedminster, Attendee Says." NJ.com, October 2, 2020. www.nj.com/coronavirus/2020/10/as-many-as-300-attended-trump-fundraiser-at-bedminster-attendee-says.html. Accessed December 10, 2022.

Yu, Janice. "Joe Biden Hosts Drive-In Campaign Event in Atlanta." Fox 5 Atlanta, October 27, 2020. www.fox5atlanta.com/news/joe-biden-hosts-drive-in-campaign-event-in-atlanta. Accessed December 10, 2022.

Zaller, John R. *The Nature and Origins of Mass Opinion*. Cambridge: Cambridge University Press, 1992.

INDEX

Abramowitz, Alan, 73, 211
activism, campaign, 57–59, 216–217, 295n10
Adams, John Quincy, 21–22
aggregate- versus individual-level data, 15, 65–68, 73–74, 161–162, 179–180, 183, 189–194, 207–208
Ailes, Roger, 18
air travel, 36–40, 268n102, 269n108
Alamogordo, New Mexico, 42
Albuquerque, New Mexico, 95
Althaus, Scott, 72, 94, 124
Amtrak, 39, 105
Appleman, Eric, 84, 91
Arrington, Benjamin, 23
Atlanta, Georgia, 12
Attkisson, Sharyl, 262–263n34
audiences, for campaign visits, 55–59, 164, 200, 217–219, 283n58
Axelrod, David, 7

Barkley, Alben, 36
Barrett, Amy Coney, 79–80
Bartels, Larry, 132
Bedminster, New Jersey, 80–81
Berg, A. Scott, 268n91
Biden, Jill, 5, 39, 90

Biden, Joe, 79–81; basement narrative, 4–12, 20, 24, 43, 97–99, 104–105, 117, 220, 262–263n34, 263n37, 264n12; campaign visits in 2008, 101, 116; campaign visits in 2012, 85–94, 100–101, 116; campaign visits in 2020, 4, 6, 9–12, 39, 72–73, 95–98, 101, 104–105, 109, 212, 262n30, 287n43, 292n24; and COVID-19, 8, 10; drive-in rallies, 10, 263n37, 263n38; effects of 2008 campaign visits, 173–176, 178, 198, 214; effects of 2012 campaign visits, 177–178, 187–189, 193–194, 201, 214; effects of 2020 campaign visits, 177–178, 185–186, 198–199, 204, 207, 291n19; strategy for 2008 campaign visits, 129, 149–150, 157–159, 166; strategy for 2012 campaign visits, 157–159, 166; strategy for 2020 campaign visits, 157–159, 166–167; virtual campaigning, 1–3, 5, 8, 259n2, 261–262n22, 262n31
Blaine, James, 27
Bourdon, Jeffrey Norman, 29
Brady, Henry, 44–45, 271n10
Brams, Steven, 120, 124
Bryan, William Jennings, 30–31
Buffalo, New York, 26

Burchard, Samuel, 27
Bush, George H. W., 36
Bush, George W., 38–39, 42–43, 67, 88–89, 131, 272–272n35
Buttigieg, Pete, 269n1

campaign advertisements, 120–121, 151–156, 169–170, 183–184, 208, 212, 270n4, 293n1
campaign donations, 64–65, 293n1
"campaign events," 274n60
campaign financing, 70–71, 270n4, 272n22
campaign messaging, 51–53
campaign rallies, 110, 117, 196–199, 292n24
campaign strategy, 46–47, 74–75; and allocation of campaign resources, 120–121, 284n2, 284n4, 285n18; and geographic distribution of campaign visits, 123–159
Campaign Visits Database (CVD), 14, 77–118, 219; dates included, 93–94; defining campaign visits, 77–85, 196–197, 274n60; documenting campaign visits, 94–96, 219, 282–283n51; frequency of campaign visits, 2008–2020, 97–102, 117; joint campaign visits, 89–93, 101–102; multiple visits to a geographic area, 91–93; surrogate campaigners, 90–91, 216; timing of campaign visits, 102–110, 117; unannounced stops, 82–83, 86–87, 94; vice-presidential campaign visits, 88–89, 93, 100–101, 148–149, 213–214
Campbell, James, 44
Cann, Damon, 67, 128
Canton, Ohio, 29
Carter, Jimmy, 52–53, 148, 264n12, 285n18
causal inference, 167–168, 177–180, 188–189, 195, 202–205, 209–210, 215–216, 218–219, 276n90
Charleston Courier (newspaper), 27
Cheathem, Mark, 265–266n33
Chen, Lanhee, 129, 145–146, 156, 287n44, 287n45

Cheney, Dick, 38–40, 67, 88–89, 120, 214, 269n108
Chicago, Illinois, 30, 33, 265n30
Chillicothe, Ohio, 50
Cincinnati, Ohio, 26
Clark County, Ohio, 94–95
Cleveland, Grover, 21, 265n30
Cleveland, Ohio, 4, 11, 25–26, 39, 79, 132
Clinton, Bill, 38–39, 50, 61–62, 131–132, 221
Clinton, Hillary, 39; campaign visits in 2016, 82–83, 100–101, 105, 108, 126, 131, 286n23; effects of 2016 campaign visits, 61–62, 64–65, 89, 177–179, 187, 189, 193, 207, 211; strategy for 2016 campaign visits, 148, 157–159, 166, 273n48; Wisconsin narrative, 3, 43, 131
Cohen, Marty, 126
Cole, Jeffrey Bryan 67, 128
"Columbia School," 271n10
Columbus, Ohio, 25–26
Conley, Sean, 78
Cook, Nancy, 78
Cook Out (business), 95
Cooperative (Congressional) Election Study, 62, 161–162, 180–181, 193, 200–201–203, 216, 219
COVID-19, 4, 8, 73, 78–81, 97–98–99, 115, 202, 218, 261n26
Cox, James, 31
Crist, Charlie, 259n2
C-SPAN, 95–96
Cuyahoga Falls, Ohio, 42

Darby, Pennsylvania, 9
Darr, Joshua, 73
Dauphin, Pennsylvania, 96
Davis, Marty, 80
Davis, Morton, 120, 124
Dawsey, Josh, 11
Dayton, Ohio, 25, 85–86, 89–93
debates, presidential, 10–11, 43, 78–79, 85, 89, 279n15
Dedrick, Mark, 20

Democracy in Action, 84, 91
dependent variables, 151, 169, 183, 193, 202–204, 216–217
Detroit, Michigan, 37
Devine, Tad, 120
Dewey, Thomas, 34, 61–62, 66, 207, 275–276n79
DeWine, Mike, 4
"Do campaigns matter?," 47, 163–164
Dole, Bob, 61, 270n4
Douglas, Stephen, 26–27, 266n33, 266–267n53
Duluth, Minnesota, 80
Durham, North Carolina, 95

early voting, 202–204, 217, 289n6
Edwards, George C. III, 125
Eisenhower, Dwight, 35, 37
Electoral College, 23, 49, 121–125, 134–140, 285n18, 286n35
Ellis, Richard, 20, 264n18, 265–266n33
Elmira, New York, 271n10
Elwood, Indiana, 265n30
Emhoff, Doug, 90
Erie County, Ohio, 271n10

FairVote, 125
Ferguson, Andrew, 2
Fillmore, Millard, 25
Ford, Gerald, 19, 38, 220, 264n12, 270n4
Fort Lauderdale, 95–96, 283–284n60
Fox News, 6, 81
front-porch campaigns, 28–31
fundamentals, electoral, 43–45, 47, 63, 163–164
fundraisers, 78, 80–83, 262n31, 279n16

Galdieri, Christopher, 285n9
Galvin, William 264n8
Garfield, James, 28
generalizability, of evidence on campaign visit effects, 69–70, 160
Gimpel, James, 49–51, 72–73, 211, 276n90

Google Street View, 95–96
Gore, Al, 38–39, 45, 270n4
Gore, Tipper, 39
Grant, Ulysses, 266–267n53
Greeley, Horace, 27, 266n33
Greene County, Ohio, 94–95

Hagen, Michael, 45
Haldeman, H. R., 16–18
Hancock, Winfield Scott, 28
Harding, Warren, 31
Harris, Kamala, 88; campaign visits in 2020, 97–99, 101, 287n43; effects of 2020 campaign visits, 198–199, 204, 214, 291n19; strategy for 2020 campaign visits, 156–159, 166–167, 187; virtual campaigning, 10, 283n54
Harrison, Benjamin, 29
Harrison, William Henry, 23–25, 27, 265–266n33
Hartford Courant (newspaper), 266n33
Heersink, Boris, 60–62, 64–66, 89, 207, 275–276n79
Herr, Paul, 54, 61–62
Hicks, Hope, 80–81
Hill, Jeffrey, 66, 88–89, 207, 290n9
Holbrook, Thomas, 44, 48–49, 51, 54–55, 57, 59, 61, 65–67, 274n60, 275–276n79
Hollywood, California, 82
Holton, Anne, 39
Hoover, Herbert, 32
Huang, Taofang, 44, 120, 124, 128–129, 146
Hughes, Charles Evans, 31
Humphrey, Hubert, 17, 263–264n6

Indianapolis, Indiana, 29

Jackson, Andrew, 22
Jacobson, Gary, 45, 291n21
Jamieson, Kathleen Hall, 45
Jefferson, Thomas, 22
Johnson, Lyndon, 264n8
Johnston, Richard, 44–45, 271n10

Jones, Jeffrey, 51, 62–64, 91, 276n90
Jordan, Hamilton, 148, 285n18

Kaine, Tim, 39; campaign visits in 2016, 100–101, 131; effects of 2016 campaign visits, 64–65, 89, 185–186, 198, 201, 204, 207, 214; strategy for 2016 campaign visits, 148, 157–159, 166
Karol, David, 126
Kennedy, John F., 37, 123, 269n1
Kennedy, Robert F., 16
Kerry, John, 221
King, David, 50, 56–57, 270n4
Kopko, Kyle, 89, 148
Kornacki, Steve, 127

Langston, Joy, 287n45
Lebanon, Ohio, 283–284n60, 291–292n23
Lieberman, Hadassah, 39
Lieberman, Joe, 39
Lordstown Motors, 79, 83
Los Angeles, California, 33
Louisville, Kentucky, 26

MacManus, Susan, 283n58
McCain, John, 37, 52, 89; campaign visits in 2008, 95, 97, 101–102, 104–106, 110, 116, 282–283n51; effects of 2008 campaign visits, 62, 64, 171, 173–174, 178, 185–186–188, 192–194, 197–199, 201, 205–206, 211, 214, 294n2; strategy for 2008 campaign visits, 124, 128–129, 150, 156–159, 164–165, 167
McClellan, George, 21
McClurg, Scott, 54–55, 57, 59, 67
McGovern, George, 52
McKinley, William, 29–30
media coverage, of campaign visits, 49–51, 57, 64, 164, 263–264n6, 268n91, 272n29, 283–284n60, 293n1
Mentor, Ohio, 28
microtargeting, 47
Middletown, Pennsylvania, 79, 197

mobilization and persuasion, 13–14, 46–48, 53–59, 70–71, 73–74, 128–130, 160, 164, 166, 200, 212–214, 218–219, 273n48; evidence, as causes of campaign visits effects, 65–68, 173–180, 185–186, 188–194, 199, 201–202, 204–211, 214; evidence, as strategy for campaign visits, 145–159; identifying as causal mechanism, 161, 168, 177–180, 188–189, 209–210, 276n90
Mondale, Walter, 148
Mook, Robby, 131
Morehouse, David, 50, 56–57, 270n4

Nardulli, Peter, 72, 94, 124
Nashville Union (newspaper), 266n33
natural experiments, 72–73, 210–212
Navajo, Arizona, 201
negative effects, of campaign visits, 176–177, 290n9
New Orleans, Louisiana, 52
New York City, 11, 26–27, 81–83, 265n30
New York Times (newspaper), 27, 96, 197
Nixon, Richard: 1960 campaign of, 35, 37, 122–123; 1968 campaign of, 16–18, 220, 263–264n6; 1972 campaign of, 18–19; vice-presidential campaigns of, 37
Noel, Hans, 126
North Bend, Ohio, 24
notification ceremonies, 265n30

Obama, Barack, 71, 89–90, 131, 263n37; campaign visits in 2008, 92, 97, 101, 104, 106, 116, 282–283n51; campaign visits in 2012, 85–86, 92–93, 98, 100, 101, 104, 107, 116, 269n1; effects of 2008 campaign visits, 61–62, 64, 66–67, 173–175, 178, 192–193, 197–199, 205, 211, 291n19, 294n2; effects of 2012 campaign visits, 61–62, 64, 173, 177–178, 197–199, 206, 294n2; strategy for 2008 campaign visits, 124, 128–129, 149–150, 157–159, 166; strategy for 2012 campaign visits, 157–159, 166

Omar, Ilhan, 80
"ornamental" vs. "instrumental" campaign visits, 132

Palin, Piper, 96
Palin, Sarah, 88–89; campaign visits in 2008, 94, 96–97, 101–102, 116, 282–283n51; effects of 2008 campaign visits, 173–174, 198, 214; strategy for 2008 campaign visits, 129, 150, 156–159, 164–166
Palin, Todd, 91, 96
Panagopoulos, Costas, 70, 73
Pence, Karen, 91
Pence, Mike: campaign visits in 2016, 102, 115–116; campaign visits in 2020, 97–99, 102, 115–116; effects of 2016 campaign visits, 89, 176, 188, 198, 206, 211, 214, 294n2; effects of 2020 campaign visits, 188, 201, 214; strategy for 2016 campaign visits, 148, 157–159, 165, 167; strategy for 2020 campaign visits, 157–159, 165, 167
Pensacola, Florida, 52
Perlstein, Rick, 263–264n6
Perry, Rick, 276n90
Peterson, Brenton, 60–62, 64–66, 89, 207, 275–276n79
Peterson, Jordan Carr, 64–65, 89
Philadelphia, Pennsylvania, 4, 6, 9, 24, 92
Pierce, Franklin, 265n30
Pittsburgh, Pennsylvania, 10, 26
Plouffe, David, 7
Pocatello, Idaho, 33
Political parties, 126–128
Polk, James, 21–22
Portman, Rob, 283–284n60
presidential legitimacy, 13, 20, 163, 212, 262–263n34
presidential mandates, 131–132

qualitative research, 217–219
Quecan, Andrew, 283n58

radio, 31–32
Reagan, Ronald, 38, 146
RealClearPolitics, 147
Reeves, Andrew, 129, 145–146, 156, 287n44, 287n45
regression analysis, 129–130, 151–157, 167, 169, 170–173, 183–185, 217, 287n44
Rockefeller, Nelson, 270n4
Rodriguez, Elaine, 66, 88–89, 207, 290n9
Romney, Mitt: campaign visits in 2012, 102, 104, 107, 116, 221; effects of 2012 campaign visits, 62, 64, 185–186, 198–199, 201, 204, 206; strategy for 2012 campaign visits, 156, 165, 167
Roosevelt, Franklin, 31–32, 265n30
Roosevelt, Theodore, 31
Rosas, Guillermo, 287n45
Rose Garden (White House), 19, 79, 264n12, 270n4
Ryan, Janna, 91
Ryan, Paul: campaign visits in 2012, 94–95, 102, 116, 221; effects of 2012 campaign visits, 198–199; strategy for 2012 campaign visits, 156–157, 165, 167

Salem, Virginia, 94, 282–283n51
Sanders, Bernie, 270n4
Sanford, Florida, 78
San Francisco, California, 37
Schmucker's Restaurant, 86–87
Scott, Winfield, 25–26, 266n33
Secret Service, 197, 263n38
Seymour, Horatio, 26–27, 266–267n53
Shanksville, Pennsylvania, 11
Shaw, Daron, 13, 35, 44–45, 49–51, 67, 69–75, 81, 88–89, 92–94, 121, 124, 128–129, 131, 146, 148, 199–200, 207–208, 211, 272n22, 275n78, 276n90, 284n2
Shorewood, Minnesota, 80
Sides, John, 44–46, 63, 212, 271n10
Smith, Al, 32

Snyder, James, Jr., 61–62, 64, 67, 73–74, 202–204, 208, 293n1
Springfield, Massachusetts, 221
Springfield, Missouri, 42
Springfield, Ohio, 87, 91–93, 94
Stephanopoulos, George, 8
Stepien, Bill, 78
Stevenson, Adlai, 37
St. Louis, Missouri, 26
surrogates, campaign, 90–91, 216, 270n4, 283n58, 285n18

Taft, Robert, 32
Taft, William Howard, 31
Tampa, Florida, 1, 42, 259n2
Television, 18–19, 34–36, 264n8, 272n29
Toledo, Ohio, 86–87, 91–93, 111
Troy, Gil, 18, 20, 34, 268n102
Troy, New York, 26
Truman, Harry, 13, 32–34, 37, 61–62, 65–66, 163, 207, 271n10, 275–276n79
Trump, Donald, 262n31; campaign visits in 2016, 97, 102, 104, 108, 115–116, 126–127, 282–283n51, 286n23, 292n24; campaign visits in 2020, 6, 10, 78–81, 83, 97–99, 102, 104–105, 109, 115–116, 197, 261–262n26, 262–263n34, 292n24; and COVID-19, 5, 10–11, 78–81, 98–99, 104, 283n56; and criticism of Biden campaign, 6, 9–10, 79–80, 97–99, 261–262n26, 263n37, 264n12; effects of 2016 campaign visits, 61–62, 64–65, 67, 89, 173, 176–178, 187, 198, 206, 208, 293n1; effects of 2020 campaign visits, 173–174, 176, 178–180, 187–188, 192–194, 206–207, 211; strategy for 2016 campaign visits, 148, 150–151, 157–159, 165, 167; strategy for 2020 campaign visits, 150–151, 157–159, 165–167
Trump, Donald, Jr., 90
Trump, Lara, 90
Trump, Melania, 78

"tug of war" (in campaign activity), 45–46, 63, 73, 211–212
Tulsa, Oklahoma, 261n26
Twitter, 78

units of analysis, 199–202, 268n91; counties, 94–95, 129, 141, 148–149, 199–202, 286–287n37, 288n49, 289n3; media markets, 199–202; states, 129, 141, 148–149
University of Toledo, 86, 111–112
U.S. Naval Academy, 52

Van Buren, Martin, 22
Van Dyck, Ted, 52
Vavreck, Lynn, 45, 63, 212
venues, for campaign visits, 94, 110–117, 197, 270n4; airports, 114–116, 197, 283n58, 283–284n60; arenas or convention centers, 111, 114–115; campaign offices, 87, 95–96, 279n16, 283–284n60; places of business, 86–87, 111–112, 114, 116, 283–284n60, 291–292n23; private residences, 291–292n23; public spaces, 114, 283–284n60; union offices, 116; universities, 82–83, 111–112, 114, 116
Vincennes, Indiana, 24
virtual campaigning, 1–3, 5, 8, 10, 72, 261n22, 261–262n26, 283n54

Wallace, George, 17
Wallace, Henry, 36
Warren, Elizabeth, 269n1
Washington, DC, 78, 83,
Washington, George, 21
Waterbury, Connecticut, 269n1
weather, effect of on turnout, 170, 184, 289bn6
Wendland, Jay, 58, 84
West, Darrell, 92, 111, 121, 283n58
whistle-stop tours, 32–34, 36–40, 268n91
White, Theodore ("Teddy"), 18, 35, 37, 40, 55–56

Willkie, Wendell, 37, 265n30
Wilmington, Delaware, 1, 9
Wilson, Woodrow, 31
Wood, Thomas, 50–51, 58, 62–64, 72, 215, 272n29
Wooden, Amanda, 66, 88–89, 207, 290n9

Yellow Springs, Ohio, 94–95
York Daily Record (newspaper), 96
Young's Jersey Dairy, 94–95
Yousaf, Hasin, 61–62, 64, 67, 73–74, 202–204, 208, 293n1

Zaller, John, 126